THE TECHNIQUE AND PRACTICE OF PSYCHOANALYSIS, VOLUME II: A MEMORIAL VOLUME TO RALPH R. GREENSON

Monograph Series of the
Ralph R. Greenson
Memorial Library of the
San Diego Psychoanalytic
Society and Institute

Monograph 1

THE TECHNIQUE AND PRACTICE OF PSYCHOANALYSIS, VOLUME II: A MEMORIAL VOLUME TO RALPH R. GREENSON

edited by

Alan Sugarman, Robert A. Nemiroff,
and Daniel P. Greenson

INTERNATIONAL UNIVERSITIES PRESS, INC.

Madison   **Connecticut**

First Paperback Printing, 2000
ISBN 0-8236-8322-2 (paperback)

The Library of Congress has cataloged the hardcover edition
of this title as below.

Library of Congress Cataloging-in-Publication Data

The Technique and practice of psychoanalysis, volume II : memorial
  volume to Ralph R. Greenson / edited by Alan Sugarman, Robert A.
  Nemiroff, and Daniel P. Greenson.
    p.   cm. -- (Monograph series of the Ralph R. Greenson Memorial
  Library of the San Diego Psychoanalytic Society and Institute : 1)
    Includes bibliographical references and index.
    ISBN 0-8236-6421-X
    1. Psychoanalysis.   I. Sugarman, Alan.   II. Nemiroff, Robert A.
  (Robert Allen)   III. Greenson, Ralph R., 1911-   .   IV. Series.
    [DNLM: 1. Psychoanalysis.   2. Psychoanalytic Therapy.   WM 460
  T255]
  RC504.T43   1992
  616.89'17--dc20
  DNLM/DLC
  for Library of Congress   91-35393
                                                               CIP

Manufactured in the United States of America

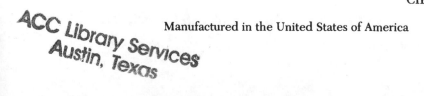

Contents

Contributors

Bernard Brandchaft, M.D., Supervisor and Training Analyst, Los Angeles Psychoanalytic Society and Institute; co-author of *Psychoanalytic Treatment: An Intersubjective Approach.*

Paul A. Dewald, M.D., Clinical Professor of Psychiatry, St. Louis University School of Medicine; Training and Supervising Analyst, St. Louis Psychoanalytic Institute; former medical director, St. Louis Psychoanalytic Institute.

Rudolf Ekstein, Ph.D., Training and Supervising Analyst, Los Angeles Psychoanalytic Society and Institute, the Southern California Psychoanalytic Institute, the Los Angeles Institute for Psychoanalytic Studies; Medical Professor of Clinical Psychology, the University of California–Los Angeles.

Daniel P. Greenson, M.D., Training and Supervising Analyst, San Francisco Psychoanalytic Institute; Chairman, CME Program, Herrick Hospital, Berkeley, California.

Alexander Grinstein, M.D., Clinical Professor of Psychiatry, Wayne State University School of Medicine; Training and Supervising Analyst, Michigan Psychoanalytic Institute.

Lawrence B. Inderbitzin, M.D., Professor of Psychiatry, Emory University School of Medicine; Training and Supervising Analyst and Director, Emory University Psychoanalytic Institute.

Sanford M. Izner, M.D., Clinical Professor of Psychiatry, University of California–San Diego; Training and Supervising Analyst, San Diego Psychoanalytic Society and Institute.

Haig A. Koshkarian, M.D., Associate Clinical Professor of Psychiatry, University of California–San Diego School of Medicine; Senior Faculty, San Diego Psychoanalytic Society and Institute.

Steven T. Levy, M.D., Professor and Chief of Psychiatry, Emory University School of Medicine at Grady Memorial Hospital; Training and Supervising Analyst, Emory University Psychoanalytic Institute.

Jack Novick, Ph.D., Adjunct Associate Professor, University of Michigan and Wayne State University School of Medicine; Faculty and Child/Adolescent Supervising Analyst, Michigan Psychoanalytic Institute; former Supervising Analyst and Faculty, Anna Freud Centre.

Owen Renik, M.D., Training and Supervising Analyst, San Francisco Psychoanalytic Institute.

Estelle Shane, Ph.D., Assistant Clinical Professor of Psychiatry, University of California–Los Angeles School of Medicine; Training and Supervising Analyst, Los Angeles Psychoanalytic Society and Institute and Institute for Contemporary Psychoanalysis.

Morton Shane, M.D., Clinical Professor of Psychiatry, University of California–Los Angeles School of Medicine; Training and Supervising Analyst in Adult and Child Psychoanalysis, Los Angeles Psychoanalytic Society and Institute; Training and Supervising Analyst, Institute of Contemporary Psychoanalysis.

Alan Z. Skolnikoff, M.D., Associate Clinical Professor of Psychiatry, University of California–San Francisco School of Medicine; Training and Supervising Analyst, San Francisco Psychoanalytic Institute.

Vann Spruiell, M.D., Clinical Professor of Psychiatry, Louisiana State University and Tulane University Schools of Medicine; Training and Supervising Analyst, New Orleans Psychoanalytic Institute; North American Editor, *International Journal of Psycho-Analysis,* and *International Review of Psycho-Analysis.*

Robert L. Tyson, M.D., Clinical Professor of Psychiatry, University of California–San Diego and University of California–Irvine Schools of Medicine; Training and Supervising Analyst (adult and child) San Diego Psychoanalytic Society and Institute; Geographic Child Supervising Analyst, Denver Psychoanalytic Institute; past President, the Association for Child Psychoanalysis.

Robert S. Wallerstein, M.D., Emeritus Professor of Psychiatry, University of California–San Francisco School of Medicine; Training and Supervising Analyst, San Francisco Psychoanalytic Institute; past President, International Psychoanalytical Association and American Psychoanalytic Association.

Edward M. Weinshel, M.D., Clinical Professor of Psychiatry, University of California–San Francisco School of Medicine; Training and Supervising Analyst, San Francisco Psychoanalytic Institute; former North American Editor, *International Journal of Psycho-Analysis,* and *International Review of Psycho-Analysis.*

Samuel L. Wilson, M.D., Assistant Clinical Professor of Psychiatry, University of California–Los Angeles School of Medicine; Training and Supervising Analyst, Los Angeles Psychoanalytic Society and Institute.

Preface

Ralph Greenson, the author of over sixty papers and articles, worked fourteen years (1953–1967) on his book, *The Technique and Practice of Psychoanalysis*, Volume I. Articles he wrote deftly and quickly; he struggled long and hard to write Volume I. He once told me, "Papers are easy, they are for now; but books are for posterity." Those who knew him were not surprised that writing a comprehensive textbook on psychoanalytic technique would be a struggle, but then he so loved struggles. An enthusiastic, energetic, vibrant man in many ways, his personality was more suited to giving papers and public lectures, and participating on panels where he could come face-to-face with his audience and potential "adversaries," than to hours, day after day, cloistered in his den. He loved audiences and, perhaps, posterity seemed "hard to get a hold of" and a long way off.

A textbook on technique was in some ways a contradiction in terms. Textbooks usually are not alive and personal, so full of detailed clinical work, which was the way he thought and wrote. Otto Fenichel's book on technique (published twenty-six years before Greenson's) was considered the mainstay of the literature of that time. Fenichel had been his analyst, and, as Greenson often noted, following in one's footsteps is never easy.

As the book was nearing completion, he became somewhat perfectionistic, doing and redoing sections, worrying about what could be left out, what had to be included, where to stop and call it a day (or perhaps a decade). Lottie Newman, his editor, feels it was his need to resolve such dilemmas that led him to conceive of the book as two volumes. The "good news" was it allowed him to finish Volume I; the "bad news" was he felt great pressure to do Volume II.

In 1970 his health began to slip; he needed a cardiac pacemaker. In 1974 during surgery to change the wires and batteries of his pacemaker, he suffered a cerebral vascular accident. He awoke from the surgery with a complete expressive aphasia (though he could understand others, he was unable to express himself). Within a week he could speak somewhat, but it took months of speech therapy before he could return to his office and resume teaching and lecturing. Those who knew him well could recognize that his speech was not as smooth and fluid as it had been. He would balk momentarily when he could not find a word, he would come up with a substitute, which would suffice somewhat, but was not quite right, and was not the word that he wanted. His ability to express himself in writing was even more severely compromised. He had written in longhand his papers and the various drafts for Volume I; now he was unable to write. His frustration, if anything, intensified his wish to do Volume II. He tried dictating. He gathered together a group of experienced analysts for a seminar on technique using his outline for Volume II and tape-recorded these meetings. He was dissatisfied with both results, but kept trying until a year before his death when he gave up the project. Included in this memorial volume are some of his post-aphasic efforts to write sections of Volume II. Readers familiar with his earlier writings will recognize the differences in clarity, fluidity, and rhythm and will be able to sense his struggles with his limitations. The editors of this book feel that, nonetheless, these sections are worthwhile in showing his thinking about technical issues even though they are far from vintage Ralph Greenson.

Daniel P. Greenson, M.D.

Acknowledgments

WE wish to thank Hildi Greenson for the dedication and perseverance that allowed this project to develop. Her painstaking archiving of her husband's papers, lectures, and seminars preserved the nucleus of Volume II around which this work is organized. Furthermore, her supportive and consistent interest in the project helped us to regain or maintain our momentum at those inevitable times of dormancy to which a multi-authored volume is vulnerable. It seems a fair testimony to her influence to say that this project would not have happened without her.

Others, too, offered crucial support on the project. Joyce Harding, Administrator of the San Diego Psychoanalytic Society and Institute, and Phyllis Baumgart, Administrative Coordinator of the Psychiatric Residency Training Program at the University of California, San Diego, provided crucial organization skills in bringing various stages of the volume to fruition. Doris Osborne and Jan Brewer performed the typing and retyping necessary in such a volume with laudable dispatch, accuracy, and enthusiasm. And Peter Graham researched and integrated the references so that the reader may more easily peruse the sources for the volume.

Finally, we wish to thank the Board of Directors of the San Diego Psychoanalytic Society and Institute. Members of the Board have supported the volume throughout its creation and have taken a clear-cut stand on the value of psychoanalytic scholarship. Resources necessary to complete such an undertaking have always been provided readily and graciously. Consequently it is fitting that this volume marks the inception of the Monograph Series of the Ralph R. Greenson Memorial Library of the San Diego Psychoanalytic Society and Institute.

Introduction

RALPH R. Greenson is considered by many to have been the foremost American clinical psychoanalyst. His textbook, *The Technique and Practice of Psychoanalysis*, Volume I, continues to be a staple in the bibliographies of most American psychoanalytic training programs. It has undergone numerous printings and been translated into German, Italian, French, Spanish, and Dutch. And the thirty-two scientific articles that were published under the title *Explorations in Psychoanalysis* demonstrate his keen interest in the theory of psychoanalytic technique as well as its implementation in the encounter between the patient and the analyst. Just a few of those articles will be mentioned here to demonstrate his clinical and theoretical versatility: "On Screen Defenses, Screen Hunger, and Screen Identity" (1958a); "On the Silence and Sounds of the Analytic Hour" (1961); "The Working Alliance and the Transference Neurosis" (1965a); "The Problem of Working Through" (1965b); "The Use of Dream Sequences for Detecting Errors in Technique: A Clinical Study" (1968b); "The Exceptional Position of the Dream in Psychoanalytic Practice" (1970). These various titles demonstrate the breadth of his clinical interests despite the well-deserved reputation he earned for his focus on the patient–analyst relationship, in particular. It would be a mistake to underestimate his sensitivity to all dimensions of the clinical encounter because he chose to emphasize areas such as the real relationship, the working alliance, and transference that he believed were underrepresented in the writings on technique that characterized his generation. Ralph R. Greenson was well aware of the multiple complexities of clinical analysis, an awareness keenly demonstrated in his works on dreams or preoedipal phenomena such as screens.

In addition, Greenson was committed to the development of institutions that promoted education in psychoanalysis as well as its extensions to other fields. Thus, he became a training and supervising psychoanalyst at the Los Angeles Psychoanalytic Institute as well as its president and the dean of its training school. He also served as a clinical professor of psychiatry at the University of California, Los Angeles. Furthermore, he served as the chairman of the Scientific Advisory Board of the Foundation for Research in Psychoanalysis for many years. His interest in extending psychoanalytic knowledge to those in other fields is particularly evident in his public lectures (Nemiroff, Sugarman, and Robbins, in press). These lectures, presented at institutions such as the Reiss–Davis Child Guidance Clinic, The Center for Early Education, and The UCLA Extension Division, made psychoanalytic thinking available to teachers, academics, and intellectuals and demonstrated how an analytic perspective was helpful in understanding and even intervening in a variety of human issues, not just the clinical situation.

Because of this interest Ralph R. Greenson offered his name as a sponsor of the Hannah Fenichel Center for Child Development when it was first created by the San Diego Psychoanalytic Society. The affection that he and his wife, Hildi, held for Hannah Fenichel made him particularly appreciative when his friend, Emmanuel Lippett, suggested commemorating her by dedicating this nursery school to her. Greenson even went so far as to enlist Anna Freud's support of this project and persuaded her to lend her name as a sponsor. Thus, Greenson played an important role in the San Diego Psychoanalytic Society and Institute from early in its inception. In fact, he had even earlier been its first scientific speaker after its organization as a training school of the American Psychoanalytic Association in 1970.

It is these affiliations combined with the close friendship between the Greensons and Emmanuel Lippett, a central supporter of the fledgling institute, that led Hildi Greenson to donate Ralph R. Greenson's professional library to the San Diego Psychoanalytic Institute in September of 1985. Among the books donated was a bound collection of his unpublished public lectures that had been saved and organized by Hildi Greenson. Finding unpublished papers by as eminent an analyst as Ralph R. Greenson was a thrilling discovery and led the library committee of the San Diego Psychoanalytic Institute to inquire about any other unpublished work. Hildi kindly offered them access to her husband's papers that she had organized and maintained.

This investigation unearthed a genuine treasure that provided the impetus for this volume—the outline for and several unfinished chapters of Greenson's intended second volume of *The Technique and Practice of Psychoanalysis*. Doctor Greenson's health had prevented him from completing the intended companion volume to Volume I. But he had planned out the book and developed detailed chapter outlines. Furthermore, he had begun work on chapters about the selection process for analysis, acting-out, countertransference, and termination. Thus, it is possible to anticipate where Doctor Greenson would have gone in Volume II had not his medical problems interfered.

Consequently, we conceived the idea of commemorating him by requesting other colleagues to write chapters about each of the topics that Doctor Greenson had planned to cover in Volume II. These topics and the outlines for the chapters as he intended to write them are as follows:

5.0 The Preliminary Interview

5.1   Historical Survey
5.2   Aims
5.3   Dangers
5.4   The Technical Problems
        5.41   The Structuring of the Preliminary Interviews
        5.42   Practical Considerations
                 5.421   The Limitations of Analyst and Patient
                 5.422   The Number of Interviews
        5.43   The First Interview
        5.44   The Question of Data Collection vs. Therapy
        5.45   The Closure of the Preliminary Interviews
        5.46   Special Problems

8.0 Interpretation

9.0 The Use of Dreams in Psychoanalysis

10.0 Working Through

11.0 Acting Out

12.0 Countertransference

13.0 Termination

Furthermore, we hoped that each author would emphasize the clinical dimensions of the topic assigned to them in keeping with Greenson's interest in the clinical process. But as we proceeded on the project this plan was changed both by intention and by happenstance. We thought it wise to include chapters on the goals of psychoanalysis that Doctor Greenson had not intended. Therefore, we include chapters on this topic by Wallerstein and by Weinshel and Renik. Furthermore, we thought it wise to take a more detailed approach to the interpretation process. In addition to the two chapters on the general topic of interpretation by Skolnikoff and by Levy and Inderbitzin, we included one on reconstruction by Tyson and one on abstinence by Dewald. In this way we tried to cover all of the salient dimensions of the interpretive process. It seemed impossible to cover countertransference without also writing about transference and we asked the Shanes to cover this area. But this topic seemed incomplete without also covering the working alliance which Bernard Brandchaft volunteered to discuss. Finally, other colleagues wanted to commemorate Doctor Greenson but preferred to write about other areas in which he was interested. Thus, Ekstein has written about the treatment of severe disturbances and Spruiell has expanded on Greenson's interest in the screen phenomena.

Consequently the completed volume is both more and less than we, the editors, had intended, a not uncommon occurrence with edited volumes. All the areas that Ralph Greenson had wanted to address are presented. Wherever possible his own incomplete chapters have been edited by Sugarman and are offered here. This editing only tried to ensure grammatical correctness and conceptual continuity. None of the ideas were modified, and wherever possible Greenson's own words were retained in an effort to convey his unique style. But not all the contributed chapters are as clinically focused as Greenson might have written them. Some colleagues have preferred to deal more with theoretical issues or to offer a survey of their areas. Still others have offered their approaches to the clinical issues, approaches that might differ from Greenson's. Nonetheless, we are confident that we are offering a volume of which he would be proud. All the clinical complexities of the clinical situation are discussed at the depth which Greenson worked. And the approaches offered represent a fair spectrum of American views on psychoanalytic technique. We are hopeful that this volume will fulfill the didactic function which Greenson intended for it, as well as his hopes for Volume II.

Thus, we begin with his own chapter on "Beginnings." This chapter makes it clear that Greenson saw psychoanalysis as an appropriate treatment for a limited segment of patients. Therefore, he created a context that would allow him to establish the patient's appropriateness and availability for psychoanalytic treatment from the very beginning. He saw the fit between analyst and patient as an essential part of the treatment and took pains to establish an analytic ambiance with all prospective patients that would facilitate a positive treatment alliance should they decide to embark upon analysis. Toward this end he developed certain policies about managing the earliest contact by the patient, their first phone call. For this reason he maintained certain hours during which he could be reached by phone, refrained from taking calls while seeing patients, and even offered tentative interpretations of resistance to patients who were ambivalent.

The subsequent consultation interviews were structured toward the goal of determining suitability for analysis. Greenson believed that traditional psychiatric categories emphasizing signs, symptoms, and diagnoses were of little use for such a determination. Instead, he tried to clarify what capacities and qualities a patient needed to possess in order to work productively in the analytic situation. These involved three major sets of criteria: (1) patients' motivations, (2) their capacities, and (3) their character traits. Greenson believed that psychoanalytically informed psychological testing could be useful in clarifying these factors. But he was also a master at using the interviews to clarify them and his unfinished chapter offers many helpful guidelines in this regard.

His son, Daniel Greenson, expands on the subject in his chapter on "The Assessment of Analyzability." He, too, finds traditional psychiatric diagnostic labels of little use in such assessment. Instead he evaluates the patient's reactions to him during the diagnostic interviews and considers their implications in regard to the factors that make for a fruitful analysis. These include the patient's ability to work, the positive aspects of their relationships, their ability to differentiate subjective from objective reality, and the severity of their symptoms. Object relations are particularly important to assess because they have implications for the patient's ability to form an analyzable transference. Affect tolerance and modulation are other important factors in determining a patient's ability to adopt an observing ego stance toward their own transference reactions. Certain character traits are also essential for a patient to be analyzable. These include psychological-mindedness, an experience of their conflicts as residing within themselves, some sense of responsibility for their problems, an ability to specify problems, adequate impulse control, a balance between tolerating passivity and yet not being completely passive, and a capacity for seeing tasks through to their completion. Motivation is another important factor. Finally, the superego and its potential masochistic ramifications need to be assessed in order to anticipate a negative therapeutic reaction.

Wallerstein goes on to examine the goals of psychoanalysis and modifies the views that he published in 1965 to take into account technical advances and research over the past quarter of a century. He deems it essential to set goals in the context of what can be accomplished via analysis versus what can be accomplished via the other forms of psychoanalytically informed therapies. Toward this end he cautions about the need to renounce perfectionistic fantasies of cure. The findings of the Menninger Psychotherapy Research Project are turned to in an attempt to study the differential outcomes that can be realistically expected from this array of psychoanalytically grounded therapies. That study demonstrated the possibility of attaining structural change through psychotherapy as well as analysis; it also revealed that conflict resolution and insight are not necessarily predictive of positive outcome. In particular, that study found that the more supportive elements of the analyses accounted for more of the therapeutic changes than would be expected. For this reason he argues that it is time for analysts to devise more tempered and modest expectations for their treatment.

Weinshel and Renik examine the goals of analysis from a different perspective. They emphasize the need to clarify scientific from therapeutic goals despite the obvious interrelationship between them. Nonetheless, an understanding of goals must take into account evolving psychoanalytic theories of pathogenesis. Because symptoms are the result of a conflict between instincts and defenses, the goal of symptom amelioration necessitates a change in the defensive process. Psychic conflict cannot be eliminated. Instead the defenses must be modified in a way that allows for a more flexible and stronger ego. Such a formulation of goals derives from ego psychology and assumes that the goal of psychoanalysis is to alter the balance of compromise formations in order to allow the most satisfaction with the least pain. Such alterations require an increase in self-awareness and make insight an important aspect of psychoanalytic success. Thus, insight and symptom relief merge into a single goal. Finally, Weinshel and Renik emphasize the value of confining our goals to treatment goals that allow the patient access to his potentialities rather than emphasizing the patient's life goals.

Levy and Inderbitzin emphasize a strategic approach to the interpretive process. They define the interpretive process as a dialogue in which the analyst broadens those aspects of the analysand's subjective life that can be discussed. As the analysand becomes a more active participant, the two parties create a narrative of the patient's emotional history. An emphasis on the analytic surface is a helpful guideline for determining the point at which to intervene in this process during any particular session. Such a surface is defined as an aspect of the patient's verbal and nonverbal behavior to which attention can be drawn in order to learn more about important conflictual issues. Different analysts may highlight different surfaces because their theoretical model leads to a different emphasis. That is, the analyst listens and initiates his interpretations in a specific way according to his conceptual allegiances. Emphases on the analytic surface promote the analysand's active involvement in creating and attending to the surface, and lead to a strategic approach to interpretation that is essential in developing guidelines for working with different types of patients. One can do so and still remain neutral by always exploring the multidetermined nature of mental elements while interpreting. That is, the analyst can remain neutral to multiple determinants while choosing in which direction to interpret.

Skolnikoff looks at the process of interpretation somewhat differently as he traces how it has evolved in psychoanalytic thinking. His review of the literature leads him to delineate two parallel and evolving concepts of the psychoanalytic process with differing conceptions about interpretation. The traditional model has evolved from a static concept of interpretation to an emphasis on the subtle reactions of the patient to the analyst's interventions. In contrast, Skolnikoff articulates an interactional model of the psychoanalytic process in which the analyst is both participant and observer; interpretations are viewed from this perspective as a series of trial interactions with the patient that are similar to ways in which a caretaker tries to relate with an infant. Thus, insight is often developed directly by the patient based upon the interaction rather than being imparted by a neutral analyst. Furthermore, such an interactional model leads to an emphasis on observing one's countertransference in order to develop insight into the patient's conflicts. Focusing the spotlight on the analyst's inner world also clarifies the fallacy of the objective analyst, according to Skolnikoff. Interpretations are often a reaction to the patient designed to master the analytic moment instead of a well-crafted imparting of insight. This view leads to an appreciation of the interaction between analyst and analysand over content.

The role of abstinence in the analytic and interpretive process is elucidated by Dewald. He points out that the classical position on the need for abstinence is due to analysts' attempts to defend the scientific status of their methodology with a consequent emphasis on the content of insight and deemphasis of personality and interpersonal interactions. Yet the extensions of analytic technique to the treatment of more disturbed patients has necessitated a greater emphasis on the relationship between analyst and analysand. Trying to accommodate findings on the intrapsychic impact of preoedipal development, he defines abstinence as a posture whereby the analyst maintains a position equidistant from drives, superego, ego, and reality. Thus, he intervenes to draw attention to whichever of these factors is most relevant at the moment without reacting to or gratifying them. In particular, Dewald believes it important that the analyst maintain neutrality while analyzing the transference. Abstinence becomes a valuable tool in the analyst's armamentarium with multiple uses such as intensifying the internal pressure of impulse, enhancing the patient's safety to express transference wishes, deepening the analytic process, reducing the patient's dependency on the opinions of the analyst, facilitating the distinction between thought and action, making resistances clearer and easier to interpret, enabling structural change, helping to compensate for developmental arrests, and avoiding the gratification of regression.

Reconstruction is a process that integrates various interpretations and clarifies the fate of the various elements interpreted as demonstrated by Tyson in his case of a man with precocious intelligence. His reconstruction allowed the patient to recover an affectively charged memory of a traumatic event that had occurred at age four. The recovery of this memory led to new material that demonstrated the conflictual origin of narcissistic character traits. In this way Tyson demonstrates the value of a classical emphasis on the interpretation of conflict. Furthermore, his reconstruction demonstrates the value of attending to both oedipal and preoedipal issues. Finally, the event reconstructed, and the memory of it, served as a screen memory to organize and bring together the patient's narcissistic difficulties with his oedipal conflicts. Thus, reconstruction is a crucial interpretive process that enhances the analytic process and provides important analytic data.

Grinstein's chapter on the rules for dream interpretation concurs with Greenson's emphasis on the importance of the dream in the analytic process. Because dreams can be so useful Grinstein advocates an active approach to the initial dream, including some explanation of its value and how to work with it. He defines four standpoints or perspectives from which dream elements may be considered. The symbolic perspective is discussed at some length given its complexity. Symbols having to do with the patient's view of the analyst or the analytic process are particularly important. Defense mechanisms must also be considered when trying to tease out the latent meanings from the manifest content of a dream. Not just the content of dreams can be revealing, however. The structure and form of the dream are also used to express unconscious strivings. Complicating the process of dream interpretation is the principle of multiple determinism, so that any one element of a dream may have several latent meanings. Similarly, the patient's comments and reactions to the telling of a dream are often revealing. Grinstein demonstrates the process of working with the symbolic implications of a dream in his second chapter. He reports that dreams in which the male genitals appear "undisguised" have special significance. Through several case examples he shows that the direct representation of the male genital in a dream indicates unusually intense affect surrounding some specific event involving a penis. Thus, such content indicates a breach in the censorship barrier.

Working through as an essential aspect of the psychoanalytic process is examined by Wilson. Despite Greenson's emphasis on the process of working through, Wilson's survey of the analytic literature reveals that the concept tends to be used so generally as to be synonymous with the process of analysis. In contrast, Wilson describes the evolution of Greenson's definition of working through. By the time that Greenson published *The Technique and Practice of Psychoanalysis*, Volume I, he saw working through as a part of the analytic process that occurred after an insight had been given. It involved the repetitive, progressive, and elaborate exploration of the resistances that prevented an insight from leading to change. Wilson goes on to consider the technical problem in working through the narcissistic resistances delineated by self psychology. He concludes that it is useful to retain the concept of working through as a way to formulate and keep one's place in the analytic process rather than reducing it to being synonymous with the analysis of psychic conflict.

Complementing Wilson's survey of the literature on working through is Izner's chapter demonstrating the utility of working through the defensive aspects of the masturbation fantasy. Izner demonstrates the importance of changes in the content of masturbatory fantasies during analysis. Transitions in content help to clarify defenses against transference and help to provide an index of the degree to which the transference neurosis has been resolved. He offers the case of a man who felt anxious around other men because of his compulsive desire to stare at their genitals as an example of such working through. The progressive working through of the changing content of this patient's masturbatory fantasies both facilitated the analysis and revealed developments in the transference neurosis. It also illuminated important aspects of the patient's defensive organization more generally. Two other patients are described in lesser detail to demonstrate the effects on the defensive structure in persons unable to use adequately masturbation or fantasy to defend against primal scene affects.

We have part of Greenson's own chapter on acting out to illustrate his stance around this central technical problem. Greenson takes pains to emphasize the need to differentiate acting out from other neurotic enactments during analysis. In particular, he distinguishes between acting out, symptomatic actions, and abreaction experiences. Acting out, proper, involves present-day actions that discharge repressed infantile impulses or guilt. Its frequent course during analysis has to do with its intimate relationship to the transference. Despite its resistive aspects, acting out can be useful in demonstrating the relationship between the adult neurosis and the infantile neurosis to the patient. Greenson goes on to clarify the technical features of the analytic process that promote acting out and states that negative transferences are more frequently acted out than positive ones. He warns that increases in resistance often presage acting out. After considering different types of acting out, he goes on to differentiate neurotic acting out from chronic and habitual acting out characteristic of borderline pathology. Finally, he addresses the technical management of acting out.

Koshkarian agrees that acting out is a common feature of the analytic process. He agrees also that it always involves both a resistive and a communicative function. Tracing the evolution of the concept shows that it parallels evolving views of transference. Their paths have currently diverged, however, so that acting out is now viewed less as a resistance to remembering than as a resistance to experiencing transference feelings. A continuing parallel with developments in the concept of transference is the shift from viewing acting out pejoratively to adopting a more positive and accepting analytic attitude toward it. It is now seen as one more source of information to be understood. Nonetheless, at times, limits must be set while continuing to analyze it. Koshkarian also discusses how countertransference reactions to the patient's acting out are often enacted before they are understood by the analyst. If care is not taken, they can complicate and prolong the patient's acting out. He takes special care to discuss cases wherein acting out has as its purpose the preservation of the analytic relationship. It can serve as a safety valve to vent feelings that the patient would flee from before expressing in the transference. He concludes that the basic tool for resolving acting out is the analysis of transference and countertransference.

Our section on countertransference begins with what Greenson had started to say in his chapter. Greenson agreed with what has come to be called the narrow definition of countertransference, reserving that term to mean reactions in the analyst stimulated directly by something in the patient—it is always based on the analyst's own unconscious neurotic conflicts. Thus, countertransference is not synonymous with all reactions of the analyst. It is the inappropriateness of the countertransference reaction that serves as the key to recognizing it in the clinical encounter, according to Greenson. In contrast, appropriate reactions to the patient are instances of empathy. Greenson reviews typical signals of countertransference and concludes with the warning that stalemates in an analysis are often caused by unrecognized and uncorrected countertransference.

Izner continues in a vein similar to Greenson in distinguishing true countertransference from other characterological reactions of the analyst that he prefers to call counterdefense. He presents a case in which exploration of a genuine countertransference reaction in him fostered analytic progress. For Izner, a genuine counter-transference reaction is both a reaction to a transference neurosis in the patient and the revival of unresolved neurotic conflicts in the analyst. Furthermore, such reactions are always enacted either emotionally or behaviorally. In contrast, counterdefense phenomena often precede a genuine countertransference reaction. The uncon-scious motive for such counterdefense reactions is to ward off anxiety and the development of transference phenomena that might generate it. That is, counterdefense reactions ward off instinctual expression while countertransference reactions allow for partial discharge of it. Often, counterdefense mechanisms have a more preoedipal color-ing. Most importantly, they are set in motion by the patient's regressive transference neurosis. They are characterological and hence ego-syntonic. Thus, they are more apt to be blind spots for the analyst than are true countertransference reactions.

The Shanes offer a somewhat different perspective on the trans-ference and countertransference interplay in the analytic situation. They seek to juxtapose Greenson's more "classical" approach with the self-psychological one. In particular, they take issue with Green-son's emphasis on the defensive functions of these phenomena and his emphasis on interpretation. They imply that his overemphasis on the tripartite model of the mind prevented him from seeing the transferential nature of the phenomena that he subsumed under the concept of the working alliance; many of these phenomena are better understood as self–object transferences from their perspective. They approve of Greenson's openness to countertransference as a source of analytic information as well as his willingness to apologize for such lapses when they caused pain in the patient. Such an approach is thought to be consistent with that of Kohut. They go on to discuss the two major countertransference reactions to self–object transferences that Kohut noted. Thus, they view Greenson as having foreshadowed some of Kohut's ideas.

Brandchaft takes a similar perspective as he reexamines Greenson's ideas about the working alliance from an intersubjective orientation. He approves of Greenson's emphasis on understanding the impact of the analyst on the patient in regard to the patient's experience of the analyst rather than the analyst's intent. Nonetheless, he believed that Greenson erred by viewing the analyst as the ultimate arbitrator of the reality of this interchange. This doctrine of an objective reality known to the analyst is antithetical to the intersubjective approach that Brandchaft advocates. Such a stance is thought to risk demanding that the patient be cured by compliance. Instead, he advocates an intersubjective approach that considers the subjective worlds of both analyst and analysand. Such an approach recasts the foundation of the working alliance to be the analyst's commitment to seek to comprehend the meaning of the patient's affects and reactions; transference is understood from within the patient's subjective frame of reference. He emphasizes the need not to interpret transference as distorted or inappropriate. Brandchaft's approach is based on a deficit model of psychopathology that stresses developmental interferences in the area of self-differentiation over intrapsychic conflict. Only a working alliance established on intersubjective principles will allow the working through of the developmentally determined invariant organizing principles and promote the structural change necessary for successful analysis according to him.

Only cursory notes of Greenson's intended chapter on termination exist. Nonetheless, he did articulate four guiding principles for the termination process: (1) one must always be considering the patient's material in terms of termination; (2) close attention must always be paid to the state of the transference, the working alliance, and the patient's real relationship with the analyst; (3) depressive reactions are expected and should be pursued; and, finally, (4) one must expect more acting out during the termination phase.

Novick emphasizes how little the termination process has been studied until recently. An aspect of termination that has particularly interested him is the problem of interminable analysis. Thus, he offers an extensive case study of the termination phase in the analysis of a man whom he had seen five times a week for more than ten years. He suggests that the patient's need to maintain a omnipotent self-image often contributes to interminable analyses, particularly with masochistic patients. The patient whose termination phase he describes was able to pick a termination date only after extensive analysis of his "delusion of omnipotence." Novick believes that insisting on the patient setting the termination date and analyzing his struggles over doing so forces the patient who is prone to interminable analysis to resolve the task of giving up magical control that he should have resolved during adolescence. And with such patients, a terminal phase can be a stimulating and fruitful period of work.

Ekstein offers a chapter to commemorate Greenson about a topic that would not have been covered in Volume II. But his excellent and detailed case presentation of the analysis of a primitively organized man is a fitting tribute to a master clinician. In a poetic manner Ekstein describes the subtleties of the interpretive process that helped his patient resolve serious narcissistic difficulties. The working through of developmentally primitive, primarily preoedipal issues, helped the patient to begin to accept reality limitations as well as to determine his own real interests. Problems of neutrality and countertransference are profound in treating patients who create such chaos around them. They also raise difficult technical questions about when to terminate treatment and how to determine appropriate treatment goals. Ekstein addresses all these issues.

Spruiell's concluding chapter is in a similar ilk. It is a tribute to Greenson and an elaboration of Greenson's interest in screen phenomena. It is also an excellent case discussion by one master clinician dedicated to another. He begins by defining psychopathology to consist of a separation in communication among psychic functions or systems that reverberates throughout those systems and causes significant problems in adjusting to external reality. Even very severe character pathology such as that exhibited by his patient is based on conflict according to Spruiell. For that reason he prefers the term *screen* to the term *splitting*, with its implication of arrest and permanent inability to integrate. The patient discussed suffered omnipotent ambitions. A screen fantasy several years into the analysis provided a catalyst for the analytic process. Patients who use screens extensively do so in order to maintain psychic equilibrium according to Spruiell. Such patients seem insatiable for new experiences and sensations that help to disguise underlying depression. Such a formulation leads Spruiell to pursue a clinical tact quite congruent with that espoused by Greenson.

In conclusion, we believe that this volume will stand as a fitting tribute and memorial to a master of clinical psychoanalysis. Experienced psychoanalysts have contributed their ideas and experience to all the subject areas that Ralph R. Greenson had intended to make the chapters of the second volume of *The Technique and Practice of Psychoanalysis*. Furthermore, some close colleagues and friends have contributed other chapters pertaining to clinical phenomena in which he was interested. Thus, we hope that this volume will prove to be as useful to the student and practitioner of psychoanalysis as Greenson had intended his second volume to be. To the degree that it is so, it will fulfill a dream of his.

Introduction to Volume II

WHEN I begin to write *The Technique and Practice of Psychoanalysis*, I had intended to explore the technical and practical problems in chronological order as they arise in the course of psychoanalytic therapy. I soon discovered that it was impossible to write intelligibly in depth and in detail about any technical or tactical procedure without having first thoroughly discussed resistance, transference, the working alliance, and the psychoanalytic situation. I hope Volume I has provided the student with a basic understanding of these fundamentals of technique so that he feels at least partially prepared to cope with the typical but complex and unexpected problems which occur during psychoanalytic treatment. No textbook, no matter how extensive and well written, can replace the complexity of meeting the patient.

It is both the bane and delight in practicing psychoanalysis that no two cases are alike once one penetrates beneath the surface. Furthermore, no two analysts work in the same way and no two of a given analyst's patients are ever handled by him in precisely the same manner (A. Freud, 1954a). This is due to differences in the analyst's theoretical orientation, his professional style, his personality and character, and also his feelings, fantasies, and attitudes, conscious and unconscious, about each of his patients. Consequently, all writings on techniques are slanted by the analyst's personal idiosyncrasies. In addition, all detailed writings on technique reveal a good deal of the analyst's intimate and personal goings-on within himself. This tends to make the analyst's own view of what he does unreliable and is apt to lead to some unconscious idealization or denigration of his work. I shall repeat what I stated in the introduction of Volume I, that despite all these qualifications, I believe that a text that attempts to depict what a psychoanalyst actually does, and why, will help to stimulate a full, open, and continuing discussion of psychoanalytic technique (Greenson, 1967).

Ralph R. Greenson

1

Beginnings: The Preliminary Contacts with the Patient*

Ralph R. Greenson, M.D.

Introduction

THERE is more variability in dealing with the initial contacts with a prospective patient than with any other aspect of psychoanalysis. This is due to several interrelated factors, most importantly that we are dealing with a meeting of strangers, and there are special stresses for both patient and analyst in meeting new and essentially unknown people. A person's competence in dealing with strangers may be very different from his ability in handling people who are familiar. Some analysts who are very capable in carrying out difficult analyses once they get under way may have unusual difficulties in the preliminary interviews. Some analysts are uncomfortable in dealing with patients face to face and others find it enjoyable,

*This chapter was left unfinished at Ralph Greenson's death in 1979. It has been edited by Alan Sugarman, Ph.D., who researched references and made grammatical changes while attempting to retain the author's unique writing style. It has been noted in the text where material had to be deleted because Dr. Greenson had not sufficiently developed that section.

perhaps too enjoyable. I believe that it is anxiety which impels some analysts to skip the preliminary interview altogether and to refer patients who "only" want a consultation and/or a referral. Then there are those who try to keep the face-to-face interviews to a minimum because of their own shyness and not primarily out of their theoretical or clinical considerations. It is anxiety or excitement which may play a decisive role, making some competent analysts poor evaluators of prospective patients.

Another complicating factor involves the need to take into account the patient's motivation to engage in an insight-oriented treatment. The preliminary interviewing of the patient is necessary for the psychoanalyst to determine whether the prospective patient requires psychotherapy and if so, what particular form of therapy is most suitable for him. I prefer to do this personally because I find that face-to-face meetings bring out subtleties and nuances that phone calls and letters do not. I also believe that it is my responsibility to make the recommendations for the therapy and the therapist for each patient referred to me. Although I respect the recommendations of the referring colleague, experience has taught me that my own evaluations have proven to have greater validity to me than those of others (this despite my having been wrong in certain cases). I explain to a patient surprised at my wish to reevaluate him that I believe each patient and analyst should have the opportunity to come to their own conclusions. As a result I try to leave one hour per week free for such consultations. If I do not have an opening, I ask if the patient's situation is urgent and if it is, I send him or her to somebody else for evaluation.

The technique of interviewing is different from the usual psychoanalytic procedure; it is even more of an art than a science. Interviewing a new patient requires the talent to relate effectively to a strange person in trouble. It is more dependent on having available the use of certain personality traits rather than on following rules. It is therefore more difficult to teach interviewing and evaluation than psychoanalysis proper. This may be one of the reasons that the psychoanalytic literature on the subject was relatively sparse until the very important book by Gill, Newman, and Redlich in 1954 on the initial interview. The only systematic and detailed writings on this subject are usually extremely condensed and limited to dynamic psychotherapy rather than psychoanalysis proper (Saul, 1972; Langs, 1973).

There are several important differences between such diagnostic interviews and psychoanalysis proper. These include the fact that the preliminary interviews are carried out face to face instead of in the traditional position of the analyst sitting behind the recumbent patient; that the patient comes with motives that may be distant from a real wish to engage in psychoanalysis; and that there is no agreement or commitment on either the patient's or analyst's part regarding their aims or goals. Nonetheless, it is necessary to explore carefully and analytically the issues involved in conducting the preliminary interviews because they may be decisive in determining the future course of the patient's therapy. If correctly handled, the first contacts offer the analyst the unique opportunity of selecting the right patient for the most suitable type of psychotherapy with the best available therapist. It also offers the patient a chance to react to and evaluate the analyst, and to decide whether or not he wishes to follow his recommendations. Being strange to one another, each party is especially sensitive and fresh to the impressions that they arouse. Above all, the initial interviews must be therapeutic and not traumatic (Gill et al., 1954; Klauber, 1972).

Unfortunately, major decisions made by the patient or analyst are often based on unexpected and ostensibly trivial occurrences which take place during the preliminary interviews. For example, an excellent prospective analytic patient whom I sent to a competent analyst refused to return to him because the chairs in his waiting room were stiff, rickety, and uncomfortable. He felt an analyst so inconsiderate of his patients' comfort outside the analytic office would be harsh in the analytic sessions. Unfortunately, the patient then turned his hostility onto me, disregarded my wishes, and went to a "hale and hearty" eclectic therapist. The analyst whom I originally recommended was a young analyst and was dead set on not being a "Beverly Hills" psychoanalyst.

I also knew an experienced and usually tolerant psychoanalyst who sent a prospective patient away after one session because he could not bear her accent and unrefined diction in the initial interview. This analyst may have correctly predicted some difficulty in establishing a favorable long-term working alliance, but perhaps some brief self-analysis might have reduced his early negative feelings and made working together possible and productive. The patient returned to me for further referral and said, "I know the analyst did not like me. I felt it in my bones."

Because of the special demands and vagaries of the initial interviews and the important impact that they may have on the later therapy, they present a serious responsibility for the psychoanalyst and require just as careful scrutiny as any other phase of psychoanalytic therapy.

The Initial Phone Call

It might seem strange to begin a book on technique with a subject that appears at first glance trivial or banal. But this emphasis illustrates a basic aspect of analysis: one cannot follow conventional or rigid criteria about what is important and what is not. The initial phone call can decisively color the patient's approach to the first office visit. I have learned from patients later in their therapy that it was my way of responding to their initial phone call that helped them overcome, at least temporarily, a longstanding and severe resistance to seeing any psychoanalyst. And I know of many instances where competent psychoanalysts lost good analytic patients by not recognizing some disturbing repercussions in the patient to some personal idiosyncrasy of the analyst, which was revealed during the first phone call. I am sure that this has happened to me when patients failed to appear for their initial appointment on which we had agreed over the phone.

I shall try to illustrate some of the main considerations through a number of clinical examples. Let me begin by stating some general guidelines that I have found useful. One is that I do not answer the telephone when I am working with a patient. This is an intrusion in the patient's hour, a disruption of his attention and mine, and a demeaning of his goings-on in favor of the unknown telephone caller. To listen to the caller with undivided attention requires that one ignore the patient on the couch. Your alternative is to give only partial attention to each which is a disservice to both. There is also an element of hypocrisy in answering the phone because it contradicts what the patient was told originally about the importance of attempting to say all his thoughts, no matter how trivial. The only exceptions I make to this rule of not answering the phone during a patient's session are when my secretary or my answering service signal me that it is an emergency. I then ask the patient to excuse me and explain that there seems to be an emergency. Occasionally, when I expect an important long distance call, I tell the patient in advance about the impending phone call. And I ask the patient to please leave the room when it comes through.

I recall a sad and amusing anecdote about the pitfalls of indiscreetly answering a phone call. I was treating a young woman whose husband was in treatment with another analyst. Suddenly one morning, from out of the blue, she asked me if I was going to Dr. X.'s surprise seventieth birthday party. I asked her how she knew about it. "Oh," she casually answered, "my husband heard about it because of a phone call Dr. Y. (her husband's analyst) answered during my husband's hour." I kept quiet because I felt that discretion was the better part of valor.

I usually receive or return telephone messages during my five- to ten-minute break between patients, so that I have ample time to listen attentively. In recent years, I have also reserved a half hour in the morning and in the early evening for receiving or making calls to which I cannot give sufficient time during my working day.

The following clinical vignettes illustrate several problems. My secretary informed me that a Mr. M. phoned and was told that I was busy. He asked when he could call back and was told he could try either at five minutes before the hour or between 11:00 and 11:30 A.M., or between 6:00 to 6:30 in the evening. Mr. M. replied he would call between 11:00 and 11:30 and did so. My secretary buzzed me shortly after 11:00 and a hesitant voice said that he was Ben M. and had been recommended to phone me by Nicholas S., a close friend of his, who had had several consultation hours with me about three years previously. Mr. S. had advised Mr. M. that he needed psychoanalysis or some kind of psychotherapy and thought that I would be the best person to consult. Mr. M. paused. At this point I said yes, I remembered Mr. S. but I wondered how he, Mr. M., felt about his friend's suggestion to see me. (I usually reserve discussion about the patient's motivation for coming until the preliminary interview, except when I suspect that a good deal of pressure may have been used to persuade the patient to make the first phone call.) He replied that he knew he needed some kind of treatment but that he was completely baffled about the different kinds of treatment. He had no real experience with psychiatrists or analysts and was a beginner compared to his friend Nicholas who seemed to be so knowledgeable. I asked Mr. M. if he felt that his predicament was urgent and he said, "Not exactly, I have been in the same mess for quite a while, but I would appreciate a fairly early appointment. I know I have stalled around for several months but I don't want to put it off again, I just don't trust myself. I know you are a busy man but I want to wait for you because I don't want to go to just anybody."

I replied that I had no regular free hours at this time, only occasional ones, but would be glad to see him and we could explore his situation if he were able to wait for my first free hour, which was 10 o'clock some five days hence. He replied that it would be fine, asked for my address, which I gave him and also the general directions in regard to where he would be coming from. Mr. M. thanked me, said he would see me Wednesday at 10:00 A.M., at which time he appeared. I shall amplify upon the personal interviews later in this volume. But for now I would like to comment on some of his reactions to the phone call which came up in the early hours of his analysis.

Mr. M. was very apprehensive when he first rang me up because he had been warned by his experienced friend, Nicholas, that analysts are very busy and that, therefore, the patient should be very brief and to the point. Mr. M. was reassured that I had a half hour for receiving telephone calls and that he didn't have to constantly watch the clock to catch me at five minutes to the hour (it is quite noteworthy how often people will miss the five-minutes-to-the-hour moment, when one is limited to that time for a phone call; resistances seem always ready to subvert one's attention). The fact that I remembered his friend, Nicholas, made Mr. M. feel good. It meant to him that I not only did not forget people whom I had seen even briefly, but also that I was not as tight-lipped and secretive as he had been led to believe. When I told Mr. M. that I had no regular free hours but only occasional ones, he felt both disappointed and relieved, and that I was kind in asking him if he was able to wait five days and if the time of day was suitable. My giving him directions to my office seemed considerate, unexpected from the straightlaced analysts whom his friend Nicholas had described. This he felt especially keenly because I was said to be very busy and he was a total stranger to me. He ended the phone call feeling decidedly less anxious and reluctant to come to the first appointment. Apparently his anxiety about how analysts behave and work had been at least temporarily assuaged by my way of answering his telephone call. He must, I surmise, have felt less like a child and that I was less of a strict and formidable grown-up. Or to put it in the patient's language, "psychoanalysts are like regular people."

Let me contrast this situation with another. I received a phone call from a Mr. C. telling me that he had been recommended to me by an analyst in another city with whom he had had a few years of psychoanalytic therapy. I told him that I had no regular free time at the moment and wondered if his situation was urgent. Mr. C. replied that it was not an emergency but he was quite upset and would like an early hour. I told him I was sorry that I had no immediate free time but that I would try to find somebody who might. Mr. C. replied that he had been given several names by his previous analyst and had already called two of them. He then asked me if I had the time to talk to him a bit longer and I said yes, I had some five minutes. Then with a sigh, Mr. C. reported that the first analyst he phoned seemed to be quite harassed, asked him abruptly if it was analysis he wanted, and when the patient answered that he was not sure, the analyst said he only had two free hours a week. If that seemed agreeable he should ring him back at 11:55. Mr. C. felt insulted and "brushed off." The man treated him merely as a "thing" to fill up his two free hours. He decided not to call the analyst back.

The second analyst whom Mr. C. phoned did not answer the phone. Instead his answering service did, telling him that the analyst was in conference and "would get back to him as soon as he could," but that she was not sure when that might be. Again Mr. C. felt that he was treated as a thing, a disposable person. He knew the answering service was not the analyst but he felt that a conscientious analyst would leave different instructions with his answering service and also would have a schedule which left room for answering people in distress more promptly or at least at a more precise time.

I told Mr. C. I could sympathize with how he felt, but I could also assure him that both analysts were decent and capable people. I repeated that I was sorry that I had no foreseeable free time until ten days later. Again I offered to find someone who had free time earlier but Mr. C. said he would rather wait, and we set up a meeting for ten days later.

I would like to discuss the behavior of the two analysts Mr. C. had contacted (I am assuming for the sake of emphasizing my point that Mr. C. reported the facts accurately). The first analyst with whom Mr.

C. spoke seems to me to have committed some blatant errors. He was working with a patient when Mr. C. phoned, and he should not have answered the phone because that is an intrusion and a disruption of their therapeutic work. It also seemed to influence the manner in which he answered the call. If he did answer the phone, he should have stated only that he was busy and limited himself to setting a time for a *telephone* appointment. He was not only impolite to Mr. C. but he also revealed to the patient whom he was treating that he handed out his hours in an impersonal fashion, a point, as we have seen, not overlooked by Mr. C.

The second analyst whom Mr. C. phones is a brilliant analyst, who works on a 50-minute "assembly line" schedule, that is, with no time gaps between patients. His working day is so full that he truly does not know when he can return a phone call. I know that from my own experiences with him. Again, Mr. C. detected that this man was under great pressure and decided against working with him, although he had also been recommended highly. I believe that analysts, no matter how busy, should have specific times when they can be reached by telephone. Prospective patients have enough internal resistances which should not be complicated by external obstacles of our own making. And there is always the possibility of an emergency situation.

There is an opposite type of telephone behavior which also evokes resistance in patients. There are analysts who are so eager to acquire patients in general, or a specific patient, that they offer extravagant concessions to the prospective patient. One such analyst was willing to interview a new patient on a Sunday or very late in the evening. The patient sensed that this behavior expressed other than professional concern and canceled his appointment. Few things scare a patient off more than feeling that the analyst needs him, a situation often correctly perceived by prospective patients and often transparent in "patient-hungry" candidates in training, or anxious analysts with too many free hours.

I was the third analyst on Mr. C.'s list, and although his need for being seen was fairly urgent, he decided to wait for me because I had given him five full minutes of my time and attention and had offered to help him find someone who might have free time earlier. He seemed to feel from this encounter that I was appropriately concerned with his plight. My behavior helped him to wait until our appointment.

An internist, Dr. X., calls me to ask if I have time to see in consultation a patient of his, Mrs. Cathy F. He had been treating the young
woman for over a year for chronic fatigue, but he had become convinced from his negative findings and her history that she was suffering from a neurotic depression. He had suggested this to her and she
had agreed. The physician wanted to set up the appointment with me
for her, because, at that point, she seemed willing and he was eager to
pin her down. In the past she had procrastinated whenever he
brought up the issue. I told Dr. X. that I would rather have her call me
directly and explained to him that experience had taught me that
patients who have to be cajoled or persuaded to come for consultation by others rarely work out in the long run and I would rather have
them run away early than later on. The physician seemed puzzled but
went along with my suggestion.

Mrs. Cathy F. phoned me the next day, told me her name, that
she was Dr. X.'s patient, and that he had told her he had spoken to
me about her and also that she had agreed to see me in consultation.
I added that I wondered if it was her wish to set up the appointment
or was it mainly due to Dr. X.'s strong persuasion. Mrs. F. hesitated
and then said that she had no enthusiasm for coming but also no
rational reasons for not coming. I suggested that perhaps her lack of
enthusiasm was really a euphemism for being afraid to come. She
laughed and agreed that this was probably so, and countered with
"so what shall we do about it?" I said we had several choices. We
could wait and see if her fatigue and depression abated with time
and then she would not have to come in at all; or she could come in
and we could explore what it was that made consulting a psychoanalyst so frightening to her. My answer seemed to please Mrs. F.
and she said: "Good, that last idea makes sense. If we can overcome
the fear then I will be able to come and if we cannot, I will be able to
stay away with a clear conscience." I agreed with that formulation
and we set up an appointment.

When Mrs. F. arrived she did not appear either fatigued,
depressed, or apprehensive. She smiled in fact and said: "You are a
very clever man. Dr. X. made me feel that I had no choice, I had to
go to a psychoanalyst and that feeling of compulsion made me more
depressed. It was oppressive. I felt frightened as though I were
being cornered. Your saying we had certain choices came as a relief.
Yes, you are a very clever man." I answered that I did not consider
my remarks clever; I had merely said what I believe. I know from

years of practice that a prospective patient's "no enthusiasm for coming" usually means they are afraid of the confrontation. I also know symptoms can ebb and flow and further, that if you offer a patient who is suffering an opportunity to explore his misery, he will eventually come if his pain is great enough and if he has the intellectual curiosity and courage to explore the frightening unknown. Most people interested in psychotherapy feel that it is better to know what you fear than to be oppressed by unknown fears. Mrs. F. agreed and added that since our telephone conversation she had begun to question her fear of the consultation herself. In fact she believed she even had some answers.

At this juncture I only want to stress two points. I always prefer the patient to make his appointment directly with me. For example, I do not arrange with a wife for her husband's appointment (or vice versa). Despite all the apparently sound reasons for the husband's not phoning, I have found that this indicates a strong resistance. If the resistance is severe enough to preclude his phoning me, his wife is only deceiving herself about the usefulness of psychotherapy for her husband *at this time*. The same holds true for physicians making appointments for their reluctant patients. Second, I try to avoid giving a patient the feeling that coming for a consultation or entering treatment is their only course of action. I always indicate there are options, some better or some worse, but options. Offering patients no choice makes for fear, flight, or submissiveness, but not for an open-minded approach to therapy (Klauber, 1972). Lastly, I believe in interpreting obvious resistances during the initial phone call.

I have not found a totally satisfying answer to a situation which occasionally arises: A patient unknown to you phones, asks for an appointment which you are able to arrange, and then asks, "Doctor, what is your fee?" This is usually an ominous prognostic sign because it indicates either a realistic problem of having insufficient funds or an irrational overconcern with money matters. My answer to patients inquiring about the fee during the first phone call (or later) is to say: "I have no set fee, my fees vary." Some of my poorer patients have later reported that they felt frightened by my reply, it sounded as if it might be an entrapment. The more affluent patients, especially the very wealthy, often felt later they might be taken advantage of and charged a high fee, one they knew was higher than that paid by other patients. They inquire about the fee on the phone in the hope of obtaining a bargain, before I know of their wealth. I do charge wealthy patients higher fees and tell them so at the appropriate time.

If I sense that a patient inquires about my fee because he is in economic distress I add to the "no set fee" the question, "Are you worried about not being able to pay?" If he answers yes, I assure him that the fee for a single visit will be within his means. I belong to that group of analysts who believe a portion of our work should be done for little or no fee. If the answer to my question is not a matter of financial hardship, I merely repeat that my fees vary and that we can discuss the matter more fully during our later appointments. I know that this will not allay such a money-oriented patient's anxiety, but he might as well face my attitude about fees without false assurances. Some patients who are not in financial straits and yet insist on knowing the exact fee already over the phone often cancel their first appointment. But, again, I would rather have a patient run away early than later on.

The initial phone call can save you and the patient an unnecessary visit if the conversation reveals that you are not able to fulfill their needs. Patients like Mr. C. will call who have been recommended to continue an analysis they have begun and have had to interrupt for some external reason. When you have insufficient time available it does present a dilemma. If they have names of other analysts suggested to them by their former analyst, they should be told to call the other analysts on their list. Sometimes patients are told to make an appointment to see me in consultation if they need analysis even when it is known that I will not be available. Their analyst believes, and I agree, that a consultation for the purpose of referral is often valuable in selecting a second analyst. I am of the opinion that a face-to-face interview with a patient can be helpful in selecting an analyst with whom you believe this particular patient can work well. The concept of "matching" a patient with an analyst is a nebulous one, and yet many analysts find it useful (Tyson and Sandler, 1971; Klauber, 1972; Holzman and Schlesinger, 1972). It is a difficult one for analysts with little experience in private practice or in teaching seminars. But even experienced training and supervising analysts make mistakes. I have often been wrong in my choices but, on balance, I have been more often right than wrong in making a good choice with the help of the single exploratory session. In general I prefer to see a patient even for one hour before making any recommendations. If this cannot be arranged I tell the patient I will give them the names of several people I consider highly, but I do so reluctantly. I then make sure I am suggesting people whom I know have free time at the moment. And also, I prefer to call the prospective analyst myself to rule out last minute changes in his or her schedule.

The initial phone call can also be an early opportunity to weed out those who entertain unrealistic expectations about therapy. I also like to get a notion of how the patient decided upon seeing me. Sometimes they say they were referred by psychoanalytic colleagues, other therapists, and former patients. These referrals are usually helpful, but when patients come to me from reading a published article or from hearing me give a public lecture, it is worthwhile spending a few extra moments on the telephone. An elderly, energetic sounding woman phones and says she must see me; she heard that I would cure her of a "sickness" that had plagued her for years and no doctor had been able to "touch." When I questioned her how she came to call me she explained that a friend of hers had heard me at a public lecture and "raved about your hypnotic personality. You see right through people, you have X-ray eyes. I know you can help me." I answered that I appreciated her friend's recommendation but I assured her (1) I did not use hypnosis, and (2) I did not possess X-ray eyes. I then inquired when she had last been thoroughly examined by a physician. The elderly woman answered that it had been at least five or ten years. I then told her that before I would agree to see her I would suggest she have a thorough physical examination and then, if her physician recommended me, I would be willing to see her. She was very disappointed and appealed to me to see her just once. "What can you lose?" I replied that from her description of her situation, I was afraid she might be wasting her time and money and, in my opinion, the correct approach to her problem was first to consult a physician. I never heard from her again.

A man in a quavering voice phoned for a consultation. His halting, unclear speech impelled me to ask him rather early in the conversation how old he was. He replied that he was 76. I then inquired about how he had come to the decision to phone me. The man answered that he is a great reader of medical books, although he never graduated from high school, and that he had come across my book on *The Technique and Practice of Psychoanalysis*. He reasoned that if I could write a whole book I might be the man to cure him of his forget-fulness, his insomnia, his depression, and his many other symptoms which had been bothering him for years. I asked if he had consulted another psychiatrist and he answered he had, but the psychiatrist whom he had seen for over ten years had recently died. The psychia-trist, whom I knew professionally, had not really helped his symptoms much but he had enjoyed talking to him once a month, it made him feel happier. I then told him that I knew his psychiatrist and thought highly of him but I did not work in the same way. I would, however, be glad to find him a capable psychiatrist who worked in similar ways to his old psychiatrist. The old man was disappointed but pleased that I would place him with someone I trusted. This I did and, thus, spared the old man and myself an unnecessary visit.

A special problem is presented to the analyst by someone asking for consultation or referral, sent by a patient currently in treatment. By and large this situation makes for a variety of transference com-plications for the patient in treatment. The new referral may be a bribe, or gift, or you are being used to exhibit your "greatness" or some other form of acting out. In any event, it contaminates the transference and countertransference if you see the new referral. It is far better to tell the person on the phone that your experience has taught you that consultation with another analyst would be best. It is a dilemma when somebody asks to see you in consultation and keeps secret that they are in treatment with another therapist. This may eventually come out in the phone call if the analyst is lucky. I tell the patient very frankly that they are not being fair to me or to their current therapist. Medical ethics require that they get permis-sion from their current therapist before we talk over how I can be of help.

There are exceptions to this rule. Potential suicidal patients, or people on the verge of acting out very destructively, can be helped by a new analyst and sometimes by a friend, spouse, or relative. One must weigh the patient's need, plight, and reliability, along with medical ethics. Sometimes the analyst may even have to give up confiden-tiality and talk to the current therapist with or without the new patient's consent.

I would like to close this brief survey of the initial phone call by stressing certain basic points. The telephone call must be taken seriously and not treated as trivial. Therefore, it should be taken at a time when it will receive the undivided attention it deserves. The first phone call may reveal strong resistances which can be pointed out and at least, partially, dealt with. The initial call can reveal the patient's unrealistic feeling of having no choice but to come to you. In such situations the analyst can reassure the patient that there are options. Sometimes it is possible to recognize that you or psychoanalysis are not what the patient needs. All of this can be handled with tact and straightforwardness, providing you give the caller enough time and attention.

I realize that some of the positions I have taken are not accepted by all psychoanalysts. Some do not have secretaries or an answering service. Many answer a phone call during their work session even with an answering service, especially those who work with no time gap between patients. Other analysts believe that it is preferable not to see a patient at all if you do not have the time to continue treatment. Many do not do consultation work at all and depend upon colleagues for their referrals. Let us not forget that there is room within psychoanalysis for individual differences in theoretical orientation, analytic style, and personality. I deal with the situation as I do because I believe it is consistent with the basic principles of psychoanalysis as I practice it.

Above all, I place great value on the "atmosphere" of the analytic situation, be it on the telephone or in the consultation room. Whatever I am trying to do should be straightforward and open, it does not have to be harsh or blunt. Tactfulness does not mean being evasive or hypocritical. From the very first telephone call, the patient should feel that, above all, the analyst is concerned with their welfare (Gill et al., 1954). This point of view suits me personally. I feel comfortable with it. This way of working may have its drawbacks and may not suit others. I may even find reason to change my way of handling these situations in the future. At this time, however, it feels to me to be a coherent and consistent part of my approach to a patient seeking help.

The Analyst's Office

The analyst's working space should fulfill two minimal but basic requirements: (1) It should be comfortable and efficient for the analyst, and (2) it should not provoke extraordinary resistances in the patient. I want to stress that the latter considerations merit greater attention in the first hours of therapy, particularly when the patient is not strongly motivated. Once the treatment is well under way and both patient and analyst have strong incentives to go on working, it is possible to work under the most adverse circumstances. I recall, during World War II, having to do some emergency analytic-type work with a fellow officer who was in an acute homosexual panic with paranoid overtones. The only room available to us had no lock, so we found it necessary to nail the door shut at the beginning of each session and to remove the nail at the end. The patient was so needful and I was so eager to be helpful, that this odd way of insuring our privacy was no hinderance to either of us.

The situation becomes more complex in proportion to the greater number of options that the analyst and patient have. Analysts who work in a hospital or university setting usually have to put up with much less comfort and efficiency than do therapists in private practice, and this does not usually cause insuperable difficulties. Patient and analyst recognize their limited choices. The remarks which follow are aimed primarily at the analyst in private practice and the "usual" private patient. The source material comes from my experiences with my own patients, the reactions of patients of other analysts who returned to me after referral, and my observations and reactions to analysts' offices I have visited.

One of the major problems we must face is how the office can be made comfortable and pleasant for the analyst and yet not destroy his "analytic incognito." After all, we have been taught that we do not want to contaminate the patient's transference reactions by revealing too much of our personal preferences or idiosyncrasies. Unfortunately, no matter how we select the location, arrangement, and decor of the office space, the final result will reveal a good deal about the analyst's personality, *even* his passion for anonymity. The last point refers to those psychoanalysts whose offices are so stark that they resemble rooms you would expect to find in a monastery or nunnery, albeit a well-endowed one. The observant patient will sense that such exaggerated austerity springs from some hidden fears in the analyst and will be made uneasy.

Other analysts try to guard their anonymity by choosing a setting and decor that is so bland and nondescript that their offices resemble rooms in a traveling salesman's hotel. This, too, cannot fail to register on the sensitive patient as a defensive maneuver at the expense of good taste. The opposite is equally objectionable—offices which are so lavish that they recall the false opulence of a Hollywood movie set. In all these instances, many patients will detect that there is something false or forced in the analyst's style of furnishing. This may well interfere with the development of a productive analytic atmosphere during the early hours.

We cannot hide our personal taste unless we resort to obvious stereotypes which then betray our wish for concealment. We also know that we cannot cater to the aesthetic preferences of all our patients. What we can do is to arrange things that please us, that facilitate our work, and that do not offend our patients. Extremes of any kind should be avoided as should relation of any intimate personal idiosyncrasies. I would not display a photograph of the biggest fish that I ever caught, but I consider it joyful and harmless to place on my desk some fresh flowers from my garden.

The office is a working space and it should be physically comfortable and pleasing to our eye, but it is not a social room, a bedroom, or a den. I want to repeat that these considerations are important particularly in the first hours of treatment, in the beginning phase, before the positive transference, the working alliance, and the therapeutic process have taken hold. Let me turn to some clinical examples.

In the previous section, I mentioned how an experienced and apparently competent analyst had lost a good prospective patient because the patient could not bear returning to a psychoanalyst whose waiting room contained only old, stiff, rickety, and straight-backed wooden chairs. I have been in that waiting room and can confirm the patient's findings. What makes this setup more disquieting is that the location of the office indicates that the analyst must have a comfortable income. I do not know this analyst well enough personally to ask him why he furnishes his waiting room and treatment room so uncomfortably and shabbily. I can only surmise from my limited personal experience, and my more extensive scientific contact with him, that his office arrangement reflects his "anti-Beverly Hills" obsession and his devotion to deeply buried psychopathology in his patients.

I try to set up my offices so they will not cause my patients any undue hardships and will also be pleasurable for me. All the furnishings in it are things I like but not things which are too intimate. I prefer to have a waiting room large enough to seat three people comfortably, because sometimes parents will come with a child or a couple with an aging parent. There are always some current magazines for reading, usually news magazines or illustrated ones, and not only the most intellectual ones. I have one or two books of paintings or cartoons for those who have to wait for a patient whom they had to accompany to the office.

In the treatment room I have a desk and two comfortable chairs on one side with another one for me opposite. The two chairs are arranged so that the patient can choose one closer or further away from me across the desk. I prefer a desk because it gives frightened patients a feeling of some protective distance and of being able to hide part of their body. It also gives me more freedom with the restlessness I often feel in my legs. I have heard the point made that no desk or a low table makes for a sense of greater openness but I believe that early in the analysis, it is the patients' feeling of vulnerability which should have first priority.

My couch is large enough to offer the patient some degree of movement without the danger of falling off. It is firm to encourage wakefulness and work and not sleep. I prefer the couch to be low so that I, sitting behind, can see the patient's face when I so desire. It also permits the patient to turn his head and see me. I have a wedge pillow for the patient's comfort and a side table for personal items such as a purse, gloves, or purchases.

In some of my previous offices where the toilet facilities were out in the public hallway, I had a small area before the exit door with a mirror and Kleenex where upset patients could regain their facial composure before having to face the public.

I prefer to have a separate entrance and exit to my treatment room so that my patients will not meet each other. My patients also like this arrangement, in general, although they seem to tolerate occasional meetings with other patients quite well as long as their reactions are brought promptly into the analytic situation and analyzed for their resistance potential. I have heard that analysts who share a waiting room do not find their patients' reactions to other patients or analysts a formidable resistance.

In summary, I believe that an analyst should work in a setting that suits him personally, in which he feels both some pleasure and comfort. I also believe he should try to arrange the office so that it will approximate a new patient's realistic expectations and will not arouse intense anxiety by being either extraordinarily impersonal or idiosyncratically bizarre. It should have the feeling of a working area which is private, comfortable, and aesthetically pleasing. One can do no more and should do no less.

I do most of my work in an office in a medical building but see a few patients at home in the early morning or evening. I supervise and refer patients to analysts who work either in professional buildings or in their homes. As a result I have some impressions about the advantages and problems in both situations. For example, practicing in a professional or medical building emphasizes the patient's awareness that psychoanalysis is a professional or medical treatment, and thus is respectable and socially acceptable. It also, however, exposes the analytic patient who comes four or five times weekly to being recognized as an analytic patient by the parking-lot people, the elevator operator, the secretaries, the physicians, and other personnel who work in that building. This can be painful for shy patients and for those who would prefer to keep their treatment a secret. This often occurs with analysts coming for more analysis, analysts' wives, and celebrities. Such potential "exposure" may evoke strong resistances early in the analysis, but if handled quickly and thoroughly, is rarely a disruptive factor.

It is worth dwelling briefly on the subject of patients who wish to keep their analysis a secret. To a married person it may mean that they or their spouse consider psychoanalysis a threat to their marriage. For many, psychoanalytic treatment indicates something shameful, something to hide. They fear that it reveals that they are "weak-minded," perhaps even "crazy," lacking in will power, sexually depraved or, at least, sexually peculiar, on the verge of a nervous breakdown, or mentally incompetent. Shame about going to an analyst was very widespread and intense in the years prior to World War II. In the 1950s and 1960s it diminished and the trend has even been reversed; I have known patients who boasted about being in analysis. (Sometimes they even claimed to be when it was not true.) Now, during the 1970s, in the United States, psychoanalysis is once more quite unpopular.

It is important to detect the shamefulness about being an analytic patient, and on what peg this shame is hung. It should be regarded as like the manifest content of a dream. And the fantasies that give rise to the particular surface manifestation need to be pursued. Some typical examples are the following: "I am weak-minded" often is derived from the notion that people will know that the patient has masturbated extensively or has an overly great need to be dependent. The nervous breakdown that they fear is often their fear of losing their internal controls. The shame of others knowing about it reflects defensive externalization and projection.

A partially realistic anxiety in this group is that felt by older analysts who would not like their patients to know they are in analytic treatment. And I do try to shield the older analysts from their own patients if it is possible. I do this by seeing them in my home, or by spacing their hours. But it is still imperative to analyze the irrational fears, even in these situations, because they produce important resistances which hinder the effectiveness of the analytic process.

Young candidates and colleagues also appreciate hiding from their patients the fact that they are undergoing analysis or supervision. I try not to humiliate them unnecessarily. But their feelings of shame should be taken up in their own analysis. If a patient is sophisticated in terms of knowing about analytic training requirements, I believe it is best to be truthful and neither lie nor be evasive. Lying and evasiveness to one's patient do irreparable harm to the real relationship, the working alliance, and the patient's capacity to develop a full blown transference neurosis.

When a patient develops a genuine feeling about what it means to be analyzed, about what it says about the analyst's personality, he will slowly recognize that the analyst also must have suffered in a similar manner for the analyst to have empathic feelings for the anxiety and depression the patient is undergoing. In a well-going analysis, the patient himself will recognize that psychoanalysis is a collaborative effort and requires a great deal of the patient and the analyst. Eventually, patients realize that the distance between patient and therapist is not as great as "analyzed" vis-à-vis "unanalyzed." Nevertheless, I try to arrange hours for analysts so that candidates and analysts will avoid too frequent contact with their own patients.

Working in one's home offers the patient more privacy but it also diminishes the analyst's privacy. The patient sees the person who opens the door, inadvertently may get a glimpse of other rooms or people, hear sounds of others, particularly children, and may even catch a whiff of what is being cooked. Such stimuli may evoke strong curiosity and voyeuristic fantasies or impulses which may be gratifying but also forbidden and, as a result, are repressed or denied. The entrance to my home office, for example, affords a view of the garden and part of the kitchen. It took several years for a male patient to admit that he often saw a female figure at the kitchen table drinking coffee. It took a bit longer to acknowledge the thought it might be my wife. He then became aware that he was afraid she might be unattractive and he would hate to tell me that. Later he realized it would be worse if she were attractive and he might have sexual fantasies about her. Only after I could show him that he had already had both sets of fantasies in his dreams did he realize he had seen her there for years but had denied the reality of his perceptions because he was looking into a forbidden area. He had "oedipalized" the situation. Toward the end of his long analysis, he would occasionally wave to her as he got into his car.

An amusing incident comes to mind. I could censor this but psychoanalysts have the tendency to portray their work as too serious, if not grim. There are moments of joy, however, not only when we have good hours but, also, from an adventitious experience. They can be very helpful if analyzed. My three-year-old grandson ran to the door when, at the breakfast table, I announced the arrival of my 8 o'clock patient. Before I could stop him, he flung open the door and joyfully yelled: "Hello, patient, hello patient," on and on until I stopped him. The patient was startled at first, but then he burst into a huge grin and said, "Hi." This hour shed some important light on how joyless my patient's way of life had been and how he envied me.

Of greater importance than these issues is the need for adequate soundproofing. It is an unanalyzable resistance if the patient in the waiting room can hear the ordinary speaking voice of the patient or analyst in the treatment room. The real possibility of being overheard will hover over the patient and inhibit his communicativeness, especially in terms of allowing himself to open up emotionally. It is not only a matter of neurotic distortions of being overheard but the real fact of confidentiality and his right to privacy. The analyst may have to resort to music in the waiting room to mask the sounds from the treatment room. I know of several colleagues who have small radios installed or have music piped into their waiting rooms.

Selecting Patients for Psychoanalytic Treatment: Analyzability

INTRODUCTION

Selecting patients for psychoanalysis is beset with many problems arising from a variety of sources. Part of the confusion is based on the uneven development of psychoanalytic theory and technique. In some areas we know more theoretically than we are able to use and in others we seem to utilize techniques we are only able to inadequately explain. For example, the theories of ego psychology seem to be far more advanced than our ability to apply them in the analytic situation. On the other hand, we often use intuition, empathy, and "hunches," activities we can only partially explain theoretically.

Then there are terms which we use frequently because they are a kind of shorthand, but because they are not spelled out they have different meanings to different people. It would be hard to get a consensus on "ego strength, narcissism, object relations, and the self" (Loewald, 1973).

In Volume 1, I wrote a chapter on "Indications and Contraindications for Psychoanalytic Therapy: A Preliminary View" (1967, pp. 51–58). I realized then that the question of analyzability is a complicated one. Freud himself used different criteria in approaching this important topic (1905b, 1913, 1916–1917). No single measure or standard, no matter how important or clear-cut, permits an accurate prediction of analyzability. One has to assess the pathology *and* the healthy resources of the patient (A. Freud, 1965). That is quite a difficult feat after a few preliminary interviews. Yet it is precisely then that the analyst has to make his recommendation as to the choice of therapy and the therapist. And yet prolonged interviews, trial analysis, and psychological testing can sometimes be of help. But they, too, can produce certain disturbing side effects (Knight, 1952; Glover, 1955; Kernberg, Burnstein, Coyne, Appelbaum, Horwitz, and Voth, 1972).

The widening scope of psychoanalysis has cast doubt on the heretofore accepted emphasis on specific symptoms and diagnostic categories as reliable indicators for psychoanalytic treatment (A. Freud, 1954a; Jacobson, 1954; Stone, 1954). Patients with clinical syndromes hitherto considered inaccessible to psychoanalysis are now found to warrant consideration. In addition, the forward surge of ego psychology has changed analysis from being primarily a depth psychology and turned it in the direction of a psychology of the self or the total personality. In this way the patient's character is now included in the diagnostic assessment of the adult patient (A. Freud, 1969b). At the same time, a number of analysts have become convinced that it is possible to deal psychoanalytically with preverbal experiences which can be revived in the transference, a view held by analysts of otherwise widely divergent views (Winnicott, 1958; Rosenfeld, 1965; Lampl-de Groot, 1967; Balint, 1968; Klein, 1975). Kohut's emphasis on the treatability of the narcissistic personality and Kernberg's concern for the borderline-narcissistic patient leave one with a blurring of traditional guidelines.

Another complicating factor in the selection process is the plethora of other "talking cures" which have gained prominence in the last twenty years. Anna Freud (1969b) has also pointed out that psychoanalysis has lost its appeal as a revolutionary movement and is downgraded, especially by the young, because it is regarded as a mode of treatment espoused by the "establishment." Brief psychoanalytically oriented therapy, behavioral therapy, biofeedback therapy, group therapy, community therapy, and transcendental meditation are also more popular with the majority of patients seeking help. They are less demanding in terms of emotional commitment, take less time, and financially are not as expensive. When we evaluate patients we now have to ask ourselves which form of therapy best meets the needs of the particular patient at this point in his life.

From all these diverse sources, our criteria and standards have become more indistinct in the process of selecting patients for psychoanalysis. It is high time to make order, or at least to make sure that we try to make analyzability better understood. Before we can proceed to technique we must first clarify the concepts and terminology. The reader is referred to five works for a more detailed picture of the problems: (1) the Kris Study Group Monograph on *Indications for Psychoanalysis*, which is the result of a seminar held in 1957 and 1958 and reported by Waldhorn in 1967; (2) "Indications and Contraindications for Psychoanalytic Treatment," a panel chaired by Guttman in 1968 (Panel, 1968); (3) "Problems in the Selection of Patients for

Psychoanalysis: Comments on the Application of the Concepts of Indications, Suitability and Analyzability" by Tyson and Sandler in 1971; (4) "Psychotherapy and Psychoanalysis, Final Report of the Menninger Foundation's Psychotherapy Research Project," 1972, by Kernberg et al., especially Kernberg's summary; and (5) Stone's (1973) thoughtful paper "On Resistance to the Psychoanalytic Process: Some Thoughts on Its Nature and Motivations." It is noteworthy how few seminars on analyzability are regular features of psychoanalytic curricula in training institutes both in America and Europe (Limentani, 1972).

Perhaps the most difficult diagnostic dilemma we face in determining suitability for analysis is that we have to make our recommendation for treatment before we can arrive at any certain diagnosis, namely, during the course of the preliminary interviews (Knight, 1952; A. Freud, 1954a). Even with prolonged preliminary interviews, psychological testing, and trial analysis, we cannot make reliable predictions of analyzability based essentially on the presenting symptoms or the presenting diagnostic category. Most of our patients do not suffer from a pure or simple neurosis but have admixtures of clinical syndromes in which cne constellation of neurotic patterns serves as a screen to hold in abeyance a number of deeper pathological configurations.

The following clinical example may illustrate this point. A woman entered analysis with the chief complaint of a fear of flying. Very soon this was revealed to be a manifestation of her repressed hostility to her impotent husband and her warded-off longings for sexual freedom. This, in turn, led to her more widespread but unrecognized fear of being trapped and helpless. We were later able to uncover her strong incestuous desires and fears in regard to her father and guilt toward her mother. This masked still deeper and repressed fears and wishes for a symbiotic closeness to her mother. At that point in her analysis the predominant clinical picture was one of an angry suicidal depression. Her phobias and anxiety states had become negligible and peripheral, and finally disappeared by the time we worked on her depression. To state this in more diagnostic terms we can say that the patient presented a hysterical facade with anxieties, guilt, hostility, and inhibitions related to her repressed and unresolved oedipal struggles with her parents. After a few years of analysis, however, we discovered that what seemed to be a fixation to the triangular jealousy, hatred, and love of her oedipalized parents, was a thin, but tenacious cover for a much more intense and enduring struggle against her depressive dependency, with great rage and guilt from her ambivalent longings and fears in regard to fusion and separation from her mother.

Sometimes, during the course of an analysis, we have to keep changing our view of what is primary or secondary, what is defensive or reactive, and what is basic and peripheral. A reliable diagnosis is often only possible at the end of treatment.

For all these reasons, and others too numerous to mention, psychoanalysts changed their major reliance on indications and contraindications based on signs, symptoms, and diagnosis, and instead tried to answer the question: What capacities and qualities must a patient possess to be able to work productively in the analytic situation? We try to isolate the demands that psychoanalytic therapy makes on the patient and we examine the patient in regard to his ability to work effectively in the analytic situation. This is the core of the concept of analyzability.

A patient is or is not likely to be analyzable depending on three major sets of criteria: (1) his motivations; (2) his capacities; and (3) his traits of personality and character (Waldhorn, 1967; Greenson, 1967, chapter 4). A fourth consideration which may be decisive for a temporary period of time, is feasibility; the patient's external situation. A patient may be unanalyzable because of his current financial, work, family, or marital situation. We must also answer the question: Is psychoanalysis the optimal treatment for this patient at this time?

PSYCHOLOGICAL TESTING

Introduction

Some thirty years ago it was standard operating procedure when a new patient arrived at one of the better sanitarium, psychiatric ward, or clinic, in accordance with their high standards, he was given a battery of psychological tests. These batteries included the Wechsler-Bellevue, the Babcock Story Recall Test, the Object Sorting Test, the Word Association Test, the Rorschach Test, and the Thematic Apperception Test. Among private practitioners, use of this battery was not quite so prevalent. Psychological testing was very time-consuming, it was costly, and it was often difficult to find a competent psychological tester.

The psychiatrist or psychoanalyst in private practice used psychological testing when he had to appear in a court of law because the results of psychological testing appeared to the lay public as "hard facts." Psychiatrists or analysts in private practice would also occasionally use psychological testing when, after several consultations, they could not arrive at a definite diagnosis. This was particularly true when you could not determine whether the patient should be treated as an ambulatory patient or as an inpatient. To put it in Knight's terms: Was the patient safely neurotic or psychotic (1953)? Did you have time enough to make a clinical diagnosis or was the patient in a precarious situation, on the verge of decompensating neurotically or psychotically, the so-called nervous breakdown?

I was never trained in psychological testing and at this late date regret it. However, I was influenced by the writings of Rapaport, Gill, and Schafer. David Rapaport, Merton Gill, and Roy Schafer published two classic volumes on psychological testing that were reedited by Robert Holt in 1968. This work was continued at the Menninger Foundation in an excellent paper by Shevrin and Shectman (1973) about (1) the controversies surrounding psychological testing, and (2) the nature of the diagnostic process. [Here Dr. Greenson intended to articulate more about the usefulness of psychological testing for the determination of analyzability. Unfortunately he never completed this section.] But the approach advocated by Shevrin and Shectman of emphasizing the form that the communication takes in the diagnostic process over a gathering of historical facts or descriptive symptoms is one I also use in interviews.

Indications and Contraindications

The use of indications and contraindications for prescribing psychoanalysis or other forms of psychotherapy is a carryover from the medical model for prescribing treatment. It was used by Freud and his early coworkers as the primary approach to the choice of treatment until quite recently and has never been entirely abandoned, although today we ask how a patient would react to the psychoanalytic situation and the psychoanalytic process.

In order to bring clarity into the confusion of concepts and terminology, I shall attempt to define the terms we shall use in this discussion. I would rather risk being considered pedantic and boring than to add to the ambiguities.

An indication refers to any sign or symptom of illness or abnormality which serves to direct the therapist to a suitable remedy or type of therapy. A contraindication refers to any sign or symptom of illness or abnormality which serves to direct the therapist away from certain remedies and types of therapy.

A *sign* is evidence of malfunction or illness which is noted by someone other than the patient. It is often elicited in the history or behavior of the patient without his awareness of its existence or its pathological nature. For example, a forty-five-year-old physician suffering from sexual impotence mentions in an offhand manner that ever since childhood he gets out of bed to drink milk and eat crackers as it seems to insure him a good night's sleep. The patient has no awareness that this may not be just an innocuous habit but a compulsive need, and a remnant of his fixation to his early oral pleasures received from his mother. He is totally oblivious that this behavior is inappropriate to a forty-five-year-old man, married for over twenty years.

Another example is a thirty-five-year-old divorcee who uses her handkerchief to brush the chair she sits upon in the treatment room, before and after each hour. She does it routinely and without any trace of self-consciousness, which makes me realize that she is unaware of her fear of making bodily contact, even through her clothes, with anything that was in contact with somebody else's lower body parts. This indicates to me the likelihood that she has a fear of being touched by some form of dirty sexuality. When I asked the patient about this "habit," the lady replied that this was typical for her and she claimed it was a sign of being fastidious.

A *symptom* refers to a change in some normal function, sensation, or reaction, of which the patient is aware. Symptoms are usually accompanied by anxiety, depression, or pain. They are usually felt as complaints and drive the patient into treatment. Sometimes the patient accepts or adapts himself to the symptom (it is ego syntonic), and only comes at the behest of outside influences. For example, a thirty-seven-year-old man arranges for a consultation with me because his wife is upset and complains that he had lost all sexual desire for the last two years. The patient acknowledges the truth of the statement but accepts it as a hereditary trait; he has heard from his mother that this "runs in the family."

A *diagnosis* is the heading or name assigned to a group of signs and symptoms which are connected together either by virtue of their common etiology or because they appear in repeated patterns and share a common clinical course. To illustrate, I shall apply this in outline form to an obsessional neurosis. It shares with all neuroses (except the traumatic neuroses) the fact that distorted derivatives of unresolved unconscious conflicts have overwhelmed the ego's defenses and have gained access to consciousness. The compromise formations of drives and defenses which have come to the surface form the signs and symptoms of the obsessional neurosis. Ego alien thoughts intrude themselves into awareness repeatedly and can be seen to have characteristics of their anal sadistic heritage as well as the typical defenses of isolation of feelings from thoughts, and reaction formation. Obsessional thoughts may be blasphemous and omnipresent, yet the patient is, on the surface, extremely pious and devout. The typical character traits of such a person are excessive cleanliness, parsimony, rigid politeness, orderliness, and punctuality, with occasional lapses. Early in the analysis, the traits are ego syntonic. It can take a long time for him to realize that these are overcompensations in opposition to his basic anal sadism drives. All of the patient's symptoms and character traits may be understood as being compromise formations, derived from his regression and/or fixation to the anal sadistic phase of instinctual drive development with its typical highly ambivalent relationship to people. For a more comprehensive description see Fenichel (1945b), A. Freud (1965), and Brenner (1973).

Diagnostic categories include more than a single diagnostic picture. Freud, for example, subdivided the neuroses into the transference neuroses and the narcissistic neuroses (1916–1917, Lecture XVI). In his view the transference neuroses were treatable by psychoanalysis because patients belonging to that category, out of their hunger for object relations, could develop and sustain a transference neurosis to their analyst and could also work analytically to resolve it. The narcissistic neuroses applied to patients who had not developed or had lost the capacity to organize and sustain mental object representations, and had no consistent external or internal relationships to people. As a consequence patients suffering from a narcissistic neurosis could not develop or maintain a transference neurosis nor a working alliance to work it through (Greenson and Wexler, 1969; Greenson, 1974b).

Other examples of diagnostic categories are the perversions, the psychosomatic disorders, the impulse disorders, the addictions, delinquency, and the largest category of all, the "borderline" cases. Recently, Kohut (1971) made an important contribution by describing a type of narcissistic character who may be charismatic, creative, and who may retain the capacity to form good object relations, and is, therefore, not borderline or psychotic. He postulated a dualistic theory of libido; above all, one which leads to higher and healthier forms of narcissism (p. 220). (See Loewald [1971b], Hanly and Masson [1976] about the question of analyzable narcissistic patients.) In all classifications, we have come to recognize a wide disparity between symptomatology and analyzability. Some patients in each of these categories are analyzable by classical psychoanalytic techniques, others require modifications or preparation and still others are untreatable. This will become clearer in our discussion of analyzability.

ANALYZABILITY: AN INTRODUCTION

Analyzability has been used in different ways by a number of writers but I believe its simplest and clearest meaning is the dictionary definition: the ability of a person to be psychoanalyzed, his fitness and aptness for psychoanalytic therapy. An analyzable patient is one who is not only understandable in an analytic sense to the psychoanalyst, but who is also able to make effective use of the analyst's interventions. Tyson and Sandler (1971) make a distinction between analyzability and *suitability*. They suggest that analyzability refers to patients who may be comprehended by the psychoanalyst but who are not able to make use of the psychoanalytic process. They prefer the term *suitability* to refer to patients who have the ability to participate and benefit from psychoanalytic treatment. To me it is the second condition which is decisive for analyzability. For all practical purposes, patients who can be understood by psychoanalysts but who cannot work in the analytic situation are unanalyzable. Patients who are analyzable are also suitable, a point of view recently expressed by Limentani (1972). It is true that patients may be more or less suitable for psychoanalytic treatment, but that is equivalent to stating that some patients are more or less analyzable. Yet, for practical reasons, we often take patients whom we think are suitable, only to find out that they are only analyzable to a superficial extent; that is, in a way comprehensible to the analyst, and yet are unable to change (Angel, 1971; Applebaum, A., 1972; Lower, Escoll, and Huxster, 1973; Applebaum, S., 1973).

The process of selecting patients for psychoanalysis began gradually to shift away from its complete dependence on the patient's signs, symptoms, and diagnosis for determining the treatment of choice. Freud began already in 1905 to consider the patient's plasticity and moral character in determining his suitability for psychoanalysis (1905a). In the "Three Essays on Sexuality," Freud noted that the homosexual who struggles against his homosexuality, that is, whose homosexuality is ego dystonic, may be more responsive to psychoanalysis (1905b). In 1945 Fenichel introduced the concept of *accessibility* as an important indicator of analyzability, especially in the gray area of severe character disorders, perversions, addictions, and impulse neurosis. In this he was joined by Glover (1954) who modified the diagnostic categories by adding the terms *accessible*, *moderately accessible*, and *intractable*. Accessibility was not spelled out by these authors but it seems clear that they were referring to the ability of the conscious and rational ego of the patient to approach the preconscious and unconscious psychic activity within himself as well as to comprehend the analyst's interpretations.

For example, some patients are able to recognize spontaneously that they are being evasive or guilty or seductive. Some may readily confirm this when it is pointed out by the analyst. They are accessible. Others remain unaware despite what seems to be clear-cut and repeated evidence of these reactions. They remain obtuse to these goings on in themselves even after frequent confrontations by the analyst. I believe that accessibility is based on what we would call today psychological mindedness, certain traits of character, and the patient's capacity to establish a treatment alliance (Tyson and Sandler, 1971). Accessibility alone does not indicate analyzability.

Another impetus for shifting away from the dependency on signs and symptoms came from the work of a number of authors who demonstrated that symptoms were not as tightly bound to diagnostic categories as had once been believed. Symptoms may be combined in many more ways than we first realized. Phobias, for example, could be found in hysterics, obsessionals, depressives, and paranoid schizophrenics (Kubie, 1948; Greenson, 1959; Rangell, 1959; Aarons, 1962). Symptoms may indicate analyzability but the absence of other necessary qualities may make a patient unsuitable, as we shall indicate later (Tyson and Sandler, 1971). Yet, I have to remind you of Anna Freud's (1970b) idea that the symptom can be equated with the manifest content of a dream. Other analysts demonstrated that the diagnosis was not necessarily a good prognosticator of the outcome of treatment. Knapp, Levin, McCarter, Wermer, and Zetzel (1960) showed in a follow-up study that the diagnosis of hysteria did not necessarily mean a patient could be successfully analyzed. Zetzel (1968) went even further and carefully distinguished four different types of hysterical patients whose analyzability varied from very good to extremely poor. Many analysts now treasure very highly the development of object relations in people seeking psychoanalysis as a more important criteria for analyzability than diagnosis. The quality of human relationships is important in predicting the capacity to benefit from analysis; that is, are they able to form a triangular relationship with a mother or father, or are they still under the influence of a one-to-one relationship, essentially child and one parent, or narcissistically oriented (Kernberg, 1972; Fleming, 1972; Kantrowitz, Singer, and Knapp, 1975; Shevrin and Shectman, 1973; Schlesinger, 1973)?

Criteria for Analyzability: Motivation

The Patient's Motivation. There are several reasons for beginning the discussion of criteria for analyzability with an exploration of motivation. First, and most obvious, it is the patient's motivation which moves him to make the initial contact. More important, it is the quality and the maintenance of a high level of motivation that makes a successful analysis at all possible. I was surprised that Greenspan and Cullander (1973) rated motivation ninth in a list of twelve criteria for analyzability. Only a patient who is strongly motivated will be able and willing to work with the determination and perseverance that psychoanalysis requires. The neurotic symptoms or the discordant traits of character must cause sufficient suffering or discontent with oneself to induce the patient to begin psychoanalytic treatment.

Up until some twenty years ago most patients came for psycho-analytic treatment because of painful symptoms (Greenson, 1955). That has changed and today it is the exception, and usually a pleasant surprise, when patients come for psychoanalytic treatment for specific symptoms that make them miserable. Instead, most of our patients consult us for more generalized and vague complaints. They usually describe a general discontent, a malaise, a not knowing "what they are all about," a sense of living a purposeless life, a lack of direction, or similar generalities, which we would classify as character disorders. Be that as it may, the patient with overt symptoms is considered a choice patient and I shall begin with a discussion of them.

The symptomatic patient comes for consultation or treatment with complaints of some specific psychological pain, either fears, guilts, depression, or inhibitions. He seeks us out to help him to overcome or to lessen his suffering. This is an important motive for entering therapy and such patients begin treatment usually with great zeal. The danger of such an impetus is that, if perchance the symptom disappears or is ameliorated before the patient's motivation is reinforced, their desire for psychoanalysis may also vanish.

There are two possible explanations for such a turn of events. Either these patients were not properly evaluated or they were not properly handled. If they came only for immediate relief from their chief complaint and had no genuine desire for the long-range changes that only psychoanalysis can offer, this should have been detected in the preliminary interviews. Such patients would have been better served if they had been referred to a therapist for brief psychotherapy. The other possibility is that the analyst failed to recognize that there were other silent but painful malfunctions going on in the patient that were hidden by his acute distress. Had this been detected early enough in treatment and demonstrated to the patient, it might have intensified his motivation to go on to long-term treatment (Gill, Newman, and Redlich, 1954).

For example, a young man urgently asks to see me. He is agonizing over whether to take a position in California or in New York; he must decide this in a few days. There are advantages and disadvantages in each of the two situations. As we talk he indicates almost inadvertently that his fiancée lives in New York and his widowed mother resides in Los Angeles. He feels very relieved when I indicate to him that the agony of his indecision stems essentially from the uncertainty about where his greater love lies. In the next several sessions I was able to show him how, throughout his life, he could never make decisions that would lead to his separation from his mother. He flunked out of college away from home, he could not get himself to have sexual relations until he was in his middle twenties, and then only when he was out of town. The patient then realized that the important decision was not the job in California or in New York, nor to be near his sweetheart or mother. The real issue was his willingness to get into treatment so that he could free himself from his infantile attachment to his mother. The patient agreed that this was crucial and I made arrangements for him to begin analysis. The point is that he would not have continued treatment if I had just let him experience the relief from the agony of indecision about the two jobs.

Here one must bring up the problem of "flight into health" and "transference cures" (Oremland, 1972). The flight into health means that the patient has, by dint of some insight, used his superficial understanding to cover over and deny the deeper determinants of his symptoms. Transference cures refers to the phenomenon whereby patients use their unexpected involvement with the psychoanalyst for a quick identification with his analytic attitudes, or as a magical cloak to cover over their more deep-seated pathology. In all such instances, the good result is superficial and temporary. These patients will either suffer a relapse of symptoms which may force them to return to psychoanalysis, or they will live a life based on denial and escape from internal reality.

The task of the psychoanalyst is to attack such quick improvements, to point out their evasive quality, and to consistently make the patient aware, within limits, of the deeper and more widespread pathology. No neurotic symptom is localized, except on the surface. An important responsibility for the psychoanalyst during the preliminary interviews is to widen the patient's view of his symptoms, and to refresh and keep alive his motivations for deep and long-range goals (Gill et al., 1954; Waldhorn, 1967). I do not wish to demean the importance of the patient's conscious suffering. It can be a most valuable source of his prolonged desire to become involved in deep psychoanalytic treatment. But if the patient is to endure the rigors of long psychoanalytic treatment, even suffering from symptoms will not suffice. Ann Applebaum put it well when she stated that the patient must also be painfully aware of the discrepancy between how he acts and feels and how he would like to be (1972, p. 56). Furthermore, the patient should have some sense of responsibility for his own misery if he is to be a good candidate for psychoanalytic treatment (Winnicott, 1963). He must be willing to bear the distress of revealing his anxiety- and guilt-laden intimate experiences; he must also be willing to spend a considerable amount of money and time to relinquish the secondary gains from his illness, and to forego quick and temporary results (see Greenson [1967], Volume 1, Section 4.1 for a more thorough discussion of these issues).

Selecting patients with the necessary motivation is no simple task. There are some tell-tale characteristics, however, which should make one wary of choosing certain patients. For example, psychoanalytic therapy is not suitable for psychological first aid, although psychoanalytic knowledge is a valuable asset. The analyst may know how to ease the pain, but it is like using a brain surgeon to cure a headache. Thus, desperation is a poor indication for psychoanalysis.

There is another group of patients who choose psychoanalysis for the wrong reasons. They are mistakenly taken into psychoanalytic treatment and become the stalemated, interminable patients in every analyst's practice. Some of these patients are insistent on psychoanalytic treatment because it represents to them the elite form of therapy and confirms their sense of personal worth (Holzman and Schlesinger, 1972). Being accepted for psychoanalysis feels an indication of their special worthwhileness, a form of snobbery, and a reassurance against inferiority feelings. Charismatic patients, glamorous or wealthy people often fall into this category (Klauber, 1972). For other patients, psychoanalysis means that they are not "crazy" and is interpreted as a guarantee of mental health (Waldhorn, 1967). Then there are lonely people who seek prolonged psychoanalytic therapy out of their loneliness. What they really want is a reliable, platonic, attentive listener, and some of them exhibit their symptoms as an antique work of art, hoping to entice the analyst's acceptance. They are patients with a strong narcissistic component (Angel, 1971; Kohut, 1971; Kernberg, 1974). Some need the analyst as a stabilizer in a world which seems to them to be going to pieces. The patient comes to the hour as a baby goes to his mother for emotional refueling (Fleming, 1972). Whenever a patient is willing to pay fees beyond their means or to come great distances which cause them severe hardship, one should be alert to the likelihood that they are not suitable analytic patients. On the opposite side of the spectrum are delinquents who hope to convert the therapist into an accomplice, or a witness for their defense. Patients who try to begin the very first interview by walking directly to the couch often do so for such a reason.

One final consideration has to be taken into account in order to evaluate the patient's motivation; that is, his secondary gain from his illness. It may be the most important source of resistance. Freud stated in 1926: "The ego now proceeds to behave as though it recognized that the symptom had come to stay and that the only thing to do was to accept the situation in good part and draw as much advantage from it as possible" (1926a, p. 99). Tyson and Sandler (1971) go on to say that: "The fact that a symptom may be a source of suffering is no guarantee that it is free from secondary gains. In some disorders the only source of gratification which the patient may experience is that associated with the secondary gain which has accrued to the symptom (Fenichel, 1945)" (p. 222). Analysis, itself, may provide a potential source of secondary gain for certain patients, particularly when it may be used as a source of masochistic gratification. Other very dependent patients may exploit the analytic situation in such a way that their need for the well-being consequent on a dependent relationship is fulfilled. However much the patient may desire help, he may have so much secondary gain to lose that analysis would not prove to be a viable proposition for him. Thus the analyst must explore, for example, the extent to which the neurosis may hold together an otherwise shaky marriage, or enable the patient to hold some power over others because of the effect on them of his problems.

I can illustrate this with the following examples. A forty-year-old woman comes for treatment at the suggestion of her internist for multiple physical ailments which keep changing, do not respond to organic therapy, and eventuate in her being so fatigued that she spends almost all day in bed and cannot accompany her husband on business trips to the East Coast or on vacations. This, she claims, depresses her, but she feels it would be unfair to keep her husband a "prisoner" of her illness. In the initial interviews it slowly emerges that her physical ailments began when she discovered her beloved husband was carrying on a number of sexual affairs. When she confronted him he admitted that although he loved his wife as a friend she was no longer sexually exciting to him. The patient was hurt, angered, insulted, and depressed but felt she could no longer compete with the younger women whom her husband preferred. She originally went to her physician with the hope he could prescribe some vitamins or hormone medication that would restore her youthful zest and vigor, in general, and her sexual desires which had been diminishing over the years, in particular.

In the five years since her husband's confession the couple had had no sexual relations and they often talked of the possibility of separation and divorce, with neither pressing for a decision. The patient would respond by developing a new physical ailment or a worsening of an old one. Her husband assured her he would never leave her as long as she was ill. It was quite obvious the patient was willing to settle for a platonic relationship with her husband provided that he lived in the same house with her. When I brought up the possibility that psychotherapy might reduce her anxiety and depression, and even relieve her bodily complaints, she became more frightened and more depressed. The patient realized that her neurosis had become a face-saving means of holding on to the facade of a marriage. She did not want to risk losing her neurosis and her husband. I recommended that she consult someone for supportive, nonanalytic therapy, to which the patient half-heartedly agreed. Apparently the patient did not feel she had the capacities to bear the possible loss of her husband nor did she have the hope of finding another. Her neurosis was a lesser evil than the real miseries she anticipated.

Some months later a man asked to consult with me. I agreed before I realized that he was the husband of the patient I had previously seen. If I had been aware of this fact I might have suggested someone else, but I am not sure. At any rate he came because he had been made anxious by his wife's report of our visits. She had told her husband that I felt her physical condition was "delicate" and that she should not be subjected to any sudden or undue emotional stress as it might produce a "nervous breakdown." I found myself in a rather awkward situation and asked him whether he had any "sudden or undue emotional stress" in mind. No, he answered, he did not want to "rock the boat." I told him that I had the impression that if he continued living with his wife the way he had, politely and asexually, and did not discuss divorce or separation, the boat would not rock. He was very relieved, thanked me profusely, praised my openmindedness, especially since he had heard that I was both a Freudian and a happily married man!

I can only surmise from my brief contact with him that his neurotic solution for his sexual and marital problems was better than anything which he imagined that psychotherapy could offer at that time. I felt that I had no right to disturb their neurotic equilibrium, that was their decision to make.

The secondary gains in this example are worth emphasizing. The wife kept up a socially acceptable facade of a marriage because it saved face. She was also never alone for long periods. The absence of sexual approaches from her husband spared her the need to confront the fact that she had some responsibility for the deterioration of their sexual life. Going to doctors and receiving physical ministrations may well have given her some indirect sensual pleasure. The physical pains and aches were a self-punishment, but also gave her a tyrannical power over her husband. She paralyzed him by threatening him with the massive guilt-evoking image of her possible nervous breakdown.

The husband's gains from this splitting off of sexuality from marriage can be understood as a return to the carefree adolescent life-style of having sex on the outside and returning home to his "mommy-wife" for his nonsexual needs. He was safely married and no "decent" woman would expect him to break up a "good" marriage. The husband could even feel virtuous in his social circle for standing by his sick wife. Small wonder neither partner wanted to risk the changes inherent in attempting any form of analytic therapy.

How different it all might have been if the forty-year-old woman had felt that she had the capacities to risk losing the platonic husband and perhaps finding someone or something better. Or how different if the husband had not been so tyrannized by guilt from her illnesses and had felt that he wanted a full life with one woman. But analysts cannot play God, and we must respect the fact that patients who consult us may have a truer inner picture of their capacities, distorted though they may be, and would prefer to live out a life that might be misery for us. We must respect the individual's right to his own neurotic life-style, as foreign as it may be to us. Above all, it is a serious blunder to try to "sell" psychoanalysis or any form of psychotherapy if a patient has inaccessible resistances (Gill et al., 1954; Klauber, 1972).

The Analyst's Motivation. At first glance it seems a simple matter to describe what motivates the analyst to take a patient. The patient is analyzable, likeable, interesting, can pay the desired fee, and can come at the time the analyst has free hours. However, certain complications may arise in the analyst which can interfere with his clinical judgment. For example, he may accept a patient for psychoanalytic treatment unaware of the fact that he was impelled to do so by intense but unconscious countertransference reactions. On several occasions I found myself working with female patients who were unsuitable for analysis. I then thought back to the initial interviews and realized, to my surprise, there was clear-cut evidence that they were poor risks for analytic therapy. With the help of some self-analysis I discovered in each case that the patient reminded me of one of my female relatives, in temperament, mannerisms, or body configuration.

We have to be vigilant about our own motives for recommending psychoanalysis. The patient's helplessness can stir up fantasies and feelings of omnipotence in the analyst which may warp his judgment (Holzman and Schlesinger, 1972). Monetary gain and narcissistic pleasure are a poor basis, if not contraindications, for taking a patient. When I was a young psychoanalyst, I took a patient into psychoanalytic treatment who was suitable, but not for me. She could afford to pay me $10.00 an hour, which at that time was more than I received from any of my other patients (it was 1938). I was delighted but so anxious that I promptly lost her, which had been predicted by my supervisor. I learned then, and have seen it confirmed countless times as a supervisor of young analysts, that nothing will drive a patient away faster than an overeager analyst.

The Psychoanalyst Must Like the Patient to Work Well with Them. You cannot spend hundreds of hours empathizing with and delving into the intimate recesses of another human being's mind, hearing, feeling, and seeing their gloomy, grandiose, delicate, ugly, and fearful fantasies, going through their joys and disappointments, enduring their hatred and contempt as well as their love and admiration, and still maintain your psychological balance if you do not like the patient. Liking is a derivative of love, limited, controllable, and durable. It implies caring. The analyst should also find the patient interesting to him in order to make sharing the work enjoyable and not boring. It also enables the analyst to hate the patient, that is, to inflict pain when necessary, but within the limits that are beneficial for the therapeutic situation (Winnicott, 1949). Charging the appropriate fee, and ending the hour at the proper time, for example, are derived from hostility and should be carried out without guilt. It is easier to do so when one maintains positive feelings toward the patient.

To understand another human being in an intimate way implies a willingness to get into the insides of another person; it is derived from both libidinal and aggressive strivings (Sharpe, 1930). To treat a patient by giving them insights and patiently bear their frequently irrational reactions to you resembles a mothering activity, a form of feeding, nurturing, protecting the patient–child. It may be a means of reparation for guilt feelings related to the analyst's past life with younger siblings, etc. It may be, in part, an antidepressant or counterphobic activity. The analyst explores the patient's unknowns in order to overcome his own anxiety about his own worries, to continue his own analysis (Freud, 1937, p. 249). No matter what its origin, the activity should be essentially a sublimation.

The analyst's *therapeutic intent* has been a matter of dispute ever since the case of Little Hans: "Therapeutic success, however, is not our primary aim; we endeavor rather to enable the patient to obtain a conscious grasp of his unconscious wishes" (1909b, p. 120). Later he wrote:

After forty-one years of medical activity, my self-knowledge tells me that I have never really been a doctor in the proper sense. . . . I have no knowledge of having had any craving in my early childhood to help suffering humanity. . . . I scarcely think, however, that my lack of a genuine medical temperament has done much damage to my patients. For it is not greatly to the advantage of patients if their doctor's therapeutic interest has too marked an emotional emphasis. They are best helped if he carries out his task coolly and keeping as closely as possible to the rules [1926, pp. 253-254].

Freud contradicted this view on several occasions (see Greenson [1967], Section 4.223). Here I wish to repeat part of what I said in Volume 1. Freud's attitude notwithstanding, I contend that the therapeutic intent in the analyst is a vital element in his makeup if he is to practice psychoanalysis as a method of treatment. I do not maintain that this urge to be a healer of the sick and miserable can be obtained only from medical school training; but no matter where it originates, it is an essential ingredient of practicing psychoanalysis as a therapy. In my personal experience, I have never known an effective psychoanalytic therapist who did not feel a strong but controllable desire to relieve the suffering of his patients. I have met M.D. psychoanalysts who were essentially misplaced researchers or data collectors, and their therapeutic results were below expectations. I have known lay analysts who were physicianly in their way of working and their patients did not seem to suffer from their analyst's lack of an M.D. degree. What I am referring to is what Stone calls the frank and evident therapeutic, physicianly commitment, the deep and thoughtful wish to help or cure (1961, pp. 119–120). I do not mean frantic therapeutic zeal. Such overevaluation of the power of psychoanalysis may tempt analysts to recommend analytic therapy injudiciously (Greenacre, 1966).

But I do believe that the therapeutic intent of the analyst is of particular importance in the analytic situation for the analyst as well as for the patient. For the patient, the physicianly analyst is a powerful activator of the transference neurosis and the working alliance (Stone, 1961). The patient's image of the doctor stirs up memories, fantasies, and feelings from childhood of an authoritative, arbitrary, incomprehensible, and magical figure who possessed the power of the omnipotent, omniscient parents. It is the doctor who takes over when the parents are sick and afraid. It is the doctor who has the right to explore the naked body, and who has no fear or disgust of blood, mucus, vomit, urine, or feces (Freud, 1926b). He is the rescuer from pain and panic, the establisher of order from chaos, provider of emergency functions performed by the mother in the first years of life. In addition, the physician inflicts pain, pierces the flesh, and intrudes into every opening in the body. He is reminiscent of the mother of bodily intimacy as well as the representative of the sadomasochistic fantasies involving both parents.

It is my contention that it is mainly the therapeutic commitment to the patient that makes it possible for the analyst to utilize consistently the various "unnatural" instrumentalities that psychoanalysis requires without becoming ritualistic, authoritarian, remote, or bored. I am referring here to listening hour after hour to free and unfree associations, paying attention to all details, listening predominantly in silence, manifesting only well-modulated emotional responses, permitting oneself to become the target of the patient's intense emotional storms, intervening only for the patient's welfare, and allowing oneself to be made love to verbally without becoming seductive, or to be vilified without defending oneself or counterattacking.

It is mainly the underlying dedication to the task of helping and healing the sick which permits the analyst under such circumstances to maintain emotional concern and compassion for the patient without becoming either overprotective like a mother or unengaged like a research worker. The physicianly attitude implies a constant awareness of the patient's basically painful and helpless condition as well as a respect for those instrumentalities, procedures, and processes which are necessary for therapeutic results. The doctor is far more reliable in assessing the amount of pain his patient can bear than mother, father, or research worker.

Yet the posture of therapist partakes partially of both mother and researcher. (I am leaving the father out of this discussion since it would lead us too far afield.) I believe that the ideal analyst is a motherly father figure or fatherly mother, the duality existing in regard to functions and not as a sexual characteristic. The analytic therapist must be in close, empathic (motherly) contact with his patients so that he can nurture their potentials, protect their rights and dignity, know the difference between harmful and harmless gratifications, the limits of their deprivation tolerance, and be willing to wait years for the fruits of his labors. As a therapist he also must be able to maintain distance between himself and the patient so that he can "research" the patient's data; that is, recall, sort, think, judge, theorize, and speculate about them. Above all, the therapist must have easy access to both mother and researcher positions, and he must be able to intervene in both capacities. Yet he must act overtly as neither, but as a composite—as a therapist.

I will conclude this section on the analyst's motivation by reemphasizing that the analyst must have a basic liking for the patient to be able to carry out a successful psychoanalysis. True, the psychoanalyst during the course of treatment will experience temporarily varying shades of love, hate, and indifference in terms of countertransference reactions. But the real relationship between the analyst and his patient should be basic liking and concern. If there were no real relationship between analyst and patient, no sustained collaborative work would be done and therapy would be ineffective. Too strong a liking, indifference, neutrality, and persistent dislike make him an unsuitable analyst for the patient. The analyst must have a wish to help the patient which is not so intense that he becomes too readily impatient or disappointed. Although the fruits of his labor may be of research value, he is basically a physicianly person treating neurotic miseries by administering insight in an atmosphere of acceptance and compassion (Greenson, 1972). (For a more detailed discussion of this problem see Greenson, Volume 1, Section 4.23.)

2

Assessment of Analyzability

Daniel P. Greenson, M.D.

s a youngster, I watched my grandfather and his friends read the newspaper or listen to the news on the radio. Their first reaction to startling news was "Is it good for the Jews?" After that was settled, or it was decided it could not be settled, they would talk about the news events from a more complete, well-rounded perspective. Many years later, I was asked to teach a course in analyzability to the first-year candidates at the San Francisco Psychoanalytic Institute. I read the literature, went over my own cases and those I had supervised (both those that had turned out to be analyzable and those that had not been), and it became clear to me that I listened in different fashion to patients when assessing analyzability than I did when listening to my patients in treatment. Usually analysts listen without any agenda, or rather with as much of an agenda as it takes to try to understand the patient's material, and then try to put what the patient is talking about together with what we know about the patient, his or her history, the analytic process itself, and where we are in it. Occasionally, we try mentally to formulate the current data with some of our theoretical notions. In short, we think dynamically. The assessment of analyzability, however, leads to an agenda, a focus. One cannot merely associate along with the patient,

43

thinking dynamically, as one usually does. As I searched for a *model* for this way of focusing, I remembered the Jewish men of my childhood. The thesis I am putting forth in this paper is that as one assesses a patient's analyzability, one's agenda must be, "Is this particular material 'for' or 'against' analyzability?"—"Is it good or bad for the Jews?" I emphasize this point because I feel it is not the way we usually listen and think. Anna Freud (1965) even went so far as to suggest that analysts might not be good at this type of listening and thinking. Where I think this approach to assessment is most useful is when one has to suggest analysis to a patient after a few sessions. One often feels one cannot take his or her time. Such is often the case for candidates who have been referred potential patients by the low-fee clinic or senior colleagues. At the other end of the spectrum it can also be true for training analysts seeing potential candidates. Often prospective analysts feel under some pressure (internal, external, realistic, unrealistic) to decide rather quickly about recommending analysis. When we are under pressure, we are less likely to be able to let our attention "evenly hover," another reason for a focus or a model to work from.

It is not my intention in this paper to get into the question of which kinds of patients are analyzable and which are not. Nor will I address the question of what is the treatment of choice for "sicker" patients, patients with severe psychopathology. Suffice it to say, after doing quite a bit of analysis, we all know there are those who take to it and those who do not, whether we call them "good patients" or whether we call them by some more diagnostic label. Even for those of us with lots of experience, it behooves us to know as much as we can about what kind of a journey we are embarking on. It helps if we know what we are getting into; certainly most patients don't have a realistic notion of what it is like to be in analysis. It is better if one of us knows some of what lies ahead. Thus, I feel the approach I offer here will be useful no matter what notions we hold as to what kinds of people are analyzable and what kinds are not.

Literature Review

A thorough review of the subject of analyzability would begin with the question of "what is analysis?" and then go on to only slightly less hefty subject matter. Suffice is to say, this chapter will stick to the straightforward and much narrower task of a practical approach to the assessment of analyzability. If one reads through the literature on analyzability, many articles have concrete suggestions (an example: dirt phobias are more difficult to analyze than motion phobias), but the articles I will emphasize are those which suit my purpose: focus.

Freud said little about analyzability directly, and what he did say mostly had to do with diagnosis. Good patients should be of "good character" and able to develop a "transference neurosis." Hysterics, therefore, were the "best" patients. (For concrete suggestions, see "Some Character Types Met with in Psychoanalysis [1916].) These ideas were echoed and refined by Anna Freud, Fenichel, and Glover, their focus being mainly on symptoms and diagnosis. Even Stone in his 1954 paper on the "Widening Scope" didn't directly discuss the question of how one is to figure out, as one's scope widens, who would benefit from analysis.

Waldhorn (1960) writing about the work of the Kris Study Group in the late 1950s spells out the problems of attempting to assess analyzability on the basis of diagnosis and symptoms. He stresses the importance of assessing first and foremost the ego's organization and function, pointing out that the superego is harder to get a handle on, and the id is "damned near impossible." (The quote is mine.) The strength of the drives seems to me something one can only guess at during an evaluation. Although emphasizing ego assessment, and rich with clinical hints, his ideas lack specific organization and focus.

Zetzel (1968) in a tour de force, "The So-called Good Hysteric," asks the question, "How come patients who present with hysterical character and symptoms can either be 'very good' or 'very bad' analytic patients?" She then describes four subgroups of hysterical patients: good hysterics, immature hysterics, depressive characters, and (so-called) borderline characters. At the end of her paper she lists *five* clues to be alert for, which may indicate severe pathology:

1. Absence of, or significant separations from, one or both parents during the first four years of life.
2. Severe psychopathology in one or both parents, often associated with unhappy marriage or divorce.
3. Serious and/or prolonged physical illness in childhood.

4. A continuing hostile-dependent relationship with mother, who is either devalued or is seen as rejecting or devaluing.
5. Absence of meaningful or sustained object relationships with either sex.

She feels the presence of more than one of the above is ominous prognostically.

Huxster, Lower, and Escoll (1975), in a paper reviewing the assessment of analyzability by committee in the Philadelphia Psychoanalytic Institute, conclude that analysts assessing analyzability may be prone, since we are so accustomed in our daily work to listening for evidence of inner conflict, to neglect the fact that information of a different order may also be needed to assess analyzability. All too often, in the workings of their committee, the members would get caught up in debate as to whether the material was oedipal or pre-oedipal, the idea being that the level of the psychosexual stage of development at which unresolved conflicts occurred was equatable with analyzability and thus received undue attention. The question is how well one assesses oedipal pathology in evaluation interviews. The authors also call attention to the idea that, on their committee, sometimes analysts interviewing prospective patients were swayed by positive feelings toward the patient in the direction of recommending acceptance in the face of significant negative information in their *own* reports, while the committee members who had not seen the patient remained "more" objective.

Tyson and Sandler (1971) feel the term *analyzability* is neither clear nor precise. Most of the previous literature, they feel, speaks of indications for analysis, which does not clarify what is to be evaluated. They prefer to use the concept "assessment of suitability for analysis." They then spell out in some detail what one needs to assess in order to make the recommendation that a patient is suitable for analysis. Their focus is on the strengths and weaknesses of the ego.

Bachrach and Leaff (1978) in an article reviewing the literature point out that most authors now seem to be saying that one should assess ego strength and object relations, but that most authors treat them in metapsychological terms rather than describe them clinically and empirically. "It is easier to argue in the abstract about the importance of ego strength than to confidently assess it."

I have borrowed from some of Bachrach's organizational format in his systematic review of the literature, hoping to move toward clinical data and away from abstractions.

As one can see from this overly brief literature review, we have moved away from diagnosis, dynamics, and symptoms to assessment of ego strengths and weaknesses.

The Assessment

When I taught the analyzability course to candidates, I explained my ideas about the differences between doing analysis and assessing analyzability. To emphasize the focus on assessing ego strengths, I asked the candidates to develop a list, a check sheet, of attributes which were either "good for the Jews" or "bad for the Jews." After we listened to the presentation of evaluation hours (either mine or the candidate's), we'd rate the patients according to the items on our list, then discuss the hours with emphasis on our ongoing assessment. The candidates found this helpful in establishing focus.

One cannot assess analyzability globally, but must have some specific characteristics in mind that one is trying to evaluate. For example, "How does this person handle affects?" In this section, I will pose possible questions, and make suggestions as to how analysts assessing analyzability might find answers to their questions. What I will not go into, because it is not within the scope of this paper, is what it means in terms of analyzability, for example, if a patient is completely overwhelmed by this or that affect, or unable to perceive particular affects. As can be ascertained from the above, I feel evaluation sessions are in some ways different from analytic sessions. I tell prospective patients that I begin therapeutic relationships with a brief evaluation period, so I can figure out whether I'll recommend therapy, and if so, what kind. I also tell them that it is hoped they will be evaluating what it feels like to work with me, not that this is quite the same as therapy, but it should provide them with some information. During these sessions, part of what I am evaluating is the patient's reaction to me, what I say and what I don't say. I don't structure the sessions. In the beginning, I am often silent for a time. But I also feel free to ask questions, freer perhaps than during an analysis proper. I try not to have the sessions turn into my questioning and the patient's responding; that has its problems. But the main point I'm making is we should feel free to question the patient, see how he or she responds to the question itself and to the fact that I've asked. Keep in mind part of the assessment is how the patient reacts to you. My list:

1. *Functioning in the World.* As I mentioned in the literature review section, analytic thinking about analyzability has shifted from a focus on diagnosis or illness to a focus on the person who has the illness. Thus, our task in assessing ego strengths is not only to look at those areas in which our patients are troubled, but to look at those areas in which the patient functions well, trying to assess strengths, abilities, and conflict-free areas.

   a. Work. Most authors who discuss either analyzability or analytic outcome emphasize success in the person's life's work as the best single barometer for prognosis (if one has to choose one barometer). People with a track record of success are more likely to be successful. Work is not meant to be restricted to a job. It can be school, homemaking, child rearing, and is often more than one thing. It is the area in life to which he or she devotes important time and energy. Our question is, first, how well does he do it, and how can we ascertain what strengths he possesses which allow him to do the things he does well. This may sound obvious, but in my experience it is worthwhile to ask ourselves first the question, "What does he work at?" then, "What enables him to be successful?" In initial interviews, patients are likely to emphasize those areas in life which trouble them. We, following the patient's lead and our own interest in psychopathology, will think a great deal about his difficulties and shortcomings. Remember to look for success! That is why I've started the assessment section with Functioning in the World.

   b. Relationships. Focus your thinking not only on those relationships which are difficult (I go into this in detail later), but on those that work. Remember to wonder why these relationships seem to work; what goes on in them.

   c. Reality testing. Obvious problems with reality testing are well known to clinicians and need no emphasis here. It is fruitful to assess capacity for observing ego functions. This can be evaluated when patients are talking about symptoms or problematic relationships. One wants to distinguish if the patient can discern the difference in the way he or she feels versus external reality. For example, a patient talks of an upsetting, ongoing battle with his boss, who is "out to get him." An attempt should be made to see if he can distinguish between "it feels as if he is out to get me; that is, the problem is a feeling within me," as opposed to "the problem is in the boss, who really is out to get me." If the patient is sure the issue is about reality, it is a good idea to check this out in regard to other relationships. In order to analyze transference, one has to be able to distinguish between "I feel as if you feel this" versus "I'm sure you really do." The same kind of thinking and inquiring are worthwhile in exploring the patient's experiencing symptoms vis-à-vis what he thinks about them. Can he get distance from the feelings which trouble him? "Sitting here I know nothing will happen to me in an elevator, but when I approach an elevator, it feels as if I will die if I get in it." Even in the phobic situation, this person can distinguish between "It feels as if I'll die" and "I know it will happen." Some people can't make that distinction sitting in your office. It still feels real to them. In ascertaining observing ego functions, one should try to clarify how much ability the patient has for distinguishing between "It feels as if it is so" and "I know it is so."

d. Severity of symptoms. From the standpoint of ego strength, one wants to ascertain how well the symptoms work and how much they cost. It is one thing if anxiety keeps one from fully enjoying romantic relationships; it is another if it keeps one from even trying to get involved in a romance at all. The latter "costs too much." A phobia which works is one that is discrete and fairly easily avoidable, as opposed to one which is generalized and ubiquitous and which leaves little latitude to live the rest of one's life (like a severe agoraphobia). In the same vein, it is a sign of ego strength if one has flexibility defensively. It is a sign of ego weakness if defenses are few, automatic, and rigidly used.

2. *Object Relations*. Many analysts feel the sine qua non of analyzability is the capacity to develop an analyzable transference. It makes sense, therefore, that we would be interested in the patient's experience in relationships, how he sees himself relating

to others, how he feels about the significant people in his life.

a. Meaningful relationships. First, does he have such relationships? One of Zetzel's ominous signs is people who don't have meaningful relationships with either sex. If they do have them, how do they talk about the important people in their lives? Do these people come alive, seem real, or do they sound pat, flat, automatonlike? Does it sound like the patient can experience intimacy?

b. Parents. Most people have fairly fixed notions about their parents, but within that, are the parents described as full, rounded, real people? How much do they sound idealized, and do you sense potential flexibility? From a historical perspective at least one healthy-sounding parent is a plus. Malignant-sounding identifications with dead, psychotic, or psycho-pathic-sounding parents is a minus.

c. Separations and losses. Early significant losses will usually come up as the patient talks about family and childhood, but significant separations from parents may not. Serious child-hood illnesses also might have to be inquired into. I'll often ask about separations, including normative ones like going to school, camp, and "staying overnight." Another line of questioning is how the patient has reacted to deaths. Most people have "lost" someone meaningful to them, or at least they had pets who have died. I'll especially ask if I have a sense an adult patient is "too close" to parents, spouse, or children.

d. Previous therapy. Previous therapists should be significant objects to former patients. I am interested not only in how the treatment went, but how the patient felt about the therapist, again paying attention to whether the patient is able to see beyond the transference to the realistic attributes of the thera-pist. Often dissatisfied patients explain their dissatisfaction as the former therapist's "problem" (be it theoretical, technical or personal). The idea "my previous therapist didn't understand me," with the implication "I'm sure you can," can be seductive. I'll often inquire into how the patient understands this misun-derstanding, paying careful attention to whether the patient has insight into the problem or is mainly externalizing and blaming. This area is rich in information if the previous treat-ment was stalemated, stuck, or ended unhappily. It can be an ominous sign if the patient feels he played no part in the difficulties.

e. The analyst as object. Prospective patients often arrive at their first hour with a preformed transference. I try to get a glimmer of what it looks like. "Why me?" is a useful entré, especially with patients who are definitive and certain before they have met with you. "You're the only one" can be most troublesome. Many authors writing about analyzability mention that an analyst's physical or psychological resemblance to important people in the patient's life can be problematic. Rapid identifications with you should be looked for. My father (R. Greenson), in a first hour, offered a patient a cigarette (in those days analysts and patients smoked). The patient declined, saying she'd smoked her own brand for twenty years and was keen on it. In the next session, she brought his brand to the hour without comment. A question I ask myself during the evaluation is, "Does the patient seem to recognize I am a real person?" It is not an easy one to answer, but when I get the feeling that I could be replaced midhour by another analyst and the patient wouldn't notice, I view it as a very "bad for the Jews" countertransference cue.

3. *Affects.* In order for a patient to analyze his or her transference, he has to be able to look at it. Inability to tolerate affect can prevent the transference from becoming a part of the analysis. Inability to modulate affect can prevent patients from getting enough distance from their feelings to look at them. Patients with primitive psychopathology often lack sufficient ego strength to regulate affects.

a. Tolerance and modulation of affects. Assessing how patients contend with anxiety, frustration, anger, depression, and excitement can be easy and straightforward. Sometimes patients in evaluation interviews have a thought-through and complicated story to tell, so that the impact of affect isn't clear or obvious. One can ask, "What happens when you become angry (or depressed, etc.)?" One can also attempt to assess affects in the session; for example, how does the patient respond to silences, especially when the patient has finished talking and looks to the analyst expectantly. Often there are poignant moments around such questions as to when to meet next or about fees. I'm not suggesting one purposely let a patient wait a bit in the waiting room or dangle in an hour, but I am suggesting that if the patient can't make the first time offered for the next appointment, much can be learned during a judicious pause before offering an alternative time. Something also can be learned about affect modulation around initial phone calls and questions about fee. The capacity to tolerate painful affect should also be kept in mind with patients who respond to silences with questions and those who, when expressing affect, quickly ask for reassurance. When people go quickly from dislike to hatred, my countertransference is "oh-oh." On the other end of the spectrum are those patients who seem affectless during the interview, especially when their narrative is short on feelings.

4. *Character Traits*
   a. Psychological mindedness. Some positive indications include the following: Evidence of genuine interest in the way the mind works. A capacity for insight and, even better, a sense of pleasure when being insightful. An ability to conceptualize experiences as meaningful and as interconnected. An ability to see oneself as others see one. Indications of an interest in how others are put together, which reflects an ability for empathy. Accessibility and interest in fantasy. A sense that dreams are important psychologically, which isn't only intellectual. When the above traits are obvious, the initial interviews are pleasurable and there is no need for further inquiry into psychological mindedness. When it is not clear, I float a trial balloon or two. I don't make significant or profound interpretations, because I don't want to make the patient anxious, or to give him or her the impression that I am going to do most of "the work" of the analysis. Rather, I try to connect things the patient has already said to each other in a way he has not thought of. Often I will do this in a general, open-ended way, such as: "This reminds me of what you were saying last time," letting the patient work on the specifics of the connection and what about last time might relate. I feel it is particularly useful to see if and how patients connect this hour to the last one, one theme to another. I am concerned when patients seem unable to sense a continuity

between one session and the next, even if we are only meeting weekly.

b. Inside versus outside. I am impressed with patients who describe the problem, whatever it is, as within themselves. Those who speak of internal conflict, as opposed to those who emphasize problems with others and who experience the problem as within the "other." Such trends in thinking can portend a propensity for externalization which is most difficult to analyze. An observing ego is a welcome ally.

c. "Unfair." This word, if used more than sparingly, has become a countertransference "buzzword" for me. It is often overused by those who feel themselves the exception, those who feel mistreated by fate, those who are seeking reimbursement for being short-changed in life. Such people often are not able to observe, take distance; they seek magic, not insight.

d. Excessive vagueness. All people, especially hysterics, when anxious, can be defensively vague. A more ominous sign is universal vagueness and habitual speaking in generalities. If in the evaluation process a patient is excessively vague, I first will try to figure out if he is more anxious than he seems. If so, I'll try to sort that out. If not, I'll try to pick an area which does not seem fraught with conflict to see if he has an ability to be more specific. If not, watch out.

e. Acting out. People with poor impulse control and a penchant for action usually make poor analytic patients. When the transference heats up, they're prone to do rather than think and talk. Clues to this propensity often come up when describing reactions to upsetting life events. A history of substance abuse is worth inquiring about; most people in this day and age have been exposed to both legal and illegal mind-altering substances. Invitations to enactment can occur during the evaluation hours. Keep this possibility in mind with patients who ask lots of questions, especially questions which feel "pushy" as opposed to those which seem to come from anxiety. Be wary of patients who too quickly want to focus on what you think or what you want as opposed to how they are feeling. A candidate I supervised was asked at the beginning of the second evaluation session, by a patient ambivalent about analysis, "Is it okay if

I lie on the couch today?" The candidate immediately felt stuck: Do I give the patient permission or do I make what feels like a feeble comment that first we should explore this request? It was the first enactment of many. People with a history of chronic, unquestioning rebelliousness can find it impossible to even try to attend to the basic rule.

f. Passivity. A history which indicates an intolerance for passivity or extreme intensification of symptoms when in a passive position can bode ill for analysis. On the other end of the spectrum are people who exhibit excessive passivity, who show no capacity for self-starting. These issues can come up during evaluation when the patient never pauses and can't tolerate your pauses. And with those who never break a pause, yours or theirs; they just wait for you.

g. Stick-to-it-iveness. I'll end this section with a character trait that bodes well for analysis. Those patients who show courage in the face of life's adversities, who show "stick-to-it-iveness," when struggling with difficult tasks, who are persistent when the road seems long; such people are "good indeed for the Jews."

5. *Motivation.* Perhaps because of my biases, professional, personal, and familial, I have not met many people I thought were too "normal" or "well-adjusted" to benefit from analysis. How could we require analysis of our candidates, if we felt otherwise? Nonetheless, I do feel it behooves the prospective analyst to attempt to ascertain whether the patient's degree of suffering warrants and will sustain such a costly (in time, money, and energy) endeavor. This is especially so with unsophisticated patients who don't know much about the differences between psychotherapy and psychoanalysis. A word about Freud's early idea that one should not analyze people with reservations about analysis. He did not mention it after he discovered the need to analyze negative transference. Most people have reservations about most of life's major enterprises.

a. Magic. One should look carefully into the fantasies of patients who seem to be seeking magical transformations. It can tell you a lot about a person if he is coming to analysis so that you will cure him, as opposed to feeling both of you will work together on his problems. It is most useful in the evaluation interviews to review specifically just what the patient wants to be different about himself, and how he expects the analysis to effect that change. A comment by Bob Wallerstein is worth remembering: "It's funny, but we still recognize our friends even after they've undergone analysis."

b. Change for others. Analysis is hard enough when the motive for change resides within the patient. When the motive resides outside, in another person, in books, in theories, in a group, the task is harder. With these people, the first analytic task is to help them become patients, which is often not easy. When a person wants to change for others (spouse, parent, etc.), the analysis starts on shaky ground. Similar difficulties can arise when people seek analysis because significant others are in analysis. Occasionally, analysis is sought because of a fascination with psychoanalytic thought or theory. This is similar to the well-written-about difficulties of the training analysis and I call it to the readers' attention because it can occur with people who are not candidates.

6. *The Superego.* It is difficult for me to articulate an assessment process for positive superego qualities. It is easier to describe the harsh, punitive, critical superego functioning we see daily. Corrupt superegos are sometimes self-evident, sometimes well hidden, but we know what to look for. A strong, but "loving" superego—how does one assess that? The best I can do for now is to say its presence is felt with people who have the capacity to experience pleasure in a loving relationship, to enjoy a job well done, the ability to savor earned rewards.

a. Masochism. In order to benefit therapeutically from analysis, a patient has to want to get better. As Freud (1937) pointed out, patients with a propensity for masochism derive unconscious gratification from their symptoms and suffering. This can lead to negative therapeutic reactions, a most difficult state of analytic affairs. Secondary gain from symptoms is usually not readily apparent, but it is a question one should ponder in assessing patients with masochistic tendencies. The question of masochism should come to mind when one hears of symptoms worsening after successes, or symptoms lessening during significant physical illness or when external events are negative. The onset of a significant depression after a loved one's death may signal mourning becoming melancholia and the presence of an extremely punitive superego. The use of one's psychic symptoms to gain power over other people, groups, or situations may be the "tyranny of the weak" and a harbinger of significant secondary gain. Tyson and Sandler (1971) point out that one should attempt to assess the role of the patient's symptoms in maintaining the external status quo; for example, in maintaining a shaky marriage.

b. Dishonesty. Blatant dishonesty is self-evident, and analytically extremely problematic. Subtle dishonesty we would probably miss, because our bias is to believe what our patients tell us and to believe they believe it. The best we can do during the evaluation is to pick up on slips, contradictions, and especially on invitations to collusion. Any invitation to finagle or finesse a third party bears close scrutiny. Be alert for possible superego lacunae. During an evaluation (in the 1970s), a former radical student now in law school mentioned in passing that he had not paid for something at a supermarket, because he was in such a hurry to get to this hour on time. When I asked, he said with a straight face, "It's okay to steal from Safeway; they steal from you." and went on with what he'd been talking about before I'd asked. I brought him back to Safeway, asking how he'd come up with the idea it was okay. He explained how they "ripped people off." I asked, perhaps not 100 percent neutrally, "So when you take from them, they lose money?" At first he said "Yes," then he said "No, they pass it on to the customers." Then he got mad at me for defending capitalism.

Clinical Illustrations

If the above can be looked upon as a "how-to" approach to assessing analyzability, the following two vignettes might be called what can happen when you "don't." What they have in common is patients referred specifically for analysis to analysts very eager to do analysis, and with no focus on assessment.

Mr. T., a twenty-eight-year-old, white-collar worker, was given the names of three analysts by his former therapist and advised to seek analysis. He was the first person who had ever called me specifically requesting an analysis. I only saw him face to face for three hours. He was well-dressed, attractive, and well-spoken. I felt he was likable and quite bright. He began by launching into the story of his failed therapy, the recommendation for analysis, and his "shopping for an analyst." The reason he was in therapy was his inability to involve himself in a meaningful relationship with a woman; he seemed to make poor choices. He was also dissatisfied with his job. Although the therapy (his third) had begun promisingly enough, it had bogged down. He felt his therapist (a man in his sixties) pushed him too much, then grew impatient with him. When Mr. T.'s behavior didn't change, the therapist gave him advice, scolded him, lectured him. The therapist also talked too much about himself and his own life, using himself as an example both of the right ways to do things, and also the wrong way to do things. The more Mr. T. felt pushed and cajoled, the less he felt like trying, and the more stuck he felt in the treatment. He felt affection for his therapist, but thought he wasn't very competent. When the therapist recommended analysis, he went and read some books about analysis. Mr. T. then somewhat abruptly asked me if I thought analysis could help him. I said I didn't know; I'd have to hear more about his problems. He then asked me several superficial questions about analysis having to do with frequency, the couch, and free association. I responded to each question asking him what he thought or knew. He then provided "the right answer." He started the second interview by launching in some detail into an account of the difficulties he was having with the managerial level above him, speaking about the business's administrative inconsistences and managerial personal shortcomings. His observations sounded insightful. He then talked about the difficulties he'd had with the people he managed, emphasizing their shortcomings, but to my mind at least, alluding to the possibility he was uncomfortable being a manager. When I asked him about this, he said it was true, and in fact he was thinking about changing jobs. He then talked about some possibilities of other jobs in other firms which interested him. He began the third hour by saying he'd seen the other two analysts and had chosen me. "When could we start?" Somewhat taken aback, I said I wanted to know more about him: "I usually see people for several evaluation sessions before I recommend analysis." He said he didn't like that, it made him feel on trial, but what did I want to know. "What was your childhood like?" I asked. "Awful," he replied, then launched into growing up in the

Southwest, in the service, the son of a career military man. He hated the military and was none too fond of his father, either. He had not seen him in years. His parents divorced when he was seven. He also hated his sister, who was three years younger. She was a "wimp" and wouldn't stand up for herself. He had been quite attached to his mother. They, in fact, moved to this area together when he was in high school. His therapist seemed to feel he was "too close" to his mother, and this might be the source of some of his difficulties with women. I asked what he thought of that, and he replied that there might be something to it. He went on, saying his mother was very critical of his girl friends, saying in essence "they weren't good enough for me." "Of course, she is at least partially right." He then spoke of how inappropriate they were. At this point, with an eye on the clock, he again asked what I thought about analysis. As best as I can remember, I thought why not? It is true I don't know that much about this man, but he wants to be in analysis (i.e., is motivated), has the time and the money; the rest will "come out in the wash." I said, "Okay."

What came out in the wash: He had *all five* of Zetzel's clues for an ominous prognosis. (1) His father was almost totally absent during the first five years of his life and he was separated from his mother six months during the first year. (2) His father was cruel, sadistic, and psychopathic. His mother sounded extremely narcissistic and unable to be intimate with anyone. After the divorce she "went through a series of men." (3) He was in the hospital for six months during his first year of life with some sort of pernicious diarrhea, which necessitated many medical procedures. (4) The relationship with his mother was hostile-dependent and she was seen as both devaluing and rejecting. (5) He had no meaningful relationships. In addition to Zetzel's "big five," he was unable to modulate affect and was easily swept away by anxiety and overwhelmed by anger. Problems resided in others, not in himself. Life was "unfair" and he continually felt mistreated. His insights were almost never about himself, but were confined to what he thought went on in others. He expected "analysis" would cure him, and was unwilling to work within the analysis. Although very bright, he had dropped out of college, lost several jobs, often after a good start.

I'm not saying he didn't benefit from analysis, or that analysis was not the treatment of choice. Had I done a better job of assessment, I think I would have had a more protracted evaluation. I would have proceeded to the couch and four times a week more slowly. The analysis would have begun more smoothly, at the very least. I would have been less caught by surprise.

The following clinical vignette was reported to me by a candidate who saw this patient fairly early in his training, when he was quite eager to do as much analysis as possible. I thought then that he was quite talented and had a "good ear." He has since graduated and I continue to think highly of his work.

Ms. A. was a twenty-two-year-old, single, graduate student, who was referred to Dr. L. by the low-fee analytic clinic. She had applied to the low-fee clinic the previous year, been accepted, and put on the waiting list. After waiting a few months, she decided to enter treatment in a short-term therapy program at a local hospital. When she called the low-fee analytic clinic to say that she was once again interested in seeking analysis, she was immediately given Dr. L.'s name. She called him that same day. When he had not returned her call by the next morning, she called again and left the following message, "I am still interested."

She arrived at the office just in time for the first session, saying she'd had difficulty finding the office. Visibly tense, she asked, "What am I supposed to talk about?" When Dr. L. suggested that she begin by talking about the reasons she was seeking analysis, Ms. A. responded saying she wanted to get to know more about herself and then fell silent. When Dr. L. pressed for some elaboration, she snapped, "What do you want to know? It would be easier if you asked questions." She said she was worried she would not be able to cover her whole life in an hour. She then said she'd been turned down for a job and she did not know why. She thought she'd undermined herself, but she didn't know how. The potential employer had explained he'd given the job to someone with experience, but she didn't believe him even though she had no experience. She went on to say that she was disappointed in her boyfriend and her friends, who aren't supportive. Therapy had made her feel better, but didn't change anything. Her sex life was dull. Her mother probably only had sex with father. "My father lives life as if it were a terminal illness; he is so unreachable." It was the end of the hour and Dr. L. suggested they meet again to see if they would agree that analysis was the right idea. Ms. A. seemed alarmed and wanted to know if there was something which caused Dr. L. to think it might not be.

Ms. A. began the second hour by saying she was disturbed that Dr. L. had said, "Maybe I should not be in analysis." Dr. L. responded, "Perhaps you have your own doubts." The patient said she wasn't sure she wanted to work on her dreams all the time and that she didn't know if Dr. L. was right for her. Then she talked of a dream she had had about a tacky, low-budget marriage. She thought the dream somehow related to an episode when she was a teenager. A family friend had agreed to let her stay with his family abroad. "At first he did it for free, then he accepted money from my parents. He was a crook; he made me dependent on him, and molested me sexually." At the end of the hour, she said, "It might go better if I were on the couch. Then I wouldn't have to stare at you."

Ms. A. knocked on the office door a few minutes before the next appointment time. She started the hour by saying she was eager to "settle the money thing," relating that she was told by the clinic the fee would be $10.00. Dr. L. responded that $10.00 was acceptable and that he would like to be paid at the end of the month. Ms. A. said she couldn't do that because she got paid midmonth, and if she had the money, she spent it. "I won't hold someone else's money for them." Dr. L. replied she could pick the payment day, as long as it was regular. She was not sure if she could do that. With some difficulty, Dr. L. realized that the patient was saying that she was not sure she could pay the fee and asked her about that. The patient said, "It is true, it is a lot of money to pay for nothing tangible." She was relieved Dr. L. had asked, she'd been planning to hide her money problems. She then talked about being angry at her boss, who would not allow her to put down more hours than she had actually worked on her time sheet. "It is unfair when he knows how much I need the money."

Ms. A. talked about misgivings about seeing a male analyst; nonetheless, she was eager to start analysis. Dr. L. agreed they should begin, explained his cancellation policy, and said they needed to make a schedule. Ms. A. said she didn't want to "get ripped off" and had a preference for early morning hours. Dr. L. said he could see her at 7:30. She responded "That is no good; I might get a job which would require me to leave earlier. (She had no particular job in mind.) It will have to be 7:00." Dr. L. sensed something was amiss and told the patient he could see her at 7:30, but not at 7:00. When Dr. L. did not agree, she became enraged. "I'm so disappointed in you. I'm sure you have a car and could arrange to be here at 7:00. I don't understand why you won't do it." She angrily stalked out.

Dr. L. was well aware of his own eagerness to begin another analysis. He recognized that he had some misgivings about the patient's analyzability and some sense that the initial interviews were "not going well." He had been focusing during the evaluation on what he thought were the patient's dynamics, an oedipal-level fixation which caused her to be afraid of him and afraid of analysis. She defended against these fears by being controlling and provocative. He thought these issues would become clearer and could be addressed once the analysis began. What Dr. L. didn't have was a thought-through approach to assessment. He did not have a focus which could have helped him ask himself certain questions which could have clarified what was going on in him and then in his patient. In retrospect, as Dr. L. went over the sessions, he had lots of questions about the patient's material and his behavior in the hours. Much of this had crossed his mind with Ms. A., but he had not sufficiently attended to it. The purpose of this chapter is to provide to analysts who are doing evaluations a focus which can provide some structure for analytic assessment.

3

The Goals of Psychoanalysis Reconsidered

Robert S. Wallerstein, M.D.

I N 1965, I published a paper "The Goals of Psychoanalysis: A Survey of Analytic Viewpoints." It had been written for an American Psychoanalytic Association panel discussion on "The Limitations of Psychoanalysis" since "any discussion of the limitations of psychoanalysis as a treatment modality necessarily raises the question of the ideal and the practical goals of psychoanalytic treatment against which its inevitable shortcomings are to be measured" (p. 748). I outlined in the beginning of that paper a variety of related considerations that I acknowledged were "inextricably interwoven with the question of goals" (p. 748) but that I, nonetheless, indicated I would exclude as specific foci in that presentation, "except as they become momentarily central to its argument" (p. 749). These excluded considerations comprised (1) the theory of technique, the relationship of means to ends; (2) the similarities and differences— including in their goals—between psychoanalysis and the dynamic psychotherapies; (3) the evaluation of results (outcome studies); (4) our various value-laden conceptions of the ideal state of mental health; and (5) criteria for termination of analysis or how we know that either theoretical or practical goals have been reached.

With this caveat, I then reviewed the analytic literature around the issue of the goals of psychoanalysis building my assessment around three major polarities, each of which at first glance seemed to pose a paradox, or, at least, a complementarity of viewpoints. These were (1) the paradox of goallessness (abstinence, the eschewing of therapeutic zeal) as a central element of procedure or technique counterposed against the ambitiousness of outcomes sought (i.e., the most far-reaching goals in terms of the possibilities for fundamental personality reorganization of any of the available psychotherapeutic approaches); (2) the distinction between goals in terms of outcomes sought (posed variously, but always ambitiously in terms of the varying theoretical perspectives, metapsychologies, within psychoanalysis), and goals in terms of the processes by which those outcomes were to be achieved (posed variously in terms of our varying theories of change or therapeutic effect, of how intrapsychic change comes about or is brought about), as well as the ways in which outcome goals (the theory of results) link to process goals (the theory of mutative procedures) to together form an overall theory of therapy; and (3) the "average expectable accomplishment" (p. 765) of analysis along the dimension between the well-known more pragmatically realistic (or pessimistic) position of Freud and the more ebulliently optimistic position of Ferenczi.

As I review and reconsider my position on those self-same issues of the goals of analysis, realistic and/or idealistic, today, a quarter-century later, in the light of the theoretical advances and cumulated clinical and empirical research experience during the intervening period, I am struck by a number of points. It no longer seems possible to me to consider (ideal or even practical) goals in relative isolation from the issues of actual outcomes (and outcome studies), of criteria for termination (either idealistic or realistic), and especially of the different or similar goals achievable within the array of psychoanalytically grounded therapies. This spectrum ranges from psychoanalysis through the psychoanalytically based expressive psychotherapies, and on to the psychoanalytically based supportive psychotherapies at the other end of the spectrum. Goals do need to be set into the context of the feasible and the actual, granted that theoretic and clinical (and research) advance can gradually alter and enlarge our understanding of what is feasible and actual.

Within this conceptual framework, I begin this reconsideration of the question of goals with the statements and guidelines provided us by Sigmund Freud, the creater of our discipline. Freud's most cited statement specifically on goals or aims is from the 1923 "Two Encyclopedia Articles. (A) On Psychoanalysis." There he said:

It may be laid down that the *aim* of the treatment is to remove the patient's resistances and to pass his repressions in review and thus to bring about the most far-reaching unification and strengthening of his ego, to enable him to save the mental energy which he is expending on internal conflicts, to make the best of him that his inherited capacities will allow and so to make him as efficient and as capable of enjoyment as is possible. The removal of the symptoms of the illness is not specifically aimed at, but is achieved, as it were, as a by-product if the analysis is properly carried through [1923 (1922), p. 251; emphasis added].

This (reasonably) optimistic or realistic (?) statement of the average good expectable outcome of analysis should be counterposed, however, against Freud's even better known many cautions advanced at the end of his active clinical career in "Analysis Terminable and Interminable" (1937) which are taken as reflecting what I have referred to as the common perception of Freud's final more problematic portrayal of the efficacy of psychoanalysis as a therapy. It is, however, remembered less well that this more guarded appraisal of analysis as a therapy is not just the overview of a lifetime of cumulating clinical experience but was also similarly expressed, albeit in more whimsical form at the very beginning of Freud's analytic work. These early sentences at issue—which are well known indeed though ordinarily not put into the context in which I place them here—are in the final paragraph of the *Studies on Hysteria* published in 1895 where he quoted himself responding to a patient's question as to how much help could be expected from analysis as follows: "No doubt fate would find it easier than I do to relieve you of your illness. But you will be able to convince yourself that much will be gained if we succeed in transforming your hysterical misery into common unhappiness" (Breuer and Freud, 1893–1895, p. 305).

Despite this very cautious tone at both the beginning and the end of Freud's active psychoanalytic career, in the very same "Analysis Terminable and Interminable," Freud did speak of an important new ego function brought into being by analysis:

Our arguments, it will be said, are all deduced from the processes which take place simultaneously between the ego and the instincts, and they presuppose that analytic therapy can accomplish nothing which does not, under favorable and normal conditions, occur of itself. But is this really so? Is it not precisely the claim of our theory that analysis produces a state which *never does arise spontaneously* in the ego and that this newly created state constitutes the essential difference between a person who has been analysed and a person who has not? [p. 227; emphasis added].

And it is this newly created state which is declared to form the basis for the patient to handle subsequent experiential vicissitude differently than prior to analysis; "we reckon on the stimuli that he has received in his own analysis not ceasing when it ends and on the processes of remodeling the ego continuing spontaneously in the analysed subject and making use of all subsequent experiences in this newly-acquired sense. This does in fact happen..." (p. 249).[1]

---

[1] It is these statements of Freud's about a newly created ego state that does not occur spontaneously that Kramer (1959) built upon in elaborating her conception of the postanalytic continuation of the analytic process via the new "autonomous, non-volitional ego function which automatically deals [analytically] with whatever is most strongly cathected in the unconscious" (p. 19). She declared this to be "a new function which is initiated by psychoanalysis and does not appear in this particular form without preceding psychoanalysis. . . . The specific capacity to solve an unconscious conflict by conscious awareness is acquired in analysis. Its continuation as a new ego function seems to depend not only on the liberation of energies currently involved in counter-cathexis, but on a sufficient liberation of such energies in the preceding analysis" (p. 22). Kramer likened this to E. Kris's (1956a) conception of the "good psychoanalytic hour" which she saw as possibly a manifestation within the ongoing analysis of the beginning of the autoanalytic function that she was describing.

G. Ticho (1967), under the rubric of self-analysis, described a similar postanalytic process, though more controlled and directed than Kramer's somewhat automatic and clearly nonvolitional conception. She built on the same quotations from Freud on the spontaneous continuation of the processes of remodeling of the ego and spelled out "the analysand's identification with the three main psycho-analytic functions: free association, objective and respectful listening, and interpretation. The final organization of these three functions into a unified whole has to be achieved by the analysand on his own" (p. 309). She stated that all this occurs "mainly on a preconscious level" (p. 318) and that it "has many characteristics of the acquisition of a new skill" (p. 317). She cautioned about the potential reach of the self-analytic work: "It is difficult to say whether self-analysis is merely limited to a continuous working-through of ever new derivatives of the core neurotic conflicts and overdetermined symptoms and behaviour patterns which serve multiple functions or if essentially new insight can be achieved" (p. 316). And she decried the "unpleasant connotations to the necessity of self-analysis" (p. 309) which can only come from the continuation of the myth of the perfect or complete analysis. And lastly, she raised the interesting question: "It is an interesting phenomenon that the science of psycho-

Perhaps Freud's final assessment on this issue is not as one-sidedly pessimistic as our usual perception of his prevailing stance, and is really in the more businesslike vein conveyed by a sentence toward the end of that same article: "The business of the analysis is to secure the best possible psychological conditions for the functions of the ego; with that it has discharged its task" (p. 250).

So much for Freud's statements about the expectable outcomes of analysis. His views on the processes by which these outcomes came about were formulated equally explicitly, and these at numerous places in his writings. They are condensed and captured most graphically in two very well-known and constantly repeated aphoristic statements. The first, that the process of analytic cure consists of rendering unconscious conscious, is the motif of the whole final section ("The Psychotherapy of Hysteria") of *Studies on Hysteria* (1893–1895). The second, the reformulation of this topographic conception into structural terms—after the creation of the tripartite, id, ego, superego, model of the psychic apparatus in the 1920s—was the sentence in the *New Introductory Lectures* of 1933: "Where id was, there ego shall be" (p. 80).

Balint (1950) characterized this particular succession as an indeed momentous shift in Freud's thinking about the process of analytic change and cure, from the earlier concern with the *dynamics* of the symptoms (expressed topographically) to the later concern with the *formal, structural* elements of character (expressed structurally). He said: "Theoretically the aim of all psycho-analytical therapy was defined by Freud—for all time to come, as we thought then [in 1922]—in his three famous synonymous formulae: 'overcoming the patient's resistance,' 'removal of infantile amnesia,' and 'making the unconscious conscious'" (p. 117). But with Freud's reformulation to "Where id was, there ego shall be," Balint stated: "In practice this meant a new, an additional task: to help the patient to repair the faulty places in his ego structure, and in particular to aid

analysis, which owes so much to the self-analysis of its creator, largely disregards self-analysis in its literature" (p. 308).

And other authors have also dealt with this cluster of issues; of analysis as always incomplete (and in theory interminable), of posttermination consolidations of the analytic work, and of the ongoing self-analytic function; for example, in three of the four papers from a panel at the 1954 annual meeting of the American Psychoanalytic Association (Benedek, 1955, p. 623; Weigert, 1955, p. 639; Windholz, 1955, p. 648). See also Grinberg (1980, p. 27) and Rangell (Panel, 1973, p. 190).

him to abandon some of his costly defensive mechanisms and to develop less costly ones" (p. 117). Balint described this as Freud's fateful shift from the dynamic (and topographic) approach with its emphasis on content, on the repressed, on the unconscious, in brief, on the id, to the "topical" (and structural) approach to the habitual defensive mechanisms, the developmental faults in the mental structure, in brief, the relative strengths of the ego and the superego (p. 118).

The significant literature after Freud (until 1964) on the very ambitious outcome goals posited for psychoanalysis as a therapy (and implicitly on the criteria for the termination of a successful, or successful enough, analysis) I reviewed at some length in my 1965 paper on "The Goals of Psychoanalysis"(see especially pp. 752–759), albeit with an emphasis on those conceptualized within the ego psychological metapsychology paradigm. There I quoted most fully Knight's detailed elaboration (in nontechnical language) of these outcome aims under the overall headings of disappearance of the presenting symptoms, of real improvements in mental functioning, and of improved reality adjustment, all broken down into ten subheadings (Wallerstein [1965, p. 753], quoting Knight [1941–1942]). Since my 1965 paper, a series of more recent articles (Aarons, 1965; Panel, 1968, 1969; Dewald, 1972; Ekstein, 1965, 1966; Firestein, 1974; Gaskill, 1980; E. Ticho, 1972) have further elaborated these considerations within the same ego psychological framework. Dewald (1972), Firestein (Panel, 1969), F. Robbins (Panel, 1968), and E. Ticho (1972) have each offered their own listings of proper outcome criteria and goals (ten, ten, eight, and ten in number respectively) that are basically but variations on Knight's original (1941–1942) effort.[2] All of them indeed can be brought

[2] I quote these in a footnote so as not to burden the thread of my own main exposition. Robbins (Beigler, Panel, 1968) quoted the following criteria for successful analysis in the Chicago Study of which he was one of the principal investigators: "(1) A clear termination phase; (2) development and resolution of a transference neurosis; (3) resolution of both positive and negative oedipal conflict; (4) dreams of resolution and/or sequestration; (5) evidence of structural change particularly of superego and ego-ideal; (6) easing of analyst's feelings toward the patient; (7) more free energy available for work and sex; (8) the emergence of an auto-analytic function" (pp. 97–98).

Firestein (Panel, 1969) summarized the views of three inquiry respondents, all senior members of the faculty of the New York Psychoanalytic Institute, to his query concerning termination criteria for successful analyses as follows:

evaluation schemas place strong reliance upon the quality of object relationships, the state of the ego and superego, and the pattern of symptoms. Under the rubric of object relationships the analyst views (1) the

together into Aarons's (1965) threefold concern with (1) the extent to which the ego functions concerned with the relationship with reality have become nonconflictual; (2) whether the patient now reacts to "often inexorable" (p. 101) outer circumstance destructively or constructively (i.e., adaptively); (3) whether the patient now exercises life's inevitable choices without distorting reality (i.e., nonconflictually). It is clear that this overall concern with an enhanced, more adaptive, relationship with reality as the touchstone of psychoanalytic success is the singular hallmark of the ego psychology perspective in psychoanalysis.

Ekstein (1965, 1966) also from within an ego psychological framework stated the overarching umbrella criterion somewhat differently, though fully compatibly with Aarons's formulation. In the successful psychoanalysis the compulsive repetition of neurotic and maladaptive behavior ("the repetition of failure," 1965, p. 68) has been transformed into the spontaneous and adaptive repetition of mastery, to wit: "a successful analysis has again set into motion growth forces in the patient which will allow him to move toward a new phase of his life, with new creative capacities, with a newly gained spontaneity by means of which he may hope to meet the tasks of life, the cycles of his life not governed by regressive and crippling repetition but by rhythmic spontaneity" (1965, p. 68). In this context, Ekstein cites Shakespeare's words from *The Tempest*, "What is past is prologue," as the epigrammatic description of the termination phase of a

---

level of psychosexual maturation; (2) the degree of impeding transference distortion; and (3) the capacity to experience pleasure without guilt or other inhibiting factors. Additional views of ego and superego are provided by (4) the degree of energy depletion by overly energetic defenses; (5) the ability to work productively and (6) to tolerate gratification delay; (7) sharpened capacity to distinguish fantasy from reality; (8) strengthened capacity to tolerate some measure of anxiety and to reduce other unpleasant affects to signal quantities; and (9) the stability of sublimations. Although (10) the pattern of symptoms is least heavily relied upon, despite the patient's greater interest in this aspect of himself, one naturally pays some attention to significant reduction of this factor [p. 225].

Dewald (1972) presented a sequence of illustrative clinical examples (pp. 316–323) to clarify the nature of the "structural changes" (p. 316) that expectably occur in a good analysis. These were (1) the increasing richness of recovery of infantile and childhood fantasy and memories with the undoing of the infantile repression; (2) the spontaneous change of derivative manifestations once nuclear conflicts have been resolved; (3) the patient's changed reactions to previously traumatic or anxiety-provoking material; (4) the increasing freedom and directness with which underlying dream thoughts and wishes can be expressed; (5) the changed (more realistic) relationships with other people outside the analysis; (6) the renunciation of previously gratifying infantile objects or relationships; (7) the enhancement or deepening of the patient's affective life and responses; (8) disappearance of the initially presenting symptoms, which though a notoriously unreliable criterion of enduring or "underlying" change, can become a more reliable indicator after the exposure and working through of nuclear conflicts; (9) changes in previously ego-syntonic neurotic character traits; and (10) the successful analysis as the preparation for the new use of the achieved results, with the epilogue of the analysis becoming the prologue for the new life. Certainly, Ekstein's idiom, more than that of the others cited to this point, seems fully compatible as well with perspectives on termination, on goals, and on outcome from within other psychoanalytic theoretical orientations. The closeness, for example, to Balint's (1936) conception of the "New Beginning" afforded by proper psychoanalysis is clear (for Balint the most significant change, conceptualized in object relational terms, is from wanting only to be loved to being able to give love [p. 216]).

Ernst Ticho (1972) in a widely remarked article has broadened the discourse in the ways suggested by Ekstein through his distinction between the treatment goals and the life goals toward which analysis is pointed. "*Life goals* are the goals the patient would seek to attain if he could put his potentiality to use. In other words, they are the goals the patient would aim at if his 'true self' . . . and his creativity were freed. *Treatment goals* concern removal of obstacles to the patient's discovery of what his potentialities are" (p. 315). And further, "Life goals can be divided into *professional* and *personal* life goals. Professional life goals refer to achievements in one's chosen work. Personal life goals refer to what kind of human being one would like to be. Both goals are, of course, dependent on conscious and unconscious ideals" (p. 320). And of course, since "we are not only interested in increasing the patient's self knowledge but also the

---

decathexis of and separation from the analyst, now seen "as a real person, free from the distortions that signify the transference neurosis" (p. 322).

E. Ticho (1972) talked of indications for the inception of the termination phase as follows:

(1) How much has the transference neurosis been reduced? (2) Have the patient's symptoms and character pathology been analyzed sufficiently so that they do not interfere with his functioning? (3) Have the patient's treatment goals been reached? (4) What is the quality of the relationship (the 'real relationship') between analyst and patient? Does it move in the direction of becoming a relationship between equals that will enable the patient to establish equally mature relationships with other people in his life? (5) Does the patient perceive the analyst in realistic terms? (6) Have the patient's separation anxieties and his approach to the new beginning been analyzed? (7) Has the patient given up his perfectionistic and other infantile expectations? (8) Have the patient's ego skills improved sufficiently? (9) What are the transference residues? (10) What is the patient's future potential, his ability to define life goals, and to follow them creatively? [pp. 323–324].

These various organizations of sets of completion criteria for analysis of course only underscore an observation of Kohut's in a Congress devoted to discussion of these issues (1966a) that,

There is no question, for example, that any single-axis approach to the analytic task will provide us with comparatively simple theoretical criteria of termination (notwithstanding the fact that the clinical variants may be quite complex). Thus, if we see the task of psychoanalysis in the Rankian mode as [only] a working through and ultimate mastery of separation anxiety, then the intrinsic criteria for termination will relate to the achievement of the capacity for psychosocial independence; if we see the task of psychoanalysis as . . . [etc.] [pp. 198–199].

application of this knowledge to his daily life" (p. 328), it should follow that in a "good enough" analysis "The successful attainment of the treatment goals enables the patient to terminate psychoanalysis and to proceed toward achieving his life goals" (p. 332). (Incidentally, Ticho's listing of the criteria for termination is importantly influenced by this stress on treatment goals vis-à-vis life goals; see footnote 2.)[3]

Among all these authors it is only Dewald who has pursued the interest earlier expressed by Gill (1954)[4] (and others) in trying to carefully and quite sharply distinguish the maximum feasible goals of proper psychoanalysis from the usually lesser goals of the spectrum of psychoanalytic psychotherapies. Basically, Dewald stated that psychotherapy (or significant life experience for that matter) can make changes in "derivative structures" but that only proper psychoanalysis can truly penetrate the repression barrier and the infantile amnesia and make changes in "core structures"—via, of course, the establishment, working through, and resolution of the regressive transference neurosis. Of the psychoanalytic psychotherapies he stated that, by contrast, "these forms of treatment are not designed specifically to expose or explore the infantile neurosis, but rather, they focus upon the manifold behaviors by which the core neurosis and structures are repeated in derivative form. The establishment of new derivative behavior patterns can lead to more effective modes of adaptation, particularly if these provide increased satisfaction, or decreased conflict with reality, and thus become self-reinforcing and self-sustaining" (p. 310).

By contrast, in psychoanalysis, change comes about both in "core" and, derivatively, in "derivative" structures: "Another indicator of

---

[3] Buhler, writing within a different theoretical (Horneyan) framework, had earlier advanced a very similar formulation including in her title ("Goals of Life and Therapy"). "We have said that the goal of therapy is to enable any adequately equipped person to clarify for himself the values he wants to believe in and the goals in life he wants to strive for, and to assist him on the way to realization of these goals" (1962, p. 168).

[4] In another paper (1989), I review the whole history of the relationship of psychoanalysis to all the psychoanalytically informed and based psychotherapies (expressive and supportive) and I develop there the crystallization of views (in America at least) in the early 1950s that led to a significant consensus within psychoanalytic ranks on the similarities and differences between psychoanalysis and the psychoanalytic psychotherapies (along the spectrum from the most expressive to the most supportive), and the distinctive characteristics of each, including similarities and differences in aims and goals.

From all of that literature, I select here only from Gill's 1954 article (which reflected well the consensus thinking of that era) for comparison with Dewald's quite comparable focus on similar sharp and clear distinctions in the 1972 article that I cite. Gill's quite full statement on core structural change is that once nuclear conflicts have been resolved, their various derivative manifestations will change spontaneously even without specific analytic scrutiny or conscious effort by the patient. . . . When the derivatives of a core conflict change spontaneously in this way, it is usually a positive sign that structural change has indeed occurred" (p. 317). It is this issue of the relationship between the kinds of changes expectably achieved in psychoanalysis vis-à-vis those expectably achieved in the range of psychoanalytic psychotherapies—on which my views are significantly different from those expressed here by Dewald—that will form the centerpiece of my exposition, based on the empirical findings of our Psychotherapy Research Project of The Menninger Foundation (Wallerstein, 1986, 1988), of my own current views on the goals of psychoanalysis, and in the range of psychoanalytic psychotherapies, in the concluding section of this article.

It is Leo Stone (1954) who, in his earlier "Widening Scope" paper that far predated the whole sequence of articles that I have now cited from the period since my own 1965 paper on "goals," gave the most tempered and humane statement of what must otherwise appear as an unduly idealized array of goals, a statement that, already back then, subtly shifted the concern from that of the achievement of the good (fully successful) analysis to the "merely" good enough. In referring to the possibilities of proper psychoanalytic work with very sick personalities who, to the very end of analytic experience, might require occasional and subtle emotional and technical concessions from the analyst—"parameters" (Eissler, 1953) that would never be undone— Stone said that, nonetheless:

If in such patients, the essential structure and relationship of analysis have been brought about, if a full-blown transference neurosis has emerged, if the

---

the goals of psycho*therapy* was set against Freud's 1923 statement from the Encyclopedia article on the goals of psycho*analysis* quoted earlier in this article. Gill said in 1954:

The goals of psychotherapy extend over a very wide range. To take first the goals in psychotherapy with a relatively strong ego. The goal may be a resolution of a crisis, assistance through a troubled period, or symptom amelioration. The more limited the goal and the more acute the situation, the more likely is the therapy to veer toward the supportive rather than the exploratory end of the continuum and the more active is the therapist likely to be. But goals may range up to more ambitious aims in cases where there is no pressing problem, but where psychoanalysis is impossible or not used for external reasons. Such are the patients who are seen, for example once or twice a week over a period of a year or more, in whom the goals are much more ambitious than in palliative psychotherapy, and in whom, as I hope to show later, more important results are achieved than I believe is often admitted.

The goals of exploratory psychotherapy with patients whose egos are theoretically unsuitable for psychoanalysis likewise extend over a very wide range. Here too there are emergency situations such as panics in psychotic characters, and again the treatment is likely to be supportive rather than exploratory and the therapist to be more interactive. But ambitious attempts at reconstruction can be undertaken with patients whose egos are unsuitable for psychoanalysis, such as the psychotic and the delinquent. Here it must be

patient has been able to achieve distance from it, if it has been brought into effective relation with the infantile situation, if favorable changes in the ego have occurred as a result of interpretation and working-through, if the transference has been dissolved or reduced to the maximum degree possible, I would say that the patient has been analyzed [p. 576].

What Stone articulated thus early is the finally now commonplace acknowledgment that the seemingly ever expanding possibilities for psychoanalysis that characterized the ebullient growth era of the 1950s[5]—despite the sober caution of Freud's final clinical legacy to the field in "Analysis Terminable and Interminable" in 1937—have by now been realistically tempered into a consensus rejection of the goal of perfectibility. Gaskill (1980), for example, has titled his paper "The Myth of Perfectibility" and has pointed out that "areas of incompleteness were discovered in nearly all patients, even when they had profited greatly from their analysis. To that degree they fell short of idealistic or perfectionistic goals" (p. 19). And Weigert (1955), before him, talked about a consensus on proper termination that can be reached "only when both collaborate freely toward goals and values that are not superhuman, but human, in full awareness of the distance from the realization of these values in both analyst and analysand" (p. 638). Ekstein (1965) summed this position up most succinctly when he stated that "increased sophistication concerning the possibility of perfect therapeutic results have made us give up the myth of the perfect Freudian man, the postambivalent genital character, and we have become more and more skeptical about termination in terms of an ideal ending point. . . . [T]his ideal ending— for example, the complete resolution of the transference neurosis, the disappearance of all symptoms, the structural changes, the perfectly integrated personality, etc.—is an overidealized goal" (pp. 59–60).

And E. Ticho (1966) attributes what he calls the "research anxiety" (p. 172) of the analyst, his reluctance to participate in research outcome evaluations of his analytic work, to the analyst's hidden per-

---

remembered that the ultimate goals may long remain in doubt, the therapist planning to go as far as he can get [pp. 785–786].

[5] A good example is Stone's wry commentary from the same "Widening Scope" paper (1954):

Among this group [of those enthusiastically devoted to psychoanalysis] . . . scarcely any human problem admits of solution other than psychoanalysis; by the same token, there is an almost magical expectation of help from the method, which does it grave injustice. Hopeless or grave reality situations, lack of talent or ability (usually regarded as "inhibition"), lack of an adequate philosophy of life, and almost any chronic physical illness may be brought to psychoanalysis for cure [p. 568].

fectionistic fantasies that will inevitably be exposed and disappointed. In his 1972 paper, he linked this issue of perfectionism to his distinction between treatment goals and life goals: "In a too lengthy analysis it seems clear . . . that the analyst's inability to keep life goals and treatment goals separate, and/or his perfectionism, play a part" (p. 328) and that "One important and generally overlooked contribution to research anxiety seems to be the analyst's unconscious confusion between treatment goals and life goals" (p. 319); that is, striving for an unattainable perfectionism.

As E. Ticho has hinted here, the renunciation of perfectionistic fantasies of cure does not come easily. A counsel of appropriately modest expectations is hard won for analysis, and is always vulnerable, yet within its frame various observations, by now commonly accepted, though news when they were first made, fall into place. In my 1965 paper, I pointed to Pfeffer's then recent series of careful follow-up interview studies of analyses judged to have been *satisfactorily* completed (1959, 1961, 1963), in which he spoke not of the shattering or the obliteration of conflict, but rather only of the loss of intensity and poignancy of old conflicts that had found new or modified solutions but were, nonetheless, still clearly discernible in the transitorily relighted transferences of the analytic follow-up interviewing procedure. This distinction is crucial, of course, to the question of what we mean when we say that a goal of psychoanalysis is the maximal *resolution* of intrapsychic conflict, and the "Pfeffer phenomenon" as it came to be called, excited various efforts to replicate (and/or refute?) it. Two other psychoanalytic research groups, one in Chicago (Schlesinger and Robbins, 1974, 1975, 1983) and one in San Francisco (Norman, Blacker, Oremland, and Barrett, 1976; Oremland, Blacker, and Norman, 1975) sought to replicate these findings using essentially the same method, with only some slight modifications, and came up with essentially the same observations and conclusions. A Panel at the American Psychoanalytic Association (Panel, 1973) and then a Discussion Group at the next following meeting (Panel, 1974) only widened this chorus of confirmations. What I am suggesting here is that some of this (for psychoanalysis, unusual) desire to replicate Pfeffer's original observations reflects the same reluctance to come to terms with Pfeffer's counsel of limitation of expectations from satisfactorily concluded analysis that E. Ticho stresses when he points to the diverse manifestations (e.g., "research anxiety") of continuingly persisting perfectionistic fantasies.

Yet within this same context many of our operating precepts, sometimes stated aphoristically, take logical place, both as admonitions and as exhortatory reminders. For example, about returns to treatment or about lives characterized by intermittent periods of treatment extended at times over many years, which is all the more commonplace than we usually openly acknowledge, it seems to still take periodic restatement as Zetzel (1966) did that, "No patient, in short, reaches *successful* termination of analysis unless he accepts the fact that he is not so invulnerable that he could not return for advice or help, if need arose" (p. 106; emphasis added). And yet, here, of course, Freud's own strong statement, in "Analysis Terminable and Interminable" (1937), that such returns to treatment would among the practitioners of analysis be *more* expectable, *more* the rule, is at once so well known, so acknowledged, so properly inherent in both the nature of analysis and the nature of life, and at the same time so widely neglected on practical, logistical, and on deeper grounds.

Of course, psychoanalysis is always a counsel of balanced consideration and we can be mindful that a return for more treatment can also have its neurotic underpinnings, in fact can reflect the self-same quest for a perfection that won't brook the acceptance of limitations built into the compromise formation that a termination always represents. This was put by Alvarez de Toledo, Grinberg, and Langer (1966) as follows: "We have already referred to the ancient phantasy of immortality. In some cases, reanalysis might be regarded as an expression of the same phantasy. Even though we agree that there are advantages to the resumption of analysis when it is really necessary, we object to the criterion that looks upon this as a rule. It is important to bear in mind the possibility that reanalysis might be pathologically used as a 'phantasy of immortality' " (p. 186)—I would say alternatively as a 'fantasy of perfection.' And at the same Congress, Aiza, Cesarman, and Gonzales (1966) carried comparable thinking about the requirements for reasonable closure of imperfect processes like analysis even further:

[T]he fundamental characteristics of the postanalytic phase: It must constitute a transition between the neurotic transference relationship and a realistic relationship with the analyst and be completed within a reasonable period of time. We wish to clarify that, when we speak of a realistic relationship with the analyst, we are including the possibility of an estrangement from him, since the mental health of the analysand will include considering the analyst as a human being, with whom he may or may not be in agreement [p. 167].

(Their statement, and caution, was of course directed to the issue of the training analysis and the subsequent life career of the candidate, and is most pertinent to that context; it is, however, also applicable more generally when realistic or neurotic reasons reignite wishes to return to treatment after the conclusion of a therapeutic analysis.)

Perhaps I can best bring closure to this section of my argument, our gradual, but reluctant retreat from the early enthusiasms and ambitions of the era spoken about by Gaskill as that of "The Myth of Perfectibility," or by Ekstein as that of the "perfect Freudian man, the postambivalent genital character," or by Ticho as the confounding of therapeutic goals and life goals into a striving for an unattainable perfectionism, by two further quotations, one from Grinberg (1980) who had been one of the protagonists in the 1966 Congress discussions of these issues, and another from Greenson (1966) as one of the closing remarks in that Congress. Grinberg's point was to question the usefulness of our whole preoccupation with setting goals and our concern then with our relative success or failure in achieving them. He said (1980):

I would like to state the doubts which I have regarding the criteria and goals as being the essence of the psychoanalytic process. Perhaps we do not realize that we "saturate" the development of the analytical relationship with the aprioristic idea of "leading" our patients to achieve the "therapeutic goals" which we had already fixed for them from the beginning. If this topic is . . . under review, we should question ourselves whether these "therapeutic objectives", as stated above, correspond to what should be our "psychoanalytic point of view", with its search [only] for truth, regarding our goals [p. 25].

Which is underlined even more emphatically as the deforming effect such preoccupation with goals can have upon the pursuit of proper analytic task in the following further statement:

Finally, I discuss the disadvantages caused, in my opinion, from bearing in mind *too much* the idea of "termination" during the carrying out of our task within the analytic situation in the closing phase of analysis. The predominance of the aprioristic thought that the analysis is "on the point of" or "should" end would obstruct the ability to detect what is authentically new in the material and what is most feared by the patient, such as getting closer to the search for truth about himself [p. 35].

This is very reminiscent of Lipton's reminder in his article, "The Last Hour" (1961), that the function of the last hour is to go on analyzing—even to interpreting new material (a significant newly recovered memory) in the last minutes—as if the analysis were to go on forever, certainly a counterbalancing position to, in fact the very antithesis of, concern with goals and their achievement. Greenson's statement was a more insouciant question posed toward the end of the 1966 Congress discussion of issues of termination and goals, how realistic, how idealistic (and perfectionistic), and by whose lights? He asked, "As I listened to the morning discussion, I had the following fantasy: What would happen if I sent a patient with whom I had just terminated analysis, very successfully in my opinion, to the different members of this panel?"(p. 263). A reminder that our illusions and our idealizations do indeed die hard!

It is within the framework of this more modern climate of foregone idealization and perfectionism that the Psychotherapy Research Project (PRP) of The Menninger Foundation (Wallerstein, 1986) was written up in book form in 1982. It was the final clinical accounting of what was learned in following the treatment careers and the subsequent life careers of a cohort of forty-two patients, started half in psychoanalysis and half in other psychoanalytically based expressive and supportive psychotherapies. They were followed through the whole natural span of their therapies, starting in 1952, to whatever natural termination point, onto 100 percent follow-up information at the stipulated follow-up point, two to three years posttermination. There was a further follow-up, as circumstance allowed, up to the thirty-year mark in 1982 for half the cohort remaining, after excluding the eight known to have died of various illness-related or unrelated causes over that time period. For each of the patients a variety of case-specific predictions (average about 50 per case) were made to the expectable outcome or range of outcomes (and to various contingent outcomes where indicated) for that patient with that character structure and that illness picture within that particular set of life circumstances, given the effective deployment of the appropriately indicated and planned treatment modality (Wallerstein, 1964).

These specific clinical predictions were geared clearly to the optimal expectations in terms of what we felt to be the appropriately realizable goals of these different therapeutic modalities; psychoanalysis as in many ways the therapeutically most ambitious and far-reaching (see Wallerstein [1965], especially pp. 750–752), as well as the expressive and supportive psychoanalytic psychotherapies in terms of what they did (or could) offer to those for whom these approaches were indicated. Set this way, in terms of the *optimal* expectations for each of these psychoanalytically informed treatment modes, each employed with the patients deemed most appropriate to it, we were clearly casting the work—and our expectations—still in the era of "widening scope" (Stone, 1954) and expanding ambition, not yet tempered by the retreat from the striving for "perfectibility."

The detailed accounting of the processes and outcomes, the therapeutic courses and the goals achieved or not achieved, is given at length, both through individual case write-ups for all forty-two patients in the project and through broader conclusions drawn across various groupings of the patients in my book, *Forty-Two Lives in Treatment* (Wallerstein, 1986). The overall conclusions were then brought together in summary form in a paper condensed from the final section of the book (1988), a paper in which I tried to reconsider the relative roles of psychoanalysis and psychoanalytic psychotherapy in terms of the actual outcomes and changes that were achieved. I can bring all those considerations into context relevant to the purposes of this paper through a very lengthy quotation from the concluding part of that 1988 paper, "Psychoanalysis and Psychotherapy: Relative Roles Reconsidered."[6]

I will bring our overall conclusions together at this point as a series of sequential propositions regarding the appropriateness, the efficacy, the

[6] The lengthy quotation which follows is an overall statement of considerably more than the (achievable, or achieved) goals in psychoanalysis—and in the varyingly expressive and supportive psychoanalytic psychotherapies. It is rather, in its central focus, a statement of the results achieved, and the bases on which they were achieved, in this whole spectrum of psychoanalytic psychotherapies being studied in PRP, from psychoanalysis at the one end through expressive and then supportive psychoanalytic psychotherapy at the other. Within that summarization of the actual results (of the varieties of psychoanalytic psychotherapies as well as of psychoanalysis proper) are embedded, of course, the realistically reached goals—at least with that segment of the patient population treated within that setting (The Menninger Foundation) during that period of time (the 1950s and 1960s).

reach, and the limitations of psychoanalysis (varyingly "classical" and modified) and of psychoanalytic psychotherapy or psychotherapies (varyingly expressive and supportive)—always of course with the caveat, as this was discerned within this segment of the overall patient population, those (usually sicker) individuals who have been brought to or sought their intensive analytically-guided treatment within a psychoanalytic sanatorium setting.

1. The first proposition has to do with the distinctions so regularly made in the psychodynamic literature between "structural change" (gratuitously called "real" change), presumably based on the interpretive resolution of unconscious intrapsychic conflicts, and "behavioral change" or change in "manifest behavior patterns" that are (invidiously considered) "just altered techniques of adjustment" and presumably are all that can come out of all the other, non-expressive, non-interpretive, non insight-aiming change mechanisms, i.e., all the varieties of supportive psychotherapeutic techniques and implementations. . . . Intrinsic to this way of dichotomizing between kinds of change has always been the easy assumption that only structural change or real change as brought about through conflict resolution marked by appropriately achieved insight can have some guarantee of inherent stability, durability, and capacity to weather at least ordinary future environmental vicissitude. It goes without saying that the commonplace value distinction automatically follows, that change brought about by expressive-analytic means is invariably "better" and this is of course the basis for the widely believed clinical operating maxim, "Be as expressive as you can be, and as supportive as you have to be." It is clear . . . that I question strongly the continued usefulness of this effort to so tightly link the *kind* of change achieved (real change, better change) with the intervention modes, expressive or supportive, by which it is brought about. If we accept the observations made from the study of our PRP cases that the changes reached in our more supportive therapies and via intrinsically supportive modes seemed often enough just as much structural change, just as stable and enduring, just as able to cope with life's subsequent happenstances, as the changes reached in our most expressive-analytic cases, then we must accept that the one way (the interpretive-uncovering way) does not have such an exclusive corner on inducing true structural change.

2. The second proposition has to do with the conventional proportionality argument, that therapeutic change will be at least proportional to the degree of achieved conflict resolution. Put this way, this proposition is almost unexceptionable, since it is clear that there can be significantly more change than there is true intrapsychic conflict resolution, on all the varying (supportive) bases through which change can be brought about, as well as properly proportionate change where the change is all or "purely" on the

basis of conflict resolution with accompanying insight—if such an ideal type ever actually exists in practice—but it would be hard to imagine real conflict resolution (and accompanying insight) without at least proportional concomitant change in behaviors, dispositions, attitudes, symptoms, etc. However, in the closely related arena of the proportionality of therapeutic change to the degree of attained insight (as distinct from conflict resolution), I have already indicated in passing that we had three instances within our PRP population of achieved "insight" seemingly in excess of induced change. This of course is a common enough problem and a frequent enough complaint, both within and about psychoanalytic treatment, and has been the subject of considerable discussion in the psychoanalytic literature. In our own three instances such concepts as undigested intellectual insights or of insights within an ego-weakened or psychotic transference state were invoked. What is meant here of course is insights that for varying reasons are not consequent to true conflict resolution and do not reflect it.

3. The third proposition, often linked to the proportionality argument, but in the light of our findings much more debatable and to be clearly separated from it, has to do with the necessity argument, that effective conflict resolution is a necessary condition for at least certain kinds of change. It is certainly clear that an overall finding from our project—and almost an overriding one—has been the repeated demonstration that a substantial range of changes, in symptoms, in character traits, in personality functioning, and in life-style rooted in lifelong and repressed intrapsychic conflicts, have been brought about via the more supportive psychotherapeutic modes and techniques, cutting across the gamut of declared supportive *and* expressive (even analytic) therapies, and that in terms of the usual criteria—stability, durability, and capacity to withstand external or internal disruptive pressures—these changes can be (in many instances) quite indistinguishable from the changes brought about by typically expressive-analytic (interpretive, insight-producing) means.

4. A counterpart of the proposition based on the tendency to overestimate the necessity of the expressive (analytic) treatment mode and of its operation via conflict resolution in order to effect therapeutically desired change, has been the other proposition, based on the happy finding, that the supportive psychotherapeutic approaches, mechanisms and techniques so often achieved far more than were expected for them—in fact often enough reached the kinds and degrees of change expected to depend on more expressive and insightful conflict resolutions—and did so in ways that represented indistinguishably "structural" changes, in terms of the usual indicators of that state. In fact, proportionately, each within their own category, the designated psychotherapy cases did as well as the designated psychoanalytic ones. More to the point, the (good) results in the one modality

were not overall less stable or less enduring or less proof against subsequent environmental vicissitude than in the other. And more important still, within the psychotherapy group (of 20), the changes predicted, though more often predicated on the more expressive mechanisms and techniques, in fact were more often actually achieved—often the same changes—on the basis of the more supportive mechanisms and techniques.

And even more, within the psychoanalysis group (of 22), in almost every case there were modifications, parameters, etc., some analytically resolved but mostly not, and all of them in the direction of more supportive modes and aspects, so that even by our liberal PRP criteria, there were only 10 (not quite half) of the psychoanalytic cases who were in overall retrospect viewed as having been in essentially unaltered analyses, six who were in substantially modified (in supportive directions) analyses, and six who were considered really converted to varyingly supportive–expressive psychotherapies. By the usual stricter criteria of customary outpatient psychoanalytic and psychotherapy practice, just about every single one of our PRP psychoanalytic cases would be considered substantially altered in varingly supportive directions. Put into overall perspective, more of the patients (psychotherapeutic and psychoanalytic alike) changed on the basis of designedly supportive interventions and mechanisms than had been expected or predicted beforehand, either on the basis of our clinical experience or our theoretical positions.

5. Considering these PRP treatment courses from the point of view of psychoanalysis as a treatment modality, just as more was accomplished than expected, and more stably, and more enduringly with psychotherapy, especially in its more supportive modes, so psychoanalysis, as the quintessentially expressive therapeutic mode was more limited—at least with these patients—than had been anticipated or predicted. This has of course been a function of a variety of factors. In part this has reflected the whole ethos of the psychoanalytic sanatorium and the psychoanalytic treatment opportunities that it is intended to make possible. The dominant theme here has been the concept that the psychoanalytically guided sanatorium, with its possibilities for protection, care, and life management of the (temporarily) behaviorally disorganized and incompetent individual, could make possible the intensive psychoanalytic treatment of patients who could not be helped to resolve their deep-seated personality difficulties satisfactorily enough with any other or lesser treatment approach than psychoanalysis, but who also could not tolerate the rigors of the regressive psychoanalytic treatment process within the usual outpatient private practice setting.

This, of course, is what has led to the concept of psychoanalysis on the basis of so-called "heroic indications," which by the nature of the kinds of patients brought to The Menninger Foundation, necessarily comprised such a substantial segment of our PRP psychoanalytic population. In our PRP experience however, the central tenets of this proposition were found wanting; these particular patients characteristically did very poorly with the psychoanalytic treatment method, however it was modified by parameters, and however buttressed with concomitant hospitalization, and they in fact comprised the great bulk of the failed psychoanalytic treatment cases. On the other hand, there were certainly enough instances of very good outcomes among the very ill and disordered in supportive-expressive psychotherapies that we can feel that the whole broad spectrum of "sicker" patients who are being talked about here can indeed do much better in an appropriately arranged and modulated supportive-expressive psychotherapy, if the ingredients are put together skillfully and imaginatively enough, and if one can ensure truly sufficient concomitant life management. That last stipulation, concerning the need for adequate enough life management, is of course one of the central keys to the success of the treatment recommendations being proposed here, and, by that token, reaffirms a proper role either for the psychoanalytic sanatorium or for some less controlled life regimen made more possible by modern-day psychoactive drug management. The big difference is in the departure from the effort at psychoanalysis per se (even modified psychoanalysis) as the treatment of choice for these "sicker" patients in that setting. On this basis, I have spoken of the failing of the so-called "heroic indications" for *psychoanalysis*, and am instead inviting a repositioning of the pendulum in its swings over time around this issue, more in the direction of "narrowing indications" for (proper) psychoanalysis along the lines marked out by Anna Freud [1954b, p. 610].

6. The predictions made for prospective therapeutic courses and outcomes tended to be for more substantial change and for more permanent change (i.e. more "structural change") where the treatment plan and implementation was to be more expressive-analytic, and where these changes were expected to be more based on thoroughgoing intrapsychic conflict resolution through processes of interpretation, insight, and working through. And pari passu, and again in terms of the conventional psychodynamic wisdom, the other part of this proposition has to do with the belief that the more supportive the treatment was intended to be (had to be), the more limited and inherently unstable the anticipated changes were predicted to be. What our research study has revealed in great detail is that all of this was (again, overall) consistently tempered and altered in the actual implementation in the treatment courses. The psychoanalyses as a whole, as well as the expressive psychotherapies as a whole, were systematically modified in the direction of introducing more supportive components in widely varying ways, they by and large accomplished more limited outcomes than promised (hoped), and, as indicated, with a varying but often substantial

amount of that accomplished by non-interpretive, i.e. supportive means. The psychotherapies on the other hand often accomplished a fair amount more, and in several of the more spectacular cases a great deal more, than initially expected and promised, and again with these cases, however the admixture of intervention techniques was originally projected, with much of the change on the basis of more supportive modes than originally specified [pp. 144–149].

I can illustrate these overall project conclusions about the goals sought and the results achieved in both psychoanalytic psycho-therapies and psychoanalysis proper, as well as the distinction between psycho*therapeutic* and psycho*analytic* goals and results within a single treatment process, through the following account from the verbatim interpretive synthesis of the original write-up of the treatment course and outcome of one of our project patients, called in my (1986) book the Adoptive Mother.

The patient had come to psychiatric evaluation presenting as her central problem her inability to be a proper mother, culminating in the return of an adopted child to the adoption agency after four months of mounting distress. Diagnostic study revealed the present-ing distress to be a reflection of core neurotic conflicts, (1) in the area of feminine sexuality, of her basic sexual identification, of activity–passivity, of her competitive rivalry with men and her need to dominate them; and (2) in the area of oral-dependent deprivations and frustrations. At the time of termination study and again at the time of follow-up study, there was general agreement by patient and analyst (and research investigators) that after three years of analysis, only partial resolution of intrapsychic conflict had occurred, although there was a very substantial and very satisfying alleviation of the originally presenting symptoms of recurrent anxiety, bitter depres-sion, and acute life crisis.

The transference models that had been activated and seemingly worked through in this analysis were clearly evident. There was the initial position of the nurse (the patient was a nurse) objectively reporting to the physician about the symptoms of a third party— herself, the patient. This was a struggle over detachment versus involvement, the struggle to overcome her distrust that any good could come from emotional closeness. Alongside this were the abreactions of penitent to priest-confessor (the patient was a devout converted Catholic), the seeking of forgiveness for her own unlovableness via a more tolerant superego figure. Once these initial positions were worked through, the main core of the analytic work revolved around the two major transference images of the terrible father who mistreated mother, and the good, kind, understanding mother who sheltered and protected. As clearly documented in close study of the analytic work, the negative mother transference, though it was clearly evident in the analytic material (for example, a dream, in the termination phase, of the patient beating to a pulp her interfering mother who had interrupted the patient and her husband at intercourse) was never fully developed or analytically worked out. In fact, the analysis ended prematurely at precisely the point when this kind of material was pressing to the fore; that is, the transference neurosis had unfolded but was never adequately resolved.

The process notes from the termination phase of the analysis amply support this view. During the same period as the dream just referred to, there were fantasies of her mother indulging in the very same forbidden sexual behaviors that were interdicted to the patient; a memory of mother having told her about the degenerates (men), and what they do; the childhood fear of mother catching her masturbating (and the association to the analyst peering at her); fear of homosexual fantasies she would have had if she had had a woman analyst. Hatred was gingerly expressed toward mother and father as partners in crime. The patient also mentioned her strong discomfort on kissing her mother-in-law in greeting or at parting after a visit. In another dream of this period, the patient spilled her jewels, and these were restored to her by the analyst. In her associations she toyed with this as the symbol of the restoration of her femininity. She associated to the pregnancy and miscarriage she had had early in her marriage, but then veered away to a bossy reaction to the analyst's presence, taking up a critical, defensive, "masculine" position. All these conflicts were active in the material of the termination phase of this analysis without concomitant evidence of insightful mastery or new ego positions.

Nonetheless, the patient felt pressured to draw the analysis to a premature close before this material was ever worked through. Her own awareness of this was caught in the complaint about "orders from headquarters" (her husband) pressing her to terminate so that she and he could move to their new home in a distant city. She asked,

"How can I go when I can't make peace with my own dead mother?" Despite this, she did leave, ascribing her decision to the increasing importunities of an ever more demanding husband or, at other times, admitting she could have stayed in treatment longer if she really wanted to, and that her husband would have been willing to delay his plans for her. At the point of leaving there was again a general agreement on the part of the patient, the analyst, and the research investigators that the analysis ended on the same note of positive attachment and sustained good feeling toward the analyst that had characterized the predominant transference mode throughout—gratitude to the fatherly analyst, who was also the good mother who cared.

What accounted for this limited outcome in terms of structural change with termination prior to the full analysis of the negative mother imago, which was so centrally tied to her core conflicts and their symptomatic expression? Research study revealed what seemed to be a number of contributory influences within the treatment: (1) The analyst was heavily influenced in the direction of a "defense analysis" that focused more on interpretation of defense and resistance and less on specific content meaning of inner impulse or its transference manifestations. Interpretive effort often seemed partial and one-sided. (2) This interlocked with a particular learning problem that seemed to characterize this analysis. This was the analyst's difficulty in showing the patient the transference meaning of phenomena, for example, of acting out, without seeming critical and punitive. It seemed that for this analyst, acting out was characteristically to be directly suppressed—or ignored. He did not rely on the patient's ability to come to understand its meaning in a way that would be sufficient to control it. (3) In addition to this specific learning problem, a particular countertransference issue seemed to operate to limit the full effectiveness of the analyst's work. The patient was a woman whom he would go to any lengths to help, from whom he was willing to take a lot, and who perhaps made him too anxious to really deal effectively with her bossy and competitive ways. (4) A last problem specifically noted within the conduct of the treatment lay in the analyst's tendency to tread lightly in analyzing the meaning of the patient's religious beliefs and feelings. In part this may have been in defensive deference to the husband's (and the patient's) anticipated fear that psychoanalysis would undermine—that is, take away—the patient's religious faith; in part it may have been a reflection of a more general attitude of reluctance to explore the meaning of religion in intrapsychic life. In any case, it is clear that the meaning of her religion and of her relationship to God was never brought into deliberate analytic focus, despite its obvious connection with the unexplored aspects of her relationship to her mother. Rather, the disappointment with her religion with which she began the analysis shifted to the same note of heightened faith and good feeling that characterized every other aspect of the ending state of the analysis. How much her renewed religious fervor represented the coin she paid to keep her husband's love; how much the relative sexual inhibition with which she ended the analysis represented the conviction that sexuality to be moral must be paid for by pregnancy, and that therefore if pregnancy were banned, so also must sexuality be; and how much aggressive charge resided in the demandingness with which she continued to "storm heaven"—all these were relatively unexplored territory.

Thus, a variety of influences within the specific conduct of the analysis could be felt to contribute to the analytically limited outcome. That they by themselves did not necessarily account for this outcome or for its specific form is attested by the other side of the coin—the limitations on the possible result of the analysis predicted at the time of pretreatment study from the diagnostic psychological test protocols, that is, from the side of the patient. It was observed that the nature and form of the acute decompensated state in which the patient had initially presented herself for treatment gave evidence of the disorganizing anxiety that could be potentially generated by the regressive experience of psychoanalysis. The patient's own awareness of this was reflected in her early panicky "fear of losing control." It was predicted that at a point of achievement of good symptom relief, and of substantial if not complete gains toward more adaptive reaction patterns, rather than face the danger of further regression, the patient would prefer to consolidate and "quit while she was ahead"—and she could do this by invoking reality pressures and supports from without, and by remobilizing her potential for counterphobic mastery from within. This is exactly what seems to have happened. Furthermore, it was specified that the area of incompleted work would be in relation to the negative mother transference and the patient's hostile identification with the malevolent, feared, and hateful preoedipal mother imago. Again, this is exactly what seems to have happened. In fact, the very life solution she came to at the end of the analysis, to have a grateful feeling to mother figures, to maintain her marriage with its problems glossed over, and to try again to adopt children even at the price of considerable inner turmoil, was in itself an expression of the unresolved identification with mother—she chose to be a martyr like mother, burdened with children and with an unsatisfactory husband.

In terms of this major limitation drawn from the nature of the patient's personality structure and of her illness across the expectable outcome of the analysis, the termination was perhaps at the best possible point of improved functioning—whether deliberately planned technically (for which there was no special evidence) or sensed intuitively and pushed for by the patient, abetted by the already stated problems within the therapist's handling of the treatment that likewise worked to keep it less than fully interpretive, and to allow significant sectors of intrapsychic functioning to remain in repression and unanalyzed.

Two corollary predictions had been made initially, one having to do with the first phase of treatment, the other with the prospects of postanalytic treatment. The first prediction was of the desirability in this case of an initial period of preparatory psychotherapy in order to help arrest the acute decompensation. Again, though this does not seem to have been done deliberately, it worked out that way. The patient spent the first two months (40 hours) sitting up rather than on the couch. She expressed herself as too anxious to accept the psychoanalytic structure directly.

The other prediction, which was based on the expectation that the analytic result would be incomplete and that the patient would be left liable to recurrent anxiety and perhaps even transitory symptom formation in the face of continued environmental triggering of her core conflicts, had to do with the form of future treatment. It was stipulated that this should not then be an effort to analyze further what had remained unanalyzed from the first treatment (for the same reasons), but that this should rather be a supportive–expressive psychotherapy aimed at helping her utilize the previous analytic accomplishments to stabilize herself in the face of new stresses.

In effect, this is also what happened. The patient did not seek further psychotherapy in an explicit way. She rationalized this on the basis of the higher treatment fee in her new community, which she could not afford. What she did instead was to call on a variety of helping hands—none specifically for psychotherapy. There was the priest who admonished her regarding her duties to her husband and to their future together, including the child he encouraged her to adopt; there was the family physician who prescribed medications to help her cope with the tensions and anxieties any such moves would generate; there was the understanding adoption agency social worker, sympathetic to her plight, to whom she could pour out her burden of grief, of worry, of discouragement. The patient thus combined the ingredients of her supportive–expressive psychotherapy, and insured that any more ambitious psychotherapeutic effort was precluded.

On this basis the patient was able to go ahead and adopt two children, albeit with considerable psychological strain. With the consolidation of the success of the first adoption, a girl, there was enough accrual of circular gratifications and enough increment to her self-esteem and her self-confidence, to enable her, three years later, to adopt a boy. Thus, with an analysis that was incomplete and with important transference components unanalyzed, the patient could nonetheless achieve her original treatment goal—to be able to be a proper wife and mother. Indicative of the nature of the incompletely analyzed transference fantasies which underpinned these significant treatment changes was the patient's voiced desire on the occasion of her research follow-up visit to see her ex-analyst and to show him her adopted daughter, the successful "fruit of his labors."

I have not here given any context either in the life history of the patient prior to the analysis or in the treatment history during the analysis for these observations and inferences from the final interpretive synthesis that relate to the themes of goals sought and results achieved. I trust that what has nonetheless emerged from this highly abstracted and summarized account is the kind of assessments of the process and outcome of psychoanalytic treatments that our research program engaged in in order to understand the changes in life functioning achieved. For this patient the treatment added up to a very satisfactory therapeutic result, since she did, after the termination of her analysis, go on to successfully adopt two children in her new community, albeit with some recurrent difficulties. At the same time, in the sense of thoroughgoing conflict resolutions, the psychoanalytic gain achieved was substantially less complete than the experienced psychotherapeutic gain.

Which brings me to the question, What did all this labor in our Psychotherapy Research Project add up to in relation to the issue of goals and results in psychoanalysis and in psychoanalytic psychotherapy? Again, I can quote from that same 1988 paper already quoted at length.

It can be most broadly generalized as follows: (1) The treatment results, with patients selected either as suitable for trials at psychoanalysis, or as appropriate for varying mixes of expressive–supportive psychotherapeutic approaches, tended—with this population sample—to converge, rather than diverge, in outcome. (2) Across the whole spectrum of treatment courses in the 42 patients, ranging from the most analytic–expressive, through the inextricably blended, onto the most single-mindedly supportive, in almost every instance—the psychoanalyses included—the treatment carried more supportive elements than originally intended, and these supportive elements accounted for substantially more of the changes achieved than had been originally anticipated. (3) The nature of supportive therapy, or better the supportive aspects of all psychotherapy, as conceptualized within a psychoanalytic theoretical framework, and as deployed by psychoanalytically knowledgeable therapists, bears far more respectful specification in all its form variants than has usually been accorded it in the psychodynamic literature. (4) When studying the kinds of changes reached by this cohort of patients, partly on an uncovering insight-aiming basis, and partly on the basis of the opposed covering up varieties of supportive techniques, the changes themselves—divorced from how they were brought about—often seemed quite indistinguishable from each other, in terms of being so-called real or structural changes in personality functioning.

In the light of the conceptual and predictive framework within which The Psychotherapy Research Project of The Menninger Foundation was planned and implemented three decades earlier, there is of course considerable real surprise to the overall project findings; that these distinctive therapeutic modalities of psychoanalysis, expressive psychotherapy, supportive psychotherapy, etc., hardly exist in anywhere near ideal or pure form in the real world of actual practice; that real treatments in actual practice are inextricably intermingled blends of more or less expressive–interpretive and more-or-less supportive-stabilizing elements; that almost all treatments (including even presumably pure psychoanalyses) carry many more supportive components than are usually credited to them; that the overall outcomes achieved by those treatments that are more "analytic" as against those that are more "supportive" are less apart than our usual expectations for those differing modalities would portend; and that the kinds of changes achieved in treatments from the two ends of this spectrum are less different in nature and in permanence, than again is usually expected, and indeed can often be easily distinguished. None of this was where, three decades ago, we expected to be today. From another perspective, in terms of the corridor comments made by practitioners in informal interchanges about the conditions and nature of professional practice, what they regularly find that they do in actual practice as against how it is conceptualized for formal presentation in professional meetings, our PRP research conclusions are far less surprising [pp. 149–150].

Which, in conclusion, circles me back to the "reconsideration" of the goals of psychoanalysis stated in the title of this paper. The detailed findings of our Menninger project (PRP) lend impressive empirical support to the gradually crystallizing consensus within the clinical and theoretical psychoanalytic literature that I have amply enough documented, that we have come through a rather prolonged era in psychoanalytic thinking (to which my 1965 paper on "The Goals of Psychoanalysis" perhaps unintendedly added) of expanding ambitions for the most reconstructive (of character as well as of symptom malfunctioning) psychological therapy yet devised to a now tempered, realistically much more modest assessment of realizable expectations. In this we have finally recapitulated the personal trajectory on this issue of Sigmund Freud, the founder of our discipline.

4

Treatment Goals in Psychoanalysis

Edward M. Weinshel, M.D.
Owen Renik, M.D.

REUD begins his 1937 monograph on "Analysis Terminable and Interminable" with what may be the briefest statement of the goals of psychoanalytic treatment, saying that "Experience has taught us that psychoanalytic therapy—*the freeing of someone from his neurotic symptoms, inhibitions, and abnormalities of character—is a time-consuming business*" (Freud, 1937, p. 216; emphasis added). Most analysts will quickly recognize that Freud's definition of the goals of analytic therapy is deceptively simple, an observation that is already implied in Freud's reminder at the end of that sentence that those goals will be achieved neither quickly nor easily. Further, although most analysts would probably agree with those aims spelled out above, it is equally likely that most analysts *today* would consider Freud's statement neither sufficiently clear nor comprehensive.

In fact, it may be virtually impossible for psychoanalysts to arrive at any consensus regarding the reasonable expectations that one should or could anticipate from a reasonably well-conducted analytic treatment. It is not unlikely that these differences have been present ever since the theories and concepts of psychoanalysis have been applied to the treatment of psychological difficulties; as those theories and concepts have gradually evolved and changed over the years, so have the goals and expectations from the treatment. With the advent of the so-called "broadening scope of psychoanalysis" and the introduction of a variety of revisions of "classical" Freudian theory and practice, those differences have been accentuated and their range extended.

It is often noted that psychoanalysis is, on the one hand, a science using its own research technique and producing its own body of theory; on the other hand, it is a therapy in which theory is applied to relieve human suffering while clinical observation provides further data for scientific examination. Therefore, when we speak of the goals of psychoanalysis we inevitably refer, simultaneously, to scientific and to therapeutic goals. To some extent these goals can be distinguished, *must* be distinguished, for ethical reasons; to a significant extent they are inextricable. When Freud spoke in general terms of psychoanalytic treatment having as one of its aims that of freeing the patient from symptoms, he addressed an aspect of the goals of psychoanalysis that it has in common with many other human endeavors, namely, the therapeutic one. However, as we try to be more specific about what we mean by "symptoms" and what we mean by "freedom from symptoms," we invariably become involved in science; in doing so, we begin to formulate those aspects of the goals of psychoanalysis that help to distinguish it from other therapeutic modalities.

Freud was usually quite circumspect about the therapeutic results of analytic therapy. Those reservations gradually became more marked as his own experience (and that of his colleagues) increased, and, after the publication of "Analysis Terminable and Interminable" (one of the last contributions published during his lifetime), many of his colleagues felt that his position on the matter became somewhat pessimistic. At the same time, others viewed these shifts rather as an indication of an increasingly realistic appraisal of the product of the psychoanalytic treatment endeavor. In any case, it is certainly true that Freud did put additional stress in his later years on the limitations of the psychoanalytic method, the difficulties inherent in the analytic procedure, and the obstacles standing in the way of analytic work.

Freud had always, in one fashion or another, been concerned with a number of factors that he believed were "decisive for the success or otherwise of analytic treatment." He organized these factors around three principal categories: the role and the influence of significant early trauma; the relative strength of the instincts *vis-à-vis* the ego (either in terms of its constitutional propensities or its relative strength *at the time*); and what he referred to as the alteration of the ego resulting from the primitive defensive measures instituted by the "immature, feeble" ego.

His emphasis, therefore, lay on the "quantitative factor," on the "economic line of approach" (Freud, 1937, p. 226), and the relative strength of the ego (and, at times, in conjunction with the superego) versus that of the instincts. Freud argued that:

All repressions take place in early childhood: they are primitive defensive measures taken by the immature, feeble ego. In later years no fresh repressions are carried out: but the old ones persist, and their services continue to be made use of by the ego for mastering the instincts. ... We may apply to these infantile repressions our general statement that *repressions depend absolutely and entirely on the relative strength of the forces involved and that they cannot hold out against an increase in the strength of the instincts*. Analysis, however, enables the ego, which has attained greater maturity and strength to undertake a revision of these old repressions; a few are demolished, while others are recognized but constructed afresh out of more solid material. These new dams are of quite a different degree of firmness from the earlier ones; we may be confident that they will not give way so easily before a rising flood of instinctual strength. *Thus the real achievement of analytic therapy would be the subsequent correction of the original process of repression, a correction which puts an end to the dominance of the quantitative factor* [Freud, 1937, p. 227; emphasis added].

Here we see the goals of psychoanalytic treatment stated in a way which is inseparable from that version of psychoanalytic theory at which Freud arrived by the end of his life; it is a version which represents the result of many years of clinical observation and experience submitted to careful scientific examination. Symptoms are understood in terms of instincts and a process by which instincts are repressed, and the aim of psychoanalytic treatment is conceptualized as an alteration of the process and the product of repression. The goals of clinical psychoanalysis have developed beyond symptom relief just in the sense of behavioral change or a self-reported amelioration of the patient's chief complaint. Thus these goals become different from, though not inconsistent with, the goals of other therapies.

For most analysts, we submit, the statement from "Analysis Terminable and Interminable" quoted above represents the principal theoretical frame of reference for understanding psychoanalytic therapy and the goals of analytic work. Not all psychoanalysts would give equal emphasis to every element in that statement but most would probably subscribe to its general concepts. It should be noted, however, that there are analysts whose orientations are in accord with significant revisions in Freudian theory and practice, and, for them, the concept of change and the goals of therapy would vary considerably from the above.

A few explanatory words are in order. It is our impression that when Freud spoke of "repression," he was referring not just to the specific defense mechanism of repression but to the whole repertoire of defensive operations undertaken by the ego, both the infantile and the more mature. Freud did not believe that psychoanalysis (or life experiences in general) could eliminate the instincts or their demands. "This is in general impossible," Freud declared, "nor is it at all to be desired. No, we mean something else, something which may roughly be described as a 'taming' of the instinct. That is to say, the instinct is brought completely into the harmony of the ego, becomes accessible to all the influences of the other trends in the ego and no longer seeks to go its independent way to satisfaction" (1937, p. 225).

Similarly, psychoanalytic treatment is neither able nor intended to eliminate psychological conflict. It has often been suggested that the elimination of psychological conflict would lead to stasis and is therefore undesirable. In any event, the reality of the "average expectable environment" guarantees that any such aspiration is chimerical. This is why Freud insisted that psychoanalysis could not be a modality for the removal of all human suffering; the best that one can expect from analytic treatment is the elimination of "neurotic" misery so that the individual could then better deal with the ordinary and inevitable human unhappiness. "Our aim," Freud stressed, "will not be to rub off every peculiarity of human character for the sake of a schematic 'normality', nor yet to demand that the person who has been 'thoroughly analyzed' shall feel no passions and develop no internal conflicts. *The business of the analysis is to secure the best psychological conditions for the functioning of the ego; with that it has secured its task"* (Freud, 1937, p. 250; emphasis added).

This formulation, centering as it does on the concepts of ego and ego functioning, illustrates again the intimate interrelation of psychoanalytic therapeutic goals and psychoanalytic theoretical understanding. It also indicates the enormous impact of ego psychology: beginning with Freud's revision of his anxiety theory in 1926; continuing with the work of Anna Freud, Hartmann, Kris, and Loewenstein, and so many others; and resulting in a contemporary perspective generally shared by analysts (even in the midst of our considerable diversity) that personality is a complex phenomenon which demands that it also be regarded from what has been called an adaptational point of view. It is also a perspective within which psychopathology and normality are not categorically dichotomized.

From this perspective, it is understandable that psychoanalysts do not speak readily of treatment *cures* and why Maxwell Gitelson offers a "counsel of modesty" for psychoanalysis (Gitelson, 1963, p. 343; see also Weinshel, 1990, pp. 277 and 284). More recently Charles Brenner has approached this same line of thought by emphasizing the role of compromise formations in psychological development, pathogenesis, and psychoanalytic treatment. Brenner emphasizes that inasmuch as psychological conflict is the product of the interaction of various psychological forces, the result of that interaction is some sort of compromise formation, wherein residues of those conflicting forces are discernible. Brenner proposes that "the mind functions so as to afford the drive derivatives the fullest expression of satisfaction compatible with a tolerable degree of anxiety and/or depressive affect . . . the guiding principle is the same: as much satisfaction and as little unpleasure as it is possible to attain" (Brenner, 1982, p. 111). Looked at in these terms, we could say that the goal of psychoanalytic therapy is to assist and to facilitate the psychic apparatus in altering the balance of the compromise formations so as to provide the greatest amount of satisfaction with the least amount of pain. A necessary codicil would be that by "satisfaction" we refer not to immediate gratification but rather long-term satisfaction and adaptation.

The evolution of the psychoanalytic theory of psychic functioning has entailed a parallel evolution of the psychoanalytic conceptualization of psychopathology and a corresponding evolution in the conceptualization of the goals of psychoanalytic therapy. A similar evolution takes place, microscopically, within every successful clinical analysis. Commonly, analyst and analysand begin their work with somewhat different views about the latter's problems. Through the dialectical interaction between the two, a consensual understanding is forged. As the investigation proceeds, the patient's ideas about what constitutes his symptoms (his "miseries") are likely to change a great deal, and the analyst's understanding will change as well.

This evolutionary process is observed by every clinical analyst and has been commented upon in a variety of ways. It can be described as an inevitable shift in focus from the analysis of symptoms, in the narrower sense, to the analysis of character. Initially, ego-syntonic components of the analysand's personality are likely to draw his critical attention; but in order for the analytic work to go forward, ego-syntonic traits come under scrutiny as well (Abrams, 1987).

Considering how the evolution in the understanding of symptoms and goals takes place within a progressive clinical analysis, some emphasis should be given to the elucidation of the analysand's transferences. After all, the potential unique benefits of psychoanalysis derive from the fact that the patient has the opportunity to become aware of, review, and alter obsolete conclusions that underlie some current maladaptive attitudes. Analytic work, when it is productive, unveils and examines certain compromise solutions which are actively operative even though they were forged under conditions long past. In his papers on technique, Freud pointed out that analysis of the treatment relationship provides both a convenient and effective vehicle for a first-hand examination of transference since it is impossible to destroy anyone *in absentia* or *in effigie* (Freud, 1912a, p. 108); and, further, the analysand's transferences to his analyst inevitably form the greatest obstacles to as well as the greatest opportunity for analytic progress (Freud, 1912a, p. 101).

When we speak of those goals that we consider to be *specific* to psychoanalytic therapy, we cannot avoid the thorny task of defining insight and delineating its place in the psychoanalytic process. Is insight a means to productive analytic work, an end, or both? Although for most analysts the acquisition of insight for the patient remains a significant goal, it is a concept about which there remains considerable controversy and uncertainty; and it is unlikely that "insight" per se currently represents *the* sine qua non for a successful psychoanalysis. Nonetheless, there is probably an area of consensus concerning the role of insight: it is generally agreed that clinical analysis aims at symptom relief *based on increased self-awareness*. One of the earliest conceptions of the goal of analytic treatment—that it makes conscious what was previously unconscious—has like many psychoanalytic formulations, never been really invalidated albeit recognized as incomplete. The achievement of insight, in the sense of heightened self-awareness, probably remains a primary operational objective for most psychoanalysts in their daily clinical work. Translated into a somewhat different idiom, the achievement of insight (or the capacity for self-analysis, self-observation, self-inquiry, and other related terms) also implies a greater and easier access to unconscious psychological derivatives.

Any number of elements are collected under the heading of realizing increased self-awareness for the analysand, the sum and substance of which constitute clinical analysis as we know it. A partial list would include investigation of fantasies and dreams; gaining an understanding of the relevant traumatic past, whether on the basis of actual recovered memories or by reconstruction; establishing the role of drives and drive derivatives; the clarification of both intersystemic and intrasystemic intrapsychic conflict; the exposition of the content of anxieties and depressive affects (and other affects as well) together with an understanding of the various ways in which these affects elicit defensive activity.

Whatever an analyst's particular theoretical orientation or emphasis, he is likely to understand analytic work as some sort of ongoing process in which the analysand's capacity for self-observation is enlarged and refined. Therefore, in clinical psychoanalysis as it is generally understood (the diversity of individual approaches notwithstanding), when analytic work proceeds, *insight and symptom relief merge into a single goal*. The analysand's resistances clarify themselves as the most immediately relevant symptoms to be studied, and no distinction can or need be made between investigation of the analysand's self-observational difficulties and investigation of his psychopathology. It becomes a matter of conviction, based not on faith but born of empirical evidence collected within analysis, that insight into the manner in which the analysand interferes with his self-examination is also insight into the causes of his pain. Increased self-awareness is accompanied by decreased subjective distress.

From this point of view, too, it can be seen that another goal of analytic clinical work is to make it possible for the analysand to engage in a form of self-observation or self-inquiry that at least approximates the analytic situation. The agreement to terminate analytic meetings, then, is best understood not as a decision to terminate the analytic process but as a judgment that the analyst's input is no longer required to maintain adequately the analytic process.

There is, undoubtedly, considerable variety among individual analysts as to their views of what shifts and changes constitute the most significant indicator that the goals of analysis have been attained. Further, it is not likely that any patient, given even the best outcome, will demonstrate *all* of them. However, it should be noted that the analytic work often affects psychic activity so as to enhance overall psychological functioning and the quality of life in ways that are no less significant for being inconspicuous.

Ernst Ticho (1972, pp. 315–333) divides the goals of psychoanalytic therapy into two somewhat loosely defined categories. *Treatment goals* deal with the "removal of obstacles to the patient's discovery of what his potentialities are" (p. 315). *Life goals* are "the goals the patient would seek to attain if he could put his potentialities to use" (p. 315). The patient, reasonably enough, is most concerned with the latter and with the hope and anticipation of a better life. Very frequently an immediate life goal is the amelioration of a particular psychic pain or the elimination of a discrete symptom or inhibition; for most patients, expressed in one fashion or another, there is the wish for greater pleasure and less pain in the realms of love and of work. Using Ticho's polarities, we would have to say that rarely are all treatment goals or all life goals achieved. Often, one of the more gratifying products of the analytic experience is the recognition and clarification by the analysand of what his life goals are—even if those objectives cannot be reached in entirety.

The psychoanalytic method is most effective and most successful when the treatment confines itself to the pursuit of treatment goals and the psychoanalyst operates by the principle that "The business of analysis is to secure the best possible psychological conditions for the function of the ego. . . ." In the final words of *Studies on Hysteria*

(Breuer and Freud, 1893–1895) his credo was enunciated *vis-à-vis* the patient in this way: "No doubt Fate would find it easier than I do to relieve you of your illness. But you will be able to convince yourself that much will be gained if we succeed in transforming your hysterical misery into common unhappiness. With a mental life that has been restored to health you will be better armed against that unhappiness" (p. 305).

5

Interpretation

Steven T. Levy, M.D.
Lawrence B. Inderbitzin, M.D.

Definitions

IN all psychoanalytic inquiry, careful definition of terms is crucial to counteract misunderstanding created by the many different and often contradictory ways words are used by proponents of different theoretical and technical persuasions. Here we will use the term *interpretation* to refer to the ongoing process whereby verbal expression is given to that which is understood about the patient and his problems. Most central is the understanding of unconscious mental conflict or activity. Interpretation is its decisive instrument: To the extent that the entire therapeutic process is a vehicle for reaching such understanding of unconscious mental life, it is appropriate to explore the analyst's comments about all that transpires between analyst and patient within the broad context of interpretation. What the analyst communicates to the patient becomes a way for the patient to think about and define his inner experiences and comes to constitute the form his new self-knowledge will take. The patient's corrections, amplifications, and other contributions to the analyst's interpretations must be included in what is considered the interpretive process.

Interpretation and the Unconscious

The analyst makes many verbal interventions that are not, strictly speaking, interpretations. Narrowly defined, only interventions that make conscious what was previously hidden are interpretations. This most restrictive definition was especially relevant during the early years of psychoanalysis, often referred to as the period of id analysis. During this phase in the development of psychoanalytic technique, emphasis was placed on uncovering the repressed wishes and traumatic experiences of childhood and the instinctual fixations which were their result. To interpret meant to undo repression, making the unconscious conscious. The latter constituted the therapeutic aim to which was attached a theory of cure that emphasized the pathogenic nature of repression in neurosogenesis and the curative effects of the discharge of tensions associated with previously avoided instinctual wishes and their derivatives, and of exposure of the repressed to the reality orientation of adult, conscious mental activity.

The development of ego psychology in the 1920s and 1930s led to significant changes in psychoanalytic technique. The unconscious as a system was replaced by a recognition that a wide variety of mental activity takes place outside of awareness. Analysis of defense became the dominant theme in technical treatises, most notably Fenichel's (1941) *Problems of Psychoanalytic Technique*. Likewise, there have been periods when the analysis of transference has been emphasized as the central activity of the analyst. Interest in developmental internal object relations, self psychology, and other familiar psychoanalytic theoretical approaches with their concomitant technical emphases have broadened the scope of the material to which interpretive efforts are addressed during clinical work. With the disappearance of "the unconscious" as a discreet entity or system, and with the diversity in psychoanalytic approaches now prevalent, defining interpretation solely in terms of exposing that which has been unconscious seems too limiting. It fails to do justice to the analyst's many interpretive efforts which aim at expanding the patient's self-understanding. Not all that the patient does not understand or recognize accurately and completely is best described as unconscious. The connections between seemingly separate or disparate behaviors, thoughts and feelings, recurrent themes, typical distortions, unexpressed yearnings, all the familiar material of analytic scrutiny are the subject of the analyst's interpretive efforts. The analyst must carefully consider timing, tact, and strategy in relation to all interpretations, not only those specifically aimed at uncovering previously unconscious material.

Interpretation as Process

Many of the restrictions on what ought to be called an interpretation are vitiated if interpretation is regarded as a dynamic process. It is certainly worthwhile to consider certain of the analyst's statements to the patient as discreet interpretations and to study them from the point of view of their clarity, evocativeness, and effectiveness. Much can be learned from a microanalysis of such interpretive statements about issues such as the analyst's theoretical positions or preferences, his countertransference, neutrality, and relative anonymity. However, few would argue that such a microanalysis could ever present an accurate or complete picture of the way the analyst helps the analysand to an expanded understanding of his or her inner life. The interpretive process is a dialogue in which both participants, analyst and analysand, talk about the latter's psychological life. In every analysis, the analyst struggles to find ways of speaking with the analysand about an ever widening and deepening range of subjects. If things go well, the analysand becomes an increasingly more active participant in the dialogue, the analyst's role focusing more and more on resistances which arise in the dialogue, especially those related to the transference. Things are repeated, revised, expanded, contradicted, forgotten, and rediscovered. The patient's relevant emotional history is reconstructed. Put differently, a narrative is created. This is a process in which specific statements by the analyst have an important role. Yet taken by themselves, they constitute only what is being talked about at the moment. The same statement, spoken at a later time, may have much greater positive impact or may become a resistance to further exploration. The interpretive process can be said to be taking place when the patient's knowledge about himself is expanding by virtue of what he and the analyst are talking about together. Viewed in this way, the analyst's encouragement, his reminders, his confrontations, clarifications, and efforts at working through (Greenson, 1967) are all part of the interpretive process.

Whether a statement is an interpretation depends on its context in the dialogue and its dynamic impact.

Interpretive Expertise

We believe that interpretation should be studied in its own right because it constitutes an important aspect of the analyst's expertise. We should note at the outset of this discussion that developing into a skilled interpreter is only one facet of enhancing the analyst's technical expertise and cannot make up for deficiencies in empathy and intuition, understanding of psychopathology, or the intrusion of the analyst's personal problems into the therapeutic work. Having said this much in the way of cautionary restraint, we do propose that the analyst's technical skill, his sense of areas of expertise, is a valuable asset in handling the pressures and ambiguities of analytic work. We believe that an overemphasis on the "art" of analysis, on the analyst's creativity and innately intuitive approach to his work has obscured the need for and value of developing a sense of expertise. Often an emphasis on technical skill is uncritically equated with mechanical clinical work. To the contrary, our observations lead us to believe that blunders occur more regularly from the absence rather than the presence of carefully developed technical guidelines. The psychoanalytic candidate emerges from his training having carried out only a few analyses, often completing only one or two cases by the time of graduation. Furthermore, each case is likely to be very different. Unlike the medical graduate of other specialty training programs who likely has treated many patients with a specific clinical problem or repeatedly carried out a specific surgical procedure, the graduate analyst, despite the lengthy training he has completed, is in many ways a novice with little of the experience of repetition behind him to feel very expert.

Given the variety, frequent surprises, emotional pressures, and subjectivity of analytic work, maintaining a sense of expertise is greatly enhanced by developing guidelines for interpretation based upon carefully thought out theoretical and technical principles. Conceptual clarity about such guidelines constitutes a kind of expertise that at least partially compensates for lack of expertise derived from experience and repetition. Guidelines are not constraints limiting creative options. Rather, they represent a distillation of accumulated experience and theoretical conjecture from which the clinical analyst derives a hypothesis regarding his decision about when and how to make interpretations. Such interpretations may conform to these guidelines or depart from them, requiring an alternative hypothesis that is tested by examining the analysand's responses to the intervention. We do not wish to give the impression that decision making about interpretation is entirely a cognitive, intellectual process. Arlow (1979) has described the genesis of interpretation in the shared unconscious fantasies of analyst and analysand. Others have emphasized transference–countertransference complementarity and its disruptions as a trigger for the analyst's interpretive interventions. The analyst's empathic, transient identification with the analysand is another source of direction regarding interpreting (Fliess, 1942). A balance must be struck between spontaneity and careful timing, between the cognitive and the affective. Such oscillation helps insure that the analyst takes advantage of his capacity for unconscious receptiveness while protecting the patient from inappropriately timed or tactlessly presented interventions.

Fenichel's Guidelines for Interpretation

The most widely known, systematically organized presentation of guidelines for interpretation is put forth in Fenichel's (1941) *Problems of Psychoanalytic Technique.* Freud mentions many guidelines for interpretation but in fact carefully avoided setting down any detailed or systematic instructions about carrying out analytic work for fear of prematurely creating dogma by virtue of his special role as founder of the science. Most of Fenichel's ideas are derived from Freud and show the stamp of Freud's (1923[1922], 1926a) structural revisions of theory. Fenichel referred to economic, dynamic, and structural criteria for interpretations. A basic premise underlying his guidelines is the idea that a predominant instinctual conflict can be determined during the analytic session. Economic, dynamic, and structural criteria then refer to the optimal interpretive approach to this conflict. Economic considerations concern interpreting "at the point of the *most important* current instinctual conflicts. It is the point of the most important conflicts *at the moment*" (p. 47). The analyst's decision about what is momentarily most important should be based on what Kernberg (1983, 1988) has described as the "patient's dominant affect disposition within any psychoanalytic session or segment thereof" (1988, p. 482). Fenichel (1941) says: "[W]e must operate at that point where the affect is actually situated at the moment; it must be added that the patient does not know the point and we must first seek out the places where the affect is situated" (p. 45). The analyst must base this decision on the patient's free associations and nonverbal behaviors, leading themes in the material, and "in the general atmosphere created by the influence of the patient's transference and the analyst's countertransference" (Kernberg, 1988, p. 482). The dynamic criteria for interpretation are best summarized by the familiar dictum that the analyst should interpret resistance before content. The removing of resistances becomes the dynamic aim of interpretation. The structural aspect of interpretation dictates that the analyst's interpretations work primarily upon the ego. The other psychic structures (id, superego) are affected indirectly through the mediation of the ego.

Fenichel's criteria for interpretation are an attempt in the direction of systematic interpretation in analysis. He is quick to point out that these guidelines refer to complex situations in which sorting out predominating affects, many simultaneously present defenses and their ever-varying manifestations as resistances, and a multiplicity of contradictory yet relevant contents is by no means simple. Furthermore, the dynamic configuration of the material is constantly changing. Nevertheless, interpretive efforts based upon rational guidelines congruent with the theory of the therapeutic action of analytic interpretation are important alongside the analyst's intuition and free floating attention; "we should always be able to explain what we are doing, why we interpret, and what we expect each time from our activity" (Fenichel, 1941, p. 52).

The Analytic Surface and Interpretation

The concept of an analytic surface as a starting point for the interpretive process was referred to by Freud (1914). He used the term *surface* in different ways, one of which was clearly related to the topographic theory: the surface of consciousness was contrasted with the depth of the unconscious. A second meaning, more relevant to our discussion, considers the analytic surface any aspect of the patient's verbal and nonverbal productions to which the analyst and analysand can profitably direct their attention in the service of further analytic inquiry.

Fenichel (1941) emphasized the importance of beginning the interpretive process at the surface. "In what other way could we penetrate to the depths than by beginning at the surface" (p. 44). His emphasis that "analysis must always go on in the layers accessible to the ego at the moment" (p. 44), the structural criterion, comes closest to defining the analytic surface as we conceptualize it. In regards to the interpretive process beginning at the surface, Fenichel also underlined the importance of *logically* scrutinizing the analytic material.

The concept of the analytic surface as a specific focus of the analyst's and analysand's joint attention has received little systematic attention in the psychoanalytic literature. Paniagua (1985) noted that surface does not appear as a psychoanalytic concept in any of the specialized psychoanalytic glossaries or dictionaries. He defines the surface as "the level of observables" (p. 323) that can be demonstrated to the analysand or to any independent observer. By analytic surface, we refer to some aspect of the patient's verbal and nonverbal behavior to which the analyst *and* the analysand can direct their attention in order to learn more about important conflictual issues. It is the beginning point of systematic exploration and interpretation, frequently recognized in disturbance, discontinuities, or disequilibria in the analytic material and relationship that attract the analyst's attention, often with an element of surprise. We assume that in the momentary here and now of the analytic situation, something meaningful from the past is represented. It is alive and immediate. This current event, perceived by the analyst, is one that with joint focused attention can also be sensed by the patient if it is to be an effective surface for interpretation. We analyze "dramatic realities" (Friedman, 1988, p. 128), and it is this very small drama that we are spotlighting as the analytic surface.

A surface approach as the starting point for a systematic interpretive process begins from *observational data* that is available to both analyst and analysand and thus is strongly empirical in its emphasis. Analysts with different personalities, predilections, and theoretical orientations would nevertheless be able to observe the same analytic data. However, this does not mean that they would choose an identical analytic surface as a starting point for their interpretive efforts. For example, Gray, in a series of papers (1973, 1982, 1986, 1987), has defined and described his choice of an analytic surface based on the structural theory, the importance of intrapsychic conflict, and particularly the analysis of observable manifestations of resistance. Gray (1986) selects "those elements in the material that may successfully illustrate for analysands that when they were speaking they encountered a conflict over something being revealed which caused them involuntarily and unknowingly to react in identifiably defensive ways" (p. 253). The analyst must judge what can be successfully illustrated to the analysand, success in this context referring to the latter's capacity to observe and comprehend without resorting to additional defensive measures. Gray (1982, 1986) outlines the sequence of interventions in his surface approach. He explains to the analysand the purpose and value of focusing attention on the conflict-based interferences with free association described above. When evidence of such inference emerges during the hour, Gray invites the analysand to consider the data as a sign of conflict and attempted unconscious solution. Next, he explores the defense as a manifestation of some unconsciously experienced risk while attempting to reveal something to the analyst. This "irrational risk" (1986, p. 251) is explored in order to counteract the automatic unconscious inhibition it gives rise to.

We have described Gray's surface approach in some detail for illustrative purposes. We have shown how other analysts have similarly described their interpretive approaches without explicitly relating them to so-named analytic surfaces, nevertheless orienting their listening and interpretive interventions to some central element (transference, free association, empathy) of the analytic dialogue (Levy and Inderbitzin, 1990). These different surfaces represent ways of organizing the data of observation more than they do different phenomena. They focus the attention of both the analyst and the analysand on a specific phenomenon from a vantage point that will allow systematic exploration and expansion of the patient's awareness of inner life. Surfaces are in no sense superficial in their subject matter or relative importance. Analytic surfaces are defined from currently observable material that one can expect to be present throughout an analysis rather than appearing only at specific junctures.

A surface approach tends to make the impact of theory on clinical work explicit, specifying as it does a particular mode of listening and a specific way of initiating the interpretive process. Furthermore, it emphasizes the analysand's active involvement in creating the surface and attending to it by organizing active participation in the analytic process. Internalization of the analytic process is enhanced by the consistency of the analyst's and analysand's attention to a specific surface, increasingly enabling the analysand to take over the interpretive function as self-analytic skill and confidence grow. A sense of mastery is developed as analyst and analysand experience a widening of awareness and insight.

Therapeutic Strategy and Interpretation

In the previous sections, we have described Fenichel's guidelines for interpretation and our reasons for advocating a surface approach as the starting point for systematic interpretation based upon observational data available to both analyst and analysand. The surface approach and Fenichel's guidelines are implicitly microscopic in their approach to the material of the analytic hour. They represent strategic approaches based upon the material as it emerges in the analytic dialogue. Strategy can also refer to a macroscopic perspective on the overall course of an analysis. One of us has explored the role therapeutic strategy plays in the theory of psychoanalytic technique (Levy, 1987). Here, we will explore briefly its relationship to the interpretive process.

In the past, talented clinicians such as Reich (1949), Sharpe (1950), and Glover (1955) described strategies from a macroscopic perspective, delineating what might be called lines of interpretation typical in the analysis of specific kinds of neurotic psychopathology. More recently, strategy in relationship to psychoanalytic technique has been advocated in the treatment of patients within the "widening scope of psychoanalysis." Kernberg (1976), Kohut (1971), and others have recommended specific technical strategies for borderline and narcissistic patients. In general, however, specific strategies for guiding clinical work with those patients traditionally

felt to be analyzable have been considered unnecessary, psychotherapeutic rather than psychoanalytic, and constricting or limiting
in their effect on the analytic process. The sources of this anti-
strategic bias have been explored elsewhere (Levy, 1987). Nevertheless, we believe that strategies for interpretation exist within
psychoanalytic practice, residing in the realm of the "wisdom" or
"art" of experienced psychoanalysts.

The microscopic view of the current analytic data as it emerges for
interpretation in the analytic session is only one way the analyst
approaches the material. A macroscopic or strategic view of the
material takes into account "the sequence in which things are taken
up, delay in interpreting certain defensive operations while exposing
and exploring others, variation in emphasis on interpreting transference, extratransference phenomena, alliance issues, feeling states,
manifest versus latent content, and other familiar sources of analytic
data" (Levy, 1987, p. 454).

A strategic overview of lines of interpretation with patients suffering from specific clinical problems may reveal sequences in "progression, regression, transference development, interpretive intervention, and elements of strategic or tactical decision making that would
otherwise remain hidden" (Levy, 1987, p. 456). For example, in the
analysis of patients with masochistic character pathology, interpretation of masochistic phenomena often begins by focusing on the
patient's tendency to be drawn toward painful and humiliating
experiences. Only later do gratifying or tension regulating aspects of
such behavior become the subject of interpretive exploration. Sadistic aims hidden behind suffering, self-control, and self-deprivation
are interpreted still later. Exploration of fantasies of magical control,
feelings of entitlement and specialness in relation to suffering, the
narcissistic aspects of such pathology, are regularly explored last
along with the oedipal issues such pathological traits regularly ward
off or are a regressive response to. Such a sequence of interpretation
is not unusual in work with such patients. It involves many strategic
choices, about what to interpret at a given time in analysis, which are
not governed solely by the sequence of emergence of material in the
clinical work. Data regarding all of these elements may be present in
the earliest analytic sessions. Nevertheless, this familiar pattern of
approach in interpretation, along with many others that are part of
the accumulated expertise of generations of psychoanalysts, repre-

sents strategic trends in interpretive technique that can be lost in a solely microscopic and unnecessarily nearsighted view, neglecting an important method of clinical observation.

We are not advocating that the analyst respond to the analytic material on the basis of a macroscopic strategy that determines priorities for every intervention. Rather, we are suggesting that some balance be established between the microscopic surface approach to interpretation and a macroscopic strategic approach that identifies lines of interpretation the analyst can utilize to advantage. A surface approach to the material of the hour and a strategic approach to the overall conduct of the analytic work are complementary and synergistic rather than mutually exclusive or contradictory. Neither should be assumed to limit the many choices the analyst makes, but rather inform his thinking about interpretive interventions. It represents an oscillation in the analyst's observational mode.

Interpretation and Neutrality

Psychoanalytic neutrality has been much debated throughout its history, beginning with Freud's (1914) introduction of the concept in his paper on transference love. In it, he states "we ought not to give up the neutrality toward the patient which we have acquired through keeping the counter-transference in check" (p. 164). Recent papers on the subject of neutrality (Bornstein, 1983; Wolf, 1983; Lichtenberg, 1983a; Leider, 1983; Poland, 1984; Shapiro, 1984; Hoffer, 1985) have focused on the ambiguity and multiple meanings of the term. Some authors have viewed neutrality as the essence of the psychoanalyst's approach to the analysand. Others have dismissed neutrality as a myth.

In many places in the psychoanalytic literature, neutrality is clearly distinguished from anonymity and abstinence. Elsewhere it is viewed as synonymous with or inclusive of these two other terms that describe aspects of the analyst's relationship to the analysand. For some, neutrality is a global or superordinate term, encompassing all of the analytic attitude. Others have linked neutrality to the analyst's interventions, referring to technical neutrality (Kernberg, 1976). Neutrality has been explored in relationship to the way the analyst listens to psychoanalytic material, in its relationship to empathy, as a characteristic of the emotional climate of the analytic situation, in relation to the analyst's values and moral judgments, and as an approach to intrapsychic conflict. Even Anna Freud's (1936) often quoted definition of neutrality as equidistance from id, ego, and superego is not without ambiguity. Absent is any reference to external reality nor is it clear how an attitudinal equidistance is related to specific instances of intervention where one of the psychic agencies is emphasized at the expense of others. While most psychoanalysts accept the importance of the concept of neutrality within the theory of psychoanalytic technique in general, it is evident that in relation to specific analytic practices, neutrality remains a problematic and complex subject worthy of further study and debate.

We will explore neutrality in relationship to the interpretive process. We believe that the nature of the interpretive interventions defines the analyst's neutrality. Because interpretation is a goal directed activity, neutrality as a concept must be considered in terms of such goals if it is to retain its value in relation to the interpretive process.

Analysis is carried out in the service of the patient. Emphasis on the research aspect of psychoanalysis and the portrayal of its therapeutic goals as nonanalytic is a serious distortion of clinical analytic work. Analysts have long-term goals such as structural change, an improved capacity for productive work, and the enjoyment of interpersonal relatedness. Likewise, symptomatic improvement, the overcoming of resistances, the elucidation of transference, and other familiar psychoanalytic phenomena are related to short-term goals and aims to which the analyst's interventions are directed. All analysts have health values that translate into what they hope to help the analysand accomplish. Freud used the German term *Indifferenz* which was translated by Strachey as "neutrality." It was Freud's intention to characterize the psychoanalyst's approach to clinical data as different from the usual physician's stance of *authoritarian* helpfulness, and we agree with this distinction. However, this does not mean analysts are either indifferent to the outcome of their interventions with patients or neutral in the sense of the experimental researcher who carries out experiments in order to discover new knowledge. In fact, distorted notions of indifference to therapeutic outcome and scientific objectivity have led many analysts to either publicly repudiate neutrality as an important psychoanalytic concept or privately question their own therapeutic aims and goals in relation to clinical work. The introduction of terms such as *benevolent neutrality* (Stone, 1961, p. 28) and *compassionate neutrality* (Greenson, 1958b, p. 201) have done little to resolve this dilemma. It is unfortunate that neutrality is not regularly defined in a way that maintains its usefulness while remaining consonant with what actually takes place in psychoanalytic practice. To label neutrality an ideal goal we can never achieve merely bypasses the issue. In fact, neutrality should be defined so that, in a well-conducted analysis, it is regularly achieved and easily demonstrable.

We believe that the interpretive process can be characterized in terms of the concept of neutrality. In this context, neutrality refers to the analyst's recognition of and focus on the multiply determined nature of mental events as expressed in his interpretations to the analysand. While the analytic process may bring to the surface the product of mental activity in a particular form, the analyst always assumes a multitude of conscious and unconscious determinants, longitudinally and historically connected, of which the current observable behavior, feeling, attitude, fantasy, etc., is an amalgam. This theoretical position considers all mental activity as compromise formations in relation to intrapsychic conflict, a view in keeping with Hoffer's (1985) theoretical position about neutrality. It is the inevitability of the presence of this multitude of factors, and the analyst's openness to them and explicit reference to them in his interventions, that constitute neutrality in relationship to interpretation, not any indifference to the outcome of the convergence of these multiple factors. We are in agreement with Poland (1984) who is critical of those who dismiss the inevitable judgments the analyst makes "with the pejorative label of 'health morality'" (p. 297). The interpretive process remains neutral according to our definition to the extent it explores in as open-ended and accepting a way as possible as many of the determinants of mental activity as are discoverable via the analytic method. When the analyst's intervention interferes with the discovery or elucidation of further material related to particular mental conflict, it is no longer neutral. Such a point of view allows room for the analyst's judgments about which direction to take in moving the material forward and helping the patient to make changes that are implicit in the material being uncovered and explored.

The therapeutic aims and goals of psychoanalysis vary from case to case depending on the exact nature of the psychological stress and/or impairment. Recently, Poland (1984), Shapiro (1984), and Hoffer (1985) have explored the neutrality concept in relation to the different aims and goals of psychoanalytic treatment. Whatever the precise nature of the patient's problems (symptoms, inhibitions or characterological difficulties), the analyst's task is to interpret the nature and origin of the underlying conflicts responsible for the patient's neurotic compromises. Inquiry and interpretation are the essence of analysis, and the analyst's rigorous pursuit of understanding in order to diminish mental conflict is based on the belief that interpretation based on this understanding offers the best possibility of achieving the therapeutic aims and goals (Brenner, 1976). The analyst is neutral in so far as his interpretive efforts are in the service of understanding the multiple and contradictory determinants of the emerging conflicts. Neutrality reflects the analyst's conviction that nothing is ever *only* what it manifestly seems to be. It does not preclude the analyst's interest in and pursuit of therapeutic aims and goals; we are not indifferent to the outcome of the analysis. Neutrality, represented by the type of interpretations we have described, contributes to a background of safety by protecting the analysand's individuality and autonomy. Similarly, interpretation reinforces neutrality by its focus on understanding rather than on moralistic judging and advising or narcissistic self-enhancement. Central pathological infantile instinctual conflicts can gradually emerge and be experienced and expressed, because of the analysand's ever growing confidence that the analyst's responses will consistently be neutral interpretations.

The analyst's interpretations are also multidetermined, and this will be revealed in the choice of words, intonation, and form of interpretation. In addition to the explicit insight communicated by an interpretation in the service of the immediate goal of furthering understanding, implicit messages are always contained in the interpretation (Poland, 1984). To put it in either/or terms for the purposes of exposition, the implicit meaning of interpretations tend, often subtly, to either pull the patient forward toward the therapeutic aims and goals, or push the patient back away from them. Interfering countertransference is often expressed in the implicit communications of the analyst. The benefit of an interpretation that is correct from a dynamic and economic perspective can be nullified by an implicit message that is antithetical to the therapeutic goals.

Conclusion

We have described interpretation as the central activity of the analyst and have explored various modes of decision making that help make the interpretive process maximally effective. We do not wish to imply that interpretation constitutes the entirety of the therapeutic effort of the analysis. Neither do we believe that interpretation consists only of those uncovering statements made by the analyst during the course of analytic sessions. The analyst's silences, his tact, the timing of his comments all serve interpretive functions. Likewise, the relationship that develops between analyst and analysand in its uniqueness plays a central role in the interpretive process and weighs heavily in determining the outcome of the analytic work. We have isolated verbal interpretive work in order to examine its theoretical and technical underpinnings. Doing so helps to reveal guiding principles of interpretation that are seen in clearer perspective when interpretation is viewed as distinct from the more complicated intrapsychic and interpersonal matrix of the analytic situation as it actually unfolds. Nonetheless, we believe that to the extent the analyst can establish for himself clear principles of interpretation based upon well thought out clinical and theoretical guidelines, his functioning as an effective therapeutic analyst will be enhanced.

6

The Evolution of the Concept of Interpretation

Alan Z. Skolnikoff, M.D.

INTERPRETATION is always thought to be the key to change in both psychotherapy and psychoanalysis. The concept has evolved markedly in recent years, in a variety of directions. As with other developments in psychoanalytic technique, instead of older concepts being replaced by new ones, a multiplicity of meanings have evolved, both along theoretical and empirical lines.

As in other areas of technique, various authors define aspects of technique according to their conception of the psychoanalytic situation. Some of these conceptualizations are complementary and others are mutually exclusive. If the reader will keep in mind his conceptualization of the process, it will be easier both to understand, agree or disagree with what constitutes an appropriate interpretative technique.

Let us start with Greenson (1967), who defines interpretation to mean an intervention that makes an unconscious phenomenon conscious. More precisely, "it means to make conscious the unconscious meaning, source, history, mode, or cause of a given psychic event. . . . By interpreting we go beyond what is readily observable, and we assign meaning and causality to psychological phenomena. We need the patient's responses to determine the validity of our interpretation" (p. 39). He also defines confrontation and clarification as interventions that precede interpretation. The first step in analyzing a psychic phenomenon is confrontation. Confrontation implies having to call to the patient's attention (his conscious ego) that there is a preconscious or unconscious phenomenon that he is not aware of. Clarification, the next step, means that the psychic phenomenon in question that is about to be analyzed is brought into sharp focus. This means sorting it out from other extraneous material surrounding it in the hour.

With respect to an interpretation, in addition to the knowledge of the patient's dynamics and derivatives of his unconscious, the analyst also uses his own unconscious, his empathy, and his intuition as well as his theoretical knowledge for arriving at an interpretation. The analyst needs the patient's response to determine whether his interpretation is valid. The final step in analyzing is working through. "This refers to a complex set of procedures and processes which occur after an insight has been given" (p. 42). The working through also refers to the repetitive, progressive, and elaborate explorations of the resistances which prevent an insight from an interpretation leading to change.

The simplest definition of interpretation refers to the topographic model: "to make the unconscious conscious." In this relatively simple conceptualization, one considers that there are certain forbidden impulses that are warded off, or specific memories that are repressed. If these are brought to awareness at an appropriate time without overwhelming the ego, this can lead to change (reduction in anxiety or symptomatology or change of mood). Simple examples would refer to an interpretation of the meanings of slips or symptoms. The structural model makes the theory of what is interpreted more complex. Here, an impulse mediated by the ego can come up against a superego prohibition. Defenses are mobilized, and theory dictates that, instead of interpreting the warded-off content, the resistance is interpreted. Here the admonition to interpret process over content speaks to the change from the topographic to the structural model; that is, the analyst looks beyond what the content is of what the patient is not saying, and rather looks at the mode with which he resists awareness of an unconscious or conflictual issue. If the resistances of the patient can be interpreted, then gradually the warded-off content comes into awareness. Greenson further clarifies the advantages that the structural point of view has over the topographic point of view (Greenson, 1967, p. 138). "Our ultimate aim is to enable the ego to cope better with the id, the superego and the external world. . . . The analysis of the patient's ego may be regarded as having two different aspects and functions. The unconscious, irrational ego initiates pathogenic defenses and is seen as the experiencing ego during treatment. The conscious, reasonable ego is the ally of the analyst and appears clinically as the patient's observing ego during the analysis (Sterba, 1934). One should analyze the ego before the id; or, putting it another way, the analyst's interventions should aim at making the patient's reasonable ego better able to cope with the old dangerous situations. With the proper sequence of interpretation, we expect the reasonable ego to expand its powers as it becomes more familiar with how it can operate in the present as contrasted with the dangerous situations in the past.

A complementary theory of interpretation with the structural theory focused on the transference is offered by Strachey (1934). The patient's id impulses directed toward the analyst are interpreted. This interpretation becomes mutative because the patient eventually realizes that the impulses are not really directed at the analyst but toward archaic objects. The analyst is then internalized temporarily as a new object leading to modification of the patient's harsh superego.

How does the therapist know or validate whether he has made a appropriate interpretation? Traditionally we hoped for an "Aha!" phenomenon, associated with a correct interpretation. In addition, we think that the correct interpretation demonstrates a change in the patient's understanding of himself (insight), and a decrease in symptomatology, and/or more adaptive behavior. Greenson suggests, from a traditional ego psychological perspective, that the analyst, through his knowledge of the patient, is able to discern whether the patient's reactions and ensuing associations confirm the unconscious meaning associated with the interpretation. The analyst also uses his own unconscious reactions or responses to the patient as confirmation of the patient's reactions to the interpretation.

Arlow (1987) has expanded on Greenson's concept. After reviewing the advantages of the structural model in conceptualizing interpretation, and pointing out how the interpretation of resistance permits the ego to bring forth warded-off contents in a systematic way which could otherwise be disturbing, Arlow goes on to study the psychoanalytic process microscopically. He shows how "examining the moment-to-moment variations in the sequence of thoughts as they emerge into consciousness shows how the same efforts to resolve conflicts in the past are repeated in the present" (p. 75). There is a particular emphasis in his conceptualization on how the analysis of conflict in the present eventually reveals unconscious fantasies from the past. It is through the patient's misunderstanding or misinterpretation, as studied through the transference reactions, that these unconscious fantasies are revealed. He emphasizes, more than Greenson, that the attempt to recover repressed memories interferes with the study of the moment-to-moment reactions that the patient has to the analytic situation. He points out how the interaction between the analyst's interventions and the patient's responses exposes the nature of compromise formations. This process deepens the patient's understanding of how his mind works and facilitates achieving insight. Although there is more of an emphasis on the here and now and on the interaction of patient and therapist in the study of the patient's unconscious conflicts, Arlow's understanding of the dynamics of interpretation focuses on the psychoanalytic process uncovering the intrapsychic dynamics of the patient from a structural point of view. He focuses on the verbal productions of the patient and his subjective reactions to the analyst in the transference, and particularly follows the response that the patient has to the series of interpretations given by the analyst as a way of understanding these conflicts.

When we look at actual, single interpretations, it is harder to judge their accuracy or therapeutic efficacy. For example, some interpretations lead to transient symptomatology, an increase in anxiety or depression, or a regression. Retrospectively we view these changes as a result of faulty technique. Interpretations that are poorly timed, or too deep with an ensuing overwhelming of the ego's defenses, can lead to maladaptive changes. Prospectively the situation is more complex. The analyst often is unclear about the meaning of the patient's immediate response. Regarding the lack of the analyst's clarity, Boesky (1989) suggests an important modification of technique. He describes the use of questions to satisfy the analyst's curiosity, which underscores the mutual inquiry that should characterize the psychoanalytic process. The use of questions by the analyst also reaffirms for the patient that the latter is not omnis-cient. In comparing notes about what constitutes a positive response to a given interpretation, analysts differ considerably. Some focus on cognitive insight and an improvement in the working alliance. Others might see the same response as a false compliance or sub-mission that will later have to be analyzed. There are further excep-tions to the rule that a correct interpretation ought to lead to a decrease in symptomatology. Such an example is the interpretation of an ego-syntonic character trait. The analyst expects to interpret features of the patient's psychic organization that will make this ego-syntonic character trait dystonic. He would consider a success-ful interpretation one that would lead to an increase in anxiety that would transiently occur as a result of this dystonicity.

Other views of interpretation show the need to carefully study and follow up the patient's response. Schlesinger (1985) demon-strated how every good interpretation, rather than resolving the neurotic process, actually furthers it. The patient becomes optimally neurotic in response to the interpretation, which can lead to a sequence of interpretations and deeper understanding as well as par-tial insight on the part of the patient. He describes how the trans-ference actually reproduces the neurosis. He sees younger, more inexperienced analysts as having difficulty with this concept, with the assumption that more experienced analysts are able to interpret this way all the time; that is to say, they expect the patient to get more neurotic with correct interpretations and continue to interpret the neurosis as it develops *in vivo*. I think Schlesinger underestimates the extent to which most practicing, experienced analysts are able to sys-tematically analyze the sequence of responses to their inter-pretations. It is my experience that many analysts feel confused about the interpretative sequence, and have difficulty in following the sub-tle interplay of their interventions and the patient's responses. Gill (1982) goes much further in recommending that interpretations focus on the subtleties of the development of the transference. In *The Analysis of Transference* (Gill and Hoffman, 1982), verbatim tran-scripts of psychoanalytic sessions are offered to demonstrate how the transference might be followed from the patient's reactions to the analyst's activity. This is similar to Schlesinger's idea about analyzing the neurosis as it develops from interpretation. Gill contributes the idea, which others disagree with in terms of what they expect ideal technique to be, that the analyst's actual activity is often perceived by the patient as provoking his feelings toward the analyst. Gill departs from the classical position, stating that the analyst in practice is often, in response to the patient, departing from what would be considered an ideal neutral position. When the patient confronts him with this, he must be ready to accept the possibility that his deviation really occurred, rather than presume that this is the patient's misperception due to a transference distortion. The sample verbatim transcripts of psychoanalytic hours offer ample evidence of the patient's perceptions of the analyst's activity. This detailed description of actual clinical process opens the possibility of a new conceptualization of what position the analyst really takes in the analytic situation. Previously, we assumed that the analyst uses his unconscious or preconscious reactions to the patient as a way of understanding or empathizing without interaction, which if it occurred would involve an overt departure from neutrality. Gill's clinical material shows frequent departures from neutrality, suggesting that the analyst's behavior may be influenced by his emotional responses to the patient. This is, of course, an expanded definition of Gitelson's (1952) use of the term *countertransference*. At that time he narrowly defined this as the analyst's unconscious reaction to the patient which made him unaware of specific actions or utterances that were deviations from neutrality and were based on unresolved emotional conflicts within himself. Gill's description of the analyst's activity suggests that these deviations might be more ubiquitous than was previously believed.

Other conceptualizations of the analytic situation deemphasize the verbal productions of both the analyst and the patient. These new concepts are based more on an object-relations or interpersonal theory. Even though the analytic goal might still be to study the intrapsychic activity of the patient, there is the conviction that this might be better understood by studying the interaction of the analyst and the patient with the presumption that the analyst, despite his attempt to remain neutral, departs from this neutrality based on his inevitable emotional reactions to the patient. These emotional reactions can possibly give us clues to the patient's intrapsychic conflicts. This could be the meaning that Freud (1923 [1922]) referred to as "to catch the drift of his own unconscious with the patient's unconscious" (p. 239). Here we understand this to mean that not only is the analyst cognitively engaged in free-floating attention but that there are inevitable shifts in his emotional reactions toward the patient. We could also think of the personality of the analyst being an important factor in his interaction with the patient, rather than presume that any well-trained analyst can treat all types of patients.

Some authors have expanded their understanding of what can be interpreted through a reconsideration of the motor activity of the patient. Boesky (1982) reconsiders the concept of acting out. He suggests that action isn't always instead of remembering. He asks us to reconsider Freud's article ("Remembering, Repeating and Working Through" [1914]). Certain activities can be in the service of remembering and are integrally linked with unconscious fantasies evoked by emerging transferences. He further states that psychoanalysis cannot take place without acting out, any more than psychoanalysis could take place without transference. Productions from the nonverbal sphere can also be understood and interpreted. In this conceptualization, paralinguistic and nonverbal aspects of the interaction between analyst and patient have equal importance with the verbal exchange. McLaughlin (1987) describes specific nonverbal behaviors of his patients that are rich in allusions and give him explanations of motivation. As part of his free-floating attention, he notes patterns of gestural and postural behavior which he feels are as much part of the patient's character as are patterns of speech and thought.

Weiss and Sampson (1986), through a study of psychoanalytic process from process notes and tape recordings, have developed the concept of *control mastery*. They suggest the patient engages in a series of tests of the transference, to see whether the analyst will respond to specific demands. These tests are ultimately designed to determine the safety of the psychoanalytic situation. The patients feel encouraged by the analyst's repeated demonstration of his capacity to remain neutral. The authors see this process as diminishing the importance of interpretations to help the patient bring forth warded-off conflicts. In this conceptualization, interpretations are designed to make the analytic situation safer instead of focusing on resistances per se. Then, warded-off conflicts emerge within the increasing safety of the psychoanalytic situation. Sandler (1976) also sees the gradual development of a sense of safety within the psychoanalytic situation. He conceptualizes safety as a facilitating process in another direction: The patient and the analyst will begin to interact with the potential for spontaneously reenacting conflicts from the past now within the transference, which can be studied and understood by the analytic pair. Sandler feels that the analyst develops the capacity to respond to the role which the patient assigns to him, and therefore plays into this reenactment.

To sum up some of the ideas that have been presented so far: There have been two parallel evolving concepts of the psychoanalytic process, which lead to somewhat different ideas as to how and why interpretations are made and for what purpose. In the traditional model, where the analyst can be presumed to remain neutral, there has been an increase in attention to studying the subtle reactions that the patient has to the analyst's interpretations and the patient's reactions to the analytic situation from moment to moment as refinements of the previous, more static concept of interpretations. This more static concept implied that a single interpretation would impart a great deal of information about a specific unconscious conflict. Now, a careful study of the patient's reactions to here-and-now feelings within the psychoanalytic situation and how these relate to past and present conflicts becomes the basis for subsequent interpretations.

A contrasting model of the psychoanalytic situation conceptualizes a two-person field with the analyst being both an observer and a participant. In this conceptualization the significance and the reasons for interpretation take on different meanings. I will try to emphasize this and other conceptualizations of interpretation that derive from ideas of the psychoanalytic situation as a two-person field.

Data from infant research have been introduced into the conceptualization of the psychoanalytic process. Psychic development has been viewed along the lines of a series of experiences with an interactional quality (Lichtenberg, 1983b; Stern, 1985). Depending on one's theoretical predilections, interactions between analysts and patients are viewed as directly reproducing a pattern between the infant and his caretaker or a defensive derivative warding off a conflict associated with that earlier pattern. Friedman (1985), in reviewing Lichtenberg's work, makes many remarks concerning similarities and differences between the analyst and the patient in their interaction and earlier care-taking experiences of the patient. Lichtenberg raises the possibility that the analyst uses interpretations not as facts but as a series of trial interactions with the patient, much as a mother seeks to help or understand what her child needs through a series of trial actions.

In a continuing bilateral search for meaning, Poland (1988) points to the dual nature of insight. He shows how, frequently, insight is not coming from the therapist and imparted to the patient, but is seen as a parallel phenomenon. The patient develops insight into unconscious motivations through things that he discovers in the psychoanalytic situation. Remarks of the analyst as well as interpretations might lead to this insight, but are not necessarily directly connected with this. We have all had the experience of giving an interpretation in which we feel that we are imparting a particularly vivid understanding of the patient's conflicts, only to be interrupted with, "That's very interesting, and I'm sorry to interrupt you, but this reminds me of. . . ." We have various responses to such a statement. At times we see this kind of response as a resistance to the interpretation—perhaps the patient is competing with what we are telling him, or trying not to listen to what we are saying. At other times we can see that a specific common theme exists between what we have interpreted and what, in the dynamic unconscious of the patient, was set in motion. Sometimes the patient's insight doesn't pertain to our own in any form. This permits us to think of the analytic enterprise in a different way. It gives meaning to the idea that the patient and the analyst learn from one another, as contrasted with the analyst as authority who teaches the patient at the appropriate moment through an interpretation about his unconscious conflicts. It also suggests that the common insight of patient and analyst might not be as central a phenomenon in leading to change as one had previously thought. More broadly, a truly mutual investigatory process facilitates insight in either party of the analytic dyad.

Another way in which the theory of technique has been altered is through the expansion of the concept and use of countertransference. The narrower definition of countertransference (Gitelson, 1952) is expanded to the broader definition of the "transferences" (McLaughlin, 1981) of the analyst. Other terms, such as the emotional responsiveness of the analyst, also apply in contrast to what was previously thought to be undesirable countertransference. Along with the narrower concept of neutrality, countertransference was previously thought useful as a signal affect. The analyst would anticipate and *control* departures from neutrality by studying his signal affects to gain some clues to the patient's conflicts. More recently, the use of countertransference has been expanded to look at shifts in attitudes and behavior. In addition to Sandler's concept of role responsiveness, McLaughlin (1988), through a careful study of the analyst's moment-to-moment attitudes and reactions to the patient, points to how the analyst can develop insights that will elucidate the patient's conflicts. McLaughlin goes further than most authors in this matter, because he is willing to look at defensive behavior on his part (which could be called countertransference acting out) to gain insight over a departure from an optimum analytic stance. In this framework, the analyst can presume that his transferences toward the patient will alter his activity and lead, by the analyst's continued self-observation, to formulating new interpretations concerning the dynamics of the patient.

Other authors study the analytic situation in an attempt to delineate what factors motivate the therapist to make interpretations and how they time them. Lawrence Friedman (1988, p. 96) suggests that if we study how a patient has to balance himself in a variety of equilibria to sustain a fantasy or stabilize self-esteem, we can also do the same thing to a therapist when we make him an object of our study. "We must learn to see the therapist's momentary decisions as efforts to balance himself when challenged by the demands of the moment." Psychoanalysts usually don't think of themselves that way; they think of themselves as craftsmen, deliberately selecting features of the patient that are germane to their theory of therapy. He agrees that the therapist's responses may be guided by explicit plans, and yet he suspects that the finer principles of the therapist's selection and response to the patient are not a matter of studied decision but rather more impulsive. Fliess (1942, 1953) studied the metapsychology of errors in analytic reactivity. He felt that the analyst could do the impossible by rising above reacting to his patients. This could be accomplished through the establishment of an analytic "work ego." The deprivation of not reacting to patients could be replaced by the higher gratification of the cause of analyzing them. In reviewing this idea Friedman (1988, p. 98) points out that the analyst never really achieves this ideal. "He is one human being locked in an activity with another." It is safest to assume that the principles of his behavior do not differ radically from those of his patient. What does differ radically is that he is not in the same position as his patient. He has, instead, another set of problems that come from being a therapist. Very carefully and elaborately reviewing extensive case examples in the literature, Friedman points out that a therapist doesn't really

know, but doubts when he is interpreting. He is unnecessarily burdened by the notion that if he guesses what's going on with a patient
and tells him, that he will unduly prejudice the patient. He suggests
that *interpretation* can be a word for a pompous guess. As an antidote
for the problem of thinking that one always has to be correct as
therapist, "undisguised guessing" could be a powerful stimulus to discover what's really going on. This reverberates with Boesky's recommendation that the analyst permit himself to ask questions.

Understanding, by making a direct interpretation or by listening
carefully in what might be called a safe analytic ambience, can have
powerful aggressive or erotic components. "Understanding is not
love, but it can act as a loving gesture" (Friedman, 1988, p. 107).

This reminds us of Stone's (1961) concept of the "primordial
transference" associated with that gratification the patient obtains by
imagining the analyst's silent attention. Friedman (1988) further
points to how one has to consider how the patient makes sense of the
therapist. This of course reciprocally includes the analyst's being
aware of what the patient is doing for him; not just to understand this
as part of the patient's pathology, but to have an emotional reaction to
it and to recognize how that emotional reaction to the patient's
attitude or feeling toward him affects how he interprets. He also
emphasizes the context in which any given interpretation is made as
being the determining factor in assigning meaning to that interpretation (p. 137). He feels no analytic communication can ever be a
transparent proposition. It is always a historical event with a vague,
unique, complex background and with multiple meanings.

Klauber (1972) goes into more depth in exploring the analyst's
reactions to his patients. There are a number of major points which
focus on various aspects of the analyst's emotional reactivity to his
patients. He feels that the analyst's transference to his patients
evolves to some extent in a set pattern which is determined by his
own personality reacting with the personality of the patient (p. 387).
One of the difficulties in studying the content of interpretations that
the therapist makes is that one loses an adequate study of the meaning of the interpretations in the complex relationship of the mutual
transferences. He further wonders about the patient's conceptualization of the analyst. After all, the patient must see the analyst as a person, and how does this determine just what he brings up for study? He
asks the corresponding question, of course, of the analyst: How much

does the analyst's response to the patient in an ongoing way affect what he is able to say? He realizes that the patient's free associations are designed to get around this prejudice as are the analyses of the analyst designed to get around the countertransference. He asks why the analyst can only conceptualize the patient's analysis after it has ended. He also wonders why the patient often does the most significant piece of analytic work, or tackles his main problem only after the analysis has ended. He presumes that this is because, first, the analyst is too involved with the patient emotionally to be able to clearly conceptualize his work with him during the analysis; and the patient because of the person of the analyst interfering is not able to complete the analytic work until after he gets away from the interfering influence of the analyst.

Klauber goes back to Strachey's question (1934) about knowing the effect of any interpretation because of what the patient does to libidinize or aggressivize it. As do other authors, he repeatedly warns about trying to understand interpretations through an analysis of their content. He points to different theoretical approaches to patients as having equal validity, and that certainly an individual from one theoretical position doesn't subscribe to the theoretical position of another analyst, but might still agree that interpretations in another theoretical framework can be effective. How else do patients treated in a totally different theoretical framework from one's own ever improve? What appears clear to the patient and the analyst in the hour is difficult to reproduce in words or in theory in some other setting, except by violating what was actually done or said. He theorizes that what happens is some unconscious accord that has to be reached between patient and analyst for them to agree on each other's theories about what went on. He is careful not to throw away the value of interpretation or construction in the classical sense. He thinks the human mind is satisfied and in some sense healed by what it feels is the truth. It is just that when this truth is studied by others, it seems to have only a relative value. It is true, however, of nearly all patients that some system of historical explanation is necessary for them to be satisfied that they are cured. He discusses some other aspects of the analyst's motivation to interpret on a moment-to-moment basis. At times, an important motivation to make an interpretation is to deny the anxiety that is aroused in the analyst by the fact that the situation that he's involved in is unknown to him, and correspondingly dangerous. He is also afraid of the impulses that the patient directs to him. He might react, for instance, with aggression; and instead of empathizing with the patient he may find himself irritated or bored. He is always in danger of being either too distant or too close to the patient. Interpretations, then, can have many meanings in this context of his endless emotional reactivity to the patient. It can be a way of getting closer to the patient when he is bored or distant, or staying further away by talking about feelings that the patient might have for him, or he for the patient (he might put this in the framework of the patient's feelings), and by saying them will keep a safe distance. Interpretation, then, can serve to reduce the danger of excessive sexual stimulation, for the analyst as well as for the patient. Interpretation can also have the role of limiting sexual desire in the patient by the analyst's talking about it rather than remaining silent. Giving some interpretations is like getting a glimpse of an inherent struggle in the analysis. Also these interpretations can feel like a tease. This concept might partially account for the ambivalent relationship which often characterizes the way a patient feels about his former analyst. This often characterizes itself in an unpleasant longing to return to his analyst.

From the preceding review it is clear how many factors contribute to the formation and timing of an interpretation. If the analyst is to report his interpretive work to others, how are they to understand the context? There are many settings in which analysts communicate to others the nature of their work: supervision, oral case presentations, articles, books, as well as personal communication. We frequently note, in listening to or reading case presentations, that we speculate about how the analyst, in giving a specific interpretation, has missed his own countertransference or a specific theme in the patient's productions because of his emotional or theoretical bias. If we question the analyst–presenter, he will often contribute new material that even more clearly substantiates his perspective or occasionally be surprised and thoughtful about the question, leading him to acknowledge a specific "blind spot" (countertransference in the narrower sense) that he was not aware of or to agree that another theoretical perspective could be more useful. Certainly from this perspective we can see how the context in which an interpretation is given really determines its validity. Even in extended presentations of a long case study where a specific interpretation is given, it is difficult to know all of the factors that have contributed to the context and determined what has gone into the analyst's thinking. Also, in other reports, or under the best of circumstances (for example, in an extended amicable supervisorial situation), there might not be consensus about what determined a specific interpretation, let alone its validity.

I would like to offer some brief examples of interpretations to further illustrate the complexity associated with understanding the context in which the interpretation is given as well as the impact that it has upon the patient.

1. A soft-spoken maternal female analyst was working with a young male graduate student with an obsessive–compulsive character structure, who had a sense of inferiority in relationships to women and difficulty asserting himself in a variety of contexts, either with other men or with reference to his ideas about his graduate studies. The analyst–supervisee appeared to understand the patient very well. She was able, through an understanding of the family history as well as the dynamics of current conflicts, to differentiate between oedipal and preoedipal conflicts. Nevertheless, in the interpretations of the transference, she consistently attributed preoedipal conflicts to his attitude toward her. Hence, her interpretations would go something like this: "You've just fallen silent now, presuming that I don't support you in this matter," or "I notice, when you tell me about wanting to have a relationship with Jane, that you think I feel you're not up to it." In discussing her always focusing on issues of support and his need for admiration as the major focus of her interpretations, I wondered why, despite some evidence in the material, she almost never interpreted oedipal themes. I further asked her how she felt about the patient personally. She said she felt in him a sense of helplessness, and, try as she might, she couldn't really imagine him being appealing to women or assertive in his work. I wondered about this with her: Was this her subjective reaction to him that she was responding to, that is, this helpless presentation of himself which defended against a more assertive stance? Was her personal reaction to him as the analyst–mother interfering with viewing him as an assertive male? In supervision we continued to look at these issues. To her surprise, the analyst began to notice provocative and assertive comments from the analysand which seemed to suggest more oedipal attitudes

toward her. When she tried to clarify this with him, he was shocked thinking that such attitudes would be disrespectful toward her. He saw them as being challenging of her or overly presumptuous. All of these feelings, he felt, belonged outside of the analysis; that is, they might be part of his personal reaction to her, which would interfere with his being able to accept her supportive interpretations. The analyst and I concluded that the patient and the analyst had colluded to isolate the oedipal content of the transference with the presumption that it couldn't be used within the analysis. Opening up this area permitted both of them to have another view; the analytic process included studying their more personal reactions to one another.

2. I worked with a young professional woman who early in the analysis said that she had the reputation of being provocative and challenging in a variety of situations, both professionally and with men. She felt that these attitudes were not consistent with success, either in a long-term relationship with a man or in professional advancement. I welcomed working with her with the presumption that I had a lot of experience with such provocative women. I actually admired her pluck and I didn't imagine that I would feel threatened by this. In the early phases of the analysis she admired my ability not to be provoked by the kinds of things she was discussing with me. This had to do with professional activities bordering on the unethical, as well as relationships with men which had manipulative self-serving elements as their major focus. Eventually, of course, her provocative style focused on my activity within the analysis. She saw my remarks as inane, things that she already knew about. She felt that my interventions were for my immediate needs to have something to say rather than for her benefit. On one occasion she was describing her inept father and how she had fooled him by consistently making him feel that he was important to her only to follow up by belittling him and demeaning him. Further she described how her mother favored her and supported her in her belittling attacks against the father. I was excited to think that this very much resembled her attitudes toward me in the transference; that is, she would frequently demean me, tell her husband a variety of anecdotes about her analysis which would deprecate me and permit them both to laugh about my ineptitude. At that point, with enthusiasm and clarity I presented to her how she did the same to me as to her father, in order to have the pleasure of defeat-

ing me; to which I added that she did this to convince herself that she needn't fear any closeness or admiration of me. After giving what I thought was a concise summary interpretation, I was surprised at the patient's remark. She briefly pointed out that I must be angry with her and felt the need to put her in place by my sharp tone and raised voice. She had noted that I had been doing this repeatedly in the last few months. It wasn't what I said but how I said it that made her realize that she was getting to me. I gamely continued: "How does that make you feel?" She stated that it "makes me feel as if I'd better go easy on you, because you can't take the heat."

At that point I recalled having felt annoyed, but thinking that the patient was trying to provoke me a little bit further and that my annoyance was because of her provocation. On the other hand I was aware of a certain justification to her criticism. I did wait until the latter part of the hour and rehearsed to myself just how I was going to make this interpretation to her, which was unlike my usual style, in which with other patients I would make my interpretations when they occurred to me. (There appears to be a great variation in how analysts conceptualize and give interpretations. Caution and preparation are probably related to the idea of the analyst cognitively weaving an integration of different themes. Here the analyst is more observer than participant. Spontaneity, on the other hand, is probably more related to the concept of the analytic situation as a two-person field where both analyst and patient are emotionally involved.) Upon further reflection I became aware that the patient was right. I was threatened by her attacks, particularly the unusually provocative nature of her behavior. I think it took a year before I became completely aware of this and continued to be provoked on numerous occasions in different ways by what I considered her outrageous manner. She continued to recognize the subtle ways in which she could get me to react to her provocations within the hours. She often correctly interpreted (to the best of my subjective understanding) my angry silence in response to her teasing behavior, or my "pointed" interpretations to throttle her outrageous behavior. As I gradually became aware of the nature of my reactions to her, the climate of the analysis changed. I found myself listening and responding more casually to what she was talking about. She noticed the difference by stating that I seemed to understand her more and be less provoked by her. She noticed that I didn't seem to feel the need to "jump in" to impart information to her because I knew something that she didn't. At the same time the quality of the silences changed. She no longer saw them as determined by my angry withholding. She began to feel closer to me, with a sense of admiration for my patience and unflappability. In the safety of this new relationship she then brought up themes associated with her wish to be her father's son (replacing a younger brother) and acquire what she assumed was more power by becoming identified with him as a man.

In these two examples of interpretive sequences, I have presented how the emotional reactions of both patient and analyst are interrelated. In both examples the analysts were not aware of the extent of their involvement until after much reflection. When one talks about self-analysis, it is certainly experiences such as these that further the analyst's continuing self-awareness. It certainly underscores the maxim that one learns from every patient, as well as presuming that the patient learns from the analyst.

In this review I have attempted to show how the concept of interpretation has changed gradually, particularly associated with changes in the understanding of the analyst as a more active, emotionally involved participant rather than observer. This leads to more carefully studying the patient's relationship to the analyst's actual behavior as well as their fantasies of what he is like. The other part of this change involves studying the interpretive sequence in which there is a focus on unraveling how the patient responds to previous interpretations. The sequence emphasizes the context in which the interpretation is given.

The simpler, more certain meaning of the good interpretation was one that created an "Aha!" phenomenon in which both patient and analyst could clearly see a dramatic change as a result of insight. Now with the added complexity of the analyst's involvement as a participant-observer as well as the study of long sequences of interpretations and ensuing responses, we have learned to tolerate greater ambiguity and multiplicity of meanings associated with clinical data.

Although the categorization of interventions that Greenson (1967) proposed is still useful semantically (confrontation, clarification, interpretation and working through), we find when we look at long excerpts of raw clinical data that we cannot easily sort our statements in that way. For example, what could be considered a working through of one conflict that has already been partially mastered could be seen to anticipate a confrontation of another one.

As we go from the theory of technique to samples of raw clinical data, we certainly will have the opportunity to continue to revise our conceptualizations of what our interventions mean.

7

The "Rule" and Role of Abstinence in Psychoanalysis

Paul A. Dewald, M.D.

Abstain: Deliberately or habitually to withhold oneself from an object or action, often with the implication that indulgence in it would be hurtful or wrong.

Webster's International Dictionary, 1959

IN recent years the issue of abstinence during psychoanalytic therapy has become "a buzz word" which evokes intense emotional responses both from clinicians and theoreticians in discussions of technique. This response is partly in reaction to observation and experience in working with patients included in "the widening scope of psychoanalysis" (Stone, 1954). With the application of psychoanalysis to the treatment of "sicker" patients previously considered "unanalyzable," many analysts' clinical experience led to the conclusion that such patients could not tolerate the levels of abstinence appropriate for neurotic individuals. Such individuals are now frequently and successfully treated in psychoanalysis, and the balance between abstinence and gratification in these cases is frequently discussed.

Freud's (1919) written technical recommendations, symbolized by his metaphors of the analyst as dispassionate surgeon, or the analyst as passive reflective mirror, do not correspond to his own informal notes of his actual technique, in which his behavior is different from the technical stance he recommended for others (Lipton, 1977). Today many of Freud's cases would be understood as manifesting significantly more difficult and primitive psychopathological organizations than the classical pure oedipal configuration, and manifestations of major preoedipal factors are clear in the clinical data of his case histories.

Eissler (1953) attempted to define classical technique as involving a therapeutic position in which the analyst's only role is to ask occasional questions and to offer interpretations. But he had to acknowledge that most patients could not be successfully analyzed if the analyst strictly followed this classically defined model of technique. Eissler introduced the term *parameter* to acknowledge the frequent need for more flexible and active intervention by the analyst, at times including various departures from full abstinence. To preserve the essence of an analytic process, the parameters themselves were to be eventually subjected to analysis and their use should no longer be necessary by the end of the analysis.

Throughout its history psychoanalysis has been on the defensive in regard to its status as a scientific method. Partly as a result of this, a variety of technical descriptions offered in the literature have emphasized the cognitive, intellectual, interpretative, content-oriented interventions made by the analyst, and deemphasized or ignored completely the humanistic, personal, idiosyncratic, and experiential components of the analytic process. Proponents of this position have maintained that theoretically the individual analyst should be interchangeable, and that the power of the analytic situation resides in the nature of the analyst's interpretative interventions. Issues of personality, style, setting, and interpersonal interactions were seen as essentially irrelevant to the main task of acquisition of insight by the patient and the modification of behavior based upon working through and acceptance of the insight. The emphasis was away from the analyst as a responsive and interactive person in the therapeutic experience and process.

Modifications of "classical technique" began with the experiments of Ferenczi and Rank (1925). Subsequently, Alexander and French (1946) emphasized the corrective emotional experience and the activity of the analyst in stimulating it, at the same time blurring earlier distinctions between psychotherapy and more classical psychoanalysis. In one sense their recommendations could be viewed as deliberately providing an abstinent response to the patient's manifest transference expectation. However, they addressed only the most superficial and simple transference expectations. This led to a very animated and affectively charged series of positions in the early 1950s when debates about these questions assumed increasingly bitter and hostile form.

Stone (1954, 1961) emphasized that the application of psychoanalysis to the treatment of more difficult and primitive cases required a loosening of the rigid attitudes of abstinence in order to allow and encourage such patients to participate in the treatment process. Loewald (1960) also began a series of ground-breaking contributions leading to the position that psychoanalysis provided a new form of object relationship for the patient and that, within the framework of the analytic situation, the analyst became a new and real as well as transference figure in the life of the patient. At the same time, Kohut (1959, 1971, 1977) began his explorations of narcissism that led to the theoretical system of self psychology and a series of technical recommendations stemming from it. Winnicott (1955) also began a series of presentations promoting the elaboration of the object relations school, subsequently adopted by contributors such as Modell (1976) with his emphasis upon the various forms of holding environment, nurturance, and support offered by the analytic situation.

Greenson and Wexler (1969) called attention to the "real relationship" between patient and analyst, and to the importance of the analyst at times acknowledging and responding in a reality-appropriate behavioral way to events in the patient's life. Application of psychoanalytic technical and therapeutic concepts to a more primitive patient population led to further departures from the narrow classical technical model in the recommendations for the treatment of borderline and significantly regressive states by authors such as Kernberg (1975), Masterson (1981), Searles (1986), and others.

The question of the role of abstinence as part of psychoanalytic technique suffers from the difficulties in gaining access to the clinical situation and to the psychological events that occur between patient and analyst, given the paucity of detailed and reasonably complete clinical data in our field. Even those instances in which lengthy clinical data are presented in some detail (MacDougall and Lebovice, 1969; Dewald, 1972; Stoller, 1979; Volkan, 1987) inevitably omit a variety of potentially significant clinical manifestations and data in regard to issues of therapeutic abstinence versus gratification. Additionally, there is a lack of a generally accepted precise definition of what constitutes abstinence or gratification, empathy and its functions, transference frustration and regression. These issues have variable meanings among psychoanalysts, dependent upon their theoretical persuasion and the technical recommendations that evolve from their basic assumptions.

Furthermore, the terms *abstinence* and *gratification* (and other synonyms) have unfortunately been endowed by analysts with a perjorative quality determined by the analyst's theory of technique. In that way each term carries either positive or negative values for analysts, depending on individual theoretical persuasion. There have also evolved theoretical models (Kohut, 1971, 1977) in which developmental deficit is emphasized as pathogenic and pathognomonic of character deviation and neurotic illness. These formulations have favored the theoretical and technical shift away from concepts of activation of unconscious mental conflict, insight, and working through, in favor of corrective "transmuting internalizations" of more gratifying, reassuring, and active growth-encouraging forms of psychological intervention by the analyst as important components of successful psychoanalytic treatment. Gedo and Goldberg (1973) propose to maintain the structural model, and the concepts of psychopathology and technique stemming from it, for those instances in which the disturbance seems to be predominantly focused at high levels of oedipal psychosexual development. But these authors suggest that examples of such high level psychopathology and function are increasingly rare in the practice of most psychoanalysts today, and that a significant increase in the number of patients seen by analysts involve cases where preoedipal, primitive, and at times disorganized borderline, narcissistic, and other forms of pathology predominate. For them the effective technical model must include departures from the previous traditional conflict-oriented recommendations, and include more reality-directed, reactive, and interactive experiences between patient and analyst than are usually included in the technical precepts of the conflict model. They maintain that technical abstinence by the analyst fails to address the problems and therapeutic issues of such patients, and that a variety of psychoanalytic interventions must go "beyond interpretation" (Gedo, 1979) and involve a type of active, reassuring, directive, or guiding intervention by the analyst, which conflict-oriented analysts might consider forms of transference gratification.

My own views on this topic are guided by the structural theory of mental function, with its emphasis upon unconscious conflict, conflict resolution or containment through compromise formation, and updated conceptualizations of ego psychology (Weinshel, 1990) which include the importance of object representation and relationships, the images of the self as elements of ego function and structure, and the theoretical advances expressed by the separation–individuation process. In this view preoedipal experience and conflict exert major impact upon development and ego or superego distortions or deficiencies, and significantly influence and organize the form and structure of later oedipal configuration. This theoretical model also includes the effects of psychic trauma and reality events upon the individual's development and organization of unconscious mental life.

During the historical period when the topographic model of mental function served as the basis for technical intervention, abstinence was directed chiefly to sexual drives at the oedipal level, relating to the patient's libidinal impulses and wishes. With the development and subsequent elaboration of the structural model and ego psychology as the paradigm of mental function, the concept of abstinence was broadened to include not only sexual but also aggressive wishes and drives, expressed as derivative impulses, fantasies, and desires for transference gratification. Additionally, there was recognition that the transference included unconscious aspects of superego function projected to the analyst as part of transference experience. Other elements recognized as part of the patient's transference experience included the ego's adaptive and defensive activities, a variety of regressive ego states, as well as regressively reactivated immaturity in ego functions such as reality testing, object relationships, regulation of conflict experience, modulation of affects, and other developmental processes.

Psychoanalysis can be conceptualized as an unfolding process, implying change and goal-oriented direction over time. It involves intrapsychic experience and elaboration within the patient, as well as intrapsychic experience, elaboration, and focus within the analyst, both occurring in conjunction with an *interpersonal* relationship taking place between patient and analyst. Analyst and patient are each active interpersonal participants, sensitive and responsive to the input from the other.

A precise, easily circumscribed, and generally accepted definition of psychoanalytic abstinence is not available at present. For me, abstinence refers to *an analytic posture of participant neutrality* in which the analyst maintains a position equidistant from drives, superego, ego, and reality functions and factors as they impinge upon the patient's mental organization and experience. The analyst avoids attempts directly to manipulate or influence the patient's reactions or behavior, and seeks instead to identify and understand the manifestations of transference, countertransference, and the interpersonal events of the psychoanalytic situation. The analyst observes but avoids active *behavioral* responses to the patient's derivative transference wishes, defenses, or expectations, and instead may draw the patient's attention to them from the equidistant position just described. This does not imply that the analyst is indifferent or is emotionally removed from the patient's experience, but that responses and interventions occur within relatively consistent and therapeutically appropriate limits.

In this formulation, transference refers to the patient's conscious and unconscious expectations, wishes, hopes, and fears that the current relationship with the analyst will become a reenactment and repetition of various infantile and childhood relationships, desires, conflicts, and adaptive modes of organization. These transferences are expressed through various derivative phenomena at different levels of form and intensity, and with progressively more conscious and fully accessible and expressed manifestations of these intrapsychic components of the patient's psychological organization. Such transference experiences are the result of a complex internal template by which the patient organizes and gives meaning to the data of internal, as well as external, perception and interaction. On the basis of the internal template (of wishes, fears, fantasies, past experiences, defenses, ego states, superego values, and demands, etc.) the patient observes, interprets and reacts to input from the analyst observed as part of the interpersonal component of the therapeutic relationship and interaction.

In this conceptualization, the patient's anticipations, fears, and wish-fulfilling desires, as well as the conflicts, affects, compromise formations, conscious and unconscious fantasy systems, and the multiple adaptive, defensive, and self organizations related to conflict expression are all experienced as part of the patient's transference phenomenology toward the analyst. Consciously and/or unconsciously the patient attempts to elicit and encourage the analyst to participate in a variety of complementary responses to the patient's transference reenactments and behavioral repetitions.

In an optimal analytic situation, the analyst maintains a position of steady analytic neutrality and nonparticipation in actively fulfilling or satisfying the patient's transference enactments, wishes, defenses, and conflicts. This means that the patient's transference expectations, hopes, and fears are *not* realized, and the analyst continues a relatively constant attitude of analyzing the transference phenomena instead. This analytic attitude and the interpersonal and intrapsychic interactions and experiences which it evokes in the patient represent a *new* form of object relationship occurring between patient and analyst. The differential between the transference expectations and the patient's actual observable experience of the analyst provides an important therapeutic arena for the interactions between patient and analyst, and for the changes which these interactions stimulate within the patients (for details, see Dewald [1972]).

In this model, the concept of abstinence refers to the analyst's continuing analytic response and therapeutic neutrality in the face of the patient's transference wishes, provocations, defenses, and expectations. Abstinence is a tool in the analyst's repertoire and is *not* a goal in itself. Although it has been described as "a rule," its use, intensity, persistence, and the ways in which it is applied are subject to a large number of variables within the given patient, the analyst, and the stage of the analytic situation and process (Cooper, 1986).

Gratifying Elements in the Psychoanalytic Situation

Before emphasizing the uses and effects of abstinence, it is important to recognize that in spite of painful or distressing periods in analysis, and in spite of the level, intensity, or duration of the transference abstinence that occurs, psychoanalysis also offers the patient a variety of gratifications and satisfactions of infantile and childhood wishes, as well as those of later life stages. These gratifications occur as a result of the structure of the psychoanalytic situation and the functioning of patient and analyst within it, some of which is expressed in the concept of "basic transference."

In addition, the role and functioning of the analyst in the psychoanalytic situation provides the patient with a complex and multifaceted "new" and "real" object relationship. The patient's transference responses and expectations of the analyst are met instead by the relatively narrow range of traditional analytic neutrality and interventions. The difference between the patient's anticipations and the analyst's observable behavior present the patient with a new and different form of object relationship, which ultimately permits new and different patterns of interaction and adaptation (Loewald, 1960; Dewald, 1976).

Greenacre (1954) has described the commonly perceived "tilt" in the analytic situation and relationship which seems to favor the analyst. Such things as the degree of revelation of self, the intensity of attachment and affective meaning, the ability to come and go, the control of the patterns of communication, the payment of a fee, the charge for missed sessions, the restraints of time, and option of silence, are often experienced by the patient as unfair and arbitrary.

There is a complementary "tilt" in the analytic relationship which favors the patient and provides for various forms of emotional gratification. These elements include the high frequency and substantial duration of analytic sessions, which means that during the course of an analysis the patient spends an unusually large amount of time with the analyst. The analyst maintains a consistent reliability and presence, seldom, if ever, being absent without advance notice. The analyst's attitude of respect for the patient as an individual and for the painful aspects of the person's neurotic suffering is often in contrast to other people in the patient's experience. The analyst is willing to listen attentively and sensitively, and to provide the patient with an opportunity verbally to express himself and any thought processes without responsibility for the analyst's needs, feelings, or internal reactions, a situation that is unique in human interactions. The same is true regarding the patient's opportunity to experience and express a full range of affects without criticism or retaliation. The analyst's appropriate and correctly timed interventions offer the patient a sense of intimate communication and understanding, relief from the isolation and alienation which the patient had previously experienced, and a sense of being the central focus of attention and concern in the relationship and situation. The analyst's long-term commitment, therapeutic attitude, and willingness to dedicate him- or herself to the rigors of the analytic work in support of the patient's psychoanalytic progress without making similar demands on the patient is another unusual feature of the psychoanalytic situation. The analyst allows him- or herself to be used as the object of the patient's transferences and accepts whatever distortions, misinterpretations of motivation, or unpleasant stresses such transferences involve without retaliation or a personal need to correct or suppress them. The analyst also protects the patient's privacy and confidentiality, without necessarily receiving a complementary attitude from the patient. And the analyst also offers noncompetitive efforts at helping the patient toward maturation and progress, at times involving levels beyond the analyst's own achievements.

Gitelson (1962), Winnicott (1955), Modell (1976), and others have emphasized the aspect of the holding environment provided by the psychoanalytic situation, and its dynamic similarity to the parent–child relationship, which for some writers is expressed in almost literal form. The patient's experience of communicating disorganized or conflicted thoughts, and having the listener organize, integrate, explain, or interpret them in a way that brings sense and coherence and allows an experience of being understood, is a rare occurrence in everyday life. Empathy and understanding are most effectively conveyed through correct interventions by the analyst, and result not only in cognitive awareness or insight (by small increments), but also in reducing the patient's sense of strangeness or alienation, the sense of isolation from others in regard to one's own thought processes, and the sense of having to cope with deep-seated internal conflicts alone and without help. The analyst's effective interventions also convey a sense of creative mutuality and help through the analytic process.

In addition, the shifting moment-to-moment state of transferences may permit the patient to ascribe to the analyst a variety of pleasurable or unpleasurable wishful or defensive meanings to current experiences in the analytic interaction, and thereby to achieve transference gratification in spite of the analyst's neutral technique and intentions.

Furthermore, if the analysis proceeds effectively and successfully, the patient will also achieve pleasure and satisfaction at his or her own expanded self-knowledge and awareness, and at the increasing depth and richness of his or her interpersonal relationships including the experience with the analyst. New capacities for mastery of conflict can also provide an enhanced self-confidence and pride.

The Varying and Various Effects of Abstinence

The impact of transference abstinence upon the psychoanalytic process has a number of features and effects. For pedogogic purposes, they will be considered individually in this presentation, although in the clinical situation they occur concurrently and/or in various combinations or sequences. The nature of the specific effects will also vary with the stage of analysis and with the intensity of the psychoanalytic situation and relationship.

The vignettes used here to illustrate the concepts being described were chosen because they are typical, common and garden variety examples of the issues related to abstinence.

1. Other things being equal, transference abstinence and the lack of satisfaction of the derivative of a wish or impulse will tend to intensify its pressured quality. The more intense or persistent the wish or desire, the more likely is it that the person will experience more direct access of that wish or fantasy to consciousness and, therefore, the greater is the likelihood that the individual will be able to observe and recognize its psychological effects. Such an intensification of conscious awareness of the nature or form of the wish is a first step toward recognition and insight into how such a wish affects the individual's psychic economy. On the other hand, fulfillment of the derivative forms of a transference wish tends to reduce its intensity and its peremptory and motivating quality, thus decreasing the pressure toward conscious recognition by the patient.

For example, a twenty-seven-year-old man, in his second year of analysis, asked in a benign way what my plans were for the two-month-off summer vacation and what my destination was. Asked to associate to the question, the patient expressed annoyance at not being given a factual answer, and contempt for the "stiff, inhumane analytic posture" and assured me, "you don't have to worry, I won't follow you even if I knew." In the next session, the patient expressed a series of fantasies as to who would be accompanying me, whether my wife or my mistress, and a fantasy of me in an intense sexual orgy while away. This led to recall of similar questions and fantasies about his father when the father took business trips while the patient was in grade school.

2. Given the nature of infantile and childhood wishes and fantasies and the conflicts that result from them, transference abstinence for such demands and desires helps to create and maintain a safe therapeutic situation in which the analytic process can unfold. Experience by the patient that transference wishes will *not* be overtly gratified by the analyst makes it safer for the individual to express such desires freely without having to take the behavioral consequences and responsibility which satisfaction of the wishes would impose. The analyst's optimal attitude and response to the expression of such wishes acknowledges their importance and impact, as well as respect and regard for the distress, conflict, disappointment, pain or frustration which the patient may experience from the therapeutic neutrality, without praising, rewarding, condemning, criticizing, or humiliating the individual who experiences them.

An attractive young woman had just invited me to join her on the couch and to make love, expressing her desire in passionate terms. Following a period of silence, she said, "I hate you for having such control and for being above it all emotionally. But if you had ever shown any sexual interest in me, I could never have said what I did, and if you ever touched me I'd walk out and never come back."

Patients carefully and repeatedly test the safety and security of the analytic situation, and also the capacity of the analyst comfortably to maintain it. Their transference wishes and conflicts, both libidinal and aggressive, tend initially to be experienced and expressed in derivative and relatively superficial form and intensity. If the patient achieves transference gratification for less intense and less primitive forms of derivative wishes, such fulfillment may create a paradox for the patient by making it "unsafe" to seek

expression of deeper, more primitive, or more threatening transferences lest they too be ultimately gratified. The final effect may
then be that the patient maintains more continuous and active
defensiveness against the emergence of deeper, more primitive
forms of transference, and maintains a relatively superficial and
"safe" level of experience and communication.

A divorced middle-aged woman who had been involved in
repeated overt incest with her father from age three to eight began
analysis with no conscious memory of the incestuous behavior. In her
transference experience, she expressed bitter disappointment and
anger at the analytic situation and at my attitude of not expressing
conscious admiration, praise, reassurance, or love for her. Her previous psychotherapist had been warm, encouraging, and openly caring. Only after many months of bitter depressive complaints at my
continuing "unfeeling and cold neutrality," could she begin to
express her previous sense of conviction that I would eventually
become sexually actively involved with her, and her relief that I had
not yet yielded to her complaints. This transference interaction
allowed the eventual recovery of the memories of incest.

3. As mentioned above, all patients tend experientially to test the
analyst and analytic situation to determine whether or not it remains
safe for free and spontaneous expression. If derivative transference
wishes, defenses, or conflicts are dealt with in an analytically neutral,
effective and appropriate fashion (without overstimulation and over-
gratification, or disapproval, criticism or humiliation) and without
avoidance or evasion of the topic by the analyst, the patient in the
therapeutic alliance is encouraged to allow more direct experience
and then expression of deeper transference conflicts and wishes. In
this way, a spiraling process of testing, recognition of the analyst's
continuing neutral analytic posture and response, reassurance that
the situation remains safe and controlled, followed by the expression
of somewhat deeper and more primitive conflicts can occur. For
many patients, this testing procedure continues throughout the
entire analytic experience including the final termination process. In
the final termination process, the most intense and ultimate tests may
often occur (Dewald, 1976).

During the second year of analysis, there was a knock on the door
interrupting the session of a middle-aged man. I went to answer the
door, and then returned to my chair without saying anything. The

patient resumed his associations at the point of the interruption and continued for several minutes. When I pointed out he had not mentioned the incident, he responded that he didn't think he was supposed to. I said that he must have had some response, to which he said that in his first analysis he had once expressed irritation at a similar incident. His analyst had changed the subject, and at subsequent similar interruptions had returned to his chair saying, "I'm sorry." The patient had interpreted this to mean that the analyst was unable to tolerate his anger, and subsequently in that analysis he had inhibited such feeling. After I pointed out his transference assumption that I was equally uncomfortable with his aggression he could begin to address the deep resentment he felt at the interruption and at his former analyst's reluctance to deal with his aggression.

4. Establishment of a transference paradigm in which the analyst, from time to time, offers reassurance, praise, or positive manifest response for "good" behavior, or offers criticism, alternative judgment, rebuke, or other forms of negative response, tends to create a situation in which the patient is encouraged to depend upon the opinion and judgment of the analyst. Such a state may exert added strength to the patient's spontaneous tendency to perform in order to achieve transference reward or punishment from the external authority in contrast to enhancing the patient's own self-determination, independence, and capacity for personal self-observation and evaluation.

A physician involved in an unconscious competitive father transference was preparing to take his Board Certification examination. He had been advised by senior colleagues in regard to what he should do in the clinical portion of the examination. The analytic session just prior to the exam ended in the usual way and I offered no comment about the exam when he left. Analysis of his blatant disregard of the advice, which led to his failing the examination, revealed the fantasy that I would be threatened by his succeeding, and would punish (castrate) him for it. If I had wished him good luck it would have meant it was safe for him to pass.

Six months later he took the examination again and in due time told me he had passed. The next session he reported a fantasy that there had been a computer error; he had actually failed, and would be receiving notice of his failure shortly. Analysis revealed his fantasy that my not having congratulated him on his success meant I hated him and would again castrate him for challenging me by passing.

These two incidents were importantly instrumental in exposing at a significant experiential level the extent of his fears of success and the projection to me of his destructive competitive wishes. Had I wished him "Good luck" the first time, or congratulated him the second (both of which would be normal "human" nonanalytic actions) it is likely that he would have passed the exam unremarkably, and the underlying conflict would not have emerged.

5. Most analysts agree that direct manipulative instructions and suggestions are inappropriate in usual analytic situations. However, the nature of the psychoanalytic relationship is such that powerful suggestive forces are continually operative. Given the general paucity of behavioral clues to personal feelings, values, and opinion, and given the relatively abbreviated amount of verbalization offered by the analyst, and given the patient's continuing attempts to scan the meager clues for meaning, everything the analyst says or does (or does not say or do) takes on significant internalized meaning and pressure for the patient. In this way, the patient correctly or incorrectly "reads" the analyst and may use such data as a guide to thoughts, affects, and transference interactions; and these "data" take on additional meaning and power for the patient since they are not offset or corrected by the usual types of feedback and information available in other forms of human interaction.

Interactions or responses conveying direct transference fulfillment (whether positive or negative) thus take on increased significance for the patient and carry the risk of manipulating or controlling the patient's thought processes and behavior, sometimes with and sometimes without the analyst's conscious recognition.

On an occasion when beginning to express a direct erotic transference fantasy, a patient heard me shift slightly in my chair. Her associations stopped sharply and a long silence ensued. Analysis of the silence indicated her interpretation that my shift in my chair meant I was angry and disapproving of her fantasy and that I wanted her to stop talking about it. I had been unaware of the trigger to her silence until we analyzed the silence itself.

6. The emergence of significantly meaningful transference wishes in the absence of behavioral fulfillment, but at the same time considering them from an analytic self-observing perspective, offers the patient an experience of repeatedly learning to separate wishes

and desires from actions. As this distinction is established, the patient can achieve a greater sense of confidence in his own capacity for modulation, control, and conscious volitional decision making in regard to intrapsychic and interpersonal wishes and desires. This confident ability in turn can permit the patient to allow further conscious access to otherwise unacceptable wishes and fantasy organization, since the threat of loss of behavioral control will be reduced. Such change may then aid in the resolution of superego prohibitions against thinking ("a thought is as bad as an act") and may also enhance ego capacity for judgment, synthesis, impulse control, and the eventual development of sublimation.

A patient late in the process of an analysis expressed this issue as follows: "When I started analysis I used to be terrified of expressing my thoughts because they were so bad. Then I worried I'd hurt your feelings, or else you'd secretly hate me. Then I felt if I expressed myself without holding back I'd be humiliated or else something would get out of control here. Now I know I can think anything I want, and I have the power to control things and my thoughts and feelings aren't so horrible and dangerous after all."

7. Gratification of the derivative of a transference wish tends to reduce its intensity for the moment, and thereby tends to decrease conflict regarding it. This diminution of intensity may result in scrutiny or associations which are attenuated, intellectualized, or at other times are reconstructions after the fact, thereby contributing to the loss of an opportunity for affective analytic experience in regard to the issue in question. Abstinence prior to analyzing the interaction tends to heighten the intensity of the conflict in question, and thereby the liveliness and affective quality in the resolution and working through of the particular transference incident.

A woman patient early in her analysis asked if I had any children. My suggestion that we look at what was behind her question and why it came up at that time was met with irritation, and a comment that analysts are too stiff, impersonal, and afraid to be human with their analysands. Several weeks later the patient asked the same question again, wondering herself why she had asked since she expected no answer. After a short silence she described a feeling of shock and bitterness in reaction to learning, as an eight-year-old, that her father had been previously married and that she had two half-siblings she had never met. At that point she could recognize her concern and fears about surprises which might be in store for her in beginning a relationship with me.

It could be argued that this same concern might have become conscious through other analytic interactions even if I had factually answered her original question. While that may be true, analysis is already long enough without wasting opportunities which present themselves for investigation.

8. Issues of gratification versus abstinence are also relevant to processes of resistance and defense experienced in the patient's associations, and in the transference relationship. Gratifying, accepting, or strengthening a particular defense or resistance, or the failure *eventually* to interpret it and bring analytic scrutiny to the issues being defended against, tends to avoid conflict and enhance a patient's transient feeling of comfort and reduction of anxiety. As a result, analytic scrutiny and experience in the working through of significant components of psychic conflict may be avoided. This is not to say that every resistance should be interpreted immediately, or that there are not times during the course of an analytic process when it is appropriate for the patient temporarily to maintain certain defenses. But this should reflect a deliberate technical decision by the analyst on the basis of a particular tactical issue, and ultimately the resistances in question would be subject to analytic scrutiny when the patient is deemed ready to confront the warded-off material. If the patient is already aware of the conflict and the resistances in question, and the analyst does not directly address the issue, the patient's understanding may be that the analyst is reluctant or fearful of confronting the material, leading to more intense or sustained resistance.

A man well into his analysis repeatedly expressed admiration, respect, affection, and idealization of me in glowing terms. His wish was to become my protege and to serve as executor of my scientific manuscripts and papers. When I pointed out that this fantasy implied he was thinking of my death, he became significantly flustered and anxious, and with great difficulty acknowledged an underlying fantasy that he considered himself superior to me, and was biding his time until I would become older and weaker so that he could take my place without fear of my retaliation.

9. Gratification of transference expectations and wishes may occur in many forms, and the effects of particular interventions by the analyst may be determined more by the nature of the patient's

total transferences than by the form or content of the intervention itself. Depending on the nature of the transference at the time, the same intervention (or failure to intervene) may be perceived by the patient as gratifying or as abstinent, and there is a similar variability in the effects of particular technical interventions upon different patients.

A patient in the midst of an angry resentful transference reenactment of feeling unloved by her mother experienced a period of my silence as further bitter proof of how I did not care for her and she was unlovable. On another occasion a few weeks later, while analyzing her sense of being expected to perform, a similar response of silence was experienced by her as my showing great sensitivity to her and to her need to feel accepted even if she performed poorly. In either case, the patient's response should eventually be explored analytically.

10. Most patients in an effective analytic process eventually experience a typical "double-bind" form of transference conflict, which recapitulates an important developmental process. Under transference pressures to repeat and/or reenact infantile and childhood developmental stages and conflicts, the patient consciously and unconsciously seeks to evoke from the analyst responses complementary to transference fantasies and wishes, or to the defensive or adaptive compromises of such wishes. Abstinence for such transference reactions may lead to feelings of hurt, disappointment, frustration, shame, or humiliation, but at the same time such abstinence provides reassurance that taboos will not be violated, and that the analytic situation is safely protected. Gratification of transference wishes and demands may lead to momentary excitement, pleasure, fulfillment, or reassurance, but may also result in shame, guilt, intensified conflict, and disruption of the therapeutic alliance and analytic situation. This represents a type of developmental conflict experienced by the child whose preoedipal and oedipal wishes should optimally be accepted and comfortably tolerated by environmental objects but for whom overstimulation and gratification of such wishes may evoke anxiety, guilt, and a variety of ego distortions. The developmental task for the child is to experience and accept the existence of its wishes without undue guilt or shame, while simultaneously accepting limitations to direct gratification and achieving tolerance for delay or substitute fulfillments.

A woman who had experienced long-term direct incestuous sexual activity with her father as a girl canceled a session well in advance. Several days later she indicated her plans had changed, and asked if the session was still available. When I said it was available, she expressed pleasure and indicated she would attend. The next day she was anxious, remote, and had difficulty associating. Analysis of her behavior indicated she had felt that my "being nice" and letting her have the session back meant I was weak, had too great an interest in her, might make some inappropriate expectation of her, and she defensively wished I had given her time to someone else. At the same time analysis of this interchange offered her the opportunity to experience a reality-based fulfillment of a request without having it result in inappropriate behavior by either of us.

11. There are frequent complex and multifaceted transference situations in which conflicting and/or contradictory transference wishes may coexist. Gratification of one wish may simultaneously frustrate another, or vice versa. Optimal management of such situations requires recognition of the complexity of the conflicting transferences, and the eventual directing of interpretive attention toward all the active transferences. Abstinence is maintained through the analytic attitude and posture.

A patient with a transference expectation of being criticized and rejected maintained a defensive posture of emotional distance and abrasiveness. In describing a complex event he presented himself as being at fault and to blame for a conflict situation with a co-worker. Rather than interpret the patient's previously recognized self-defeating behavior (which the patient expected and consciously sought to elicit) I instead interpreted his wish to put himself in an unfavorable light as a way of feeling misunderstood and criticized by me. This would further have justified his wish to maintain emotional detachment. The patient responded with a sudden burst of tears and deep expressions of gratitude for being understood; this was immediately followed by an angry accusation that I was tricking him and he would be a fool to let his emotional guard down and give in to his temptation to trust me more. The ante had just been raised and he resented my increasing the intensity of his conflict.

12. A significant conscious experience of regressive transference yearnings and conflict in regard to infantile and childhood wishes and fantasies is an important part of every successful and well-conducted psychoanalysis. However, analysis is a therapeutic procedure

designed eventually to promote replacement of such wishes and fantasies by more age-appropriate levels of expression and object choice in regard to basic human needs and wishes. If the psychoanalytic process provides active and sustained real fulfillment of derivatives of infantile and childhood fantasies, and if analytic interactions become an end rather than a means, the patient's fixation to the past may be enhanced and maturational change in psychic structure through renunciation of inappropriate objects and wishes may be significantly delayed. At times this can lead to interminable psychoanalysis and stalemates in which the original analytic goal is lost to an on-going mutual living out of transference and countertransference forces, and at other times it may enhance a tendency toward acting out, particularly if the patient's transference pressures upon the analyst have successfully evoked significant sustained gratifications and loss of the analyst's neutral position.

A middle-aged woman, seen in consultation at the request of her internist, described being in analysis four times per week for the past fourteen years with the same analyst. In the first five years she had obtained significant symptomatic relief and some insight and characterological change which now allowed her to accept pleasure without her former sense of guilt. For a number of years recently she had experienced the analyst as a personally invested friend to whom she could talk more easily and safely than to her spouse about the various events and concerns of her life. She saw him as the replacement for a much loved uncle who died when she was a child. "It makes me feel happy to have my uncle back, and since I have the money to pay for analysis I plan to continue it indefinitely so I can enjoy this relationship and never have to give it up."

13. Even if the patient's major pathology is at preoedipal and/or preverbal levels, and even if these conflicts have resulted in arrest of development of various ego functions, the adult patient in analysis is *not* the same as a young child. As primitive preoedipal transferences and conflicts are mobilized and intensified by the analytic process, appropriate levels of transference abstinence encourage a gradual shift in the patient from nonverbal, preverbal, or yet unremembered experiences and feeling states to verbal description and communication. As part of the analytic process, such adults can increasingly use whatever meager verbal and communicative skills they have to describe their immediate transference experiences; such even falter-

ing attempts at verbalization serve as early precursors of interactional communication, modulation and synthesis. The use of language to communicate such needs and feeling states (in contrast to action) leads to the more effective acknowledgment of separation between individuals, and to further development of more precise and sophisticated forms of linguistic expression.

A young woman with major dyadic and preoedipal conflict and pathology began regressively to experience a variety of oral symptoms including severe bulimia, chronic bruxism, sensations of the Isakower phenomenon, distortions of body image, intensified separation anxiety, and various reenactments of the separation–individuation process in the transference. Maintenance of the standard psychoanalytic situation with abstinence except for verbal interpretation of the regressive behavioral phenomena resulted in the patient gradually verbalizing her affects and ego states in increasingly complex and descriptive form. With such increasing capacity for verbal expression there was a reduction in the acting out and altered body image, and eventual progression toward triadic oedipal levels of conflict.

14. Not infrequently the effect of the patient's overall transference behavior is to elicit in the analyst an impulse to respond in an affective or behavioral way that complements the patient's original transference expression. Such subjective countertransference responses can be used by the analyst as a signal of the transference provocation and as a stimulus to subject his gratifying countertransference response to self-analytic scrutiny rather than immediate intervention or action.

A man in the middle phase of his analysis had for several sessions expressed a series of complaining, derogatory, and angry reactions toward the analysis and toward me. I became aware of feeling irritated at the continuing litany of angry disappointment and asked myself why the patient bothered to come to his session or didn't get up and leave if he was so bitter. This awareness allowed me to restrain my initial irritation and wish to confront and reject the patient, and instead to interpret the patient's behavior as a defensive wish to provoke rejection in response to having verbalized feelings of love and admiration during the previous week.

15. There are some eventually analyzable patients whose psychopathology and character structure are such that any even mild

frustration or disappointment of their wishes is experienced as intolerable. For them the level of transference abstinence appropriate in more usual cases may threaten their willingness to participate freely in the analysis. The tactical need may be for the parameter of gratifying a derivative transference expression, but the effects of such gratification should subsequently be subjected to analytic scrutiny after the incident in question has occurred. By analytic attention and interpretation of the issues surrounding the active gratification, a process is initiated whereby the patient's need for direct fulfillment of derivative wishes can slowly be replaced by verbalization, and activity can slowly and repeatedly lead to reflective awareness and gradually increasing impulse control. In patients for whom acting out has been a major characterological form of adaptation, this may be a long, taxing, and disruptive process. But unless it is ultimately successful and transference gratification is gradually replaced by appropriate levels of abstinence one may question whether a genuine psychoanalytic process has occurred.

The wife of a physician acknowledged in the third year of her analysis that her husband had been prescribing sleeping pills for her since the beginning of treatment. When asked about it she said she knew I would disapprove and not allow her to use them. At that point I told her I would prescribe the pills for her and that once per month she was to remind me of her need for the prescription. Over the next eight months the writing of the prescriptions served to bring active analytic scrutiny and understanding to the multiple meanings of her insomnia, and ultimately her need for the medication disappeared.

16. If the analyst usually maintains a neutral observing abstinence as previously described, but provides transference gratification at times of intensified distress and regression, he may inadvertently reinforce and encourage symptomatic regression. The patient consciously or unconsciously perceives that pain, suffering, and disturbed behavior elicit more direct evidences of the analyst's concern and active involvement. If this pattern cannot be reversed by interpretation, a spiraling iatrogenic and disruptive transference regression may ensue, interfering with the analytic process. And once initiated such a process tends to become self-sustaining.

A young woman with borderline personality characteristics was in her fourth year of analysis when she began to recover extremely painful memories and conflicts around a major childhood trauma. She had a very meager social support system and experienced increasingly intense separation anxiety and abandonment feelings during the weekends. In a countertransference-inspired attempt to help her cope with the sense of alienation and abandonment, I would participate in her occasional weekend phone calls with a conversational style similar to that of the analytic sessions. In spite of my efforts to deal with the calls during her regular analytic sessions, they became more frequent, more desperate, and eventually occurred on week-nights as well. Her regressive dependency and disruption increased steadily until the analysis eventually had to be interrupted.

Another patient in her second analysis described how her former analyst, at times when she experienced acute anxiety or feelings of being "cut off," would hold her hand "to maintain a feeling of connection," or allow her to hug him briefly at the end of her sessions. These behaviors relieved her acute distress, and she felt increasingly desperate in her need for these signs of his presence and concern. However, she also became increasingly aware of a perception that she could never express her conscious sexual fantasies since they too might be ultimately acted upon with the analyst. She felt herself to be the one who had to maintain control of the situation between them, and in spite of her feeling of attachment to the pleasures involved ultimately (with the help of a friend) recognized her need to interrupt the treatment if she was ever to face her deeper neurotic conflicts.

Summary

Abstinence by the analyst is not synonymous with stiffness, rigidity, emotional coldness, or punitiveness toward the patient nor is it synonymous with long periods of silence or inactivity by the analyst. It relates instead to an attitude of curiosity about motivations and meanings, a recognition of the multidetermined nature of human behavior, acceptance of the concept of all behavior (whether "normal" or "neurotic") as representing a compromise formation of conflicting tendencies, and a willingness to place the overall goals of analysis ahead of immediate relief or reduction of distress. The most effective way of maintaining abstinence is through appropriately conveyed interpretation which demonstrates understanding and at the same time shows respect for the patient's conflict and distress.

As the analysis proceeds and as the patient becomes aware (through experience and/or through the analyst's interventions) of the effects of abstinence, there develops an increasing identification with the analyzing function of the analyst. The maintenance of transference abstinence eventually enhances the solidity of the therapeutic alliance, and encourages the patient's efforts at self-analysis, working through, and renunciation of archaic and age-inappropriate wishes and objects.

8

An Example of the Reconstruction of Trauma

Robert L. Tyson, M.D.

HE patient's task in analysis is to remember, that is, to provide traces from the past. The analyst's work is to discern what the patient has forgotten from the traces left behind or, "more correctly, to *construct* it" (Freud, 1937, pp. 258–259); with constructions he builds the missing bridges of experience that fill in and connect the traces the patient provides. The analyst makes these links in the patient's mind when he conveys his constructions (or reconstructions—Freud used the terms interchangeably) to the patient; the effectiveness of these bridges is codetermined by their content and by the timing and manner in which they are made, a matter of technique.

Looking more closely at the process of reconstruction, the traces or fragments provided by the patient and with which the analyst works appear in various forms. Freud (1937, p. 258) listed them succinctly as appearing in dreams, in allusions contained in the patient's associations, and in the patient's actions inside and outside the analytic situation. He regarded the transference as "particularly calculated to favour the return of these emotional connections" to the patient's forgotten material. As for what the analyst does with this material, "it is the psychotherapist's business to put these [fragments] together once more into the organization which he presumes to have existed" (Breuer and Freud, 1893–1895, p. 291). Thus this organizing activity on the analyst's part depends on his having thought out to some degree the pattern of the patient's psychic history, a matter of theory. As Kennedy (1971) pointed out, Freud used the terms reconstruction, or construction, in these two senses—to refer to a process in the analyst's mind, and to a type of verbal intervention made by the analyst.

Following Freud, Greenson (1967, p. 16) stressed the need for the analyst to do some intellectual work with the data provided by the patient. The analyst puts together insights resulting from his intuition and empathy so as to reconstruct larger segments of the patient's life. For him, as for Freud, the transference neurosis provided a clinical organizing focus; in it, says Greenson, the patient relives and works through oedipal and later editions and variations of his childhood neurosis (p. 185), even though it might be years before the analyst realizes that a piece of behavior represents one of those traces which connects to forgotten experiences (p. 265). The implication is clear in this statement that the guiding principle of the analyst's intellectual work is the oedipal pattern, though in his clinical examples Greenson gave much evidence that he also took account of factors in the patient originating earlier than the oedipal phase.

Freud (1937) further distinguished between the interventions of interpretation and of construction, or reconstruction. Interpretations deal with single elements or aspects of the patient's unconscious psychic life and have the aim of making them fully conscious so as to be better understood. Reconstructions bring together various interpretations and, as Greenson put it, deal with the life going on in and around the patient which would explain the fates of those elements (1967, p. 323). Greenson added that the analyst, in making his reconstructions, may even conjecture regarding the parents' emotions, behavior, and motivations if these factors are intimately related to what was going on in the patient at the time.

In this paper my principal aim is to present an example of how the analyst is called upon to do his work and to reconstruct portions of the patient's past so as to enhance and further the analytic process. I will describe selected segments from the analysis of a highly intelligent thirty-four-year-old man who came to treatment with many clear-cut neurotic symptoms as well as a narcissistic character disturbance. This rather condensed account is designed to highlight the interweaving of the patient's preoedipal and later neurotic psychopathology; it also stresses the ways in which they were reflected in the development of the transference and in the appearance of the traces of the past from which a significant aspect of the patient's childhood experience could be constructed. Following a particular reconstruction, the affectively charged memory of a traumatic event from the age of four was recovered. Once available, it was possible to see how this experience and the memory of it served as a screen memory to organize and bring together the patient's earlier difficulties in the narcissistic sphere with his then current oedipal conflicts. The defensive, adaptive, and developmental uses to which the patient's superior, perhaps extraordinary intelligence were put are also described.

Background

Mr. A. was referred by a colleague who had the patient's wife in analysis. Mr. A. requested help because his marriage was breaking up, and since he felt responsible to a degree, he too wanted analysis. He implied but did not elaborate other reasons why he wanted treatment and was clearly terrified of what analysis might hold for him, saying that he wanted an analyst whom he could take home for cocktails. Fearing that he would feel completely defenseless, he wanted at first to decrease the proposed frequency from five to four times per week. But after questioning himself whether he could get through the coming weekend without seeing me, he agreed to the higher frequency.

A brief history gleaned chiefly from the analytic work is as follows. Mr. A. was the youngest of three children in a well-to-do Jewish family. A much older brother was exceptionally talented and academically gifted, married, and had established a remunerative business of his own. A sister four years older was described by him as a "B" student. She was for the most part ignored by parents and siblings, unable to compete with them in any sphere. The competitive climate in the family is well illustrated by the patient's description that, when he was two-and-a-half years old, he used his quite precocious intelligence to recite perfectly and from memory his sister's elocution lessons with which she struggled in an effort to correct a speech defect.

The patient's father, a self-made man, repeatedly declared to his son that it was important to do well in school, to make a living, to be the boss, and by offering himself as an example, it was important not to reveal to anyone how much money one had or what one felt or thought. His father was secretive, remote, often absent, and given to temper tantrums, yet idolized by Mr. A. who saw him as a paragon of intelligence and virtue. He complied with his parents' wishes for him, as well as obtaining his share of their attention and care, by performing superbly in school, even better than his older brother.

Mr. A.'s mother, though more attentive and certainly more vocal and openly admiring of him than his father, nevertheless provided the children with her own version of her husband's philosophy that one always has to take care of oneself, not trusting the task to anyone else. For example, she is said to have put her older son, though dressed, in his cot into the severe winter snows for hours at a time "in order to toughen him up" as an infant. For years the patient's sister slept outside in the unwindowed and unshuttered porch in all seasons. The patient was the most protected, sleeping in an unheated attic with the windows open. Particularly in the winter time this complicated his bed-wetting and he recalled feeling that his back was freezing; this sensation returned as a somatic symptom early in his marriage when he felt sexual disappointment with his wife, and on occasion in the course of the analysis, when he felt rage at being betrayed or let down by a woman.

In addition to the enuresis, it emerged that Mr. A. had other symptoms in childhood including phobias such as fears of feces, shoe polish and the smell of shoes, heights, and birds. Some of these symptoms persisted into adult life relatively unmodified.

Mr. A.'s recollection was of an intensely lonely and sad childhood. His parents seemed always to be battling. They moved into separate bedrooms, and eventually the father left the home permanently during the patient's early adolescence; in response to this the patient consciously felt no loss but only relief. His brother was always preoccupied with his own pursuits and had no time for him, and the patient treated his sister in the same way, perhaps with more disdain. At school he felt an "outsider" for various reasons, added to by his manifestly superior intelligence that complicated his school career and put him far ahead of his peers.

Mr. A.'s mother was very ambitious for her sons, and with her "encouragement" he succeeded in gaining entrance to a prominent university at the age of fourteen, graduating two years later to enter professional school that he completed successfully in the prescribed time. He began work with a prominent company in his field at age nineteen. Because of his innate ability and gift for creative thinking, he attracted attention and soon began an affair with the daughter of the president who was not Jewish. Mr. A. was ashamed of his Jewish background, and the prospect of marrying a non-Jewish girl was quite consciously one way to get away from it. Moving to a distant city when the opportunity arose was for him yet another way to distance himself from his Jewishness, which he identified with his mother. Within a year after moving away, Mr. A. married this girl after he had made her pregnant on a return visit. The course of their marriage was marked by an increasing disillusionment with each other, and by an increasing mutual sexual dissatisfaction. Although Mr. A. was often sexually unfaithful, he was slow to realize that she, too, was having affairs until he discovered a letter from a lover she had left open in the house. Subsequently he was humiliated when his wife told him that the older man involved, an Arab, was able to give her much more sexual pleasure than he did, and he requested a referral for analysis.

The Analysis

When the analysis began, Mr. A. lay on the couch but kept one foot on the floor and said he felt like a roller-coaster without wheels. I commented on his fear that the analysis might send him off the rails. He responded by putting his foot together with the other one on the couch and by describing many instances of his struggle to achieve control of his internal and external worlds, including his fear of heights. He told of an attempted suicide at the age of twenty-two when he tried to drive his car off a bridge at high speed, but the car was stopped by the railings. The patient was knocked unconscious, recovered soon after, and went on his way unapprehended and untreated. Since then, and especially since encountering recent serious financial difficulties, Mr. A. had fantasies of suicide that he controlled by the counterthought that he would do it only after everything, financially and personally, was "cleaned up."

The first six months of the analysis was characterized by a kind of "reportage" that Mr. A. came to call "The Court Gazette" in which he recounted everything since his previous visit. We were able to see that this reporting had the defensive function of controlling the analysis and keeping him "on the rails." It also represented his wish for me to have a perfect picture of his life and experiences. For many weeks he struggled to get everything into the time allotted, complaining that the sessions were not long enough, while increasingly idealizing me and the analysis. As he and his wife drew further apart, Mr. A. felt closer to me, thus stimulating his unconscious homosexual desires.

His resultant anxiety precipitated defensive acting out in an intense and sudden sexual affair with an ex-secretary, in search of the perfect sexual experience and to prove himself the perfect lover. The theme of seeking perfection in others, in himself, and in his experiences and performance ran throughout the analysis and his life.

When Mr. A.'s wife and children moved out in the second month of analysis, I could interpret his identification with the helpless aspects of his mother who was ineffectual in dealing with his father, and this was then linked with his fears of becoming dependent on me and the analysis. But he wanted me as a friend without any such complications and thought of a homosexual man with whom he had once worked closely before coming to the city, an experience which worried him because of his conscious homosexual excitement at the time. During this work, Mr. A. began still another heterosexual affair, this time with a young woman whom he knew still continued a lengthy liaison with an older man. Indeed, the excitement involved in triangular affairs became quite clear to him, but the very process of talking about it further stimulated his excitement and all the concomitant anxieties. This was a clear example of Mr. A.'s tendency to sexualize his anxiety, a defense which frequently presented technical problems in the analysis.

In the sixth month of treatment, a holiday was approaching and Mr. A. reported a dream in which a friend fell off a tall building. On waking, he had the fantasy of coming to the session and calmly shooting me dead. Associations before and after the dream were concerned with doubts about my ability to deal with him, and with how he seemed to feel nothing about me and the analysis for a time before and after holidays. It was then not difficult to show Mr. A. how this dream encompassed not only his fears of becoming too dependent on me and of his homosexual excitement in the sessions, but that he also feared that his anger at my leaving would destroy me.

Just at this moment, the patient suddenly reported with shock the curious sensation that I had "dropped out of sight," that I no longer existed where I was, that there was a hole there, and that he felt as if he were floating on the couch. Mr. A. reported he was now watching himself having this feeling and in essence doubting its reality, just as he had doubted feelings at times of emotional crisis earlier in his life. Among the subsequent intellectualizations and rationalizations, feelings of disillusionment with his current girl friend came to mind and he wondered how he could have idealized her. He described how he seeks a woman who appears to be a mirror image of himself, but she always turns out to be unattainable because, on approaching her, he finds fault with her and the illusion of her perfection disappears. Soon he reported a dream in which he was penetrating this girl by inserting his two hands into her vagina. He associated to his experience in intercourse as being a mutual masturbation.

After considerable work on the use of his sexual relationship with his woman friend to deflect his sexual feelings about me, I was able over several months to interpret some aspects of his anger at me for disappointing his idealized expectations, his use of idealization to defend against his anger, his difficulty in controlling his impulses to masturbate in the hour, his masturbatory use of the analysis as a consolation and as a focus of his excitement, and finally to approach his wishful fantasy of getting inside me as an idealized source of gratification, safety, and comfort. In the course of this work Mr. A. reported another dream in which he traversed a labyrinthine path through many dangers, finally to discover a word in code on the wall saying, translated, "The End." He then became aware of an anxiety consequent on the belief that if he talked about homosexuality and masturbation with me, he should talk about it with everyone else and act on it as well. This was for him a dramatic demonstration of what he had unconsciously felt to be the magical power of words. It was a reflection of his identification with his most secretive father, and of the idea that letting something out would leave him depleted and vulnerable.

This piece of analysis threw into relief Mr. A.'s efforts to control me and our work by editing his associations and by isolating his feelings. The fantasy emerged that I controlled him and his life and thus we were bound close together. Because of the timing and the desperate quality of his controlling efforts, it began to occur to me that, perhaps more important than the anal aspects of his character, Mr. A. might have had to contend with very early fears related to traumatic separations in childhood.

Confirmation of this idea seemed to appear as the summer holiday approached and Mr. A. complained he felt the analysis was moving too fast and would be over too soon, and that something awful would then happen. The same features again became dramatically apparent in the fourteenth month of analysis when, approaching the next holiday, he became aware that he was anxiously reaching for some kind of response from me. This culminated in a second occurrence of the keenly experienced feeling that I had suddenly disappeared, that there was a hole where I had been. Mr. A. felt some anxiety at this moment and then reported that it was almost as if he enjoyed this feeling of anxiety. I said that his anxiety actually seemed to relieve and reassure him that *he* was still there. To this I added it seemed likely that as a child he had had a number of experiences similar to those he had with me in which he felt let down by his mother, in that he felt her not to be reliably safe, supportive, or even understanding, and that he managed to be reassured at those times that the pain of his anxiety meant that he was still alive.

Before presenting the patient's responses to this reconstruction, I will pause to sum up my impressions at this point in the analysis. The patient's relationship to his mother was reflected in mother figures as seen in his relationships to his wife and past and present girl friends, and in the development of the transference. A yearning for his father was present as well, not so much as a man and a person as for the admiration, approval, and confirmation that he received abundantly from his mother, beginning before the age of two when he became the center of attention in his intellectual performances which brought glory to her. Clearly he felt he received very little emotional warmth from either parent in his rewards for these exhibitions. Mr. A. seemed to need these kinds of responses from me too, most particularly on the approach of separations in the analysis. When my responses were inadequate for his needs, he experienced the anxiety and sudden sense of my absence that I have described.

What I have not so far brought out concerns Mr. A.'s difficulties in sustaining any empathic kind of relationship with his wife, colleagues, or girl friends, after initially promising beginnings. While the haughty, cold aloofness of some narcissistic personalities was absent in Mr. A.'s character, a sense of moral superiority and the typical anal traits of obstinacy, frugality, and orderliness were clearly there. He could handle neither time nor money rationally. He collected clocks and compulsively kept them on time but was himself habitually late for everything. He was repeatedly in financial difficulties, withholding his payments to me and others for months at a time, paying in one huge amount. At the outset of the analysis, he didn't know his income, charging his expenses to the company he established himself, and drawing money as needed for other purposes, but in fact spending significantly below what his income would warrant. This incidentally recreated his relationship to his father who never gave him a regular sum but insisted that Mr. A. come to him whenever he needed money, and gave just what was required. Early triadic relationships, in which Mr. A. competed with his older brother and father for his mother's adoration by exhibitionistic displays of his powerful intellect and retentive memory, were repeated with his girl friends both before and after marriage, and in courting his wife. The narcissistic humiliation he suffered when his wife made it clear that an older man was a better lover than he, demonstrated how he so often seemed to believe that he had won an oedipal victory[1] in many areas, but these were tenuous victories constantly in need of being rewon. Faced with a battle which he could not deny having lost, he was somehow able to endure the humiliation of asking another person for help when he asked for analysis.

The last point in this summary of my impressions is as follows: Interpretations along the lines of his exclusive wish to possess the mother for whom he also felt contempt, his guilt over his sexual wishes for his mother, and fear of father's retaliation for his murderous wishes toward him, and the safety of an identification with the mother and of a homosexual position, were acknowledged by Mr. A. as making sense to him but not emotional sense. The obstacles in the way of further analysis of Mr. A.'s oedipal instinctual life and object relations appeared to me to have two origins. The first is related to Reich's (1949) description of the resistance of the "phallic-narcissistic

---

[1] "Among analyzable individuals, at least, a narcissist might be defined as one who has to reorganize his life around the belief that he has won an oedipal victory" (Spruiell, 1974, p. 276).

character,"[2] which in Mr. A.'s case seemed more closely linked to fears of loss of the object rather than to castration anxiety, as evidenced by his fantasies of our being bound closely together, for example, and by his sudden sense of my disappearance at particular times. I came to understand that his requirements of me in the developing transference reflected an intense hunger for a globally idealized object. Thus any transference interpretations were reacted to as a disturbance of this need or else deflected in a variety of ways. The second resistance, related to the first, was a consequence of Mr. A.'s pervasive tendency to intellectualize[3] and this required me to be cautious in making interpretations without access to the patient's genuine feelings and the availability of abundantly clear material.

Now to return to the clinical scene. In response to my having reconstructed the reassuring function of his feeling anxious, Mr. A. began to talk of his experiences of separations from his mother. A pattern emerged in which we could see how he came to take an active role in leaving women who had grown attached to him, or in engineering their leaving him, rather than be taken unawares by their sudden departures. In the course of this work, he found his third woman friend since the beginning of analysis, a person who was noted for her promiscuity but with whom he managed to maintain a relationship in spite of feelings of intense jealousy because of her continuing contact with her many former lovers. Soon the patient reported a dream that he was a little boy again, eating cereal in the kitchen at home. After telling the dream, he recalled that at the age of four years two months he was sent to school for the first time. The family lived about two blocks from the school but the patient had

---

[2] "The analysis is always successful if one succeeds in unmasking the phallic–narcissistic attitudes as a defense against passive–feminine tendencies and in eliminating the unconscious tendency of revenge against the other sex. If one does not succeed in this, the patients remain in their narcissistic inaccessibility. Their character resistance consists in aggressive deprecation of the analysis and the analyst in more or less disguised forms, a narcissistic taking over of the interpretive work, and in the denial of and defense against any passive or apprehensive tendency and particularly the positive transference" [Reich, 1949, pp. 206–207].

[3] Abraham (1919) has given an apt description of this form of resistance exemplified by Mr. A.'s efforts to be a model patient by preplanning his communications and by always having something to say. Of such patients he says:

> They speak as though according to programme, and do not bring forward their material freely. Contrary to the fundamental rule of analysis they arrange what they say according to certain lines of thought and subject it to extensive criticism and modification on the part of the ego. They seem to show an extraordinarily eager, never-wearying readiness to be psycho-analysed. Their resistance is hidden behind a show of willingness [p. 304].

never been there before. Even though he wanted her to, his mother did not take the patient on the first day because it was laundry day. She took great pride in doing her laundry by hand although machines were available, and she boasted that her laundry was the cleanest on the block. The patient manfully and without protest trudged through the rain to school only to be told he looked too young, and that he should go home and get his birth certificate. He came home crying only to be met by an unsympathetic mother who gave him the certificate, turned him around, and sent him off again.

Mr. A. reflected on how incredible it was that such a little child should be sent to school for the first time alone, when, like a curtain dropping, he began to idealize the experience as being a marvelous one, making for great independence. At the same time, he began to have fantasies of killing his girl friend and dismembering the body, then having intercourse with it. He recalled having a similar fantasy twelve years before when living alone. There were many features in this memory of going to school and in the jealousy of his woman friend's attachment to other men which enabled us to understand better his murderous fury toward his mother, a fury which was frequently but not always expressed in phallic terms. As we gradually came to see, the episodes of fury toward a "loved" woman followed after he felt that he had been treated by her with a surprising, almost intrusive indifference on her part. Only on a few occasions were these experiences linked with the woman's interest in another man.

Mr. A. provided some background with which to understand this material by telling me for the first time of his childhood enuresis. Until the age of six, he said, he wet his bed quite frequently. He told me that when his mother tried to cure the enuresis by giving him cold showers, he screamed and protested but finally resolved to end his discomfort, stopped screaming and stopped wetting. The sublimation of the patient's erotic urethral pleasures thus seemed to be strongly linked with feeling brutally treated at the hands of a woman. The sight of his cold and shriveled penis and his deep feeling of murderous revenge toward his mother were connected with efforts to recover his humiliated phallic potency.

From this time on, the patient became an avid reader in an attempt to quench his insatiable curiosity. He was a living example of the belief that knowledge is power and found himself living out the equation "intellect equals penis." He quoted a motto that he adopted from a book he read, "The best thing for being sad is to learn." He said that from childhood he would sometimes become conscious of homosexual feelings toward a boy or a man, accompanied by a wish to fondle or kiss the other person's penis. But most of the time while not conscious of this side of the equation, Mr. A. felt attracted to men whom he felt showed intellectual potency and he found himself wishing to come into contact with this aspect of them mentally, comparing his power with theirs. If he felt himself finally to be the stronger, he experienced a short-lived elation. If they were stronger, he attached himself to the man in sycophantic fashion. Needless to say, the transference reflected the many vicissitudes of this aspect of his life.

Mr. A. was aware of his mother's investment in his precocious intellect, and her attention together with his mental functioning provided him many pleasures, protections, and compensations from early childhood. From this material, and from an example from the age of eleven, I wondered if Mr. A.'s intelligence may have served him as a kind of latter-day transitional object. As for the example, one day Mr. A. described his belief that there was nothing he could not do if he set his mind to it, and at the age of eleven this was put to the test by his attempting to read a textbook on electronics. After the first ten or twelve pages, he discovered he could go no farther and was stumped, chiefly because he did not have the mathematics at his command necessary to understand the material. He felt with much humiliation that this was his first failure, and he felt totally abandoned by his intellect just as if it had been taken away.

A safeguard against such traumatic experiences developed in the formula of never saying to himself, or anyone else, that he planned to accomplish a particular task because this "killed off" the ability to do it. This safeguard also protected his grandiose fantasies of perfection, which were now more frequently related in the analytic sessions. For example, in regard to his work, he often said that no one could do the job "right," whatever the job, but only *he* could. I understood this to be linked with his childhood experiences, particularly as we began to see that he did not always feel so very well taken care of as a child. I interpreted that he was telling me that only he could do his analysis, not me; and that it was not only that no one but he could do a job "right," but only he could keep himself alive. I went on to interpret his wish to find the omnipotent object who could take perfect care of him but that now, just as when a child, he would repeatedly find himself disillusioned and have to fall back on his own resources as he so often felt he had to do in the analysis.

The patient responded to this reconstruction over the next several weeks with an immense sense of well-being, feeling as if a load had been lifted. It was as if, for a time at least, he had temporarily given up some of his grandiose fantasies and the demands that these fantasies imposed on him. He seemed very much to relate to me now as an emotionally starved child might, taking in my every word. He said, "Your words are a revelation to me," and he wondered if we could meet on weekends. Mr. A. acted out his transference wishes with his mistress and told me how he would voraciously take her in via his eyes during intercourse and he became conscious of a wish to curl up inside her. He remembered that when he was about four, his mother had a practice of lying down beside him until he fell asleep for his afternoon nap. She would then get up and go about her business. The particular day in question he remembers waking, finding his mother gone, feeling an intense sense of abandonment, searching anxiously for her throughout the house and going out on his tricycle and sadly riding up and down the sidewalk looking for her.

About this time, the patient's life with his colleagues was made more difficult by his outbreaks of rage which were so severe that during them he could hardly breathe. These outbursts were associated with feelings that he had been betrayed by one or another of his partners. Along with this went fantasies of leaving them all—leaving his company, leaving his analysis, and cutting his own throat with a knife. His fantasized perfect or ideal man never became so uncontrollably angry, and Mr. A. was most distressed at this departure from his strict standards. Using these memories, fantasies and feelings, I could show him the connections between the way he handled his feelings of rage currently, and the way he split off his feelings of helpless abandonment, subsequent rage, sadness, and then self-sufficiency beginning in childhood. I also had in mind the negative transference and his well-defended anger against me, and I went on to interpret that his loss of feelings before and after separations in the analysis were a way of destroying me in retaliation. I said that this repeated with me the way in which he would become the active one and destructively abandon the people who became attached to him like he had felt abandoned before, much as he had seen his father doing to the family. Shortly after this, the patient announced he was leaving for two weeks on a business trip, with the conscious wish to prove that he was not dependent on me. He said, "I have no belief whatsoever in what you say about separations."

Returning to analysis, Mr. A. reported that on the day before resuming his sessions, he had had an anxiety attack with the idea that I wouldn't be at the first session waiting for him. Then, as if to try out the validity of this experience as well as to reassure himself that by leaving me he did not destroy me, he left on his Easter holiday two days before I left on mine. This time he returned with feelings that he had lost me and the analysis, suffering what he called "an infinite depression" and again fantasizing suicide. In our discussing his intense feelings of loneliness, I wondered if he had also felt that I had asked him to take care of himself too much and too soon. The patient profoundly agreed with this, saying that he felt I should have prevented him from leaving. He went on to tell me that he now understood more about why he delayed his payment of fees. He had a wish that I would take care of him for love and not for money, and in fact he had the fantasy that I was very rich and didn't need the money at all. This wish and the indebtedness that resulted also served as a way to ward off separation, and he could see one of the reasons why he has continued to owe a small sum of money to his father for many years.

Just before the summer holiday, nearing the end of the second year of analysis, the patient was able to describe that his picture of me was of someone very much like him, a coprofessional, but one who did not have any of the many faults that he did, and one who indeed represented the ideal he would like to achieve for himself. But then some feelings of anger and resentment toward me began to surface, connected with the thought that the only way to achieve the ideal state he had just described would be for him to do the analysis perfectly himself, without me, and himself to become an analyst. Of course, we had gone over this ground before but Mr. A. seemed unaware of it at this point, and it seemed to have a different quality to it. In any event, the summer vacation was about to begin, and in the last session, he said he felt that if he retained his anger he became energetic, and it gave him a drive to organize and to perform, just like the retaining of his feces.

After the summer vacation, Mr. A. volunteered that, for him, analysis is the kind of "pain in the ass" that he likes, and that he was aware of having missed me and the analysis. While there was little evidence to confirm it at the time, it seemed to me as if I had become part of the patient just as his retained feces had served to help him maintain a sense of control over himself, and especially as a separate person. The issue of his anal homosexual transference is yet another theme, but I want to return to the topics of idealization and of reconstruction in keeping with the aims of this paper.

Mr. A. continued his description of various ideal self-images he has had over the years, gradually revealing more ideas of grandiosity and omnipotence illustrated from segments of his past and current life. This material began to emerge in the second year of treatment and could be linked up with more clearly oedipal themes. There were many such waves of narcissistic concerns, followed by periods in which his involvement in triadic situations was paramount, and in which his feelings of rivalry, jealousy, and anxiety *vis-à-vis* the analyst and other important persons in his life formed the focus of the analytic work. Transitions to this latter kind of material were often marked by the appearance of defenses which involved me. For example, at one point I sensed I was caught up in a countertransference reaction in which the patient and I were analyzing a third person. I told the patient it seemed to me that for a while we had been analyzing somebody else. Among his subsequent associations, he began to recall experiences which involved his older brother, how much he had admired him and wanted to be like him, and even to surpass him, and he remembered how proud his mother was of this brother. He was abashed to realize that he had never really gotten into this very important topic in the past three years. In retrospect I could see how the narcissistic preoccupations for some time had served as a resistance to analyzing the subsequently appearing oedipal themes and conflicts, in this instance, rivalry with the older brother.

In regard to Mr. A.'s images of his ideal self, or selves, I will summarize the material which gradually emerged, delineating two sets of antithetical images beginning in childhood. He continued to feel confronted with both images, first striving toward one and then the other. Very briefly, one is represented by a football star, a tycoon heading a conference of business leaders, a perfect scholar getting perfect marks, an orderly man who plunges in and makes order out of things. In spite of the male gender attributed to this image, many of its elements were derived from his experience of his mother. One day he remarked, "You are just that kind of a person, quite suitable for an analyst!" However, Mr. A. more often felt contempt for this image, a feeling which persisted whichever goal he strove for, and which was manifested in the transference often enough. When the patient cast himself in this first image he would allow people to come to love him unconditionally, and then he would leave them, or feel them to be worthless because they loved him.

The second image was of a reclusive person who enjoyed his private pleasures in solitary fashion, a professor, contemptuous of the first type, but a brilliant and inspired scatterbrain followed by a retinue of people who clean up the mess. He described a childhood fantasy in which he believed there was great knowledge hidden in the works of certain writers and, in coming to understand them, he felt he would gain great power especially in his relationships with others. He would be withdrawn and aloof, a nonparticipating observer in life, and his power would give him immense perception and understanding of the world. Mr. A. told how this omnipotent knowledge depended on a precious store of power to "know" something instantly and perfectly without having to calculate, to think, or to look it up. However, it was always important to conserve this precious store of power because using it up would leave him helpless and powerless, and he made it clear that this fantasy was still influencing him. One of the ways the basic fantasy was manifested was in the belief of power being enhanced by the incorporation of the penis, the incorporation being accomplished by oral, anal, or other modes such as by learning, while the penis itself appeared concretely in dreams, fantasies, and in displaced forms such as powerful and desirable motor cars, planes, or knowledge.

At this point, Mr. A.'s associations took up the theme of the "ideal woman," especially those attributes in his wife which had led him to believe she fulfilled this role, and he described similar fantasies about my wife. He had an anxiety dream in which a woman appeared with an uncircumcised penis. He next recalled an incident in adolescence; while working in a photographic darkroom, he cut off the end of a finger. At the sight of blood he almost fainted and felt he was losing his mind. He also remembered shamefully how he avoided a close boyfriend during latency after this boy had become crippled by polio. His fears that I would take away his intellectual potency through the analysis became more clear and for some weeks the analytic work centered around the further interpretation and working through of his castration anxiety. While this encompassed early fears of his father's unpredictable rages and his identification with this aspect of his father, his infantile sexual wishes seemed as remote from the analytic work as ever.

The intense repression to which these sexual wishes had been subjected was evident in his description of his forcing himself to masturbate at the age of fifteen, "to find out what it was like," allegedly never having done it before. Up to this time, he said he "knew nothing" about sex, and only now did it strike him as rather remarkable that he had preserved this gap in his knowledge while taking in so much information about so much else. At age sixteen, while at university, he attempted to have intercourse with a girl but was humiliated to find himself impotent. It was two years before he tried again, but his attitude toward academic learning was now characterized by the need to make "no effort." He played endless card games, sunbathed, and in general gave the appearance of magically producing the needed knowledge necessary to obtain his degree. When he was able to have successful sexual intercourse, and especially after he impregnated one girl, Mr. A. was also then capable of studying and working in the more conventional fashion, though some of the magical intellectual potency fantasy continued.

During the third year of treatment, following much analytic work on his castration anxiety and his homosexual fears and feelings, Mr. A. reported beneficial changes in his life, changes which he attributed to the analysis. These included a remarkable shift in his relationship to his father with whom he was surprised to find he could talk in a friendly way without anxiety, less overwhelming curiosity about his woman friend's sexual activities with other men, and a somewhat more reasonable attitude in his work and the financial affairs of his business. But now the focus of the analytic work again revolved predominantly around themes of the patient's disturbances in narcissistic development and in object relations, though with more apparent oedipal coloring.

For example, Mr. A. described a fantasy from the age of nine in which he believed himself to be a concealed prince of the English royal family, and that some day he would be discovered and made King of England. He recognized that a current partial derivative of this fantasy was that he would come across a "bonanza" in his work and suddenly become as rich as Howard Hughes. What made his family romance fantasy feasible for him was a family legend that his father was a foundling, therefore possibly not Jewish, but clearly in fantasy the source of Mr. A.'s concealed power. The possession of an uncircumcised penis was therefore a precious store of potency. By marrying a non-Jewish girl who had affairs with non-Jewish men, and by repeating this circumstance with many girls, as well as by "taking in" an analyst he was convinced was also not Jewish, Mr. A. revealed how he attempted to redress the narcissistic injuries of his early years via his homosexual feelings and fantasies as well as by the phallic grandiosity of the fantasies on which he based his life. Thus further analysis of his homosexuality was followed by the appearance of renewed longings for his father together with wishes to spend more time with me and the sensation that the analysis was clearly not just limited to the analytic hour. Less depressed, he felt as if his emotions were now in color, as it were, instead of black and white, and in his words, it seemed to him that "the arctic ice was breaking up."

With the increased sense of well-being and power that came with these developments, Mr. A. one day expressed the not unfamiliar idea that he didn't really need analysis and that in any event he was the only one who could do it. But he thought it must really be a pleasure for me to have such a talented patient as he was. These pleasurable feelings of absolute efficiency and invincibility were soon rudely interrupted during a session in which I stumbled in my speech. It took a week for the patient to tell me how shocked he was, "as if a rock had dropped" on his head. He felt that even telling me about it was too grossly aggressive. Painful lonely feelings now developed, and he recognized that he had learned to expect this when threatened with the loss of his feelings of omnipotence, just as with the threat of the loss of his intellect. But I was puzzled by the intensity and extent of his response to what was certainly not the only nor the first demonstration of my fallibility. Earlier analytic work gave the background which suggested that this was another example of Mr. A.'s narcissistic rage which had contributed significantly to his suicide fantasies. These fantasies, however, had not appeared for over a year, and it occurred to me that the unusually direct focusing of this rage on me, and his attempts to protect me against it, might actually be an indication of analytic progress in the narcissistic sphere. Yet the concrete description of his shocking experience, preceded as it was by agreeable feelings of my taking pleasure in his talents, strongly conveyed to me a sense of these events being a reenactment of some childhood experience which included his having been "dropped."

In the weeks that followed, Mr. A. was more aloof and distant than usual, with occasional feelings of anger and resentment toward me. He dreamed his car was stolen and he couldn't reach me because his phone was dead. He had a fleeting fantasy of a body without a head, a hole being where the neck should be, which I interpreted in the transference, in terms of his feelings of my disappointing him and of his destructive wishes toward me. He tried to "run" the analysis, saying he no longer felt the obligation to bring all his thoughts to me. He began to feel that I was going to tell him something absolutely terrible. After some time, following his expression of concern that he should do something to prevent his business from "falling apart," I said that it seemed he was trying to protect himself against a painful surprise, and that his feeling distrustful of my being able to "hold" him safely in the analytic situation suggested that as a child he had had a painful experience of being dropped. With a rush of feeling, Mr. A. recounted a story he had blithely told me two years before, but which he could now date to a time just after his fourth birthday, two months before the painful experience of first going to school without his mother's support.

In the story as he now told it, his parents were taking him and his sister by car to their maternal grandparents for a week while they went on holiday alone. He and his sister, who was asleep, were in the back seat. He was playing with the door handle, the door opened and he fell out onto the center of the highway. According to what he was told later, neither of his parents noticed his disappearance for some miles, when they turned around and went back to find him lying on the other side of the road. Mr. A. experienced peculiar dizzy feelings in going over this event, and a diffuse anxiety. He recalled a fantasy from latency of being impaled on the hood ornaments of cars, like a bullfighter impaled on the horns of a bull. He remembered his efforts at the age of five and after, of trying to learn how to drive a car even to the extent of turning on the engine when the keys were left in the ignition, before his feet could reach the pedals. In short, this memory had come to serve for him an organizing function in which a number of his preoedipal conflicts, narcissistic disappointments, and the anxieties evoked by his mother's actually life-threatening indifference came together with a number of his contemporary oedipal conflicts. With such an organization of his experiences, it seemed he was then better able to employ his considerable natural endowments in a life-long attempt to control his environment in an effort to make it safe, to anticipate the unexpected, even to bring about near-catastrophic situations of abandonment, academic, or financial disaster. From these he would repeatedly rescue himself with feelings that he was truly alone in this world and should never again rely on anyone else, and that the risk of striving for the idealized object of his oedipal desires was too great.

Discussion

A great deal of clinical material is required to provide sufficient background for the demonstration of a reconstruction. In Mr. A.'s case this makes it possible to discuss related aspects, such as the role of his gifted intellect in skewing his developmental progress, beginning preoedipally. The analytic work helped him understand some of these effects as well as the many meanings of the power of his mind and the uses to which he put it.

Often encouraged by Mahler's work (Mahler, Pine, and Bergman, 1975), many authors have contended that preoedipal determinants constitute an integral part of the infantile neurosis (Blum, 1977; Coltrera, 1980; Tyson and Tyson, 1990). The interweaving of persisting preoedipal with oedipal themes in this patient's analysis is permeated by the effects of his precocious intelligence, and the samples of reconstructions made in the course of his treatment, facilitating the analytic work, support Rangell's declaration that "reconstruction has always been to the oedipal and preoedipal period" (1980, p. 92).

James (1960) sheds some light on the reasons why intelligence might develop precociously rather than in a balanced, phase-appropriate manner, and Keiser (1969) has thoroughly discussed the ways in which superior intelligence participates in the formation of neurotic conflicts. Analysts often seem to assume that superior intelligence necessarily entails precocious intellectual development, but clinical experience makes clear that no such simple relationship exists. In James's case the infant's early feeding experiences, including interchanges with her caretakers, significantly influenced many aspects of her later personality development and prompted the precocious development of her intelligence in ways that made it appear to be a constitutional given. In the present case, there were indications of a high family intellectual endowment as well as some hints that the mother's on-going depression in addition to her sometimes bizarre child care attitudes might have contributed to an accelerated mental unfolding in the cognitive sphere. Keiser gives examples of how cognitive precocity confronts the small child with problems for which they are emotionally unprepared, experiences which came to light later on in Mr. A.'s analysis.

It is no surprise that a family's reactions to a gifted child's intellectual feats influence the child's development and his attitude to his own mental powers. However, different from Mr. A., Keiser's cases had what he called a "destructive attitude" toward their intellects, even if their families' attitudes in this regard were positive. Mr. A. was expected from the beginning to perform at a high level, having been preceded by a brother with notable intelligence and other members of the family being similarly distinguished. Just like his family, he expected his mind to perform faultlessly and regarded it with affection since it seemed to him so often to respond as he wished. Thus he repeated in the relationship to his own mind the relationship of his family, especially his mother, to him. His response to what he viewed as a failure of his mind at age eleven, when he was unable to comprehend mathematics for which he was not prepared, illustrates several aspects of this relationship.

First, the powerful threat of abandonment can be read in Mr. A.'s analytic material, not lessened as his development proceeded, and concretely represented in the experiences of suddenly feeling I had disappeared. Next, the safeguards he adopted to protect against the threat of abandonment and the resulting pervasive fury involved both a turning of aggression against himself and a form of denial in fantasy in the refusal to acknowledge any ambition, aim, or objective so as to avoid the risk of intellectual failure. And finally, in this, his intellect was like his mother whose sudden and unexplained disappearances formed a leitmotif in his life and thoughts. His perfectly functioning mind was like a bridge to his mother in her absence, like Winnicott's (1953) transitional object. Its failure was felt as if he were being abandoned by her, as my failures to be perfect were concretely felt in the analytic sessions as my disappearances. The reconstruction of his early experience of being dropped then gave him renewed access to the affect attached to his organizing screen memory of falling out of the car. This marked a turning point in the analysis which subsequently proceeded to other areas by means of the complex interaction between interpretation and reconstruction (Kris, 1956a,b), including the regressive homosexual love for his father, the several sources of his insistent rage and destructive impulses, and the consequences of his precociously heightened perceptual acuity.

Summary

By presenting aspects of the analysis of Mr. A., I have illustrated the role of the analyst's reconstructions in enhancing and facilitating the analytic process. I have traced the way in which Mr. A.'s precocious intelligence was involved in the development of a defensive narcissistic "shell" which represented far-reaching efforts to deal with profound disappointments in his early object relationships, especially with his mother. The evolution of the analytic work with the patient showed slow swings between preoedipal and narcissistically centered material, on the one hand, and rather clear-cut oedipal conflicts, on the other. The transference evolution illustrates how the later conflicts were always colored and deeply influenced by the earlier ones. Although the patient's suicide fantasies disappeared and his ability to work improved, only extended analytic work enabled his ability to love to surmount the burden of early infantile rage with which he had to cope.

9

Basic Technical Suggestions for Dream Interpretation

Alexander Grinstein, M.D.

I N the course of the first volume of his book, *The Technique and Practice of Psychoanalysis*, Ralph Greenson cited many excellent examples from his analytic practice to illustrate how various facets of the individual's dynamics are revealed in dreams. His eminently convincing examples, presented in an inimitably readable style, are so typical of him that they clearly reveal his charm and his relationship to his patients. Candidates and even more experienced analysts often wonder how they could emulate his work in their approach to the dreams which their patients bring into their therapeutic sessions.

The purpose of this chapter is to outline various technical suggestions in a concise and systematic way to help the therapist in his work with dreams. In general, I have followed the basic organization of my book, *Freud's Rules of Dream Interpretation* (1983). Bibliographic citations, references, additional technical suggestions, and examples may be found in that work.

Dreams in psychoanalytic therapy are but one of the many sources of material that are used by the analyst to help his patient. In his book

Greenson uses examples of patients' dreams to demonstrate where the patient was in the treatment and to confirm or elaborate the analyst's understanding of what was going on. Yet, even though at times dream material may help the analyst to feel more comfortable in his understanding of the patient, we must emphasize that under no circumstances should it be regarded as having such an inordinately special value that when the patient does not bring up dreams for a period of time, there is nothing of value taking place in the treatment. Freud (1900) wrote that "the interpretation of dreams is the royal road to a knowledge of the unconscious activities of the mind" (p. 608). But, we may add, they are by no means the only road, nor are they necessarily a paved highway.

To be sure, if a patient brings in no dreams, at some appropriate time it would be proper for the analyst to ask him if he has any dreams. It has been generally agreed, however, that if a patient brings in no dreams whatsoever in the course of a lengthy therapy, this may indicate some serious ego disturbance or major resistance.

The subject of recall of dreams is invariably raised by patients early in their treatment. They ask if they should record their dreams, either by writing them down or by dictating them into a tape recorder. Such procedures are contraindicated as they only create further resistances. Besides, if one deals with the patient's resistances, the recollection of dreams often finds its way into the material. The point is that we are not really interested in having a patient preserve his dreams, nor is their content as important as the material that lies behind them.

Generally near the beginning of an analysis, patients will bring up a dream unless, as I said earlier, there are serious problems associated with the recollection of dream material. Initial dreams are very important as they immediately alert the therapist to the patient's underlying problems and may indicate the nature of his early manifestations of transference and resistance. Often they spell out the determinants of the patient's neurosis in condensed form. Because initial dreams are so significant, it is generally a good idea for the therapist to acknowledge this by some appropriate comment even if the specific content cannot be adequately understood, or the patient is not ready to deal with all that the dream may reveal.

When a patient brings in an initial dream, it is essential to inquire what he knows about dreams and how to work with them. It is self-evident that whatever explanation the therapist gives the patient or whatever suggestions he makes will depend upon his patient's knowledge and sophistication about dreams.

For those persons who are not sophisticated about dreams, a brief explanation is in order, one best couched in simple terms, indicating that dreams in an analysis are a means of communication that patients use to tell the therapist about themselves. We tell the patient that he may disregard the story line of the dream and proceed to relate whatever comes into his mind about any of the parts or elements of the dream. He may begin sequentially from the very beginning of his dream, or he may choose any element in the dream that is particularly vivid or impressive to him, or the very opposite, one that is especially vague; or, he may begin with an element that has to do with something connected with the dream day. This may be something he saw, heard, said, or read. The last suggestion is valuable because there is always at least one element in the dream that refers to the dream day. By calling attention to this, the therapist is able to bring the analytic process into a close connection with the patient's life. Moreover, in every dream that is reported during the course of therapy there is at least one element that contains some reference to the previous analytic session. This then enables the therapist to maintain a continuity between the previous session and the present one. In this way, the patient is helped to observe the flow of material from one session to the next rather than regarding each session as separate and entirely unrelated to the one that preceded it.

Sometimes in the course of the session a patient may recollect a piece of the dream that had not occurred to him before, or that he had not mentioned earlier when relating his dream. It is then a good idea to turn one's attention to this new piece of dream. The reason for this is that apparently certain resistances have been overcome and the patient, by bringing up the additional dream material, is, in effect, indicating that he is now ready to deal with the underlying material with which this particular dream is connected.

While these suggestions are helpful in getting the patient started in his work with dreams, especially early in an analysis, as time goes on and the patient is more familiar with working with his dreams, he will spontaneously associate to various dream elements as they occur to him.

It need not be of concern to the therapist if the patient ignores the dream altogether but continues his associations along some other line of his choice. It may well be that while the dream reveals much about what is going on in his unconscious at the time, the patient's primary concerns relate to some current reality problem. That is what is on his mind, what he wants to talk about and what the therapist must deal with. The unconscious can wait! Other dreams will occur that deal with the same topic. There is an exception to this, however. If the content of the manifest dream suggests that there is a serious problem of a threatening nature or some major resistance, the therapist must address himself to that matter.

While the therapist considers the patient's associations to the various dream elements, there are other matters to which he must pay close attention. He must not neglect the patient's general demeanor, his parenthetical remarks, his changes of posture and his other behavior. When the patient's behavior coincides with some element in the dream, it is important for the therapist to point out the connection.

In one instance a patient arrived ten minutes late for his appointment. He apologized stating that he was delayed because of a traffic tie-up and besides his alarm clock did not go off on time. Then he related that he had had a dream the night before in which he had a business appointment for which he was ten minutes late. It was possible to point out to him the connection between his coming late for his analytic appointment and his coming late for his business appointment in the dream.

We said earlier that no special emphasis should be placed on dreams which a patient brings into his treatment. Nevertheless, the associations to specific elements in the manifest dream content are very important as they may allude to present-day situations that are of particular significance to the patient, to important historical events or experiences in his life; to fantasies or thoughts that he may be hesitant to discuss. Also included among these are the patient's attitude about his therapy and/or therapist. The therapist should be particularly aware of any dream material that indicates the patient's hesitations or anxieties about the treatment or about the therapist. When these are pointed out and discussed openly with the patient, there is often a sense of relief and a reduction in tension as he realizes that his hesitations and doubts may be freely talked about. As a consequence, the working alliance between the patient and the therapist improves. The therapist's candor in dealing with material that may be difficult or offensive to the patient encourages the revelation of painful or embarrassing material and is beneficial in resolving the patient's neurotic problems.

There may be a negative side to this in some instances as the patient may feel that his therapist is unduly insightful and that his dreams have been too revealing. As a result, the patient may stop having dreams altogether or may have heightened resistance to further exploration. In these instances the therapist is required to deal appropriately with the resistances from whatever available material is at hand.

Basically, the problem is that while dreams in therapy serve as a means of communication between the patient and the therapist, a part of the patient's personality is dedicated toward concealing precisely the very material which has been responsible for his difficulties.

Thus far we have considered rather general matters in connection with the interpretation of dreams. Let us now explore some of the more complicated and challenging aspects of dreams. The therapist, in his efforts to understand his patient's dreams, must appreciate that any element in the manifest content of the dream must be considered from *four* different standpoints: (1) whether it is to be taken at "face value" that is, in a positive sense or whether it is to be viewed by its opposite meaning; (2) whether it is to be considered historically; (3) whether its interpretation depends on its wording; or (4) whether it is to be considered symbolically.

In connection with the first of these considerations, whether a dream element should be viewed in a positive or negative sense, I am reminded of the following incidents.

Many years ago Ralph Greenson gave a lecture before the Michigan Psychoanalytic Society. As he talked, he paced back and forth, cigar in hand, in a kind of a Groucho Marx manner. Then he stopped abruptly and said in his characteristic way: "You know, after all, psychoanalysis must be a Jewish science. Why is it a Jewish science? Because only a Jew would think that if a patient said 'Things are terrible,' that there must be something good. And the reverse is also true. If the patient said everything is going well, the analyst should think, 'So, what's wrong.' " Naturally, the audience was much amused.

On another occasion, in an address to the Michigan Association for Psychoanalysis, Theodor Reik spoke of the Talmudic approach in dealing with difficult dreams. That meant, he said, when something was not understandable one should "Turn it about" or "Turn it around" in the spirit of the Talmudic scholars.

Whether the "Jewish approach" applies or not, the fact remains that in many instances a dream element must be considered both from the standpoint of how it appears, as well as by its opposite.

The existence of polarities in the unconscious facilitates the consideration of any element from both standpoints, as "to love or be loved" or "to love or to hate," "to look at or to be looked at," "to attack or to be attacked." The reversal of impulses is especially prevalent in those instances where an unconscious impulse must be repressed because it is too anxiety-producing. Patients, especially men, find the wish to attack or to take the active role in sex relations much more ego syntonic than the passive component of such impulses. Knowing that the passive component is more frightening and ego alien alerts the therapist to be on the lookout for such possibilities and to be especially careful in bringing them up to his patient. Discussion of passive impulses requires timing and tact. Presentation of such formulations must be made from the standpoint of the side of the ego rather than as a direct confrontation of an id wish. An expression such as "You are afraid that I am going to assault you" is much more ego syntonic than saying to a frightened patient, "You want me to assault you." This technical suggestion is well demonstrated by many examples in Greenson's book.

Dreams in which one element is reversed often have other elements reversed as well. Sometimes it occurs because of a dreamer's style and many of the elements in his dreams are reversed. Dreams in which there is reversal of elements frequently deal with passive homosexual wishes and fantasies.

At times, dreams in which the subject and object are reversed indicate that the dreamer is using projection as a mechanism of defense. If this is the case, then it is the defense mechanism that must be considered first, before any effort is made to deal with the specific content.

In general, the consideration of an element from a historical standpoint is much easier to deal with than one which must be viewed from both a positive and a negative standpoint. Historical events include all past events from any period in the dreamer's life including recent events. Attention to past events helps to bring about an understanding of the patient's life and is particularly useful in reconstructing early determinants that have a bearing upon his problems.

In one instance a man had a lengthy dream in which the setting had to do with long tables and men sitting behind them. When asked about this particular element, his initial reaction was a very casual one. "Oh!" he said, "It reminds me of the draft board where I went after World War II was declared. I had been called up for induction and the setting in the dream reminds me of going before the draft board and being given an appointment to get a physical for induction." At this point he stopped and it was obvious that he was reluctant to pursue the matter. Encouraged to proceed, he said, "Well, I did have my physical and I was rejected because of a history of an allergy." While he was content with having ended his associations with this revelation, his obvious discomfort suggested that there was more to the matter. Upon investigation he then revealed that, at the time, he had been having a great deal of difficulty in his relationship to his wife. Unbeknownst to her, he went to a physician who was a friend of his and asked him to write a letter to the draft board indicating that he had been in treatment for a mild allergy but that he no longer had any symptoms. Without telling his wife or anyone else he then took this letter back to the draft board and informed them that he was no longer symptomatic and that he was willing to serve in the armed forces. He was promptly inducted.

He had never told anyone what he had done because he was ashamed to have used this ruse to get into the service in order to effect a legitimate separation from his wife, whom he did not dare to leave for fear of social disapproval. At the same time he succeeded in winning the praise and admiration of his friends for serving his country, and in getting some consolation from his family for having to leave for the armed forces. After he had revealed the story, he said ruefully that he would have preferred being assigned to active duty to the hell he experienced being married to his wife, whom he could not bring himself to divorce.

While the material in this instance referred to an important historical event, it also succeeded in providing insight into the intense discord in his current marital situation. He did not feel he could admit how bad his marriage really was but covered it up by repeated protestations of how much he loved his wife and how deeply he cared for his children. He was reluctant to discuss his marital problems because he felt that if he did, he would have an extramarital affair and get a divorce. The dream thus alluded to a parallel situation in his past. He had wanted to get out of his marriage but did not dare to do anything about it. He had kept his action a secret by getting a doctor friend to facilitate his separation from his wife. There were transference implications in that parallel as he had secretly hoped and yet feared that I, or his analysis, would make it possible for him to get out of his marriage legitimately.

In another example, a woman who had been in analysis for some time dreamed of a sink over which there was a clothesline with some clothes hanging on it. She had great difficulty in talking about this dream. Finally, she revealed that the sink in her dream reminded her of a sink over which wet bathing suits were hung to dry. She then related that on one occasion she had invited her former psychotherapist to visit her at the family beach house. While he was there, they had gone skinny dipping one night and the incident had culminated in their having sexual relations. She felt so guilty about this experience that she had not revealed it before. While the dream referred to that event, there were important transference implications: that a similar situation would occur in her present therapy.

In both examples, there were allusions to material which the patients knew about and which had been so disturbing to them that they had tried to suppress it. In these instances, the material referred to events in their adult lives and dealt with situations that they were initially unwilling to discuss for fear of where such revelations would lead; for example, criticism by the analyst or sexual involvement with him.

Manifest dream elements frequently refer to specific childhood events that may have been repressed either completely or partially—relegated as it were to the fringes of the patient's memory so that they could only be recalled with a great deal of difficulty. In these instances the specific dream element, when explored, brings to light the entire painful event and with the therapist's help enables the patient to deal with it appropriately. Traumatic events are legion, but what constitutes the particular difficulty for the individual can only be ascertained from the patient's associations.

One day a woman in analysis related a dream in which she is looking out of a window and sees a figure that looks like Santa Claus standing on the ground. Her associations led to her hospitalization when she was a child. Because she had a communicable disease, she was quarantined in a hospital with a group of other children, none of whom were allowed visitors. She recalled that the nurse held her up to the window so that she could see her parents outside waving to her. It was Christmas time and her parents had left a number of toys for the hospital Santa Claus to give to her. One of the gifts she particularly remembered with a special fondness was a soft cuddly doll she kept in bed with her. When she recovered from her illness and was allowed to leave the hospital and go home, she was not allowed to take any of the toys with her. Much to her sorrow, she had to leave her cuddly doll behind. She often thought of it and, even as an adult, found herself wishing that she still had it. Her dream alluded to the entire traumatic experience of her hospitalization and her being left behind just as the doll was. It became paradigmatic for subsequent incidents of separation and loss.

One of the most interesting and delightful aspects of working with dreams is understanding the significance of words or expressions used in them. Here, the dream work makes use of mechanisms that are common in jokes, puns, and in the most primitive type of wit. It is really not technically difficult for the therapist to utilize his insight into the way some words are expressed as pictures or as phrases. A non-Jewish friend of mine, also an analyst, related the dream of a woman patient in which there was a wasp present in her underpants. The pictorial representation of the insect stood for her view of her non-Jewish analyst as a WASP (White Anglo-Saxon Protestant) and the obvious sexual wishes connected with him.

Dreams make liberal use of pictures to express ideas or thoughts. In a previous communication I reported a number of instances in which the convertible car in the manifest content of dreams in men was a switch word used to express sexual convertibility: the unconscious wish and fear of being converted from a man to a woman, from having active sexual wishes to passive ones. Since that publication I have had an opportunity to observe the same picture used in dreams to connotate a wish or a fear that the patient might be converted to another religion or to a different political persuasion.

The last specific consideration that the therapist must make with respect to a given dream element is whether it should be viewed from a symbolic standpoint. Here, our view is that the symbolic reference must include: (1) its metaphoric significance, or (2) its reference to some intimate aspect of the individual's life or body.

The first consideration of symbolism, that is, having metaphoric or allegorical meaning, is actually closely allied to or even identical with the use of the dream element in accordance with its wording. In this respect it is to be regarded as a means of representation which we will discuss shortly. We may view in this category such objects as a flag standing for the country, a church for religion, or a governmental building standing for the government itself or some agency within it, a uniform for a particular branch of service and the like. This type of symbolism must always be heeded first because there is a tendency for many therapists to jump to the other type of symbolism without due consideration for the more general applications which may be closer to what the patient had in his mind at the particular time.

The other consideration of symbolism, as it is generally understood in analytic circles, refers to the direct translation of a given dream element to mean a specific object or activity. The objects symbolized are the dreamer himself, his body as a whole or some part of it as the sexual organs, or a member of his family. In addition, certain basic aspects of life, such as sexual relations, birth and death, are also symbolized.

While a knowledge of symbolism is very important in the understanding of dreams, a direct translation of dream symbols without taking the dreamer's associations into account is a highly risky business as it bypasses any specific understanding of their significance for the individual. To avoid this, some analysts have gone to the opposite extreme by eschewing the use of symbols altogether. This, however, is also a mistake as it deprives the therapist of an important tool in his work with dreams. The understanding of symbolism should always be used as an *auxiliary method*, one that augments the understanding of a patient's associations but does not preempt them. After all, a pistol can be a pistol and refer to aggression or defense. The therapist is well advised to pay close attention to what the patient says even with the most obvious of symbols.

A Jewish businessman, in analysis for some time, had repeated affairs with women and from time to time consorted with prostitutes with whom he often adopted a passive position. One day he brought in a dream in which he sees a nude woman who was wearing a chain around her neck from which some object is suspended. His initial remark after telling the dream was, "I suppose that you will think that this was a woman with a penis. Well, she was a woman all right and very shapely and she sure didn't have a penis." After a moment's pause he said, "Say, that reminds me of a joke. There was this Jewish fellow who went to Vegas and picked up a prostitute. When they got up to the room and undressed, he noticed that she had a chain around her neck from which was suspended a Jewish star. So he said to her, 'Say, are you Jewish?' When she replied that she was, he said to her, 'So am I. How about a discount—half price.'"

The patient readily saw that this joke was an association to his dream in which the woman was wearing a chain around her neck from which some object was suspended. He could go no further, however. He had had the dream shortly after the first of the month when he had been given his monthly statement which he had not as yet paid. During the time he had been coming for treatment he had not complained about his fee but had paid his bills promptly. Initially, various attempts at exploring a connection between the joke and his analysis led nowhere and he finally said: "After all, a joke's a joke. Can't you hear a good joke without analyzing it?" It was not until some time later that the patient was able to deal with his feelings about his fee.

By his dream and his associations to it, the patient had equated his analyst, who was also Jewish, with the prostitute. The analyst had asked for one fee, but because both he and the analyst were Jewish, he had wanted to use this as a basis for having his fee reduced to half the amount. There was also a sexual implication in the material that had to do with his passive homosexual wishes in the transference.

What I want to emphasize here is that simply translating the manifest dream element of the chain and object suspended from it as a penis, which the patient actually saw himself but denied, would have led nowhere and would have only intensified his resistance to dealing with the transference situation in his analysis. What was important to take up in this material was his reaction to the fee and his inability to deal with that subject at the time. His passivity and his wish to be loved at all cost and to avoid creating the impression that he would haggle about the fee had initially prevented him from bringing up the subject.

There are typical symbols in dreams that represent members of the dreamer's family. Siblings are often represented by vermin or by small animals. Parents are represented as figures of authority of all kinds, their gender determining whether the reference is to the father or the mother. It is essential to note the specific attributes of the authority figure that are used to represent the parent—whether the figure is benevolent or cruel, loving or hateful. A patient dreamed of Alexander the Great and told me that he had been reading a book about him the night before. He spoke of him initially as the great leader, the great conqueror. Then, he recalled that he was also a cruel and violent man, that he had epileptic seizures, that he was homosexual, and that he had had incestuous relations with his mother. After some moments he realized that my name was identical to that of the great conqueror. In a condensed fashion, his dream of Alexander the Great represented me as that important historical figure whom he had elevated to greatness while at the same time attributing to me extremely negative characteristics. Actually, this proved to be identical with the highly ambivalent attitude he had about his own father. However, to interpret to the patient ad hoc that the figure of Alexander the Great in his dream stood for his father would only have facilitated his intellectualization. It would have missed many of the nuances that were expressed and were in the process of being worked through in the transference situation.

A good deal of the individual's view of himself or of important figures in his environment is expressed by symbols of the body as a whole. The human figure is often symbolized in dreams as a house, as an automobile, or as some article of furniture. Again, as with symbols of the parents, close attention should be paid to the description of this symbol as the terms used by the patient will often reveal many important aspects of how he views himself or important persons. Deformities, current or belonging to some earlier time, will often find their way into the description of the symbol in the dream. A man with a somewhat deformed leg often had dreams in which a house had something wrong with one side of it, that he was in a contrivance of some kind (car, bus, boat, etc.) and it listed to one side (he did limp on occasion). Another man whose lack of organization was virtually legendary and who described his life as being in total shambles often had dreams of houses which were messy and cluttered. He identified these with his mother's house. This woman, who periodically drifted into psychotic states for which she had to be institutionalized, lived as a recluse in a dirty, dilapidated house when she was out of the hospital. Her personality, he stated, was like the house in which she lived, and he was identified both with his mother and with her house.

The greatest number of symbols in dreams are sexual symbols. These are the most readily and frequently recognized. The breasts and buttocks are symbolized by objects that bear some similarity to them in shape or size. The male genital organ is symbolized by objects that resemble it in either appearance or function (penetration, emission, impregnation, urination). Symbols for the female genital organs may refer to the *external* genitalia, including the hair, or to the individual's conception of the *internal* sexual apparatus that involves the vagina and/or uterus. Objects that are in some way capable of enclosing or containing other objects, either in appearance or in function, are readily used in dreams to represent the female genital. The therapist should keep in mind, however, that such dream elements may often refer to the anus, rectum, or lower bowel. It is therefore necessary to distinguish whether the reference is to anal material or to the dreamer's view of the female genitals.

It should be noted that because of constitutional bisexuality and the fact, which we discussed earlier, that any element in the dream can stand for its opposite, the therapist must be continually vigilant in order to recognize that a symbol which at first sight seems to obviously belong to one sex, may on analytic investigation refer to the opposite sex. Thus a dream in which a male figure occurs may refer to the dreamer's childhood view that a woman possesses a penis (e.g., the phallic mother). Dreams in which a male figure has a protuberant abdomen may refer to the dreamer's childhood theory that a man is capable of becoming pregnant and having a baby.

Sexual activity is frequently symbolized in dreams by some reference to a rhythmic activity, such as climbing, rubbing, sawing, filing, or playing scales on a musical instrument. The therapist should note from the associations whether the specific symbols refer to some autoerotic activity or to sexual relations, as well as whether the activity is consummated with pleasure or whether some inhibitions are present. In one dream, for example, a man was trying repeatedly to put a male plug into a female receptacle but somehow was not able to make it go into the hole.

Dreams of castration, expressed in various ways, are extremely important in analysis. Sometimes such dreams include an authority figure who will punish the dreamer for his forbidden wishes. Castration in dreams is symbolized in various ways, usually by referring to a loss of, damage or injury to some body part or by an addition or multiplication of some appendage. At times, castration is implied in the dream by the presence of some instrument that is capable of inflicting damage as an ax, knife, sword, or razor, without any further details being present in the manifest content. In these instances the instrument serves to symbolize what is dreaded by the dreamer. On other occasions, castration is implied and a man will dream directly of being a woman.

Pregnancy symbols are very common and include dreams of poisoning, infection, or infestations of all kinds. In addition, dreams of having cancer or some other type of growth within the body often refer to pregnancy. Large animals, especially if they are heavy, and kangaroos clearly represent a pregnancy. Inanimate objects used for carrying things like carts, baskets, or bags, often refer to this, too.

Dreams of pregnancy are often followed by or associated with dreams wherein there is an allusion to intrauterine life or to the birth process. The former dreams have as their content some reference to a claustrum, a submarine or a diving bell. The latter characteristically describe some passage through a narrow channel or opening, or the coming out of a body of water. At times birth is symbolized by gifts or by a new arrival. Dreams of rescue or rescuing are generally connected with birth: either giving birth to a child or the wish to be a mother.

The other end of the life cycle is also commonly symbolized in dreams. Dreams of death are symbolized by departure, by a trip or some reference to silence, stillness, or blackness. In connection with dreams about death, it is extremely important for the therapist to ascertain whether the dreamer is expressing a death wish toward someone, some anxiety about an individual, as a sick child, or whether the material about death concerns thoughts about his own state of health, or reveals a depression with suicidal ideation.

From this brief discussion of symbols one may see how many of the basic problems that concern people are expressed symbolically in their dreams. The therapist must utilize his knowledge of dream symbolism to recognize allusions to a particular conflict or a particular experience. Using this as a basis, he will then be able to elicit further material that the patient may have been initially unwilling or unable to divulge directly by exploring the patient's associations to a particular dream element. Thus, for example, it is not enough to simply ascertain that an individual had a sexual wish. The therapist must look further to discover what the nature of the particular wish was, its object and the reason for its appearance in the dream at the particular time.

Associated with symbols in dreams are various other means of representation utilized by the manifest dream. Earlier we stated that dreams have a special function in psychoanalytic therapy because they serve as a means of communication with the patient's unconscious in the therapeutic process. Bearing this in mind, we can see how essential it is for the therapist to pay particular attention to those manifestations in the dream that bear direct relationship either to himself or to the therapeutic process. Symbols used in a metaphoric sense may represent the therapist as someone who is a helpful figure for the patient, or the reverse. Various allusions to a teacher, a doctor, or a service person, for example, often have direct reference to the therapist in a positive sense. At times, when the reference to a particular person is explored, one may find that the therapist is compared with or equated with someone who is incompetent, dilatory, who charges too much, or who in some way is not performing a good, adequate, or helpful service. Sometimes the therapist may be represented by a person of the opposite sex. Thus, it is by no means unusual for a male therapist to find himself represented as a woman in patients' dreams. Once again it is important to ascertain whether he is portrayed in this manner as the good and giving maternal figure (as "granny the good"), or as the vicious witch.

Since dreams are basically egoistic, the patient is always in them and in many he finds himself in one way or another in a therapeutic situation. I have had a number of patients who have dreamed of famous persons who have been in psychoanalytic therapy. In these dreams the patient equated himself with the famous person and identified his therapist with the analyst of that person. A number of dreams in this connection had to do with Marilyn Monroe and, as is so well known, with her therapist, Ralph Greenson. In these instances the patient identified with her, not only as a prominent person and an attractive sex symbol, but also as someone who was in analysis and who had committed suicide. The similarity of my last name with that of Ralph Greenson also provided an important vehicle for the patient to express his or her ambivalent feeling toward me and the therapy. If Marilyn Monroe, who was seeing a famous analyst, could commit suicide, it could also happen to them as well.

The treatment situation itself, often represented by a journey of some kind and the conveyance in which the dreamer finds himself, provides the therapist with an important clue about what the patient's view is of his therapy at the particular time: whether the journey is fast or slow, easy or perilous. In this connection, all equipment used for communication (telephones, radios, televisions, intercoms, etc.) can also be pressed into the service by the dream as a metaphor for the treatment situation. Here it is important whether the message that was coming through was clear or blurred and whether there was a good deal of static affecting the reception.

One patient dreamed of being in an airplane that seemed to be out of control. He was frantically talking to the tower and crying that he could not understand what was coming through on the "squawk box." The reference was to the treatment situation and his feeling that he was getting out of control and panicky. The message that he was receiving from the control tower (i.e., myself) was not clear. His associations led further to incidents in his childhood where he was terrified and cried to his mother for help only to be told to "quit squawking." In the dream he equated me with his umempathic mother who was not helping him with his anxiety and who not only let him cry but admonished him for it by telling him to "quit squawking."

It is not uncommon for the patient to project his own problems upon the analyst. This is especially true if these are of a pathological or a characterological nature. Attributes of a negative nature such as dishonesty, certain abnormal or gross sexual behavior, or violent aggression, are often displaced upon the analyst. In one instance, the patient whose mother was psychotic had repeated dreams in which there was something wrong with me and he wondered if I, too, was suffering from the same type of condition that his mother had but was covering it up. As time went on we came to understand that he secretly feared that *he* might actually become like his mother, female, psychotic, and deranged. His fear of his own impulses was transferred upon me and at the same time he repeated in his relation to me his fear of his mother in her pathological condition.

Dreams may use the mechanism of projection to express various feelings and impulses that the individual is unable to reveal directly. We may find, for example, that the patient expresses some of his own affect by projecting it upon the therapist. It is not he who is afraid, it is the therapist. It is not he who is angry, it is the therapist. In these instances it is important to bear in mind that inasmuch as affects can be reversed, some of the anxieties which are expressed may indeed refer to the opposite. A patient dreamed that my wife had died and that I was very sad. His associations led to his fantasies about *his* wife being killed in an automobile accident, and led to his further thoughts that then he would be free and would be able to pursue inhibited and unrestrained sexual gratification. He had projected the whole scene upon me but provided me with the opposite and more acceptable reaction to my wife's death, thus repressing his own feelings about which he felt guilty and ashamed.

When the patient projects his own ideas, wishes, or characterological problems upon the therapist, it is especially important for the therapist to take them up directly. If this is not done, the patient may feel that the therapist is being defensive, that he does indeed have something to conceal, and that there is some truth to his allegations. Frequently, the advantage of such a move is that the patient, realizing that it is acceptable to discuss his concerns, will feel much more inclined to reveal his own problems in this respect.

The mechanism of reversal of affects in dreams should also be taken into consideration in dreams that are frankly pleasureful. A male patient dreamed of a highly erotic scene with a woman and the dream culminated in his having an emission but no orgasm. The initial view of the dream was that it was the acme of sexual pleasure: that it fulfilled his fondest dreams. His associations, however, led to his anxiety about being involved with women in general and his problem with premature ejaculations. He went on to relate how frightened he was in so many situations. On one occasion, when he was taking an important examination in college, he had an emission during the written test. He stated that he had been terrified of what would happen to him if he failed the test: He would be laughed at by his colleagues and condemned by his parents. His ejaculation in the dream was like the emission he had had when he was taking the important examination in college. While the scene in the dream was pleasureful and erotic, the affect that was repressed was extreme anxiety. He was as anxious in the erotic scene with the woman in his dream as he was during his college examination and he feared that he would be laughed at and condemned by her as he had feared he would be by his colleagues and parents.

Another patient had a somewhat similar dream of being in a highly pleasureful, erotic situation with a woman and also having an emission without any orgiastic pleasure. His associations, however, led him to recall an episode that had occurred when, as a young man, he was hitchhiking and was picked up by a man who had put his hand on his thigh. Realizing that the man was making a homosexual pass at him, the patient got out of the car but immediately afterward had an emission. In this instance, his emission was also based on anxiety, but the anxiety here was his fear that he might be a homosexual and that he might have been aroused had he stayed with the man. His dream expressed his pleasure in heterosexual wishes, reversing his unconscious wish and fear of his homosexual strivings.

Sometimes an affect appears in dreams in which the individual finds himself unable to express his feelings or to pursue a necessary course of action. In talking about the dream he will state that he was unable to move, he was "frozen to the spot," or "paralyzed," that he was unable to talk, or that he could neither run away nor attack. These dreams are very characteristic in that they express a conflict which the individual has about doing something. Most often these dreams refer to an inhibition based upon a superego prohibition for the particular wished for impulse. In one such example a man found himself, in his dream, beside his mother's bedside. He knew she was dying: that she had had either a heart attack or a stroke. He knew that he had to call a doctor right away but he was unable to move in order to make the necessary phone call. He was very frightened in the dream and awoke with anxiety. The patient then related that ten years before he had indeed visited his mother in a distant city. She had been ill and was under a doctor's care. The trip to see his mother was most inconvenient for him because he was involved in some extensive business negotiations and at the same time was having some serious marital problems.

At the time of the dream this patient's analysis had reached a point where he was dealing with problems connected with his relationship to his mother. He recalled with difficulty that when he had gone to see his mother, he had wished that she would die and free him from her incessant demands. He recalled feeling resentful at having to drop what he was doing to visit her and went on to describe many instances of her unreasonable impositions on his time and freedom. Prior to this dream, he had not been able to confess these feelings either to himself or in his analysis because he felt that they were shameful and that he would be criticized for having had such thoughts. Brought up in a strict, religious home, he took the commandment to honor one's father and mother quite literally and firmly believed that any infraction of this commandment would be severely punished. The dream represented his conflict. He knew that he had to summon the doctor immediately so that his mother would be saved. Yet there was the opposite wish to delay calling the doctor until it would be "too late." It would then not really be his fault if she died. The two conflicting wishes resulted in paralysis.

Thus far we have focused our attention on the content of dreams. It is also very important, however, for the therapist to keep in mind the *form* of the dream and the various techniques that the dream uses to express certain unconscious strivings. In many dreams the content and the form of the dream are very closely related. Yet, in some dreams the underlying significance of the dream can only be ascertained by the form in which it is presented rather than by its specific content. The therapist should therefore note the dreamer's style in describing his dream as well as its general characters.

This is especially noteworthy, for example, in long, rambling dreams that take up the better part of a session. In listening to such dreams, the therapist is often hard put to know where to begin or what to say with regard to them. Actually, the important point about such dreams is that they are not to be understood in terms of their specific content at all but rather by their form. The lengthy, rambling dreams, filled with innumerable details, reveal the dreamer's state of mind at the particular time in the treatment or refer to an earlier time in his life when he was confused about various matters. He may be trying to express the bewilderment he felt at that time as well as what he experiences at the present time. In recounting such dreams the patient may be attempting to make the therapist as confused as he (the patient) was at an earlier time in his life. The feeling of confusion which the therapist experiences under such circumstances, his countertransference reaction to the patient's dream productions, is in and of itself indicative of what the patient is trying to express but is unable to do in a direct way. He cannot remember how confused he was when he was a child, he can only repeat it and make the therapist as confused as he felt then.

If such dreams persist over a long period of time, however, they should raise serious questions whether they are expressing something characterological about the dreamer: His ego is in some way weakened, he is inundated by material of all kinds from his unconscious and is unable to synthesize it or bring it to some kind of understandable focus.

Some patients proceed to describe particular minutiae regarding various dream elements or express doubts about the dream itself. They seem, as it were, to get stuck on particular points of content in the dream and never really get to a broad view of the total dream picture. By expressing their obsessive preoccupation with details, these patients reveal some of their underlying characterological problems. At times the content of the patient's dream or his associations when viewed in connection with his obsessional preoccupation with minutiae in the manifest content of the dream may provide clues to the underlying reasons for the obsessional behavior of the patient. Thus, after one lengthy dream that took up most of his session, a patient indicated by some fleeting comment that he was involved in some questionable business practices. The purpose of the obsessional preoccupation proved to be, in his words, "a filibuster" to avoid dealing with the "real" problems.

Another aspect of form in the manifest content of dreams may be that temporal relations are transformed into spatial ones. Events that occurred long ago, as in the dreamer's childhood, may appear as far away or very small. The individual may find himself in a large room, in a large building, or surrounded by very tall giantlike individuals. The dream uses this mechanism to refer to events that had occurred a long time ago in the dreamer's childhood.

It is rather common for a manifest dream to represent early times in the dreamer's life by setting the "story line" of the dream in some early time in history, as the Dark Ages or the Middle Ages, or in some "early civilization," or by some reference to a prehistoric period, as the time when there were dinosaurs. The latter reference may not only be to the "prehistory" of the patient's life, but also to his view that his parents were like those huge beasts—incapable of feeling and having incredible aggression.

Another rather specific allusion to a particular age of the dreamer may be made by the picture of a clock in the manifest content of the dream. It should be noted that the representation of age as a time of day is in and of itself a childlike expression. In the description of the time in such a dream, one patient commented on the hands of the clock pointing to "half-past five." While the reference to age was to five and a half, his association to the "hands" was to his touching his sister's genitals at approximately that age and to masturbation.

Dreams in a night or in a given period in an analysis, as over a weekend or over a vacation, are always related.

In a series of dreams a woman dreamed of looking for an object that she had lost. She was not certain what the object was but went on in her associations to describe many material things that had disappeared over the years. She spoke of going through periods when she was "always losing something" and related that during the previous several weeks, she had indeed lost a number of items. One day she had lost her glasses, another day, her purse, still another day, her wallet, and even some article of jewelry. She had left her wallet at a clothing store and had left one of her rings on the counter in the ladies' room of another store where she had gone to wash her hands. Analysis revealed that the dreams referred to a period in her childhood when her mother was gone for several months. At that time, the patient felt that she had lost her mother and that she herself was lost without her. She remembered, too, going from room to room in her house, wondering where her mother was. When a member of the family would take her for a walk or shopping during this time, she wondered where her mother was and whether she would ever see her again.

When working with dreams in analysis it is important for the therapist to bear in mind that material is often represented by similarities and parallels in the manifest content of dreams. These similarities refer to situations which are equivalent emotionally in the patient's mind or to people who, in one way or another, have certain common characteristics. The therapist is well advised to consider such parallels as, very frequently, these have to do with the transference. There are many variations in this process. Sometimes, when two people are mentioned who have similar characteristics, it is essential for the therapist to look for another person who may have similar characteristics. At other times, the characteristics are distributed among several figures in the dream and these then may point to another individual who may have all of these qualities. Besides this, it is important for the therapist to note that while the patient may be expressing his feelings about the characteristics of another person, including the therapist, it may well be that he is projecting his own characteristics, which he finds intolerable, upon the other person.

When patients in a session report having had a number of dreams, the therapist should attempt to ascertain the relationship between them, or their connection with other material presented in the course of the session. Dreams may be presented in pairs and this form repre- sents a way of expressing a connection between the two dreams or parts of dreams. Causal connections such as "since, therefore," or "because so and so occurred, the consequences were" or "if I had done so and so" or "if something had happened then something else would not have occurred," are frequently indicated in this way. These dream sequences often provide an understanding of the basis of a patient's symptomatology.

A man brought in the following pair of dreams. In the first dream, he is going to India where there are several villages in which there is a good deal of starvation and babies are dying of malnutrition. In the second dream, he is in a social situation and his wife is being extremely friendly with another man who seems to be making advances to her. The patient is very irate with this man and tells him in a loud voice to stop and to leave his wife alone.

He promptly connected the first dream with a television program he had been watching the evening before on the starvation of babies in India. He had heard, some years before, that infants could actually die from being neglected and unloved. Since then he had seen numerous articles in the paper about babies and children who developed malnutrition as a consequence of being uncared for and who subsequently died. He expressed his bitter anger at women who did not care for their children.

After a time, he went to the second dream. Some years ago he had indeed been jealous of his wife's relationship with a male coworker in their church group. He had realized even then that there was no realistic basis for his jealousy as was borne out by a good deal of factual material. The patient was not paranoid but what came out in great detail was that he had projected upon his wife a situation from his childhood. His parents were divorced when he was a small boy and his mother, who drank excessively, frequently consorted with various men. She would often go out in the evening, leaving him completely alone and uncared for. At times she would lock him out of the house. He saw her being propositioned by men at different times and, on occasion, when he came home from school heard his mother and a strange man talking behind her locked bedroom door. She remarried and divorced several times after her divorce from his father. On some occasions he observed scenes of intimacy between his mother and her current husband. During many periods in his childhood and adolescence she did not prepare breakfast for him nor did she provide him with lunch money when he went to school. Sometimes she was not home in the evening and he had to go to bed hungry.

During the course of the session in which he related the two dreams, he was reminded of another recent dream dealing with similar material. In that dream he had gotten into some confrontation with one of his mother's husbands. In his associations to *that* dream he remembered that on one occasion he had seen this man going to the bathroom with a "large erection" and was furious with him.

While the dreams clearly alluded to the man's oedipal problems and to primal scene observation, his reaction to the first dream about going to India pointed to his feelings of deprivation by his mother not just for preferring another man, but also for neglecting him altogether from the time he was very small. It was this experience of maternal neglect with which he was constantly confronted when he felt his wife was not paying sufficient attention to him.

On some occasions patients will report a dream within a dream. Compared to other dreams, these dreams are not as frequent, although they are likely to occur in virtually every analysis at some point. These dreams have a very special significance in that the dream within the dream refers to some reality that had taken place. Its being put into the dream within the dream part is a way for the dreamer to distance himself from something in that material. For this reason, the therapist should explore the patient's associations to that portion of the dream.

Inasmuch as manifest dreams having few elements are generally considered to be highly condensed, it is necessary to look for the multiple allusions in the patient's associations to the particular elements that appear in them.

A man (mentioned earlier) dreamed of a woman dressed in gaudy clothes and being heavily made up. He thought she looked like a prostitute. He had actually seen someone who looked like that on television as he was flipping through the various channels. This led him to many associations of prostitutes he had seen and with whom he had had sexual relations. Ultimately, his associations led to his having witnessed his mother "entertaining" a strange man in her bedroom when he was a boy. When he told a schoolmate of the incident, his friend told him sarcastically that everyone knew that his mother was a whore.

Condensation may be seen in dreams that are particularly vivid or in dreams wherein a specific color is mentioned. In many instances the color follows rather traditional usage: yellow meaning cowardice; green meaning jealousy; red meaning passion; blue meaning depression; purple meaning royalty; black alluding to death, and white to purity or innocence. The therapist should not be content with understanding color in the manifest content of dreams on the basis of some standard significance, however, but should explore the patient's associations to why a particular color is chosen. Quite often he will find that the reasons are overdetermined.

Numbers in dreams may also be overdetermined. These may refer to various specific stimuli during the dream day or are references to particular associations in which the numbers appear. Special attention should be paid to numbers referring to such things as the analytic fee, the number of sessions, to addresses and telephone numbers of people in the dreamer's life, to anniversaries and important dates.

Usually, speeches in dreams refer to something which has been said, heard or read during the dream day. These intrusions into the dream are often torn from their original context and distorted to fit in with the requirements of the dream. The therapist, therefore, need not be concerned about the accuracy of the speech in question. At times, speeches in the dream are actually thoughts which the dreamer may have had during his waking state and are carried over into the dream. Obsessional commands, stemming from something in the dreamer's past and having been taken up by the superego, may also appear in the manifest content of a dream. In one instance a man with a masturbatory perversion of tying himself up dreamed that someone in a loud authoritative voice was yelling, "Don't you ever do that again." The words were a direct quotation from his father who had caught him attempting to explore his baby sister's genitals. One determinant of his perversion was that he was tying himself up to prevent himself from doing something sexual with a woman. By tying himself up, he was also playing out his father's command of tying him up (verbally) so that he would never "do that" again.

When listening to a dream being reported by a patient in the course of an analysis, it is important to pay attention to whatever comments or glosses are made about the dream or some element in it. Such comments may be interpolated in the telling of the dream or in the dreamer's assessment of it before or after having related it.

Under the general heading of comments about a dream the therapist should note the patient's behavior as well as his verbal associations. One man, who had great difficulty in his interpersonal relations and was prone to make inappropriate remarks in social situations came to his appointment one day carrying a plastic cup. He deposited it in the wastebasket in my consulting room saying somewhat belligerently, "I brought this in to throw it in your wastebasket. I had some coffee while I was driving here for my appointment but I didn't want to leave the cup in my car. I hate to have stuff like that littering my car."

After he had assumed his position on the couch, he promptly launched into recounting a dream. "It was a nothing dream," he announced. "You may say it was a nothing dream. It had to do with our dog. He had made a mess in the living room—right on the carpet. He deposited a pile of shit on the oriental rug. My wife cleaned it up. The dog doesn't do that very often. . . ." The patient's comment that the dream was "nothing" served to belittle its significance in his mind. Yet, such a judgment hardly fit in with his behavior. He had, in effect, acted out with me what his dog had done. He had brought in his soiled plastic cup, his worthless nothing, his refuse, and deposited it in my wastebasket, expecting me to clean up after him as his wife had cleaned up after the dog. Behind this material there were vague memories of his mother's insistence on his cleanliness.

Quite frequently in relating a dream the patient uses the alternative "either/or" in describing a particular element. The therapist should treat this alternative statement as an "and." A man dreamed that he was "either in the bedroom or in the bathroom." He was not sure which. His associations led him to recall observing his mother in the nude in *both* the bedroom *and* the bathroom.

At times, comments are made referring to something about the dream such as: "There was something left out" or "There was a big part in the dream that seemed to stick out in my memory but I don't know what to do with it." These remarks, when viewed from the standpoint of the patient's associations, provide the therapist with additional information about what the patient is alluding to. In the brief illustration given above, the male patient was struggling with his reactions to his observation of the female genitals when he was a boy and his recollection of having erections.

The therapist makes no judgment about a patient's remarks that he or she is uncertain about a particular detail in the dream. Whatsoever the statement is, it is taken entirely at face value and the associations to the particular element are explored. Doubt concerning an element in the dream may have specific significance. It may represent the patient's view of the particular element in question, what somebody had said to him, doubts about either what the dream has to do with, or some general doubts about himself or his own veracity. Essentially, the same holds true with judgments that are expressed in a dream. The dream itself does not express a judgment but the dreamer imposes a judgment about an element or about the dream in its entirety. This usually means that there is some material in the latent dream thoughts about which the dreamer is expressing a judgment. A patient may state, for example, "I had a good dream last night" or "I had a confused dream last night." These judgments refer to the person's reaction to the material contained in the dream. The remark, "a good dream," may mean that the patient understood what was behind it, or that there was something in his latent dream thoughts such as a decision about some course of action that he felt good about, or that the therapist, as a transference figure, would approve. It is by no means unusual for a patient to dismiss a dream as insignificant if it reveals a problem about which he is particularly ashamed or finds unpleasant. By so doing he dismisses the importance of the material with which the dream is concerned. The patient who deposited the plastic cup in my wastebasket was doing just that.

The patient may comment that a dream is absurd and, very often, some dream element or group of elements or situations in the dream do appear to be outlandish. This has specific significance. The comment should alert the therapist that the material with which the dream is concerned is the dreamer's judgment about the absurdity of some wish or impulse in the latent dream thoughts. Not infrequently this absurdity relates to an aggressive attitude which the dreamer has had about one or the other of his parents and expresses a similar kind of criticism against other figures of authority. The patient may use this mechanism in his dream to express a similar attitude toward the therapist as a transference figure.

In our clinical work we find that there are a number of dreams that, with variations, appear with some frequency. The cautionary remarks expressed earlier about symbols in dreams are pertinent here as well. It is essential for the therapist to inquire into the patient's specific associations to the various elements of such dreams. In most of these dreams, while their gross manifest content is similar, their significance, as far as the latent content of the dream is concerned, varies. Among such dreams are those dealing with being naked, of being subject to some type of examination, or of the death of someone. Other dreams deal with the loss of teeth, with flying or falling. Any of these dreams are capable of having multiple meanings and may derive from any level of the dreamer's psychological or emotional development.

Rescue dreams, another type of dream, are commonly connected with material dealing with birth but may also be associated with other situations from which the dreamer wishes to be rescued, or from which he wants to rescue someone. It would be a travesty of therapeutic, let alone interpersonal, sensitivity to interpret a patient's dream of trying to rescue a friend or relative from a totalitarian state as a wish to give birth to that person rather than expressing the ego wish to help give him a new life.

Observation dreams, those in which the individual is watching some figure or some performance as through a window, on television, or in an auditorium of some kind, frequently occur in the course of many analyses. Such dreams may refer to the observation of the genitals, usually of a person of the opposite sex, or, rather typically, may refer to the observation of the primal scene. While these dreams refer to a historical event, they also occur very frequently when there are separations in the analysis. In this instance they deal with the prototypical situation from which the dreamer felt excluded (Izner, 1959).

In the case of punishment dreams, it is important for the therapist to ascertain for what deed the punishment is being imposed. A man related that when he attempted to have intercourse with his wife he was impotent. That night he dreamed he was attending a party and there was a beautiful girl with whom he wanted to have sexual relations. As he approached the girl, a man came up to him and threatened him with a saber. The man then executed some deft movements with the saber which sliced through the patient's trousers on both sides of his fly. He experienced no pain. On awakening he felt that his penis had shriveled up and was like a clitoris.

The patient's associations immediately following his report of the dream were about his father's exceedingly strict attitude about his sexuality. He spoke of his father's service in a European army and his having been adroit in foil, saber, and épée. His father had repeatedly threatened to take him to a doctor if he masturbated. The patient was fully convinced that he would be punished for his sexual wishes by castration and by being turned into a woman.

Another rather common dream is the so-called reconciliation dream. In such a dream the individual finds himself returning to a love object from whom he had been separated as after a divorce. Typically, the dreamer greets this person with a great deal of pleasure and often reports to him events of importance that had happened since their separation. Characteristically, in the dream or shortly after awakening, the dreamer experiences the wish that the separation had not occurred but often this feeling is then followed by a sense of realization that the separation was indeed inevitable. Frequently, too, there is also a feeling of sadness that the relationship had not worked out. These dreams are attempts to master the separation that had proven to be painful and are part of the process of mourning the loss of a love object.

One woman, after separating from a man with whom she had had an affair that proved to be "totally impossible," dreamed repeatedly of meeting him under various circumstances, being joyous at the reunion, and briefing him on the events in her life since they last met. On awakening she was angry with her former lover and desperately wanted to "tell him off in no uncertain terms" about his intolerable behavior that had made the separation necessary.

Another fairly common type of dream is the so-called affirmatory or corroborative dream in which the patient dreams of agreeing with an interpretation that had been made in a previous analytic session. While these dreams may indeed seem to be corroborative, the therapist must be on the lookout for a compliance which serves to obscure a diametrically opposite point of view. Under these circumstances, it is important when following the patient's associations to be on the lookout for negative remarks and associations.

As the therapy progresses, the patient will bring up material at various times to indicate that the end of his analysis is in sight. Often the material in the manifest content of the patient's dreams at this time brings into focus many of the individual's basic problems. Typically, termination dreams use imagery to indicate the end of a process: a building that is under construction is almost finished; the patient is packing boxes and suitcases ready for a move; the patient is reading a book and he is coming to the end and so forth. The end of a journey, the end of a trip are commonly used metaphors in the manifest content. The therapist must then ascertain whether the implied termination is based upon a resolution of the individual's problems or whether it is a wished-for termination to avoid dealing with important but conflictual or embarrassing material. Although termination dreams often use the metaphor of death, it is essential to understand why that particular metaphor is used as, for example, is the patient concerned that he will die as a result of the termination, or that the analyst will die. Previous experiences with the death of a love object are often revived in the process of termination and the material about that person emerges in the patient's dreams.

One woman patient finally agreed to terminate her analysis after a long and difficult treatment during which the issue of termination was raised many times. She wanted to set dates but found herself unable to live up to her proposed intentions. As she considered the dates of termination at some point in the future, she became inundated with tremendous anxiety and indicated that under no circumstances could she possibly stop. She was extremely frightened that if she terminated she would become profoundly depressed and would commit suicide. During one such hour in which she cried that she could not possibly terminate, she brought in a dream in which she is riding in a car that is being driven by some man. The car seems to stop. A black woman puts her hand through the side window of the car grasping the patient's hand. The patient tries to free herself but is unable to do so because of the iron grip with which her hand is being held by the black woman. As the car is moving forward, *she* finally tears the woman's arm off. She then looks behind her and sees that the arm, severed at the elbow, is lying on the back seat.

She realizes that the dream is reversed. It is not the black woman (who is myself in the transference) who is holding on to her but rather that she is holding on to the black woman. She would like to tear herself loose but is afraid to do so. From her associations it became evident that for her to give up her analyst was tantamount to castration: Either she or I would be castrated.

In this chapter I have presented a number of basic suggestions for the therapist who is working with dreams in the course of analytic work. Initially, the therapist's work is to facilitate the emergence of the patient's associations to the various parts of his dream. Once the patients associations are brought forth and studied carefully, then it is up to the therapist to provide constructive suggestions or interpretations about the significance of the material derived from them. As dreams are often multilayered, and as such are capable of various interpretations, it is quite likely that different therapists as well as the patient himself may see the material in different ways, not one of which may in and of itself necessarily be the only correct interpretation. It is essential that the therapist provide his patient with the opportunity to either accept or to modify the interpretations that are suggested. The interpretation may thus be considered in the nature of a hypothesis which can then be verified or rejected on the basis of subsequent material.

10

The Male Genital in the Manifest Content of Dreams*

Alexander Grinstein, M.D.

R ALPH Greenson was always interested in observations of clinical material that might add to our psychoanalytic understanding. The following paper is presented as a tribute to his interest in furthering the spirit of such exploration.

While dream elements symbolizing the male genital in the manifest content of dreams are extremely common, dreams in which the male genitals appear directly are by no means as frequent. They may occur in the same night or in the same period of time as do the more usual dreams that utilize symbols of the male genitals. It is my impression that dreams in which the male genitals appear "undisguised" have special significance.

The following clinical examples are presented to illustrate some possibilities.

*This material was presented to the Michigan Psychoanalytic Society on October 25, 1990.

Case 1

After she had been in analysis about two years, a young woman, living with a man who had refused to marry her, had the following bipartite dream.

In the first part of the dream she is walking with her man friend. They pass some people and she notices a man with his pants unzipped and his penis "hanging out." The penis is turgid. She looks at it intently and calls her friend's attention to it. In the second part of the dream she is in some fancy restaurant with her friend and they are going to join another couple at dinner. The man of the other couple is the same man whom she had seen with his penis exposed, but now he is properly dressed. There are a number of tall tables and stools in the restaurant.

She was curious about the dream and reflected about whose penis it looked like. She was certain that it was not her lover's, nor did she think it resembled that of any of the other men with whom she had had sexual relations. After a few moments and with some difficulty, she recalled that it looked exactly like her father's penis when she had showered with him when she was around four years of age. Her mother was pregnant at the time and had told her father to shower with her because she herself could not bend down comfortably to bathe her in the tub. It was an unusual situation as her father was a rather formal and fastidious person. She did not recall ever having seen him in the nude before, nor afterwards. She remembered that on some of these occasions while they were showering, her father's penis became turgid and she was curious about this change in its appearance. "I never saw him have an erection though," she added. The showers continued until one day her father told her mother that she (the patient) was too old for them to shower together. After this the showers abruptly ceased. She did not know what precipitated the sudden change in the routine and wondered whether she may have touched her father's penis but indicated that she did not remember if she did or not. "I could have, it was right there," she said.

Then, after a short pause in the session, she related that when she was a teenager, a boy in her class had asked her to go as his date to a house party during the Christmas vacation. When she asked her parents' permission, her father indignantly refused to let her go but instead he took the whole family to New York City. Even though she was under age, he took her and her mother to the Stork Club. She recalled that there was a bar, tall tables and chairs like the ones in the second part of the dream. She had not been to that restaurant since that time.

She went on to relate that she had had no sexual enlightenment as a youngster. She remembered that when she had asked her mother about her protuberant abdomen she was told that her father had "planted a seed" and that she (the patient) would have a baby brother or a sister. At the time she thought that her father had gone to a store, bought some seeds and that her mother swallowed them.

Her subsequent associations led her to recollect a number of instances from her childhood, adolescence, and young adulthood when her father clearly indicated that he was opposed to all her male playmates and friends. He was very possessive of her and when she began to date, he often made derogatory remarks about the men she dated, implying in various ways that he would have been a better choice.

While the patient's father did not engage in any overt sexual behavior with her as far as she could recall, his taking her into the shower with him was, for her, tantamount to a seduction and one which was followed by a sudden forceful expulsion and rejection. Her associations dealing with her mother's pregnancy and her classical theory of impregnation alluded to a repressed fellatio fantasy involving her father whereby she, too, could become pregnant and have a baby.

Case 2

The patient, a middle-aged man in the process of divorcing his wife, was having an affair with a woman his own age. While his sexual relationship with his wife was unsatisfactory, his sexual relationship with his mistress was extremely satisfying. He felt guilty about the relationship, however, and did not know whether a continuation of the affair would result in marriage.

After he had been in analysis several months, he had the following dream. His mistress is stroking his penis which gets longer and larger until it is so huge that he can put it into his mouth and suck on it. As he does this, he awakens from his dream. He is very disturbed by the dream and hesitates to talk about it because he is not certain whether the dream meant that he was a homosexual and that he wanted to suck another man's penis.

He talked for a short time about his wife having performed fellatio at his request, which she did reluctantly on rare instances. He had had an affair with another woman who had no hesitation about oral sex and they had found it mutually satisfying. The relationship terminated because of his intense guilt feelings about the affair.

He went on to talk about having discovered his wife in bed with his best friend, a man with whom he shared many thoughts and feelings. The relationship between them was at no time overtly homosexual. After the incident, he often wondered if he was a latent homosexual and had engineered the situation to bring his wife and his friend closer together so that they would become intimate and he would discover them. He then remembered that, when he was a boy, the boys kidded one another about performing fellatio, although to his knowledge no one actually did.

Suddenly, he recalled a dream that he had during adolescence. There were two men in the dream whose identity he did not know. One was older than the other. He had the thought that the men would be performing fellatio on each other. He remembered that during adolescence he had often wished that his penis was long enough so that he could suck on it himself. He tried in various ways to do this but was unable to succeed.

He went on to consider the identity of the two men in his dream and believed that they referred to his older brother and his father— both of whom he had often seen in the nude and whose penises he had admired. As he said this, he again expressed his concern about whether he was a homosexual. This led him to tell me about his father who used to photograph adolescent boys in the nude in various poses. He raised the question whether his father was a homosexual and if so, he wondered, whether he (the patient) had wanted to engage in some homosexual activity with him, that is, to perform fellatio on him. The patient realized that his train of thoughts included his friend who had had the affair with his wife, his adolescent playmates, his father and his brother—all men toward whom he had homosexual feelings. Both his wife, in reality, and his mistress, in his dream, provided him with a conduit to another man. His attempt to perform autofellatio in the dream represented his wish to play both participants in a homosexual act. The appearance of this dream at this time in his analysis heralded the emergence of homosexual feelings in the transference.

Case 3

A young woman in analysis for some two years had a long childhood history of sexual overstimulation. There was a great deal of nudity in her home. Her father frequently walked around dressed only in his undershorts from which his genitals protruded, either from in front, or, when he sat down, from below. Although he had never fondled the patient sexually, he made many suggestive remarks to her. During her childhood, her aged grandparents lived in the house with them and she remembered overhearing some conversation that led her to suspect that her grandfather may have fondled her sister's genitals.

The patient had repeated dreams of nude men whose penises were clearly evident. In a number of the dreams she is in a shower with a man who orders her to kneel down before him and to perform fellatio on him. In some of these dreams she indicates that she did not know what to do. She related dreams in which the penis appears small and thin; others where it appeared to be huge. In some dreams it seemed to be wet and slimy.

In her associations to the dreams in which the penis is small, she recalled the penises of baby boys and remembered that when she was an adolescent, she had stimulated a baby's penis to watch it get erect. She then recalled that one day when she was a child she had been playing with a group of boys and one of them had showed her his penis.

Her associations to the dreams in which a large man with a big penis commands her to, or actually puts his penis into her mouth led her to wonder whether someone actually did this to her when she was a child, whether she saw this done, or whether it was entirely a fantasy. There was no way of determining which of these possibilities was valid. She thought that the presence of a wet slimy penis in some of her dreams referred to her having seen someone's penis after intercourse.

Case 4

A married woman, who had been in analysis for some length of time dreamed that she and her husband were walking in a zoo. There were no other people around. Although she was fully dressed, her husband was completely nude and she saw his penis. Suddenly, a wild animal (a lion or a tiger) came after them. She was frightened and ran away leaving her husband unprotected and at the mercy of the wild animal. She was convinced that the animal would bite off his penis. Her associations led her to recall that when she was a little girl she often played with some other children in a garage in the neighborhood. One day a little boy asked her to go behind the garage with him where they were alone. He exposed himself and asked her to touch his penis. She was frightened and ran home but did not tell anyone about the incident.

After a short period of silence, she remembered a joke about a man swimming in the nude who yells in a loud masculine voice, "Help!" and then in a feminine voice, "Sharks!" Evidently a shark had bitten off his genitals. This led her to a flood of associations dealing with her obvious envy of boys and men: their advantages in a male chauvinist society and her feelings that, as a girl, she had always been disadvantaged. Her parents had desperately wanted a boy and when she was born her mother had scornfully tossed her aside with the comment, often reported to her, "Another piece of shit." Secretly she hated all males who acted or were treated as though all their brains were in their penises. When she herself was pregnant she was fearful that she might give birth to a son whom she would reject, just as her mother had rejected her. In her sexual adjustment she was frequently unorgasmic, especially after some argument with her husband who she felt had demeaned her. She revealed that she often had thoughts about men having their penises cut, chopped, or bitten off. It was only after this dream that she was able to deal with her own orally aggressive wishes to bite off her husband's penis.

Case 5

A male homosexual, who had innumerable homosexual experiences, dreamed in the course of his analysis that he was in a cubicle of a men's room. An erect penis protrudes from a "glory hole" in the partition. He becomes sexually aroused, performs fellatio, simultaneously masturbates, has an orgasm in the dream and awakens. The dream recapitulated many of his experiences of a similar nature. A few days before, he had been in a men's room at a rest stop on an expressway. While there he saw a man performing fellatio on another man and when he entered a cubicle by himself, a man whose face he did not see and whose identity he did not know had thrust his erect penis through a hole in the partition which the patient referred to as the "glory hole." He had been tempted to suck on the penis, but was deterred because he would have had to relate what he had done in his analysis. The reason for his embarrassment as well as his not performing fellatio on the man, as he had done under many similar circumstances before, he reluctantly recognized, was that at this point in his therapy, he would have been acting out his homosexual transference toward his analyst, the man whom he did not see in the course of his sessions.

Case 6

Another man, not a manifest homosexual, who had been in analysis for several years, had been struggling with obsessional thoughts of a passive homosexual nature. He scrupulously avoided any type of activity that might betray his homosexual interests. He did not read or look at any pornographic material or watch video cassettes dealing with homosexual relations, let alone go to a gay bar, or even drive through areas of the city known to be frequented by homosexuals. In his manifest dreams and fantasies, however, he often pictured himself caressing or kissing someone's penis and mouthing it. After some length of time, he revealed that when he was of preschool age, his parents had engaged an older boy to be his sitter. This boy had performed fellatio on him and on one occasion had thrust his erect penis into the patient's mouth. He never told his parents what the boy did, but told them enough so that they never had the boy sit with him after that. The details of this event had only emerged as an association to one of his many homosexual dreams which had often been seen as expressing such wishes in the transference.

Case 7

A woman who had been in analysis for a number of years had the following dream.

She is in a room, looking at a bed on which a man is lying with his penis exposed. As she watches, his penis gets larger and larger and becomes enormously erect.

She recalled that as a young adolescent her parents had her share her bedroom with her brother who was several years older. She had often wondered whether anything sexual had happened between them because her brother frequently touched her, and often hit and pinched her upon the slightest provocation. Their relationship was very close and later in their adolescence she often went out with him as his date. She was very much in love with him and had frequent fantasies of their being married.

In the course of her associations to the dream she recalled that some years earlier her husband had gotten a pornographic movie which they watched together. In the movie a man is lying on one bed and is masturbating while a woman is lying on another bed and she is also masturbating. The scene in the movie was similar to her manifest dream. She did not remember what other sexual material was present in that movie, as, for example, whether the couple had any other sexual activity. She could recall no other details about the movie except for that particular scene. Although she had seen other pornographic movies which involved various types of sexual activity, she could only remember this particular scene in this movie.

At first, the patient said that she suspected that her brother probably did masturbate in her presence and that it was very likely that she had watched him doing this. But then, as the session went on and she thought about it further, she became convinced that she must have observed her brother masturbating and that it must have been sexually exciting to her. She wondered whether she had ever touched his penis or whether, like the woman in the movie, she had masturbated herself while watching her brother masturbate.

Case 8

Another man, who suffered from hypospadias as a child and had repeated surgery on his penis, had many dreams in which he saw his own penis, or that of someone else, being sewn, probed, pulled apart, or bandaged. Sometimes the penis appeared bloody. In every instance these dreams led to his memories of the details of many of the complicated surgical procedures performed on him intermittently over a number of years into adolescence.

Case 9

One male patient who suffered from occasional impotence recalled a dream in which he saw his genitals, which had been severed, lying on a tree stump. His associations led him to recall an incident when he was about five years of age. He had been masturbating. His father had walked in on him and yelled at him, threatening that if he played with himself, he would drive him out to an Indian reservation where a medicine man would chop off his penis with a tomahawk. Several months after this dream he took a woman home after a Christmas office party and had sexual relations with her. Some days later he learned from one of the men at the office that she had the reputation of being sexually promiscuous. He became frightened that he may have picked up some infection from her. That night he dreamed that he was looking at his penis and there was a deep abrasion, "almost like a crater," on his glans.

As I review the above clinical material, and other examples of a similar nature in my practice, my impression is that the pictorialization of the male genital as such in the manifest content of the dreams occurs under special circumstances. Thus while the male genital is usually represented symbolically in the language of the dream, the intensity of affect in the latent content of certain dreams evidently seems to require its direct representation. The associations to these dreams refer to some specific event involving the penis: an observation, a seduction, a trauma (real or threatened), or an intensification of some highly charged sexual material emerging in the transference. This latent material, due to its intensity, seems to break through the censorship barrier resulting in direct rather than symbolic representation.

This communication has been presented as an observation that must be validated by further experiences of other analysts.

11

Working Through

Samuel L. Wilson, M.D.

Introduction

IT is with a feeling of pride, humility, and a sense of nostalgia that I approach my task of contributing a chapter to this volume which assumes to honor the memory and work of Ralph R. Greenson, M.D.

Dr. Greenson was, I am sure, the first psychoanalyst that I actually met. It was through my friendship with his son, Daniel P. Greenson, M.D., one of the editors of this volume, while we were both first year medical students, that the meeting occurred. Having been invited to the Greensons' home in Santa Monica one weekend, I can still remember the unabashed and unbridled sense of joy as Dr. Greenson threw open the door, arms outstretched, promptly bear-hugging his son, whom he hadn't seen for a week. Comparing this scene to my more restrained family background, I thought, "If this is what psychoanalysts are like, I want to be one."

My relationship with Dr. Greenson evolved from that moment to one of teacher, supervisor, mentor, and esteemed friend. It is indeed a pleasure for me to be able to honor his memory and his work.

I am indebted to Mrs. Hildi Greenson, Dr. Greenson's widow and partner for many years, and to Daniel P. Greenson, M.D., Dr. Greenson's son, for access to a verbatim transcript of a seminar conducted by Ralph R. Greenson, M.D. (1960).

221

The issue of work was one of great importance for Dr. Greenson. Following Freud's dictum that to be mentally healthy one must be able to love and work, Greenson was indeed a worker. He was not passive; he loved to work and had little tolerance for those who would not join him in this endeavor. One of his most enduring contributions was his paper on the "Working Alliance" (1965a). His penchant for work was also, I'm sure, a part of what motivated him to pursue the topic of working through, which he did at various times throughout his life. His paper of 1965, first published in *Drives, Affects and Behavior* (1965b) and then republished in his book *Explorations in Psychoanalysis* (1978), remains as one of the most often quoted contributions to this most important topic.

In reading the literature of psychoanalysis, it would appear that the term *working through* has achieved a status analogous to that of a generic pharmaceutical. It cuts across all theoretical persuasions and is apparently accepted as integral to the process of analysis, no matter what analytic language is being spoken. In achieving such a universal status, the concept has tended to lose specificity. This specificity was important to Greenson and occupied a central position in his attempts to define the concept. Much of the literature that mentions working through does not define it. In general, it seems to imply repetition of achieved insight in a variety of permutations and combinations. In some cases, it seems to be used synonymously with an equally vague but assumed familiar term *analysis*. In Greenson's 1965 paper, he reviewed the literature, which, at that time, he considered to be sparse. Charles Brenner, M.D., in his major review (1987) of this concept, has included a more recent and exhaustive literature search of the now existing data available.

I would first like to review Greenson's evolving understanding of this topic and then review other contributions that have been made. I will conclude with some ideas of my own. My comments regarding Greenson's evolving view of working through are derived from three sources. The first a verbatim transcript of a seminar Greenson conducted in the Spring of 1960 for candidates of the Los Angeles Psychoanalytic Institute. The second is Greenson's (1965b) paper, and the third is his 1967 work *The Technique and Practice of Psychoanalysis*.

In the 1960 seminar, Greenson addresses an issue that was uppermost in his mind at that time, the corrective emotional experience, as put forth by Franz Alexander, M.D. (Alexander and French, 1946). This technique, which suggested a conscious manipulation of the transference in order to provide an experience that was held to be therapeutic by the analyst, was felt by Greenson to be anathema to working through. Such an experience did not, in Greenson's view, include insight, which was one of the essential ingredients in the working through process. He also felt that the school of neo-catharsis, as developed by Ferenczi and Rank (1925), which promoted the experience of abreaction and catharsis at the expense of analysis of resistance also fell under the same criticism; that is, the achievement of insight was not viewed as necessary. Greenson opined that while analysis would certainly be easier without having to deal with working through, such treatment would prevent any real change from occurring in the personality. "Abreaction without insight is insufficient," Greenson said. Abreaction per se could be helpful, Greenson felt, if it led to insight, but not if it stopped before insight was achieved. Greenson then put forward to the seminar a preliminary definition of working through. "Working through refers to the variety of repeated attempts to achieve insight about any given phenomena in opposition to various sets of forces which oppose it. Working through is a heterogeneous group of procedures and processes and goings on in which we are attempting to establish insight against forces that oppose it. As long as insight is not fully achieved, we're dealing with working through." He then went further in describing how working through was achieved. "It [working through] is carried out by interpretation, confrontation, and condensation—but it's a *repetitive* event to gain insight against forces (resistances) that oppose it." "Working through is completed when we feel that the insight gained is readily accessible to the patient." In the seminar, Greenson pointed out that working through was an ego activity that resulted in the strengthening of its synthetic functions. Working through needs to be viewed in relation to specific insights and in terms of specific libidinal and structural levels. The need for working through illustrates the fact that resistances return and must be dealt with again and again. In this way, working through describes a particular extension of the concept of analysis of resistance. Greenson felt that the dimension of time was an essential element in the working through process. By pointing out past examples of a patient's resistance, the analyst shows how resistances exist on a continuum that needs to be appreciated if structural change is to occur. "The alternating focus of attention from present to past to present is essential if what we are doing is to be labeled working through." Greenson felt that some analysts, such as Horney, use defense analysis in the present to avoid the more difficult and complex issues involved in the working through process. Although he felt that resistances which could be identified, either in or out of the analytic situation, were all part of working through, he emphasized that the transference resistance was of particular import in alerting both analyst and patient as to the exact nature of what needed to be worked through next. In a second seminar, which occurred on March 9, 1960, Greenson and the group continued to expand on the topic of working through. Greenson emphasized the importance of making connections in the working through process. These connections need to occur between different libidinal zones, behavior, and defenses. When this occurs, the analysis deepens and the patient achieves mastery over previously warded off affects and ideas. Greenson saw working through as an activity of the ego, in which it (the ego) must regress, test, and then move forward again. By so doing, the reasonable ego gains in strength and is better able to judge and observe. All of this helps explain why analysis takes time. The area of ego capacity is important in assessing how much each patient needs from the analyst in order to work through recurring resistances. Some patients will need less assistance in the working through process than others. This need will, of course, vary over time in the analysis. One way to judge whether the analysis is reaching a terminal phase is an awareness of the relative amount of working through that is being done by the patient. As the latter becomes more adept at working through and is doing more of the work with less help being required from the analyst, we have an objective measure of increased ego strength and capacity to carry on the function of the analyst. The eventual goal, of course, is to end the actual analysis and see the working through process transferred into one of the aspects of eventual self-analysis.

Greenson, like Fenichel (1941) and Rado (1925), compared working through to mourning in that both involve separation and a loosening of past reactions. He said: "In giving up past reactions, we free cathexes to the past attachments. This results in energies being made available for new experiences, new objects, and new perceptions" (p. 80). Here he gave the example of one of his patients who suddenly noticed a picture on the wall that had been there for three years and had remained unnoticed until that time. Antedating Kohut's work, Greenson emphasized the importance of being empathically in tune with the patient's subjectivity as a definite aid to the working through process. Greenson saw the analysis of transference resistance as the most fruitful means of pursuing all of this. He cautioned the seminar group, "We should never become tired of asking 'And how do you feel about me today?', 'Who am I now?', and 'What is the feeling here?'." He added that this type of inquiry required the analyst to have worked out his major resistances around issues of narcissism.

In Greenson's 1965 paper on "The Problem of Working Through" he had refined, and to some degree changed, his definition of working through. Succinctly put, his definition was "Working through is the analysis of those resistances and other factors which prevent insight from leading to significant and lasting change in the patient" (p. 231). The analytic work is not considered to be working through before the patient has insight. It is the goal of working through to make insight effective so that enduring changes in the patient's personality structure will occur. By making insight the central focus, it is possible to distinguish those resistances that prevent insight and those that prevent insight leading to change. Greenson called the analysis of resistance that prevented insight, analysis proper, while that analysis that dealt with resistance to using one's insight to produce change was to be known as working through. Greenson noticed that in some patients working through proceeds almost silently as the various resistances are interpreted over and over. In other cases, new or specific resistances prevent the insight gained from being used.

Greenson emphasized the necessity for having a reliable, working alliance before a consistent working through process could be put into motion. He felt that when an analysis was stalemated, the problem was usually one of a deficient working alliance or a special problem related to the working through process. He illustrated the latter by detailing the case of a patient who could not identify with the analytic attitude outside of the treatment sessions. When this specific, tenacious resistance was analyzed, movement again reoccurred.

The third major source used for obtaining Greenson's views on working through was *The Technique and Practice of Psychoanalysis* (1967). In this, the major work of Dr. Greenson's professional career, he further refines the concept. In it, he states that working through is the fourth procedure (along with confrontation, clarification, and interpretation) which together make up the insight furthering techniques which we know as analyzing.

"Working through refers to the complex set of procedures and processes which occur after an insight has been given. The analytic work which makes it possible for insight to lead to change is the work of *working through*. It refers in the main to the repetition, progressive and elaborate explorations of the resistances which prevent an insight from leading to change" (Greenson, 1967, p. 42). In addition to the broadening and deepening of the analysis of resistance, reconstructions are also of particular importance. A variety of circular processes are set in motion by working through, in which insight, memory, and behavior change influence each other (Kris, 1956a,b).

Greenson reviewed the importance of the repetition compulsion and the death instinct, as well as the interesting relationship between the work of mourning and working through, in his 1965 paper. In regard to the former, Greenson cited Freud's 1917 and 1926 elaborations of "special resistances," which make working through necessary (1917a, 1926a). In 1914, he called this the "compulsion to repeat"; later in 1920, this became a manifestation of the death instinct. In the Introductory Lectures in 1917, Freud referred to the "adhesiveness of the libido"; that is, the tenacity with which the libido hangs onto particular objects and channels of discharge. In 1926, he called it "the resistance of the unconscious," and, later on, "the resistance of the Id." Finally, in 1937, in "Analysis Terminable and Interminable," he connected this adhesiveness of the libido to an instinct of aggression. Although he had previously called this force the "resistance of the Id," he now went even further and described an ultimate phenomena attributable to the behavior of the two primal instincts whose distribution cannot be confined to a single process of the mental apparatus. He went on to describe a force at work, which is defending itself by all possible means against recovery and is clinging tenaciously to illness and suffering. He called this force the "unconscious sense of guilt and need for punishment" which he, again, derived from the aggressive or destructive instinct which is a manifestation of the death instinct of animate matter.

Greenson did not elaborate on these ideas of Freud in the 1965 paper. In his book of technique, however, Greenson stated that the discussion of the presence or absence of the death instinct was beyond the scope of Volume 1. He did say that, in his experience, he saw no need to postulate such a death instinct and that it seemed possible, to him, to explain repetitiveness within the bounds of the pleasure–pain principle (Schur, 1960, 1966). In regard to the comparison of working through with the work of mourning, Greenson was in essential agreement with Fenichel (1941). He pointed out how, in one case, a young man is unconsciously clinging to his lost mother, preventing him from making the new identifications necessary for change to occur. When these were worked through in the transference to Dr. Greenson, the patient's clinical depression and stalemated analytic process remitted. Glenn (1978) has gone even further with this connection in postulating that working through is a "vehicle for mourning lost objects" (p. 41) (see also Fenichel, 1941; Lewin, 1950; Kris, 1956b; Stewart, 1963).

Other Major Contributions to the Literature of Working Through

The most far-reaching review and elaboration of the concept of working through since Greenson's 1965 paper is that of Charles Brenner (1987). Brenner concludes that working through is not a special kind of analysis, it is ordinary run of the mill analysis as we know it today. Nor is it the analysis of one or another component of psychic conflict. It is "analysis of psychic conflict in all its aspects, now one, now another." Brenner believes that a patient's failure to improve requires no special kind of analysis, but rather good solid analytic work carried on primarily through a systematic focusing on the transference. Brenner points out that before the concepts of defense and superego analysis were known, Freud in two short paragraphs laid out the definition and function of working through. He meant by these terms the work of helping the patient overcome resistance. The naming of resistances was not enough to free the person from the underlying repressed, instinctual impulses. There must also be time to allow the patient to work through the resistances in order for an analytic cure to take place. Brenner states that the resistances that Freud was most likely talking about were those represented by repressed childhood wishes. Later on, Freud referred to these as id resistances, or manifestations of the repetition compulsion. Brenner includes in his paper an exhaustive review of the psychoanalytic literature of working through. I include here only the highlights of this scholarly undertaking. The reader is referred to Brenner's work for a more detailed consideration of this topic.

Freud (1914) stated that after naming the resistance, the patient must be given more time to become conversant with it. Only when the resistance is at its height can the analyst, working with the patient, discover the repressed, instinctual impulses which are feeding the resistance. This arduous task of working through is necessary and is what separates psychoanalytic treatment from any kind of treatment by suggestion. Freud correlates working through with the abreacting of affect, which was necessary to make hypnotic treatment effective. Fenichel (1941) focused on the defensive attitude of the patient. The patient must be shown that this is an evasion of something and is at base willful. Working through was essentially a deepening of the analysis of resistance. He did not believe that a special type of resistance made working through necessary.

Greenacre (1954, 1956) related working through to transference analysis and made the important addition of emphasizing the import of reconstructing childhood events and "organizing events, in latency." Novey (1962) states that it is not so much the ego defenses that resist change, but the affective infantile core which resists change and which accounts for the time lag between insight and change.

Stewart (1963) interpreted Freud to mean that the term *working through* applied only to change involving the id and the tendency to repeat patterns of instinctual discharge. This lies beyond the patient's will to change. Change occurs by virtue of the patient's continuing the analytic work in defiance of the defensive resistances and as a result of being opposed by the equally "biological" forces of maturation and development that work toward "cure." For Stewart, working through is an activity of the patient only. Stewart maintained that working through was different from mourning in that in the latter, one must come to grips with the loss of a love object, while in the former the goal is to alter the modes and aims of the instinctual drives. Stewart also felt that as patients approached the areas of infantile conflict in analysis, they feared a loss of stable ego functions. In this latter view, Stewart came closer to the view of Fenichel. Ekstein

(1966) saw working through as a form of learning which required endless repetition in the service of adaptation. Brodsky (1967) suggested working through is a function of the time lag between understanding and being able to tolerate the intense unpleasure of anxiety or of severe narcissistic mortification. Karush (1967) seemed to anticipate some of Kohut's (1971) ideas in recognizing the need for the patient to come to see the analyst as an idealized object who influences by example. This, along with other factors, resulted in new identifications and restructuring of the ego ideal. Glenn (1978) agreed with Fenichel's ideas that working through was a repetition of the undoing of defense. He also added the concept of working through as a vehicle for mourning lost objects. As the analysis proceeds, the patient progressively decathects infantile (archaic) object representations. Dewald (1976) felt that it was the analyst's tolerant analytic attitude that provided a new, real experience for the patient. The repetition of this phenomena leads to a progressive undoing of defenses against drive derivatives. This describes working through. Shane (1979) asserted that working through can best be understood via a developmental approach. He sees analysis as a developmental maturational process, therefore, pathologically oriented development is gradually changed via the process of analysis. This, like normal growth, takes time. The lag between insight and change is best explained by the concept that development takes time. O'Shaughnessy (1983) is one of the writers who emphasizes the role of the patient in the working through process. The patient must be able to put the analyst's words into his own affect-laden words for change to occur. This takes time. Sedler (1983) also emphasizes the part played by the patient in the working through process. It is the patient's will to remember that is the most powerful element of overcoming resistance. Valenstein (1983) defined working through in terms of the patient's actions. He felt that patients must convert insight into action and then practice these actions for changes to occur. The habitually used analytically informed action eventually becomes ego syntonic and relatively autonomous. This results in enduring changes in the ego and character structure. This process is especially important for those patients with "development neuroses" (previously narcissistic neuroses) who wish the analyst to do the work for them.

Summarizing in this review, Brenner sees each author focusing on what, for them, best describes the analytic process. All agree that analysis is slow work and that working through takes time. Why this is so is not known, for, as Brenner points out, just changing one word for another does not provide an adequate explanation. (Example, analysis is slow work, defensive analysis is slow work, etc.) In Brenner's view, we can say this much about working through: "Neurotic symptoms and character traits that are accessible to analysis are the result of psychic conflict originating in childhood. They're compromise formations among id, ego, and superego" (p. 101). The analysis of these compromise formations is working through.

Brenner compares the modern view of working through with that of a similar modernization of the term *transference*. In Freud's 1914 paper, both working through and transference had two meanings. On the one hand they were seen as a type of nuisance. Example, transference as resistance and working through as a type of "regrettable delay" in moving from insight to cure. Brenner now feels both to be in error. He sees transference as ubiquitous in life, albeit handled differently in analysis. Similarly, working through *is* analysis. It is the interpretive work. The analysis of psychic conflict in all its aspects is what should properly be called working through.

To bring this back to the work of Greenson, Brenner describes a case that Greenson used in his 1965 paper. Brenner reanalyzes the data and concludes that all that has happened is that more analysis of a resistance expressed in the transference has taken place.

Hans Loewald (1980), in discussing working through, takes a somewhat different tack. He at first agrees with Freud that working through involves the overcoming of the id resistance as manifested by the repetition compulsion. He goes on to say, however, that in the working through process "the ego, and not necessarily the conscious ego, works over old conflictual experiences and this compulsive repetition in current life, particularly in the transference situation is what constitutes the working through process" (p. 67). This statement makes it appear that he uses working through in a more general way to describe a part of the analytic process that occurs by virtue of an ongoing action due to the interplay of analyst and patient. This process need not be conscious to be effective. In another place, Loewald states "Working through is the work of the ego to redo or rework actively what was once experienced passively, to repeat on a higher level, a level of more dimension and further differentiated and integrated experience and functioning. Working through has to do with redoing not reworking the past" (p. 67). (Repetition is recreation.)

Rangell (1987) also takes up the process of ego alteration by the working through process. He adds an original twist to the process in postulating that the repetition compulsion itself becomes less id oriented and more ego oriented during the course of the therapeutic process. In this way, the repetition compulsion itself becomes more of a force for the overcoming of anxiety and the seeking of more adaptive solutions. Rangell sees this as an unconscious willingness of the ego to surrender secondary and tertiary gains of symptoms.

Robert Waelder (Guttman and Guttman, 1987), another highly respected clinical theoretician, focuses primarily on the interpretive aspects of working through. He describes the process in the following way:

In spite of its special name working through consists of nothing more than interpretation. One point makes it special. This is that working through is a specific type of interpretation, having the capacity to finish the analysis. The successful end of an analysis is a result of having worked through the interpretation given previously. If skillfully handled it gives assurance that the symptoms, character traits, neurosis or patient will not need further analysis. An interpretation that involves working through is different from other interpretations by virtue of its function. That is it shows the patient how he repeatedly acts or reacts in a particular unconsciously determined way. While interpretation proper shows "what you really mean is" working through has the meaning of "There too, There again" [Quoted in Guttman and Guttman, 1987, p. 60].

All the above examples are derived from what, for most, would be considered the mainstream of American psychoanalysis. As mentioned in the introduction, the concept of working through has seemed to achieve catholic or universal utility for each and every school of psychoanalytic thought. For example, Hanna Segal (1981), in her explication of the school of Melanie Klein, describes the working through process in terms of object relations and "positions." She speaks of manic defenses keeping the sense of depression from the ego and preventing the working through of the depressive position. The working through of the depressive position in normal development requires that reparation be achieved. Again, the importance of repetition was stressed. "These oscillations between the paranoid-schizoid position and depressive feelings underlie, in my opinion, the process of working through. In the analytic situation, the patient relives his relation to his original objects. His attachment to them must be relived again and again and again" (p. 20). Dr. Segal also compares working through with mourning. "A mourning process is necessary to give up the earlier pathological relationship with the object."

Working through also appears rather prominently in the writings of Heinz Kohut (1984). In "How Does Analysis Cure," Kohut's last major work, published posthumously, eleven references to working through are cited. In each case working through is described as a crucial piece of the analytic process. However, it is never defined nor is it clear how it differs from the general term *analysis*. Kohut does distinguish one difference in regard to working through when compared to traditional theory, that is what it is that is necessary to be worked through. Kohut emphasizes the importance of selfobject transferences in addition to the more familiar transferences which arise from conflict and compromise formation. These transferences, according to Kohut, stem from an arrest in development, which occurs in preoedipal times and which needs to be understood and handled somewhat differently than those more traditional transferences originating in the oedipal era. The logical extension from this supposition would be that since in most systems working through deals primarily with resistances that involve transference the same type of approach advocated by Kohut for the handling of selfobject transferences would be necessary for the working through process of the resistances based on these transferences. Another problem arises when we consider that, like more traditional transference phenomena, there also arises resistances to the development of selfobject transferences. Are these to be handled differently than the resistances due to selfobject failure? I believe so. Resistances to the development of selfobject transference seem to me to require the more familiar combination of confrontation, identification, clarification, and interpretation, as what is being addressed is an inability of the patient to allow the regressive state of mind, or the degree of dependency necessary for the reactivation of these archaic selfobject configurations to occur in relation to the analyst. On the other hand, in dealing with the resistances caused by selfobject failure, a somewhat different approach would seem to be necessary. One of the difficulties is, again, the problem of translating the language of one theory to another. While selfobject failure is not described as resistance per se, in self psychological theory it produces the same effects in the analytic flow. The difference may be in the notion that in traditional analytic theory, resistances have to be interpreted so that they are overcome, thereby allowing a deepening and progression of the analytic process, as described in Greenson's 1965 paper. This overcoming of the resistance to the use of insight is what constitutes working through.

In the working through of selfobject transferences, one hopes to achieve a similar end by following a somewhat different path. Whereas, in overcoming the resistance to using insight, the transference resistance must be transformed or changed by being made conscious again and again, in the working through of selfobject transferences it is by the understanding and explanation of the derailments of the selfobject transference via empathic failure which gradually results in maturation of the selfobject transference from its more archaic forms to those that are more mature. When this process occurs repeatedly, a new type of working through is seen to take place.

In postulating the concept of the bipolar transference, Stolorow, Brandchaft, and Atwood (1987) describe an analytic process in which both selfobject and residual (traditional) transference phenomena alternate in a background–foreground arrangement. The concept of working through and its elaboration would seem to be expanded by viewing all analyses as combinations of these types of transference phenomena.

Discussion

It seems to me that specificity of analytic terms such as working through serves a valuable function. It makes us look at what we are doing or think that we are doing under higher magnification. We no longer live in the world of oil immersion microscopy, but rather in the era of electron microscopy. While it may be parsimonious to think globally as Brenner does and relegate working through to just good analysis of all the aspects of psychic conflict, I would cast my lot with Greenson and others who have found value in honing and refining this particular type of analytic work. The advantage of such a position is experienced in the clinical situation in a way that helps the analyst keep his place, as it were, in the flow of the analytic material. In my experience, this concept acts as an organizing focus for the analyst and helps to preserve a modicum of hope when the analysis is mired down in a sea of what appears to be repetitive defensive derivatives. To be able to think of such a concept as working through at such a time can have the effect of helping the analyst and, at some point, the patient, to maintain enough optimism to see such an impasse as having a specific and particular function for the analysis. To view such an event as only more unanalyzed psychic conflict is, in my opinion, to miss deeper levels of resistance that, if illuminated, will facilitate the movement toward acceptance and resolution in the analytic work.

With the proliferation of varieties of analytic theories, there is an ever increasing tendency to pull back into our familiar enclaves and smugly, but perhaps anxiously, declare ourselves to be the true bearers of the revealed truth. If, instead, we can attempt to refine and define our language, there is the possibility that we may find more areas of agreement than has heretofore been possible. It is hard to see how this can be anything but beneficial to our continuing attempts to expand psychoanalytic knowledge.

I would postulate that what lies in the future is more likely the discovery of additional types of transference phenomena, that, together with the associated resistance functions, will necessitate the continued refinement of the concept of working through. Just as Greenson, and Freud before him, continuously worked to refine and perfect the concept of working through, it behooves us to carry on their work, and the work of plunging deeper and with a spirit of adventure into the expansion and refinement of our analytic, conceptual tools.

12

Some Defensive Aspects of the Masturbation Fantasy and the Necessity to Work It Through

Sanford M. Izner, M.D.

MASTURBATION fantasies and the problems revolving around an understanding of masturbatory activity have held a place of interest for those associated with psychoanalysis since the early writings of Freud (1900). In his elaboration of infantile sexual life (1910c), Freud clearly indicated the importance of early sexual functions and interests on the part of the developing child. In these phenomena, masturbation and the fantasies related to this activity played a significant role.

Since that early period in psychoanalytic development, there have been occasions where discussions and writings concerned with masturbation have been granted primary consideration, namely the Symposium of the Vienna Psychoanalytic Society of 1912 and many important papers (Eidelberg, 1945; Lampl-de Groot, 1950; Kris, 1951; Arlow, 1953) devoted to the subject of masturbation and its relationship to neurotic symptomatology. It is the particular concern of this presentation to attempt to demonstrate the importance of changes in the content of the masturbatory fantasies during analysis, and to relate these changes in fantasy life to the defensive, regressive phenomena occurring in relation to the transference and corresponding to the unresolved oedipal problems from childhood recapitulated by these fantasies. Transitions in the content of these fantasies should lend themselves to some clarification of the transference relationship, from the standpoint of attempts to ward off certain transference manifestations, along with clarification of the level of defensive organization in operation at that point in the analysis. As masturbatory fantasies undergo further elaboration and change during analysis, they should provide some index of attempted resolution of the transference neurosis, along with attempted altered mastery of the oedipal problem from childhood. Freud (1920) expressed these thoughts clearly in his discussion of the evolution and use of the transference neurosis in psychoanalytic treatment when he directed attention to the development of the transference neurosis and how it becomes both the illness and the means of attaining a "cure" in the analysis. Of necessity, as important as these elements may be, no special effort will be made to deal with the problems related to the compulsive type of masturbation, the significance of aggression in masturbation, or the economic aspect of the discharge function of the act, so as to limit the scope of the discussion that follows.

In order to introduce the subject adequately, a brief review of some of the more pertinent literature seems to be in order. Tausk (1912), in his contribution to the 1912 Symposium on Masturbation, mentioned the role of masturbation in barring the "individual from reality," introducing some elements of defensive function in relation to the act, but he seemed to be most concerned with the elements of guilt related to the fantasies accompanying the masturbatory act, especially revolving around the child's incestuous wishes for mother and his defiance of father.

Annie Reich (1951a), in her discussion of the symposium, emphasized a number of significant points pertinent to the discussion which follows, namely: that because "Masturbation is an auto-erotic form of sexual gratification, when a certain maturation of object-libidinal strivings is reached, masturbation cannot supply adequate gratification" (p. 84). She added that the nonexistence of masturbation in adolescence is a sign of serious illness and that, "Reappearance of masturbation in the course of analysis is frequently a sign of the lifting of repressions and a forerunner of therapeutic improvement" (p. 87). She stated further that masturbation in adults, except under special circumstances, must be considered a symptom. Fenichel (1945b), in his remarks on the subject, stated, "Masturbation does not cause neurosis, but may well be a symptom of neurosis. Whenever an adult prefers masturbation to intercourse, this can be considered neurotic" (p. 101). In summarizing Freud's (1912b) Comments on the 1912 Symposium, Annie Reich pointed out that in the masturbatory fantasy, the step from fantasy (idealized) objects to reality objects is not made and these are the "lightly disguised" incestuous objects.

Anna Freud (1949) stressed the importance of the "double struggle" against masturbation, that is, "the struggle against both the physical activity and the content of the fantasy, which may become unconscious, or become transferred to ego activities and acted out in this way, or the fantasies may emerge as symptoms" (p. 202). Ernst Kris (1951) emphasized that it was not the autoerotic activity itself but the fantasy content which was of greatest importance in the understanding of masturbation. Arlow (1953) discussed most clearly the ideas developed in Freud's paper (1908) on "Hysterical Fantasies and Their Relation to Bisexuality" and related them to the deeper oedipal meaning of the masturbation fantasies. Arlow demonstrated the role of masturbation in the formation of symptoms, indicating that the defensive functioning of the ego may separate the physical (masturbatory) and psychical (fantasy) activity of masturbation in an effort to ward off any impulse to carry out the act. This results in the formation of symptoms of rather specific nature, with repression of the fantasies or their later appearance in the form of dreams. And most importantly, as pertains to this discussion, he pointed out how libidinal impulses freed in the transference relationship can result in the development of defenses, often of a regressive nature, in an effort to ward off impulses to masturbate.

It was Jeanne Lampl-de Groot (1950) who described and summarized so clearly how, "in the course of sexual and physical maturation, the fantasy life undergoes dramatic change, from the early fantasies of a pre-oedipal relationship with mother, to be fondled and nursed and cared for passively, to the desire for gratification on an anal level and finally into the oepidal period in the genital organization" (p. 155). She also emphasized how, in order to avoid the castration threat of the oedipal period, regression may occur in the fantasy life to preoedipal states of desire and fantasy fulfillment. She discussed the point that the decisive factor with regard to health or sickness in relation to masturbation "lies in the conscious or unconscious fantasies, feelings (guilt feelings) and impulses which accompany the masturbatory act. Oedipal fantasies are of primary significance in the neurosis due to their being the first fantasies revolving around the parent of the opposite sex as a gratifying object in the sexual sphere" (p. 162). She elaborated further the development of this fantasy life with the statement, "In normal development, the oedipus complex is distinguished by the fact that genital masturbation has become the only (or almost only) act of auto-erotic gratification. At this point, a boy's desires and instinctual impulses are expressed in fantasies whose abbreviated content is *I want to take father's place with mother*" (p. 162). These phenomena may be demonstrated in clinical material obtained during the analysis of a young male adult who entered treatment in his twenty-ninth year because of intense anxiety related to disturbing libidinal and aggressive impulses. These impulses were most manifest in a tendency to become very uncomfortable in the presence of other men and because of the anxiety arising from the desire to stare at their genitals.

At the time of his entry into analysis, the patient was living in a city far removed from his original home and was preoccupied with feelings of loneliness. He was unable to progress in his professions or to attain his graduate degree and had difficulty in establishing social relationships, especially with his peers. He felt strong rivalry with the people in his office and continually experienced intense difficulty with authority figures in his profession. He was most concerned with his inability to form a mature kind of love relationship with a woman. This patient was the youngest of three sons and the only one who felt the need to leave the city of his birth, the others remaining quite close to the family, although the patient always considered himself to be the favorite of his parents. He left home to complete his education and because he felt he could not remain in the family business. The patient did not get along well at home and complained that when he lived there, he and his parents would argue all the time. He considered his mother to be an aggressive and domineering woman who ruled her husband and the household, and also directed the business. His father was experienced as being weak and passive since the time of a business failure early in the patient's life, during the Depression years. It was following this failure that mother seemed to take charge.

The family resided in a deteriorated portion of the city in which the patient was born. The contact between parents and children was always quite close, and the quarters in which they lived rather intimate. In this connection, the analysis brought to light many screen memories concerned with the patient's early experiences involving aggressive and libidinal strivings. Most of the early memories relegated the older brother to father's position in the family and were concerned with primal fantasies and early masturbatory practices. For example, the patient recollected a memory from his early teens when he and his oldest brother came upon the brother's oldest son masturbating on the back stairs. The patient asked his brother what he was going to do about it and the brother replied, "What do you expect me to do, I'm no expert on these things?" In other memories of this nature, mother was usually represented as an aggressive woman, and quite frequently as a prostitute who drank with and entertained "Negro men." When father himself appeared in these recollections, it was generally in the form of a physically strong but depreciated, broken, characterologically weak and passive person in whom the patient felt disappointed and let down. Many other early memories revolved around the patient's intense feelings of competitiveness and rivalry in relation to his "bigger and more privileged brothers," the older of whom came to be identified with father and the middle brother often being experienced as a substitute for mother.

In the transference neurosis, all of these relationships were recapitulated and reexperienced time and again and all of these fantasies projected onto the analyst. Early in the analysis the patient became aware of the homosexual components in the impulse to stare at men's genitals, which was directed at both his superiors and his contemporaries. He could also see his need to defy and depreciate these men and the resultant inability to make progress in his work and professional studies because of these feelings.

During the years preceding puberty and early adolescence, the patient had been masturbating with regularity. The masturbation was accompanied by a rescue fantasy that persisted into this period of analysis. In the fantasy he is a successful and well-to-do owner of a gambling house in a city in the West. A beautiful young girl comes into town seeking employment and wants to become a prostitute, or in other variations is a prostitute. The patient offers her an honorable position and thus rescues her from sexual promiscuity.

Lampl-de Groot (1950) explained the development of this type of fantasy of latency during which time masturbation is usually sporadic due to anxiety related to "forbidden incestuous desires." These fantasies revolve around "being grown up; in the center of the fantasies is the ambition to be a powerful man both in an heroic love life and in all life situations" (p. 170). In the transference relationship it became clear that this fantasy represented the patient's competitive struggle with father, wherein the patient became the powerful and heroic protector of mother in preventing her from falling prey to the villainous father or to the patient's brothers. In this connection it is important to note that the patient frequently referred to his first experience in sexual intercourse. He recalled how he feared that he had injured the girl with whom he had intercourse, as she found it necessary to visit a doctor for an examination the following day. His concern that intercourse was a violent and destructive act directed against the woman seemed evident.[1] In the analysis, at this time, the patient had begun to frequently hold or scratch his genitals or to cover them with his hand. He would often remark about the "itching" in the genital area and the need to "scratch," which he resorted to during much of the time on the couch. It had become clearer too that masturbation indulged in by the patient at this time was a defensive act directed at both the discharge of the oedipal libidinal impulses and attempts to ward off further oedipal fantasies. In addition, it had become a form of defiance of father and also a punitive act in a more or less controlled type of self-directed aggressive behavior as if to say, "See, you don't have to do anything to hurt me, I do it myself." His concern with regard to masturbation at this time was related to a fear of going insane.

After several months of analysis, when the patient's passive feminine homosexual strivings in the transference had been clearly

---

[1] The aggressive component directed at the object of the libidinal impulse in the fantasy (mother in this instance) is clear. R. Sterba has demonstrated this element of the fantasy in his (1940) paper entitled "Aggression in the Rescue Fantasy," wherein the libidinal object is placed in a fantasied position of danger by the rescuer.

established, along with the persistence of the masturbatory rescue fantasy, he began to evidence many dependent and orally tinged feelings directed toward the analyst. He seemed to have initiated a regression to an earlier state in the libidinal organization, apparently out of defense against the anxiety generated by his competitive oedipal struggle with the analyst and the resultant danger of castration. It was at this time that he recollected an earlier childhood fantasy with which he used to masturbate. In this fantasy, the patient is at the bottom of a flight of stairs and mother is standing near the top of the stairs talking to a male boarder. The boarder is complaining about his sore and scarred feet and mother sympathizes with and feels sorry for the boarder. The patient was stimulated to masturbate at the time when he recollected the fantasy at home before telling the analyst about it. The implications of the fantasy are quite clear. The regressive retreat in the analysis related to the oedipal struggle and the homosexual strivings and castration anxiety that accompanied it, seemed to have forced the patient into a position in the transference where the analyst had come to represent mother. His plea for love and pity and his need to be protected and cared for because of his inadequate and helpless state in comparison to father seemed evident. The patient's feelings of impotence, castration, and inadequacy were manifested by expressions of lack of sexual interest in his wife, many pleas for food and warmth from the analyst, and repeated expressions of the need for care and interest on the part of the analyst, who now so evidently represented mother. In the transference, the libidinal impulses toward mother expressed in oral terms represented a defensive retreat from the competitive oedipal position in the father transference which had been manifested by the rescue fantasy accompanied by masturbation. Mother at this point in the analysis was experienced as the powerful and protecting authority figure and father was looked upon as a depreciated and weakened person who was governed by mother. The patient obviously sought protection and rescue for himself from his own instinctual impulses toward the incestuous love object of early childhood. The desire for pity and help and rescue by the analyst as mother from the same depreciated and castrated fate suffered by father in the fantasy seemed clear. In this connection the patient recalled an incident from early childhood wherein he was watching father play cards and one of the players, a smaller and weaker appearing man initiated an argument and struck father. Father did not strike back and the patient felt very let down by father's failing of him on this occasion.[2]

With the ensuing frustration and disappointment of his demands upon the analyst for additional care and love in the recapitulation of his early childhood relationship to mother, the patient would once more shift in his transference relationship. He developed many anal, hostile, competitive feelings manifested by dreams of bombardment and fear of anal attack from behind in retaliation. These feelings were most clearly expressed in a series of dreams, a typical one of which pictured the patient fighting and wrestling with a physically powerful man, the struggle culminating with this man inserting a finger into the patient's rectum. These dreams not only represented the patient's competitive, hostile feelings in the transference based on his angry feelings toward father, but also his desire for gratification of his libidinal impulses, gratification he felt that father gave to mother, and that both mother and father denied him. As a child he seemed unable to tolerate or cope with this frustration. Following these dreams the analyst came to be experienced as the disappointing, depriving and interfering father, who could really satisfy no one. At this point, there was a return to the rescue fantasy of the early period in analysis, but the accompanying masturbation seemed much less gratifying.

As acts of masturbation decreased and the fantasies seemed less arousing, the patient dreamed of attempting to rescue his wife from a "chief." In the dream he fights with the "chief" for possession of his wife, who was in a "fenced-in area." He understood the transference implications of the dream, relating the "chief" to both the analyst and father, and his wife to mother. This dream occurred at the time of the analyst's vacation and the primal scene aspects of the dream were rather clearly concerned with feelings of exclusion in relation to his parents and the analyst (1959). The patient soon came to realize that he had experienced mother as a kind and giving person and because of his hostile, competitive oedipal feelings toward father and his older brothers, had always experienced them as persons who came

---

[2]The representation of father as a characterologically weak and depreciated person presents the boy in the oedipal period with the fear that control of incestuous impulses remains more or less with him alone. Intensification of homosexual strivings may result along with the increased propensity toward regression to preoedipal defensive states where care and control would then rest more completely with the domineering and strong mother.

between himself and mother. He then dreamed of being "in an office and talking to this very attractive girl with whom he works. He is interested in making love to her, but a large powerful man walks into the office and she begins to talk to this man. The patient becomes very depressed and leaves the office, disappointed, hurt, and dejected. The girl soon follows after him, looking for him." He realized at this point that he wished for love spontaneously from mother, that he should not need to compete for and struggle for the love from mother or his wife and that in the transference, father is a person who did not attempt to come between the patient and mother, but that mother (in reality) preferred father as a sexual object. The patient became aware that he too could feel love and compassion for his father, as mother did in the fantasy of the boarder with the scarred feet, because it was his own introjected "father figure" that kept him from mother, not father himself, as a defense against the real damaging feeling "that mother never really wanted me as a sexual partner." In addition, his fear of his incestuous impulses toward his mother forced him into the "defensive use" of father as a restrictive and interfering object. This entire picture was recapitulated in his relationship with the analyst in the transference at this point. An interesting incident at a different phase of the analysis served to illustrate this patient's need to reenact in the repetition compulsion another situation of trauma from childhood in an effort to master the feelings described above. The patient arrived at the end of the hour for one of his regularly scheduled appointments. This was on the day following the cancellation of a previous appointment. He was made aware of his error coupled with the fact that this sort of confusion had never before occurred in the preceding three years of analysis. At the time of his next appointment, he expressed the feeling that he had not wanted to come for this following hour and that he was very angry with the analyst. He had the thought that he wanted to be rid of both his wife and the analyst. He had dreamed the night before and the dream, when analyzed, revealed these feelings along with the thought that the analyst did not care for the patient and must have preferred to see someone else, since he had granted permission for the cancellation of the previous appointment. At the same time, the patient related an incident of the previous night that had occurred with his wife. He had wanted to have sexual intercourse and she at first refused him. He became furious with her, and when she went to bed and called to the patient to come to bed and have intercourse, he continued to read and did not go to bed until after his wife had fallen asleep. When he finally went to bed, he felt sexually aroused and began to fantasy having intercourse with several attractive women. This culminated in his masturbating. He realized that his anger was the result of feeling that neither the analyst nor the patient's wife cared for or were interested in him as a sexual object, and must prefer someone else. The desire to masturbate was designed to master the feelings of rejection as a love object that he had to reconstruct in the analysis and in the acting out with his wife. The angry feeling that accompanied the masturbation and his return to the analysis the next day was expressed by him in the following terms: "If you don't care about me, the hell with you. I'll show you! If you don't want me, who needs you?"

Masturbation continued for a time during the analysis, the fantasies arousing these activities revolving around thoughts of intercourse with attractive females with whom the patient worked. He began to take a more realistic attitude toward his relationship with his parents, his wife, his brothers, and the persons with whom he had contact in his work. He became more independent in his activities and less concerned with desires for financial assistance from his parents and brothers. At the same time, he began to insist that his wife give up work and remain at home with the anticipation that she might become pregnant. He had strongly resisted any desires on her part for children up to this point. It seemed, too, that he was less competitive with his brothers and peers in his struggle for attention and recognition from his parents and superiors. He was deriving less gratification from masturbatory activity which seems to coincide with the comments of Annie Reich (1951a) concerning the maturation of object libidinal strivings and the resultant decreased gratification from masturbation mentioned earlier. In this regard, it is of particular interest that his rescue fantasy became sublimated to a degree in a change in his work, where he undertook to help delinquent boys and girls who had come into difficulty with the law because of their aggressive and libidinal strivings. It was clear that the rescue fantasy revolved also around a desire to be rescued from his own disturbing instinctual impulses from childhood.

As the resolution of the transference progressed, more adequate mastery of the oedipal struggle progressed accordingly, with the formation of more appropriate and realistic object relationships by the patient. With the onset of the termination period of analysis, there was a return to masturbation and oedipal and preoedipal fantasies which were recognized as defenses against the process of separation. In the elaboration of the fantasies related during the analysis of this patient, it became evident that the analysis followed the course of the transition in the fantasies that seemed to arouse this patient to masturbatory activity, fantasies that served defensive functions on many levels during the analysis. Eidelberg (1945) in an excellent discussion points out that, "the study of changes in the masturbation fantasy as they occur in a successful analysis, indicates the progress of the treatment"(p. 128). He adds, "under favorable conditions, the masturbatory fantasy becomes more and more boring to the patient and finally disappears. In cases where it is not completely analyzed, it may interfere with good therapeutic results" (p. 128). This certainly appears to be the case and boredom along with the continued existence of the fantasy would seem to represent the introduction of another defensive function. Greenson (1953) has demonstrated the defensive aspect of boredom rather clearly, and it would seem that the development of this type of reaction to the fantasy might be indicative of something other than adequate working through the masturbatory problem.

The levels of libidinal organization to which regression occurred in the analytic process described above recapitulated many of the early attempts on the part of the patient to defend against the anxiety of his oedipal problems from childhood. His need to control and master the impulses related to his wish for mother as a love object and his desire to take father's place with her was clear throughout the entire analysis. The preoedipal fantasies and masturbation itself seemed to be only a defense against this. In reality, the existence of "primal fantasies" (Freud, 1900; Jones, 1955) in the dream material and thinly disguised in some of the fantasies themselves seems to provide a basis for the impression that masturbation as a symptom, the conscious fantasies that lead to masturbation whether directly oedipal or preoedipal in nature, or unconscious fantasies related to masturbation, may all be attempts to ward off what is both the most provocative and stimulating situation of all, and at the same time, the most disturbing to the child: that of the visualization or fantasy of the primal scene. In fact, as a decision regarding termination of analysis was arrived at, the patient reacted with a dream of masturbating during the analytic hour and the analyst being angry because the patient had fantasied sexual intercourse involving the analyst and the analyst's wife. He was aware of the implications of the dream in relation to the transference and his childhood oedipal problem. But the dream was of great significance from several standpoints. First, in relation to the termination of the analysis and the separation anxiety that usually accompanies this decision (Izner, 1959). Second, and directly concerned with the major thesis presented here, the anxiety of the patient attributed to the anger of the analyst as father in the dream was not really relegated to the masturbatory act itself, as much as to the fantasy of intercourse, which fantasy seemed to pertain rather directly to the visualization or fantasy of the primal scene. The fantasy was accompanied by the guilt and anger of the patient, anger projected on to the analyst as father in the transference. Third, from the standpoint of the resolution of both the transference neurosis and the oedipal problem from childhood, the castration danger seemed to have been mitigated into a situation of what appeared to be rather ordinary and mild anger, without the severely threatening consequences of the oedipal incestuous wish, along with the wished for destruction or elimination of father (and the analyst too in the analysis) and the fear of retaliation for this desire.

Jones (1955) refers to the letters to Fliess (Bonaparte, A. Freud, and Kris, 1954), where Freud as early as 1897 emphasized the defensive function of fantasies in his discussion of the "Architecture of Hysteria." Freud stated:

The aim seems to be to hark back to the primal scene. This is achieved in some cases directly, but in others only in a round-about way, via fantasies. For fantasies are psychical outworks constructed in order to bar the way to these memories. At the same time, fantasies seem to serve the purpose of refining, of sublimating them. They are built up out of things that have been heard about and subsequently turned into account; thus they combine things that have been experienced and things that have been heard about past events and things seen by the subject himself [Freud, 1897, Letter 61].

Fenichel (1945b) too, in speaking of conversion, pointed out the defensive aspects of masturbation, in the attempt to ward off the anxiety related to an early memory of the primal scene. He added:

Between the oedipal fantasies and the symptoms of the adult, the intermediate formations of daydreams are interpolated. And between the original oedipus fantasies and the later daydreams are inserted infantile masturbatory fantasies whose oedipus character is sometimes distorted. The conflicts which were originally connected with the oedipus complex frequently are displaced into the act of masturbation [p. 231].

The situation of another patient may serve to further illustrate the defensive aspect of masturbation and the fantasies associated with it during analysis. This patient was unable to masturbate in his adult life. He had been exposed quite frequently to primal scene situations as a child wherein he recalled sitting up nights outside the bedroom of his parents, listening to the sounds coming from there. He recollected the desire to go into their room and ask what was going on in there. His fear of masturbation resulted in an inability to resort to masturbation as a defense to ward off the anxiety related to his oedipal incestuous impulses or to even develop waking fantasies of an oedipal nature. During the analysis, he began to dream innumerable dreams of primal scene content. Some of these dreams were accompanied by nocturnal emissions. In his intense anxiety, and related to the unavailability of more adequate mechanisms of defense during the regressive process in analysis, this patient developed a paranoid psychoticlike syndrome in which he projected his incestuous impulses in the transference and from his early infantile life onto the external world. The projection of these impulses enabled the patient to avoid the recognition of them as being his own and this distortion of reality, related to impairment of ego function in this area, permitted him to avoid the anxiety attendant to reexperiencing the primal fantasies of early life and to deny the existence of the impulses to masturbate to which these fantasies might give rise. Lampl-de Groot (1950) has pointed out that "if the fantasy life constitutes a danger—an inhibiting or even destructive effect on the entire ego development may result" (p. 160). In this regard, it is important to note that patients who enter analysis and abruptly stop masturbation most often do so in order to avoid dealing with the entire problem in the analysis.

Another illustration will further clarify the thesis. A third patient who had an extremely rich waking fantasy indulged in constant "presleep" fantasies of being a heroic athlete. He would "save and win" the ball game or golf match at the very last moment and then fall immediately into a state of sleep. His sleep for a long time while in treatment was disrupted by vivid dreams of a "Medieval" (amid-evil) nature. These were court scenes involving the king and queen, their activities and struggles, the patient himself being frequently involved as a hero. Often the "wicked king was slain or driven away." This patient, too, was unable to masturbate, but utilized instead, as a defense, the satiable need to gamble and be rescued. The cards, representing the family in the form of the King, Queen, and Knave, crept into the "Medieval" primal scene dreams repetitively during his analysis. His waking fantasies revolved around the rescue of young girls from becoming prostitutes. He was able to ward off masturbation and actual primal scene fantasies, prior to falling asleep, by the development of relatively "innocuous" fantasies of being a successful and heroic athlete. At one point in this patient's treatment, long after the symptom of gambling had been relinquished, he presented a dream. In the dream, someone parachutes out of a plane, falls into shallow water and is rescued. They enter a rowboat and say, "Don't let me go back to that again." The patient associated the dream with his wife's pregnancy, which would be culminating within a month. He and his wife had not engaged in any sexual intercourse for several weeks and he was confronted with the prospect of sexual abstinence for another two or three months and felt an increasing interest in going out to gamble again. He was aware that the dream expressed the wish that he would not be permitted to be driven by his impulses to engage in the same kind of defensive activity he had found necessary to utilize in the past, that of gambling to avoid sexual fantasies or activity. He recognized that he really wished for help in the control of both his impulses to masturbate and the fantasies that might result in masturbation, for which gambling had served him as a substitute for such a long period of time.

To summarize, clinical material concerned with the defensive function of masturbatory fantasies, appearing during the analysis of a patient who was able to verbalize and associate quite freely to these fantasies has been described. At the onset of the analysis, the patient expressed a rescue fantasy involving a gambler and prostitute, a fantasy so frequently connected with the period of latency. This came to be associated with the patient's expression of his passive feminine homosexual strivings in the transference, manifested by compliance, hostility, and a highly ambivalent anally tinged relationship to the analyst. As the process of uncovering progressed, a regressive retreat soon occurred to a fantasy of an earlier period in the libidinal organization. This fantasy of the boarder with the scarred feet or "injured third party" was related to a desire for pity and love from the analyst, who at this point in the analysis had come to represent mother. This retreat had occurred in defense against the dangers inherent in the problems existing at the oedipal level. The patient represented himself as a helpless, impotent, and castrated child who required rescue from his incestuous strivings. In the process of working through, a return to the anally oriented rescue fantasies occurred, accompanied by a great deal of competitive hostility along with many fears of attack from behind in retaliation by the analyst, as father. As the patient progressed in the analysis, his masturbation fantasies altered to fantasies of chains of love objects concerned with sexual thoughts and interests in the attractive women with whom he worked and other women with whom he came into contact. With the advent of the terminal phase of analysis, masturbation had virtually ceased. The dream of the patient masturbating in the office of the analyst accompanied by the feeling that the analyst was angry because the patient fantasied intercourse between the analyst and his wife then occurred. At this point, all semblance of defense against the situation which had to be mastered in the disguised fantasies and masturbatory activity of childhood, that of visualization or fantasy of the primal scene, was gone. The patient's need to defend against these thoughts and feelings was greatly altered and the need to master the situation of trauma by masturbation appeared to be abrogated. The resultant formation of more adequate object relationships seemed to have eliminated almost all need or desire for masturbation. The analyst was now experienced in a more realistic fashion, as were the patient's parents, with whom his relationships appeared to be much more adult and his relationship to his wife became more satisfactory and mature. The working through of the masturbatory problem and the related fantasies had revealed much of the structure of his defensive processes, and at the same time resulted in a relatively satisfactory resolution of the transference neurosis along with a more adequate mastering of the oedipal problems from childhood. At this point, a problem of fundamental significance merits consideration, concerned with the feeling that the threatening figure of father in the Oedipus complex and the castration anxiety itself was utilized as a defense by this patient in order to avoid confrontation by the damaging "blow" to his narcissism that mother never really wanted him as a sexual object at all. In order to avoid the recognition that father was preferred by mother, and to ward off the angry impulses that arose in relation to this knowledge, this patient was able to project his anger on to father and use father "defensively" in order to prevent the expression of the impulses that could result in disillusionment, helplessness and further feelings of impotence in relation to mother. In this connection Freud, as he expressed it in "Moses and Monotheism" (1938), felt that, "The intensity of the fear of castration experienced by the boy . . . is *un*accountable if we consider it as a reaction to the actual threats to which the boy is being exposed in the phallic phase; only the memory of the race will explain it" (p. 124). Hartmann and Kris (1945) and Hartmann, Kris, and Loewenstein (1946) state, "However, the intensity of the fear (of castration) is not only linked to his present experience, but also to similar experiences of the past. The dreaded retaliation of the environment revives memories of similar anxieties when desires for other gratifications were predominant and when the supreme fear was not that of being castrated, but that of not being loved" (p. 32).

The clinical observations concerning the second and third patients serve to illustrate some of the effects on the defensive structure in persons unable to adequately utilize masturbation or disguised fantasy as a defense against the feelings revolving around primal scene fantasies. Freud (1910c) summarized the course of oedipal love in his statements on the psychology of love. He remarked that "Neurotics suffer with the persistence of the Oedipus Complex" and described the conditions of love due to this phenomenon, which are "the need for an injured third party, the love of a harlot, the formation of long chains of love objects, the fantasies revolving around 'rescuing the beloved', and the cleavage between tenderness and sensuality." This course or hierarchy of defensive fantasy formation seems to have been recapitulated rather completely during the analysis of the masturbation fantasies in the first clinical example. Freud added further (1924) in speaking of the Oedipus complex in boys that "masturbation is only a genital discharge of the sexual excitation belonging to the complex, and throughout his later years will owe its importance to that relationship" (p. 176).

13

Acting Out

Ralph R. Greenson, M.D.

Definition and Description

CTING out can be defined as actions of the patient which offer
belated discharge possibilities for repressed infantile impulses
or guilt feelings of the past in present-day situations. These
situations are associatively connected to the past but the patient is
unaware of the connection. The action or behavior has the unconscious purpose of warding off the memory of the past experience. The
patient is conscious of his activity or behavior but not cognizant of its
meaning. The action is well organized, not bizarre, and is felt as ego
syntonic to the patient. Although it is a distorted repetition of the past
experience, it is only thinly disguised. The situation which is repeated
in the acting out is a total experience, a unit of experience, not just a
fragment of an experience.

Acting out has to be differentiated from other neurotic actions
which occur during analysis. In particular it has to be differentiated
from symptomatic actions and abreaction experiences. Acting out
differs from symptomatic actions in that the symptomatic act is ego
alien and usually refers to part of a past situation. The symptomatic act
is also a repetition in a distorted form which serves the purpose of
maintaining the original situation in repression. The patient, however, often is unaware of his actions in the symptomatic act, not only
of its meaning.

For example, a patient during an analytic hour may unconsciously be making certain rhythmical movements with his hands which may be an unconscious repetition of one aspect of his childhood masturbation. If this is pointed out to him it becomes clear that: (1) He was not aware of it; (2) the moment he is aware of it he stops this action, and the action is felt as ego alien; (3) if one analyzes this action it is found to be a repetition of only one small feature of his childhood onanism.

A parallel to this illustration can demonstrate the difference between symptomatic action and acting out:

> A patient begins his analytic hour with much excited and scattered speech. During the speech one can observe certain rhythmical movements of his hand. This is followed by feelings of anxiety, tears, and silence. Attempts to interpret the silence do not lead anywhere. It is only when one recognizes that the entire sequence of events described above form a cohesive unit and remind the analyst of certain previous patterns of behavior in the patient that one comes upon the idea that we are dealing with acting out. This hour then can be understood as a distorted repetition of sexual excitement, masturbation, guilt, punishment, and resentment. The patient may well defend his object, his actions, his emotional outbursts, or rationalize them as being appropriate to one or another event of his daily life. He does not find any of these actions bizarre or strange or inappropriate. Interpretation of any component of this hour is fruitless. It is only the interpretation of the entire pattern which offers the possibility of leading to past memories. If the interpretation is correct in its content and if the transference situation is properly positive, only then can one expect that interpretation will lead to the original event or events which were repeated in the acting out.

Abreaction also may consist of behavior or actions of the patient which are repetitions of past events. The outstanding quality of abreaction, which differentiates it from acting out and symptomatic actions is that abreaction is an undistorted repetition of the past history. The affects which are relapsed in abreaction are always of intense, even traumatic proportions. The abreaction is felt as painful but not as ego alien, and the connection to the past is usually transparent and the patient is usually quite eager to find the connection to the past. An example of abreaction in an analytical hour would be the following:

> The patient, full of vague but intense anxiety in his associations, comes closer and closer to material which seems to point to some homosexual fantasy or experience. During the course of this hour, the patient recalls a memory of a male servant who was once in the employ of the family when he was a young boy. As he describes this servant, the patient becomes terrified, shakes, sweats, writhes on the couch, coughs, sputters, becomes cyanotic and then gags. He sits up, bathed in sweat, pale, catches his breath. He has just reexperienced a traumatic homosexual attack perpetrated upon him by the male servant. He experienced it in the present but instantly connected it to the past. It is this ease of establishing the connection to the past and the lack of distortion that distinguishes abreaction from symptomatic actions and acting out.

During analysis we see acting out, symptomatic actions, and abreactions often in combination with one another. The most difficult to recognize and the most difficult to interpret is the acting out.

Acting Out During Psychoanalysis

Acting out occurs very frequently during analysis. It should be remembered, however, that it also occurs outside the realm of psychoanalysis, but then it is not available for investigation and interpretation. The main reason for the frequent occurrence of acting out during the course of analysis is bound up with the transference. It is important to recall that transference feelings are repetitions of feelings toward persons in the present who are misunderstood in terms of the past. Not only feelings are reenacted and reexperienced, however, but also actions in accord with these feelings are repeated. It is therefore inevitable that with the development of transference we are bound to have some amount of acting out of the transference during the analysis. Although acting out in the strictest sense is always a resistance, since one of its main functions is to ward off memory, it should not be forgotten that acting out is a help in the course of the analysis. The transference situation, and, even the actions which may be stirred up in regard to the transference feelings, offer the patient a transition between his adult neurosis and his infantile neurosis. As Freud puts it, we offer the patient a playground in the analytic situation where he may repeat provisionally and temporarily certain actions of his past, now in regard to the analyst. By recognizing and interpreting the meaning of acting out, we hope to open the road to those memories which, until then, have been covered by the infantile amnesia. Thus in the transference neurosis we are bound to have some acting out; but if the transference interpretations are handled adequately, this acting out gives the analyst a possibility to reconstruct the infantile events.

Another general factor during analysis that leads to acting out involves the analyst's interpretation of the control mechanisms of the patient; that is, the defenses. Modification of the defenses corrects the distortions of the infantile impulses and affects which lie behind them, and can lead to their expression via action. Furthermore, the analyst mobilizes the instinctual drives of the patient by offering him the permissive and tolerant atmosphere of the psychoanalytic situation. These three factors, the attacking of the defenses, the mobilization of instinctual drives, and the permissive atmosphere stir up the tendencies to act out.

In general, during the course of analysis, there is apt to be more acting out of negative transference than of positive transference. Most patients are better able to verbalize the positive transference than the negative transference; and since acting out means a putting into action instead of words, the more verbalization, itself, becomes difficult, the greater the tendency to repeat rather than to remember. Usually, more intense transference reactions also increase the readiness to act out.

Increases in resistance often presage acting out. Persistent resistance may be a sign of acting out, but may also be the forerunner of acting out. Mistakes in dosage, and in timing of interpretations, lead frequently to destructive acting out. I have seen instances where too superficial interpretation by the analyst has led patients to break off the analysis. In part, this breaking off of the analysis can be understood as a repetition of the patient's leaving home because they felt misunderstood.

A young woman patient, who had run away from home when her parents refused to discuss important questions about sexuality, found it difficult to discuss openly her sexual dilemma with her analyst, despite many obvious hints in this direction. She came to me after she had seen this other analyst for three hours. In her third hour with her former analyst she told him of an overtly sexual dream with undisguised sexual excitement in the manifest content of the dream. That analyst avoided asking her about the dream and almost deliberately distracted her to something less pertinent. The patient left his office knowing she would never come back. She was furious with him far beyond what the situation would have called for. It became obvious to me that the patient was repeating with this analyst what she had experienced with her family. Unfortunately the analyst had made it very easy because he had behaved so much like her parents.

Acting Out of the Transference

As stated above, transference reactions are often acted out instead of being expressed in feelings or words alone. The situation of choice is when the patient acts out his transference feelings and impulses during the analytic hour. This gives the analyst the opportunity to observe the acting out, and to make the interpretation early, before it leads to complications. This kind of acting out is the most rewarding during analysis. The simplest examples are patients who act defiantly, or stubbornly, or bashfully to the analyst; they are usually repeating past experiences to important parental figures. The interpretation, "Where have you felt this way before?", or "To whom have you felt this way?" usually leads directly to the significant figure in the past, provided the interpretation is given in the correct intonation and without reproach. Such a point needs emphasis because acting out of intense transference feelings in the analytic hour may be more difficult to interpret than it seems. Thus, it is important that the analyst maintain a calm and firm attitude in the face of the patient's intense emotions and actions.

A young woman patient early in her analysis violently proclaimed her love for me, insisted, pleaded, and demanded that we stop the analysis and "beating around the bush," in order to engage in sexual relations. My calm but absolutely firm insistence that I must remind her of someone toward whom she had these very intense feelings led after her many protestations to a vague memory of a man who had the same quality of voice that I had. This tone of voice made her think of the morning coffee aroma which she could smell in her bedroom when she was a little girl; it then led to her first memory of her father's voice when she was a little child lying in bed, full of sexual fantasies about him. The calmness and determination of my attitude that these reactions happened to her in the past were decisive in getting the patient to work with this feeling rather than give in to her momentary impulse to gratify it.

One can also give examples of negative transference acted out during the analytic hour where the patient may become intensely aggressive, pugnacious and belligerent. Again the analyst's calm, firm, and imperturbable attitude of wanting to work out this emotional state, and his insistence that these feelings must have happened before, are prerequisites for getting the patient to give up the acting out and to attempt to understand it.

A more difficult form of acting out of transference occurs outside of the analytic hour. In these situations we also have the patient engaging in behavior which repeats a part of the past through feelings felt toward the analyst; but these feelings are displaced further onto a person or situation outside of the analysis. A typical example can be seen very frequently in training analyses. Candidates in analysis with me may make a teacher in a seminar the scapegoat for all the hostility felt toward me. The hostility toward me, itself, is a repetition of an earlier hostility to a childhood object.

For example, a candidate constantly reproached one of his teachers with being sloppy, ineffectual, too easygoing, and too timid. These were the same reproaches he had against his father, but which he was loath to talk about in the analysis. He never even felt these criticisms against me; quite the contrary, he considered me to be the most brilliant, efficient, competent teacher of the group. Eventually he began to berate himself for his lack of progress in the analysis. I then brought up the possibility that these reproaches toward his teacher, his father, and now himself, really were felt toward me. Only after he could express these feelings to me could he remember, with appropriate affect, many experiences of this nature with his father.

Acting out of the transference outside the hour is a means of warding off the patient's awareness of his transference feelings. It can be an attempt to dilute the transference intensity. Often it can simultaneously serve as a defense against the transference and a defiance of the transference figure. It is an important resistance in the analysis, and has to be handled energetically because it can lead to complications in the patient's external situation which may jeopardize the analysis.

Acting Out Not Connected to Transference

Although the most frequent source and situation for acting out occurs in connection with the transference, not all acting out stems from that relationship. Acting out which occurs in the analytic hour is usually a transference acting out; but acting out may occur outside of the analytic hour and may not be connected with the transference. All situations with love objects or sexual objects are prone to be repetitions which have the same structure as acting out. This is particularly clear in the sexual foreplay of many neurotics, and in the perversions of those patients who suffer from them. Consequently, it is not only necessary to interpret the instinctual activity in terms of instinctual zone, instinctual aim and meaning of the sexual object. It is also important to bear in mind that the whole sequence of events may be a thinly disguised repetition of a repressed sexual episode.

A patient had the following pattern of behavior in his sexual life with his fiancée: he would insist that she lie completely quiet and inert upon the bed. She was not to respond with any sign of desire or excitement until he gave her a signal. Then, he would stimulate her digitally around the labia and clitoris. Finally, he would insert his fingers into the vagina and dilate it. Only after the completion of this next part would he develop an erection and be able to perform intercourse, although only briefly. The forepleasure sequence in this patient was a repetition of the patient's fantasy about childbirth and the doctor. He read medical books as a child and saw photographs of doctors delivering babies. In his fantasy the doctors not only delivered babies, they also made the babies, and even made the sexual excitement. In this way he denied that his father really did sexually stimulate his mother, and that his mother did not really enjoy sexual relations. Only doctors brought sexual excitement, made babies, and delivered them in his fantasy. He acted out, via the forepleasure with his fiancée, the role of the doctor with his mother. He made her lie quietly in order to demonstrate that she had no sexual feelings; then he created the sexual feelings, he brought the baby for inserting his fingers, and he delivered the baby by dilating the vagina. Only through this symbolic triumph over his father was he then able to have a temporary erection of his own.

Similarly in perversions the entire sex act has an acting out meaning and has to be interpreted as such besides analyzing the specific meaning of each component of the sex act.

THE WORK SITUATION

The work situation is another typical context for acting out outside of the analytic hour and outside of the transference. Figures of authority in the work situation are apt to provoke the remobilized and deep-seated feelings which stem from the parental figures. Instead of being remembered, these feelings are repeated in the work situation. Inappropriate defiance, stubbornness, or other work problems can often only be completely understood when one recognizes the acting out function that the behavior serves.

The Predisposition of Acting Out

It is important to differentiate the more or less normal amount of acting out that we see in every analysis once the transference neurosis has developed, from the chronic and habitual acting out characteristic of the impulse-ridden, borderline patient. Fenichel and Greenacre have stressed the dynamic, libidinal, and structural characteristics of the latter type of patients. The patient who is given to habitually acting out tends to be orally fixated. They constantly seek gratification and are relatively unable to bear postponement or frustration. These patients display a great readiness to action and an inability to translate impulses into thoughts. They tend to dramatize and to have strong strivings toward exhibitionism. Problems are solved alloplastically instead of autoplastically. Thus, they try to enlist their environment into their difficulties instead of modifying their own behavior or actions. Such patients usually have difficulties with speech. They may be very verbal but will misuse their verbosity for exhibitionistic purposes instead of for communication. Silence during sessions is not uncommon because they have difficulty in putting their impulses into thoughts and words. They tend to present rather confused and amorphous pictures of themselves because their ego identifications or their self representations are unstable and labile. Furthermore, they will have difficulty in distinguishing past from present because their ego functions are poorly developed. Their thinking is apt to be magical and, in many ways, one sees indications that primary process thinking has invaded the secondary process. Although they may seem to be gregarious, these patients' object relationships are shallow, and are really pseudo-object relationships. They are traumatophilic and, therefore, accident prone. Such patients do not learn from painful experience, and are not able to modify their behavior on the basis of past painful experience. All of these traits are indications of early and severe trauma in infancy which led to oral fixation, narcissistic object relations, defects in ego functions, and rudimentary superego formations.

Management of Acting Out

Psychoneurotic Acting Out

Under this heading I refer to those patients who occasionally act out under the impetus of the transference neurosis, although there may be some occasional acting out apart from the transference reactions. The first step in management is to recognize the occurrence of acting out. The second step is to interpret it as far as possible. The interpretation, however, is dependent upon the fact that the patient has some rational observing ego when the interpretation is made. Acting out experiences cannot be interpreted successfully while they are still intense. The analyst must wait until the after-storm subsides in its intensity; then we expect that some portion of the observing ego will return. A firm and calm attitude of the analyst is of great importance in hastening the return of a rational ego. By offering this model of our behavior we calm the patient's fears and we also give them the opportunity to temporarily identify with our own rational ego. Interpretations of acting out in the absence of an observing ego are wasted and will be misused by the patient.

If interpretation is not feasible, or if interpretation proves to be ineffective, it may be necessary to suggest the patient desist from the particular behavior or action because it jeopardizes the analysis. It is best to avoid making these suggestions sound as if they are prohibitions. Nonetheless many patients will react to the suggestion as though it were a prohibition. But putting such statements in the form of suggestions and explaining the reasons for making them may help minimize the remarks from being felt as prohibition.

The Habitual Acting Out Patient

These patients pose a special problem because they are prone to readily give up mature ego functioning for more primitive and infantile ego functions. Consequently, our main attempts have to be directed to strengthening the ego functions of the patient. Greenacre (1950), similarly, suggests attacking the narcissism of the patient while Fenichel (1945a) points out the need to make the acting out ego dystonic. I believe that both are striving for the same aim, namely, to at least temporarily establish a rational ego. We can help to achieve this goal by acting as we want the patient to act. It is imperative that we be firm, and even forceful, including being forcefully calm. Above all, we must make some contact with the patient. We can appeal emotionally to the patient's intellect to help us with the acting out. Asking the patient for help with this problem in a clear-cut and unwavering manner may gratify his narcissism sufficiently that he will pay attention to us. It is important not to make too many interpretations with such patients and to keep the interpretations simple. In addition, the analyst must communicate concern without it being felt as anxiety by the patient.

A candidate recently described a problem with the acting out of a depressed patient whom he was treating. The candidate correctly recognized that this man's intention of giving up a twenty-year marriage and two children for a young woman was an acting out of an adolescent experience when the patient ran away from home. The candidate correctly reminded the patient that this intention to leave his wife and family was a repetition of what the patient had done when he was fifteen years old. The patient accepted this interpretation intellectually, but with no real emotion and with no change in his intention. He agreed that he ran away from home when his mother and father were so preoccupied with their business and he was so much in love with a young girl that he could bear it no longer. It was suggested to the candidate that he say to the patient that this current intention of the patient's to run away from his family worried the candidate; the candidate was to say that he was worried that it would hurt the patient and the patient's family. The addition of this word, *worried*, produced a dramatic effect in the patient. He was visibly touched and began to talk about the incident in his adolescence with great feeling. At the end of the hour the patient decided that he was not going to leave his family, and more than that, he was going to tell the young lady, who was in analysis, that this was childish behavior which ought to be analyzed and not acted upon. The small amount of narcissistic gratification which the candidate offered him with his concern for the patient felt so different from the parental lack of concern that the patient was willing to really remember this traumatic period of his adolescence in the relative safety of the analytic relationship.

As a general rule in analysis, we tell our patients early on in the analysis, perhaps at the first relevant moment, that they should make no major changes in their lives until there has been ample opportunity to analyze with the analyst the most important determinants for this change in behavior. Many patients would, if not warned by this suggestion, embark frequently upon dangerous or damaging changes in their life situation under the pressure to act out their conflicts rather than understand them. Since the acting out is a relatively well-organized, ego syntonic piece of behavior, it is particularly dangerous for the course of the patient's life. It is important, therefore, that we warn our patients about this tendency, and that the analyst constantly be alert for the possibility of acting out situations whenever there are stubborn resistances which do not change by interpretation, and when there are either persistent and intense transference reactions or a persistent lack of transference reactions. Rigidity and lack of change during the course of analysis is often due to unrecognized acting out.

14

Acting Out and Its Technical Management

Haig A. Koshkarian, M.D.

Definition and Description

ACTING out, like other psychoanalytic concepts such as transference and defense, if defined broadly enough can be viewed as a ubiquitous and all encompassing phenomenon, referring to much of what goes on in psychoanalysis and even life itself. After all, all of us, not just so-called acting out characters, those people of action, live out and play out important issues and conflicts in our lives and in our own treatments. It is a matter of content, kind and degree. It is good to remind ourselves of this, not because there is any particular merit or usefulness in viewing acting out in this broader more diffuse way, but because it makes more understandable the range of definition of acting out as it has been written and spoken about by many psychoanalysts.

This range exists even when we speak of acting out in its usual more limited way. We ordinarily think of acting out as those behaviors or actions of the patient, in contrast to the mere expression of feelings and thoughts, that occur in the treatment setting. That is, whether the behavior occurs inside or outside the session, it is released by or is in response to the psychoanalytic process. However, the term *acting out*

263

is still used by some to refer to "acting out characters" and their habitual modes of acting on their impulses, in or out of treatment.

There is also a range of how different psychoanalysts view and respond to acting out in the clinical setting. At the extreme, it is viewed by some as just a resistance, something that is always and mainly detrimental and negative to the progress of the treatment and therefore something to be discouraged and stopped whenever it happens. Whether it be by limit-setting or interpretation, the goal is primarily to stop the acting out. However, for most analysts, acting out is seen as having a mixed function. In this view, acting out always represents in some way a resistance to some aspect of the analytic process and therefore a possible obstacle to treatment. But it is also viewed as expressing something, a communication, a source of information, and therefore possibly serving a useful function, a preliminary step to insight. The way we view it at any one time, of course, depends on the patient, what the acting out behavior is, how extreme, destructive, or dangerous it is to the patient, others, or the treatment, what it means, and what the ability of the patient is at the moment to engage in looking at it. Depending on these factors, our response may range from thoughtful observation to interpretation to limit setting.

The Evolution of Acting Out as a Clinical Concept

While in respect to clinical specificity versus diffuseness of definition, the concept of acting out over the years has come full circle to return to Freud's restriction of the term to behavior which is a response to the analytic situation, in reference to its meaning and function in the analytic setting the concept of acting out has continued to evolve beyond Freud's initial descriptions.

In "Remembering, Repeating and Working-Through" (1914) Freud stated that the aim of the psychoanalytic technique was, "Descriptively speaking . . . to fill in gaps in memory, dynamically speaking . . . to overcome resistances due to repression" (p. 148). Thus, Freud emphasized and continued to emphasize remembering as the important aim of psychoanalysis. While the central place of transference in analysis was asserted, it was viewed as a resistance to remembering which had to be overcome by interpretation. Freud noted that rather than remember what had been forgotten, the patient often repeated it by "acting it out" in the treatment situation in relationship to the analyst. If this repetition remained in the psychic arena of feelings and attitudes, Freud viewed it as transference and a legitimate and expected resistance to remembering, which when interpreted led to the awakening of infantile memories. If this repetition involved action outside of the analysis, Freud viewed this also as a resistance to remembering. However, he cautioned that such behavior could be permanently harmful to the patient and was often aimed at obstructing the analysis. Thus Freud viewed acting out as a resistance to and replacement for remembering. No negative judgment was placed on it as long as it remained in the psychic sphere and was directed to the person of the analyst, at which time acting out and transference were one and the same. But if it occurred outside of the analysis and involved behavior relating to persons other than the analyst or occurred inside the analysis but with more extreme behavior directed at the analyst, what today we would respectively call acting out outside the analysis and acting out inside the analysis or acting in (Zeligs, 1957), it was discouraged.

The continuing evolution of our view of the meaning, function, and place of acting out in the analytic setting has been a result of the growing emphasis, beginning with Freud, on the development, expression, analysis, and resolution of transference and the transference neurosis as the central drama of psychoanalysis. Related to this has been a shift in emphasis and importance from direct remembering of the past (after the transference resistance has been interpreted) to the reexperiencing of the past via the transference. We are of course speaking of transference as a here and now experience, a contemporary enactment and reconstruction of important past experiences and conflicts and how they have been unconsciously and problematically carried forward to the present. As long as transference and acting out were both seen as resistances in different spheres to remembering, it of course made no sense to view one as a resistance to the other. However, with the increasing emphasis on transference as the most important vehicle for communication of information in the analysis, acting out has come to be viewed operationally not as a resistance to remembering, but as a resistance to experiencing transference feelings; that is, as a resistance against the anxiety of reexperiencing those memories and issues currently in the transference.

With this has come the further emphasis on viewing acting out as a compromise and more generally as multidetermined. Blum (1976) has pointed out that acting out, like dreams and symptoms, are a compromise between defense and gratification. He has also suggested that while acting out must first be considered a resistance to the analytic process, that it is always overdetermined and can represent a seeking of approval or punishment or a plea for controls, limits, or help; in other words, an attempt to get a particular response from the analyst. Others too, such as Boesky (1982), Erard (1983), Greenson (1967), and Rangell (1968), have emphasized that all acting out is multidetermined, a complex end product that serves the purpose of both resistance and communication in varying degrees, whether it occurs in or out of the analytic hour.

Acting Out and the Attitude of the Analyst

As analysts, our technical handling of acting out follows in large part from our attitude toward acting out. With the direction of changes in our view of acting out that has already been described, it is easy to see how in general our attitude toward acting out has become less negative and has become more positive and accepting. As Blum (1976) has noted, from a sometimes disparaging attitude toward acting out and acting out patients, a more neutral and objective understanding of acting out has reappeared. Not unlike the history of our view of transference, acting out has come to be seen as less of an obstacle, something to be circumvented, but as something to be understood and interpreted, an important source of information. This attitude has much to be recommended for it. It is consistent with what Rangell (1968) and Schafer (1983) have referred to as the analytic or affirmative attitude in psychoanalysis. That is, and as it refers to acting out, acting out like any other phenomenon in treatment has a meaning and even value. It is a behavior that needs to be understood. At some level, it is the patient's attempt to adapt to some psychic reality, however unsuccessful it is or negative its appearance. Like resistance in general, it is an avoidance but also an expression of something. And like resistance in general, it is something that should be understood and interpreted. As Rangell (1968) has noted, we do not forbid "thinking out" or "feeling out" even when they occur defensively outside the analysis and are only brought into it through hints and other incomplete material which can then lead to insight. Obviously that is another of our attitudes toward acting out, that it be brought into the analysis as something to be understood.

This is not to suggest that we should sit back and be blind to the obvious destructive potentials of certain acting out behavior, whether it be to the patient, others, or the analysis. It is to suggest that it is important, whatever the behavior, to maintain for ourselves and the patient the attitude that the behavior has meaning that can and should be understood, even while we are confronting the patient or even setting limits.

A patient during her first year in analysis, in response to her growing feelings that I hurt her by not sharing with her more of myself, would return to the waiting room after her session and sit there crying noticeably but quietly for about fifteen minutes. Sometimes she did the same in the outer building hallway, sitting on the floor with her back against the wall. Sometimes I saw her when I went to get my next patient and always I heard about it from other patients, some of whom wondered what I had done to the "poor woman." Some of them had interesting fantasies which led to some useful work, but in the main it was a distraction.

On the surface, the meaning of the patient's behavior was obvious. It was a public demonstration and announcement to me and others, not without some hostility, that I had hurt her very much. This was interpreted, including her wish to have impact on me and others by her picketing-like behavior. It was also important for me to better understand what her hurt was and what I had done to cause it, in the transference and in reality. But at some point her behavior had to stop, not the expression in the session of her feelings of hurt and anger, but the acting out of those feelings after the session, because it was intruding on the therapy of other patients.

This affirmative attitude toward acting out is also a separate question from the issue of analyzability. Some patients can only act out and are unable to control or reflect on such behavior, making analysis difficult to impossible.

Acting Out and Transference

While in a general way, we define acting out as the expression of some unconscious conflict through action, in practice in the analytic setting we most often relate acting out to some aspect of the transference (and sometimes to its counterpart, countertransference). It is an enactment inside or outside of the analysis rather than a verbalization of feelings and fantasies arising in the transference, whether the acting out represents a defense against the development, expression, or awareness of transference feelings or whether the acting out is a fairly direct expression of transference feelings but without recognition or acknowledgment of them as such.

When this occurs inside the analysis, whether it be in the form of coming late or a way of dressing, acting, or behaving, it is obviously more accessible to our view, understanding, and interpretation. In fact, there is not always a sharp dividing line between what we refer to as acting out inside the session (or acting in) and ordinary transference.

> A female patient, during her second year of analysis, rather than speaking of her attraction and seductive feelings for me, began to act in a little girl seductive way in her tone and manner of speech, as well as the expression on her face and the way she looked at me as she entered and left my office. When this was pointed out to her, she at first was surprised, then denied that it meant anything, and then was able to speak of her sexual feelings for me. Ultimately her acting out behavior came to be understood as her oedipal transference feelings as a little girl toward me, her father, as well as an avoidance of more "grown-up" sexual feelings for me. In all of this, her acting out behavior in the session was both an expression and avoidance of transference feelings and was well within the view of analytic scrutiny.

The following is an example of how acting out can take the form of postures and actions on the couch.

> An obsessive patient, early in his analysis, would toss and turn on the couch, going quickly from one position to another, like a child tossing and turning in bed trying to find a comfortable position. As

this was pointed up and analyzed it came to be seen as his wish that I would indeed see him as just a floundering little boy, a most comfortable role and position for him throughout his life, rather than as an adult oedipal threat to me (and others).

Even when the acting out occurs outside of the analysis, it is still most often behavior that gets reported or detected or is brought into the session in some way and is thus within our analytic view. This kind of clinical experience which most of our patients present to us, along with acting out inside the analysis, could be termed the acting out of everyday analytic life. It has been called "small to medium acting outs" by Rangell (1968) and "partial acting out" by Rosenfeld (1966) to differentiate between these more common, ordinary, expected, and even necessary forms of acting out and excessive or more extreme acting out which clearly threatens the analytic process. The following is an example of acting out outside the analysis which was easily, and in fact seemed meant to be brought into the analysis.

The same obsessive male patient just spoken of, at a later time in his analysis, began a brief affair with the wife of a local physician. He spoke of it with obvious relish, but he saw little connection between this and me and more specifically denied the obvious displaced transference feelings of oedipal victory over me. However, at the next session I could hear him whistling in the hallway even before he entered my suite door. I suggested that this behavior (another piece of acting out) sounded like that of a little boy whistling in the dark so as to calm his fear of my anticipated anger and to again defend against all of it by saying, "But I'm just a little boy. I'm no threat." This led to useful exploration of his transference feelings.

It is important to distinguish here between a mere displacement of transference feelings in which case the patient might have spoken of his wish or fantasies about having an affair with the physician's wife. Instead, the displacement of transference feelings was actually acted out. The following, like the previous patient's whistling in the hallway, is an example of acting out outside the analysis but not so very outside and very much within analytic view.

A female patient in the midst of a regressive negative transference experienced painful and acute feelings of jealousy about what she imagined I felt for my other patients, in contrast to her. She centered on the exact time of the start and finish of our sessions for evidence that she was being shortchanged or even being given only the ordinary amount of time in contrast to patients I cared about. The acting out that followed was an attempt to avoid these feelings of jealousy as well as even more extreme feelings of anger at me and hostile jealous destructive fantasies toward my other patients (her rival siblings). She began not to wear her watch to the session, and after the session she would sit in her car for a while before driving off just in case she then did see a clock. In addition, she began to take more and more circuitous routes in the building to get to my office, including using a seldom used stairway instead of the elevator, so as to avoid seeing someone in the building she might imagine was a patient of mine and who might have a happy look on her face indicating the wonderful relationship she (the other "patient") and I no doubt had. Some of the meaning of her behavior was obvious to her from the start. Some became more clear as the behavior continued, became more extreme, and was explored.

This patient's acting out behavior, like most acting out, was an attempt to avoid transference feelings, to protect herself and me from them, but it also clearly expressed and revealed those feelings. And while it continued for a period of time, it did not disrupt the analysis. In fact, it advanced it.

Acting Out and Countertransference

There is not always a sharp distinction, but when we speak of the analyst's countertransference and its relationship to the patient's acting out we are referring both to the analyst's countertransference (or counter acting out) reaction to the patient's acting out and the analyst's countertransference that may contribute to or encourage the patient to act out. It is obvious that a patient's acting out can, and indeed may be designed to induce varying feelings in the analyst, whether it be worry, anxiety, impotence, anger, or a wish to protect the patient. Such countertransference feelings can be most helpful in understanding the meaning of the acting out. However, the first sign of such countertransference feelings may be our own counter acting out in the form of such behaviors as increased silence, interpreting as an attack, our own lateness, or frequent changing or missing of hours. Such behavior if noted can be the first clue to countertransference feelings which can then lead to an understanding of the patient's acting out. However, if not taken note of and addressed by the analyst, it can prolong or complicate the patient's acting out.

> A young man, in the middle of his analysis, began to call at the last minute to cancel his sessions with little reason at a frequency of once or twice a week. He had been a difficult patient, often quick to temper and anger. He was a successful and good-looking man, but he carried with him a sense of having an ugly core that prevented people from really liking him. This was in part related to his feeling that he had never been able to please his father despite his own extreme efforts, and that his father may have loved him as a son but did not like him and even despised him. This had been a theme in the transference.
>
> At the sessions he attended I tried to get him to explore some obvious current issues that he was trying to avoid, but the cancellations continued. It was not, however, until I became aware of my countertransference feelings and behavior in response to his missed sessions that I was able to better understand its meaning and my contribution to its continuing. I first noted my relative passivity in confronting him with his behavior and then became aware of some relief when he cancelled. His were difficult hours and they were the last of the day, meaning I could go home earlier when he cancelled.
>
> At this point I was now able to interpret to him an additional meaning to his acting out, that is, as with his father, he felt I despised him and did not wish to see him, so he cancelled his sessions. He felt I would prefer that to his coming and being difficult. But he really wished that I would not accept his behavior and would even insist that he come. With this, the cancellations ceased.

This example approaches the more extreme situation in which the analyst's countertransference not only may prolong but actually stimulate the patient's acting out. All acting out, just as all transference, is a reaction to some reality in the analytic setting, but we are now talking about acting out which is contributed to at least as much, if not more, by the analyst's than by the patient's transference. Some, including Bird (1957) and Langs (1976) have referred to this as interactional acting out. Obviously, analysts who tend in general or with particular patients to be seductive or excessively permissive, forbidding, depriving, or frustrating can induce acting out behavior in their patients.

In more subtle ways, the analyst's unconscious needs or impulses may be acted out through the patient. Bird (1957) gives the example of a therapist whose own acting out impulses and promiscuous wishes are active and strong, but unconscious and hidden. Such an analyst may attempt to gratify his or her impulses by unconsciously encouraging the patient to become promiscuous. An analyst's own unconscious feelings about his or her own life situation may lead the analyst to make interventions with the unconscious goal of influencing certain life decisions the patient is in the process of analyzing and making. A special example of an analyst acting out his or her own needs through the patient is sometimes seen in analytic institute settings where analysands in training are sometimes unconsciously encouraged to fight the battles of their analyst with other analysts. In a general way, just as any time we experience a stalemate in analysis we should consider the part of countertransference, any time there is seemingly out of the blue a sudden burst of acting out by the patient we should consider among other things the possible contribution of our countertransference feelings and behavior.

Acting Out to Preserve the Analytic Relationship

Thus far in this chapter we have emphasized the mixed function of acting out. It is both a resistance to some aspect of the psychoanalytic process, but it can also serve a useful function in that often it is a source of information, most often about the transference. Let us turn now to a particular meaning and function of acting out which may often be implicitly noted in the literature and discussions of acting out but which usually is not explicitly noted or illustrated. I am speaking of acting out which has as its purpose the preservation of the analytic relationship so as to continue the treatment. Anxiety about transference feelings, for some patients, can reach the point where it is a choice between acting out, and remaining in treatment, or fleeing treatment. The acting out is a partial temporary solution and a delaying action until the patient is able to tolerate and experience the transference feelings. To some extent this could be viewed as an inherent part of most acting out behaviors. In the case example to follow, however, along with other meanings, it appeared to be the most important aim and purpose of a major piece of acting out.

More specifically, in the case to be described, in an attempt to avoid growing sexual and dependent transference feelings early in the analysis, the patient impulsively got married, disregarding the suggestion that she postpone such a major life decision until it could be analyzed. Such a piece of behavior, however much we might search for the positive, would most usually be viewed not only as a resistance against the transference but the work of the analysis as a whole, especially since it was not initially available for interpretation and had the potential for such great impact on the analysis and the patient's life. However, material which followed the marriage pointed toward an important adaptive function of the acting out.

A young single woman came for analysis with complaints of chronic depression, unhappiness, and an inability to find satisfaction in relationships. She had fled a series of relationships with men, leaving them feeling bewildered and abandoned. When her father left her mother when the patient was fourteen years old, the patient felt abandoned and depressed. An older sibling had already left the home, and she was left to live with her depressed and unhappy mother.

In the early transference she alternated between seeing me as depriving her (like her parents did, she felt) and as a good idealized parent who could give her a loving, caring, and feeding relationship. It became evident that she took diet pills, a past sometime habit, prior to her hours to combat feelings of deprivation and hunger in the sessions. There was also evidence of anxiety about sexual feelings, which however she denied. She spoke of lying on the couch and feeling stiff and thought that it would be easier to talk with me if I were an old man. She feared the outcome of centering on me to the exclusion of others but could not elaborate. In her sessions, she felt a sense of urgency, a feeling that there was something she could not control.

In the ensuing weeks, growing sexual and dependent transference feelings, associated to the fear of rejection and abandonment if those feelings were fully experienced, led to a major piece of acting out. She had met a new boyfriend who, for a number of reasons, did not seem to be a fitting object choice. But she saw him as a caring and concerned person, in contrast to the way she was viewing me at the time. She wanted to keep her new boyfriend a kind and gentle nonsexual object, but following several dreams in which the theme was that a person who can't face or handle situations flees to marriage, she prompted a marriage proposal from him and announced her plan to get married in several months. At this time she had been in analysis for just two months.

In the ensuing sessions, this decision was interpreted as her attempt to flee from her loving and sexual feelings for me. She acknowledged this with tears and embarrassment. She felt undone, she said, by such feelings, for example a fantasy of my taking her away with me, and so she tried to push such feelings and fantasies aside. And, she felt, she would only be rejected by me if she voiced such feelings. However, at other times she denied any relationship between those feelings and her decision to get married. Or at most it was a small part and she was going to get married. At such times she defiantly stated that I, like her father, thought that nothing she did was right and that she would make her own decisions. She was a big girl. At other times material from her dreams pointed to a wish that I rescue her from such an action. However, following an hour in which she voiced a feeling of particular closeness with me, felt the interpretations about her marriage decision were correct and that it was too soon to get married, she missed the next two sessions and impulsively got married, months before her previously projected date.

At this time she had been in analysis for just three months and her marriage lasted another three months before she filed for divorce. Almost immediately she felt that her marriage was a mistake, but she went back and forth on her decision before eventually getting a divorce. She revealed that when she had suddenly gotten married, she had done so with the feeling that it was then or never. If she had waited, she was sure she would have changed

her mind. She acknowledged the aptness of the previous interpretations, and I was able to add that with her increasing feelings
toward me she feared that I, like her father, would leave her and
so she had partially left me by fleeing to a marriage. However, during these months, as she would approach a decision to end her
marriage, feelings for me would become more evident (sexual or
dependent wishes that I take care of her and keep her from making any more bad decisions) and she would decide again to try and
make a go of her marriage, stating that she was tired of the chaos
she had felt in her life prior to the marriage.

A dream just before she filed for divorce finally and most
clearly highlighted the central meaning of her acting out. In the
dream she was on skis and able to ski and get through the snow
only because her husband was ahead of her in a snowmobile
packing the snow down. Without his help, she would have had
to leave the slope. In the same dream she took only half of a diet
pill and half of a birth control pill. In a previous dream, skiing
had been a metaphor for the analysis with packed snow representing packing feelings down and skimming over the surface. I
interpreted this dream as her having felt that she could not get
through or even stay in the analysis without her husband, a person to displace feelings onto. Married, she only had to feel half as
hungry and deprived with me and only feel half the sexual
feelings for me.

This was followed in the next session by open feelings of love
for me, the wish to be my wife, feelings that were hard for her to
speak of because they could not come true in reality. In the
following session, she had a dream in which she could not keep a
baby by me because I saw her as a child. It became more clear to
her that she feared that if she centered on me, showed how much
she really needed me, I would find out what a helpless and needy
child she was and would leave her. Her divorce soon followed and
shortly after this she gave up the use of diet pills signaling her conviction that she no longer needed to so much avoid her feelings in
therapy but could now face them. She remained in analysis and
successfully terminated three years later. The remainder of her
analysis, in comparison to the first months, was a much calmer
time. Transference feelings further developed and deepened and
the obvious genetic connections were made without recourse to
major acting out.

In this case, the patient attempted to avoid growing sexual and dependent transference feelings associated with the fear of rejection and abandonment if those feelings were fully experienced and expressed, by fleeing into marriage. She was unable to tolerate the anxiety of her growing transference feelings of deprivation, dependence, hunger, sexual longing, and the associated fear of rejection and abandonment. The use of diet pills and a relationship with a new boyfriend were not enough to satisfactorily defend against and displace her transference feelings, and she sought more complete refuge in marriage. Her dream about skiing dramatized her feeling that her marriage was essential to her being able to deal with her transference feelings and to remain in therapy. Thus, in this case the patient's acting out, while multidetermined, allowed her to remain in treatment, rather than breaking it off which would have been the ultimate acting out. With the safety of her marriage, a sort of safe harbor for displacement, she was able to remain in the analysis and gradually to be able to tolerate and experience her transference feelings, at which point she was able, in her dream, to more fully reveal the meaning of her marriage and then to give it up.

Summary

In this chapter we have discussed the mixed and multiple functions of acting out in the context of the analytic setting. Acting out is in some way and to some extent always a resistance to some aspect of the analysis, and therefore, especially in its more extreme forms, it can be an obstacle to treatment. But acting out is also an expression of something, a communication, a source of information, and so it can serve a useful function and lead to meaningful insights. This is especially so in the many instances of minor acting out, in and out of the analysis, which are often a regular and expected part of our daily analytic work with patients. Even in more major pieces of acting out behavior, such as in the last case example, the acting out may serve an important adaptive function and ultimately be a source of important information.

Most important in this is our attempt to maintain, in the midst of whatever acting out is going on, an analytic relationship and attitude with the patient. This includes the view that the acting out is not merely something to be circumvented or stopped, but is something which has meaning and is to be understood and interpreted. It is both an avoidance and expression of something. This is not inconsistent with the need at times with some instances of acting out behavior to step in with limits so as to protect the patient and/or the treatment. Ultimately, our basic tool in usefully understanding and resolving acting out is the analysis of transference and countertransference.

15

Countertransference

Ralph R. Greenson, M.D.

Definition

COUNTERTRANSFERENCE is a phenomenon in the relationship between the patient and the therapist in which the therapist's reaction to the patient parallels the patient's transference reactions to the therapist; it is the counterpart to the patient's transference reaction. To be more specific, countertransference is an inappropriate reaction of the therapist to his patient. The inappropriateness stems from the fact that something in the patient has remobilized some unconscious neurotic conflict in the psychoanalyst or therapist. Both these criteria must be fulfilled in order for an analyst's reaction to qualify as countertransference: (1) The analyst's reaction must be to something in the patient; and (2) it must be based on some unconscious neurotic conflict in the analyst.

There are other inappropriate and neurotic reactions of the therapist's which would not be defined as countertransference phenomena. Gitelson (1952) has described transference reactions of the analyst to the patient in which, as a result of his past conflicts, the analyst reacts inappropriately to the patient as a whole. He distinguishes these reactions from countertransference reactions in which the analyst reacts to some material of the patient. According to the definition above, however, these transference reactions of the analyst would be considered countertransference phenomena. It is conceivable, however, that other reactions do occur which are inappropriate but which *are not* countertransference reactions. For example, the analyst may displace a reaction to an external situation onto the patient. Such reactions may not be due to any specific characteristic of the patient, but are due instead to the unfortunate circumstance that the patient happens to be the accessible target for the bizarre emotional response of the analyst. Such instances do demonstrate an inappropriate response, perhaps even a neurotic response or a symptomatic act. But it cannot be considered a countertransference reaction because it is not mobilized specifically by the patient, and it does not necessarily come out of the analyst's past.

In addition to the occasional neurotic or symptomatic actions that the analyst manifests to the patient, the more habitual characterological traits of the analyst can be mobilized by the patient–analyst situation. One common example is the rigid, wooden, nonfeeling reaction of the analyst to the patient. There are analysts who have a generalized fear of their own spontaneous emotions and fantasies which is carried over into their work with their patients. This should be considered a neurotic character trait of the analyst, and not a countertransference phenomenon. However, there are also analysts who do not have this generalized lack of empathy, fantasy, and feeling in their ordinary social relations; instead it occurs specifically in response to certain patients or to all their patients. This is a countertransference phenomenon and actually can be considered a fear of countertransference. Such analysts tend to feel enormously fatigued by their analytic work, have great difficulty in remembering the analytic material, make frequent slips of the tongue, and experience frequent mistakes in memory. Their difficulty with empathy disrupts their timing and dosage of interpretation so that their interventions feel tactless and inaccurate. They have great difficulty in keeping their patients in treatment. Usually these analysts have patients who are predominantly masochistic. Another characteristic of these analysts is their readiness to doze or fall asleep. These analyses go on interminably, usually seven years or more, and are interrupted only by some external event.

Recognition of Countertransference

The key to recognizing countertransference reactions in the analyst has to do with the inappropriateness of the reaction. Ordinarily in one's analytical work one finds oneself paying interested attention to the utterances and behavior of the patient on the couch. As the patient produces the material we oscillate between empathizing with what is going on in the patient and making self-observations and judgments in order to evaluate the productions of the patient. During this course of events, one becomes aware of a rise and fall of various emotions in keeping with the patient's utterances. These emotions in the analyst are neither so strong that they impel one to action, nor so mild that one is tempted to daydream. One recognizes one's countertransference reactions when one becomes aware of the inappropriateness of one's emotional responses, or one finds oneself feeling intense emotions or feeling bored and inattentive. More obvious are impulses to act which seem not to be founded on the patient's productions. Or one finds oneself reacting aggressively or sexually to the patient's productions. The recognition by means of self-observation of inappropriate affect, impulse, or action is the key to recognizing the possibility of a countertransference reaction. A series of steps has to be taken in order to be sure that the response to the patient is or is not countertransference. First, we have to experience the reaction in ourselves. Second, the analyst must ascertain what stimulus in the patient set this off. Third, the analyst has to judge whether this response is appropriate to the stimulus. If the response is appropriate to the stimulus, the analyst is having an empathic reaction which may be valuable for making the proper interpretation of the material. The likelihood is that we are dealing with a countertransference reaction if the response is not appropriate to the stimulus. During the analytic hour it is not possible to analyze this countertransference reaction any further. Usually it is sufficient to become aware of the countertransference reaction and to restrain oneself from reacting outwardly in any way inappropriately to the patient. The method of dealing with the countertransference further will be discussed later on.

Typical Signals of Countertransference

INAPPROPRIATE QUANTITY AND QUALITY OF AFFECTS AND IMPULSES

Anger, sexual feelings, boredom, sleepiness, restlessness and uncontrollable laughter are all indications of the possibility of countertransference. Dreams about one's patients and, particularly, repeated dreams are usually indications of some stirring of one's past neurosis by the patient. Frequent slips of tongue, errors of judgment, mistakes in appointments, etc., also may be signs of some neurotic involvement with the patient. None of these reactions are necessarily countertransference, but each of them has to be scrutinized and the differential diagnosis established.

THE ANALYST'S REACTIONS TO THE PATIENT'S TRANSFERENCE

In discussing the problem of handling the transference above, it was stressed that it is imperative in order to handle the transference properly that the analyst "not enter the game" with the patient in the transference. This means that it is imperative for the analyst to recognize the transference and to analyze it at the proper time and in the proper dosage to the patient. It is recognized that transference reactions are imperative for the progress of an analysis and that the transference neurosis is our major therapeutic weapon in our struggle against the neurosis. But it is equally important to recall that the proper management of the transference depends upon the analyst's proper reactions to the transference phenomena in his patient. One of the most frequent signals of countertransference reaction is the analyst's reaction to the patient's transference feelings or behavior. Finding oneself unduly enjoying the positive transference or reacting sexually or narcissistically to the transference manifestations may be an indication of a countertransference reaction. Conversely, when the analyst finds himself unduly avoiding interpretations or confrontations which might stir up negative transference, hostility, or also positive transference, this, too, may be an indication of countertransference. The enjoyment of either the positive or negative transference is usually an indication of a countertransference reaction and has to be recognized and analyzed by the therapist. The danger in not doing so is a twofold one; on the one hand, unanalyzed countertransference reactions of this sort may lead the analyst to act out with his patient and inadvertently create unanalyzable situations either by gratifying the patient unduly or by excessively frustrating the patient. Such enactment changes the analytic situation from a transference situation to a real situation for the patient and is unanalyzable as such. In these cases it is necessary for the analyst to recognize his errors and, occasionally, to acknowledge them to the patient in order to at least have the possibility of analyzing in the future.

The other potential danger of a countertransference reaction is that the analyst does not thoroughly and systematically analyze the transference. The therapist leaves unanalyzed important segments of the patient's transference neurosis because of his feelings for the patient which are unrecognizable in himself. As a result, the infantile neurosis is not completely analyzed and second, there is a great likelihood that the patient will continue to repeat some of his neurotic past, probably to the detriment of the analyst as well as the patient. There are many unhappy situations which arise in psychoanalytic circles due to incompletely analyzed transference in the candidate because of countertransference problems in the training analyst. The result has been incompletely analyzed psychoanalysts who form a circle of devoted admirers to their former training analyst, but because this idealization is based on transference it is ambivalent, unreliable, and therefore, usually leads to unfortunate consequences both for the young analyst and for the training analyst.

THE LACK OF PROGRESS IN THE ANALYSIS

A frequent cause of stalemated situations in an analysis is often countertransference. Therefore, I discuss countertransference with younger colleagues who are conducting analyses which seem to make little progress, or which have apparently come to a standstill, and which for long periods of time have been stalemated. Discussing the case with the colleague usually makes clear quickly that at least part of the difficulty was due to the colleague's unrecognized countertransference reactions to the patient. It may be that he was disappointed that what started out as a very promising analytical problem turned into one requiring long, consistent and arduous work. He did not recognize this disappointment but unconsciously flavored his interpretations with reproach and criticism, so that the patient's hostile reactions were no longer transference reactions, and instead were due to the reality of the analytic situation. Thus the consistent interpretation by the colleague that the patient felt as though he, the analyst, were hostile was incorrect. The analyst actually was hostile. I have seen such situations change markedly when the analyst recognized this attitude in himself and was able to acknowledge it to his patient. I have also seen situations in which the analyst was afraid of the patient and yet was not aware of his fear. This is particularly true with patients who are prone to impulsive and violent acting out. Thus, a younger colleague continued to work fruitlessly for a long period of time with a patient who had made some suicide attempts because the young analyst was afraid that terminating the treatment would provoke a repetition of this event. Once he was confronted with this attitude, he could then consciously decide as to whether or not he wished to treat the patient. As he did want to treat the patient, he then had to decide that he was willing to take the calculated risk and perhaps bear the anxiety of the patient's making another suicide attempt. This new awareness on the part of the younger colleague made it possible for the analysis to begin some forward progress.

16

Transference, Countertransference, and the Real Relationship: A Study and Reassessment of Greenson's Views of the Patient/Analyst Dyad

Morton Shane, M.D.
Estelle Shane, Ph.D.

Introduction

Rᴀʟᴘʜ Greenson was at first our loved and respected teacher and supervisor, and subsequently our loved and respected friend and colleague. An important reason for the love and

This paper was presented on January 18, 1990, to the Los Angeles Psychoanalytic Society and Institute as a commemorative to Ralph Greenson on the Tenth Anniversary of his death.

respect he engendered, not just in us but in so many people, was the open-minded, tolerant, lively spirit with which he engaged psychoanalytic ideas, whether old or new. He constantly berated his more laggardly colleagues for not sufficiently sharing this attitude, once chastizing the group of twenty-two analysts with whom he shared offices with the observation that unfortunately their most widely read journal was *The Wall Street Journal*. Such direct and provocative criticism obviously did not endear him to everyone, and, indeed, Greenson was a controversial figure.

Be that as it may, had Ralph Greenson but lived to the ripe old age he deserved, he would have been the first among us to participate in the reassessment and updating of his own contributions to the theory and practice of psychoanalysis. Moreover, Greenson deserves our respect, and the greatest respect that can be paid to a contributor in any field is to not just use his or her contributions, but to continually reflect upon and question them. Greenson's books and papers continue to be used most extensively in the curricula of institutes throughout the psychoanalytic world. His writings also deserve to be reflected upon in the light of more recent formulations. It is with these views in mind, then, that we engage in our present endeavor: to review, evaluate, and update Greenson's creative ideas about transference, countertransference, and the real relationship.

First we must note that the theory with which Greenson organized his ideas was the classical model as it was at that time conceptualized. That is, underlying his contributions were: (1) an instinct theory based on the dual drives of libido and aggression with derivatives pressing for discharge, transference phenomena being understood as stemming from such a state of instinctual frustration; (2) a developmental model described by a predictable epigenetic unfolding of oral, anal, phallic and oedipal phases, each with its own aim, object, and mode, and each organized in characteristic fantasies which were anticipated to emerge in the transference of any successful analysis; (3) a structural theory based on the tripartite model; (4) a utilization of the five metapsychological points of view; (5) a technical approach heavily indebted to Fenichel (1941, 1945b) which stressed the understanding and interpretation of defense or resistance before content; and (6) an appreciation of the inevitable existence of ambivalence both in the transference and the countertransference, which ambivalence was based not only on life's vicissitudes, but also on the vicissitudes of the libidinal and aggressive drives.

The theory and technique that he most often heavily counter-poses to his own (e.g., Greenson, 1974b) is that of the Kleinian school. Yet Klein's influence on Greenson is unmistakable, her ideas being visible in his emphasis on the preoedipal mother, and on hate in the transference and countertransference, the origin of which ideas Greenson readily acknowledges. Greenson's chief argument with Klein lay in the assessment of analyzability, and in tact and timing of interpretation.

We should add for the sake of completeness, however, that Anna Freud (1965) was always a significant influence. Later in his life, some years after his major contributions on technique which are our main focus in this paper, Mahler's (Mahler and Furer, 1968; Mahler, Pine, and Bergman, 1975) insights on separation-individuation replaced more classical and Kleinian formulations in regard to object relations in the first few years of life. While Greenson did not live long enough to review and assess Kohut's later work, he was quite aware of *The Analysis of the Self* (1971). In a private communication Greenson was somewhat dismissive of Kohut's contributions, saying, with uncharacteristic taciturnity, that he did not understand the man's work. But, despite this, and with his unfailing openness to new ideas, Greenson was always ready to hear and discuss our own early attempts to integrate Kohut into the mainstream. One aspect of this review will be to clarify the basis of Greenson's differences with Kohut. In addition, we will use the ideas of more recent contributors to present contrasting as well as confirming conceptions of trans-ference and countertransference phenomena. We do this in order to speculate upon how Greenson himself might have updated his own ideas had he experienced these later influences.

With this as introduction, we will proceed with the review and assessment of Greenson's work.

The Positive Transference

Greenson (1967)* defines the positive transference as love in any of its forms, the nonsexual, nonromantic, mild forms of which he sees as contributing to the working alliance. Transference love, Greenson

---

*Unless otherwise indicated, references to Greenson's writings will be from *The Technique and Practice of Psychoanalysis, Volume I*, published in 1967.

tells us, occurs because patients have had painful object experiences in their childhoods, which experiences are repressed and then reemerge in the analysis in a form which manifests as more "irrational" and more "infantile" than "real" love.

Thus, we are confronted with one problematic assumption that may be seen to run throughout Greenson's work despite his cogent awareness of the complexities that seem to belie his own definition: the assumption that a distinction may readily and unassailably be made between rational and irrational, real and unreal, adult and infantile, along with the assumption that the final arbiter of these distinctions is the well-functioning analyst. Of course Greenson did not live to experience the current era in which reality is conceived as something to be negotiated between patient and analyst (Gill, 1982; Schafer, 1983; Goldberg, 1988). His assumptions allowed him to define the transference as a clearly neurotic formation, and, as we shall see, a phenomenon somewhat distinct from the real relationship and the (therapeutic) working alliance.

Another variety of positive transference identified by Greenson is idealization, which he viewed as an attempt on the patient's part to preserve the analyst from primitive, destructive impulses. "It is so," he tells us, "with all fixed and unchanging transference reactions; the rigidity indicates that emotions and impulses of the opposite nature are being held in check. The worshipful attitude hides a repressed loathing which covers primitive hatred" (p. 229). Consistent with this perspective, Greenson viewed all transference phenomena as ambivalent, a necessary part of a complete analysis being the release of both loving and hating drive derivatives.

This view of idealization as defense, a reaction formation against primitive, pervasive aggression, remains consistent, more or less, with current classical and Kleinian understanding. During Greenson's lifetime, though after the publication of Greenson's major work, Kohut (1968, 1971) postulated a different view of idealization, one that sprang from the basic and healthy narcissistic needs for objects that could be admired and looked to for soothing, protection, and self-enhancement. While these two views of idealization, as reaction formation and as necessary developmental experience, need not be mutually exclusive, the way idealization is handled in the analysis certainly is based on how the analyst conceptualizes the particular manifestation. If the specific instance is viewed as reaction formation, the idealization is interpreted as defensive against aggression toward the analyst. If, on the other hand, it is viewed as a necessary prerequisite for self-enhancement and structure building, the patient's experience with the analyst would not be quickly interrupted by interpretation, even were the idealization viewed as unrealistic aggrandizement. Instead, the idealization would be considered tentatively as having a possible meliorative effect in and of itself. Only when its function is clarified would the idealization become an appropriate matter for interpretation either to make explicit the developmental needs that are being gratified by the experience, or to make explicit its use as a defense against aggression. This is an important distinction creating a technical difference between the classical and Kleinian approaches on the one hand, and the self psychological approach on the other. It permits a wider range of interpretive possibilities than if idealization is always viewed as reaction formation.

Greenson's assertion that idealization in the transference always defends against aggression would appear to be based on an underlying assumption of a dual instinctual drive theory; the reason that idealization hides aggression is that all psychological manifestations must contain, if not equal parts, then at least significant mixtures of love and hate. Indeed, Greenson made clear his conviction that hate in all of its various forms must be made manifest and be analyzed within the transference or the analysis remains woefully incomplete, as, for example, in his consideration of the negative transference. More currently, Brenner (1982) makes the same point that all transference is ambivalent. Brenner goes so far as to say that it is not useful to classify transference in the categories of either positive or negative at all, given the ubiquity of ambivalence. The postulation of destructive aggression as inherent and therefore ubiquitous, in the same way that libido is conceptualized as inherent and ubiquitous, is seriously challenged, however, by infant research not available to Greenson during his lifetime (Parens, 1979; Shane and Shane, 1983; Lichtenberg, 1983b, 1989) and by self psychology (Kohut, 1980). If destructive aggression is not a basic building block of the personality as this infant research would suggest, then one might consider first that it is feasible for love and admiration to appear at times unmixed, and, second, that where destructive aggression is present, one might look for and expect to find some form of provocation, either from the past or in the present.

Finally, in terms of the category positive transference, Greenson tells us that it is always, unless it is sublimated and desexualized, accompanied by libidinal strivings, which strivings should be elicited in the analytic situation at all developmental levels. Here Greenson's fealty to stepwise epigenetic unfolding of libidinal stages of development leads him to expect manifestations in the transference on oral, anal, phallic, and oedipal levels in some distinct manner, for example, in an Eriksonian (1950) stepwise progression. Again, the more recent evidence from child observation not yet available to him (Stern, 1985) might have led Greenson to question the neatness and elegance of this phasic view. Infant researchers observe manifestations of libidinal interest arising in a fashion characterized as parallel rather than sequential, which would seem to indicate that not every libidinal phase has its day, that is, its time of preeminence. An experience focused by the developing child in one zone need not then be reprocessed at a later time in another zone; more variety and less certainty regarding individual sensual–sexual experiences must now be conceptualized both developmentally and in the transference.

The Negative Transference

Turning to the negative transference, according to Greenson, it is based upon hate in any of its various forms. It is always present, though often defended against, in the analysis; when it is not uncovered it is the result of the analyst's collusion with the patient's defenses, and most commonly results in a stalemated analysis. Therefore, early negative transference must be pursued vigorously. However, says Greenson, once the working alliance is established, a negative transference can be viewed as a sign of progress. Consistent with the Kleinian school (Segal, 1973, 1985) and many classical analysts as well (Brenner, 1982), he believed that an intense and prolonged hateful reaction should emerge before termination is thought of, that interminable analyses and negative therapeutic reactions are examples of insufficient analysis of transference hate. Also in agreement with Klein (Klein, 1957), Greenson writes of the patient's fear of the analyst as best explained by the patient's projected hostility. A potential difficulty with this set of contentions, also based upon the ubiquity of aggression, is that if the analyst tends to view a persistent and strong negative transference as inevitable and salutory, then his own contribution to the patient's hatred might be overlooked.

Aspects of the Tripartite Model as Transference: Superego, Ego, and Id Manifestations in the Transference

In addition to using the positive and negative transference as organizers of the experience of the patient's relationship to the analyst, Greenson employs the various aspects of the tripartite model in a similar fashion. That is, as has been commonly noted, the patient may perceive the analyst as a superego figure. Because Greenson conceptualizes the superego as significantly cathected with aggressive drive energies, he anticipates that such a transference reaction would be mainly hostile and critical, resulting from either a transference of the patient's experience with his parental objects or a projection of his own hostility. Perhaps it is because of this theoretical proclivity that Greenson underplays in the transference the idealized and loving aspects of the superego, the identificatory resultants of more accepting, encouraging, and affectionate childhood experiences with parental figures. Sandler (1960b), for one, offered a corrective to this often overlooked aspect of the superego, and Kohut, with his selfobject transferences, offered another.

As another application of the tripartite model to organize transference experience, Greenson writes of the analyst being viewed by the patient as an extension of his or her ego, which, as an early form of identification, functions to improve reality testing, particularly in borderline patients. In fact, the role that identification plays in the transference reactions of all patients was explored and advanced by Greenson, and most particularly as a building block for the working alliance. In making an interpretation, what the analyst expects of the patient is that the latter is able to give up temporarily the experiencing, free-associating ego in order to join with the analyst's perspective; that is, as Greenson asserts, to temporarily and partially identify with the analyst. While this process is at first only accomplished upon the analyst's request, soon such imitation and then identification becomes automatic and preconscious, patients asking themselves what they might possibly be avoiding when they become aware of their own resistances. Greenson sees this as the mark of being "in analysis," and as a harbinger of self-analysis.

Other types of identification in the transference include identification with the aggressor; identification to establish closeness and love, to be like the idealized analyst and become one with him; identification to achieve a new identity; and, as a counterpoint, the struggle against identification as a fear of being taken over by the object. Greenson also invented the concept of disidentification in relation to the little boy's struggle to establish a gender identity different from that of his mother's (Greenson, 1968a). Such a process might figure into and contribute to the struggle in the transference to avoid engulfment and loss of separateness and autonomy.

Greenson's view of the analyst as auxiliary ego is consistent with Anna Freud's (1965) view of analysis as providing a smorgasbord of functions and transference opportunities from which the patient, child or adult, may choose. Moreover, Greenson's perspective of this abiding ego potential provided by the analyst sets the stage for more recent developments in this field, such as the more modern view of "corrective emotional experience" (Schlesinger, 1988) built into the analytic relationship.

Such experiences have been conceptualized in various ways; for example, the selfobject experiences of Kohut (1971, 1977, 1984), the holding environment of Winnicott and Modell (1988), container experiences of Bion (1970), and other developmental conceptualizations. In fact, Greenson's ideas here were remarkably sophisticated. In thinking about the patient's struggle both against identification and against being empathized with, he indicates how the potentially meliorative effects of being understood can be resisted out of fear of being taken over, destroyed, engulfed, or unmasked. Thus our recent emphasis on the patholytic effects of being understood à la Kohut and self psychology is confronted by Greenson's challenge that some patients, out of their own character difficulties, resist this very process. Modell (1988) makes this same point.

Greenson introduces another aspect of ego functioning manifested in the transference when he designates those cases wherein there appears to be no transference reaction whatsoever as instances of a defensive transference; that is, a repetition with the analyst of a set of defensive reactions derived from the past and persisting into the present which together serve as a resistance to the uncovering of underlying instinctual and affective components. These reactions are ego syntonic, often unconscious, and difficult to analyze. We can see Gill's (1982) indebtedness to Greenson in the latter's conceptualization of the resistance to the awareness of transference, which Gill contrasts to the other of the two large categories of transference he identifies (resistance to the resolution of transference).

In relation to the id aspects of the tripartite model, Greenson is scrupulous about the avoidance of gratification of desire within the transference. Such gratification, he says, has the effect of rendering the analysis of that desire, on whatever level and in whatever form, less important to the patient to the point where the patient may renounce completely any interest in working on the matter. (We must say that in practice Greenson was much less rigorous than in his writings in this as in other matters, as he himself was the first to point out.) Again, it would seem that this clearly articulated and unequivocal stance is the natural outgrowth of the classical analytic theory of mental functioning articulated by Freud (1900) and later by Hartmann (1955) and Rapaport (1967): Mental activity originates in primary process, and presses for discharge in hallucinatory gratification or in action; it is only through blocking and frustration of automatic discharge that secondary process thought can be achieved. Infant observational studies beginning with Wolff (1966) and more recently summarized by Stern (1985) and Lichtenberg (1989) present an alternative view that primary and secondary process develop concurrently in the infant, remain active concurrently throughout life, and that activity in one mode need not interfere with activity in the other. This would suggest that the patient can both be gratified in terms of pleasurable desire and still not be dissuaded from or depleted of the energy required to talk about it. More recent views (Sandler, 1976; M. Shane, 1979; Bacal, 1985; and Lichtenberg, 1989) of the technical handling of acting out and enactments both within and outside of the analysis would indicate that the actual activity desired by the patient can both be gratified and analyzed; enactment may neither militate against nor mitigate discussion and analysis, but may actually be facilitated by it. Obviously, we do not mean to suggest that the ordinary interdictions imposed on both the patient and especially the analyst be rescinded by these findings; there remain the need to preserve the analytic relationship, to provide an arena wherein the patient may feel free and safe to express every and any emotion, and the requirement to protect the patient from the advantage analysts may otherwise take of transference-based feelings of love (or hate) and trust. But more benign gratifications such as responding verbally to the patient who urgently demands it, or accepting a gift which is heavily narcissistically invested, may not preclude, but, in fact, may actually enhance, the analytic process in those cases wherein the gratification is then analyzed.

The Working Alliance

As a "full and equal" partner to the transference in the analytic situation, Greenson introduces the concept of the working alliance. When the goal is to produce lasting change, he tells us, it is not sufficient for the analyst to just gather historical data and to provide insight by means of interpretation; an alliance must be established between patient and analyst, which alliance constitutes a different reaction to the analyst than the transference per se. The importance of the working alliance was discovered by Greenson in work with patients who either could not get into analysis at all, or who, though in analysis and possessed of copious insight, could not improve and therefore could not get out. The working alliance concept describes the relatively rational ("non-neurotic") rapport of patient with analyst (and of analyst with patient). It is derived from Zetzel's (1956) concept of the therapeutic alliance, though Greenson's accent is more on the rational (real) relationship between patient and analyst than, as in Zetzel's formulation, on early nurturing experiences with the mother. The concept owes a debt also to Stone's (1961) physicianly commitment, and to Fenichel's (1941) rational transference.

Greenson sees multiple factors at the core of the working alliance, including the motivation to overcome illness; the acceptance of a sense of helplessness; and a conscious and rational willingness to cooperate, to follow the analyst's instructions, and to consider the analyst's interpretations. It is an alliance, in effect, between the rational (observing) ego of the patient and the analyzing ego of the analyst, facilitated by the patient's partial and temporary identification with the analyst's approach. Greenson explains the process as follows: The patient's observing, analyzing ego is separated from his experiencing ego via identification with the observing ego of the analyst. This conception derives from Sterba (1934) who was the first to distinguish between the observing ego and the experiencing ego. Greenson adds that the analyst's interventions disengage the analysand's working attitudes from neurotic transference phenomena, just as these interventions separate the analysand's reasonable ego from his or her irrational ego. Greenson makes clear that his distinction between the working alliance and the transference neurosis is not absolute—that the working alliance itself may contain neurotic elements which then require analysis. Moreover, he adds, the working alliance may be used defensively to ward off more regressive and unacceptable transference phenomena. Yet the concept itself remains important to him.

Greenson observes that in the well-functioning analysis, the working alliance is formed and evolves almost imperceptibly, relatively silently, and seemingly independent of any special activity on the part of the analyst. With the analyzable patient, that is, one who neither suffers from narcissistic pathology nor severe impairment of ego functions nor a rigidity in object relationships, a realistically based partnership with the analyst forms easily, parallel to the patient's capacity to connect with others in his or her outside life. The analyst is then able to perform his or her appropriate tasks in the opening phase of pointing to and exploring fairly obvious resistances and inappropriate affects, and making connections between the past and the present. As a consequence of these prototypical analytic activities, the patient feels understood. Then the patient begins to regress in the transference. When the transference phenomena are appropriately analyzed, a reasonable ego and working alliance are established in the patient, alongside the experiencing ego and the transference neurosis. Henceforth, the patient experiences oscillations between the transference neurosis and the working alliance in this one area, just as he or she experiences oscillations between the experiencing ego and the observing ego. It is because the working alliance functions so silently and unobtrusively in the well-functioning analysis that the case examples Greenson provides to illustrate the concept are drawn from instances in which the working alliance has faltered or failed, that is, in which irrational transference intrusions have become manifest in the relationship, either in the patient or in the analyst.

Greenson's working alliance has certainly drawn a great deal of attention, both positive and negative. It has parallels with a number of earlier and later concepts, including Winnicott's (1955, 1965) and Modell's (1984, 1988) holding environment; Sandler's (1960a) background of safety; Bion's (1970) container; and Weiss and Sampson's (1986) passing the test. Luborsky (Luborsky, Crits-Christoph, Mintz, and Auerbach, 1988), in researching psycho-analytic psychotherapy, correlates the strength of the therapeutic alliance with a prediction of success in treatment. Schlesinger and Robbins (1983) elaborate on the concept, formulating it as the analytic alliance, and focusing on its potential for facilitating the patient's development within the analysis.

Other contributors have been less impressed with the concept. For example, Brenner (1976) and Stein (1981) do not distinguish Zetzel's therapeutic alliance from Greenson's contribution, viewing both as inimical to the analysis of the transference. Brenner writes that the use of alliance concepts interferes with an understanding of the transference phenomena pervading all human mental activity. He contends that an artificial separation of categories of rational thought and reaction to the analyst from neurotic compromise forma-tion misleads the analyst into the belief that some psychological phenomena do not need to be explored analytically. Furthermore, he feels that such a distinction directs the analyst into educational byways that have the effect of exhorting the patient to be more reasonable. Stein focuses his criticism on the failure to analyze cooperative and reasonable attitudes on the patient's part which appear to facilitate the analysis, but which, in reality, carry with them neurotic, analyzable aspects too often overlooked in the analytic process. Concepts such as the therapeutic alliance and the working alliance, Stein argues, create a haven for unconscious conflicts hid-den within such presumably "unobjectionable" attitudes.

In Greenson's defense, it should be obvious from our review above that Greenson himself was aware of both neurotic intrusions into the alliance, and the danger of the patient's using the alliance for defensive purposes. Spence (1982), in an ironic discussion concern-ing the nature of controversy in psychoanalysis—how concepts come into being and are ordered out of being by fiat and without benefit of clinical data—concludes that alliance concepts are likely to endure because they address some essential aspect of the analytic situation. In that sense, Spence can be seen as agreeing with Greenson.

However, Spence argues that the alliance concept is so vague that individual analysts put their own unique definition to it, and this inevitably reduces its value.

Gill (1982) speculates that the reason analysts have invented alliance concepts is the necessity to distinguish between the transference and the realistic relationship, but that the difficulty with such concepts has been their failure to make just this important distinction, and their failure, as well, to distinguish clearly between present and past determinants of the patient's attitudes. Thus, it would seem that, for Gill, the core of the alliance is the realistic relationship between patient and analyst. He emphasizes the need to acknowledge such realistic aspects of the relationship, notwithstanding the fact of inevitable transference intrusions which require analysis. Unlike Greenson, Gill dismisses from the definition of the "real" the idea of "genuine." (However, this "genuine" aspect of the real relationship prefigures Modell's [1984, 1988] emphasis on authentic and inauthentic exchanges in analysis.) Also, unlike Greenson, Gill introduces into this complexity the idea that "reality" in itself does not exist as an absolute, and that, in any case, the analyst is certainly not its arbiter; when Gill speaks of reality, he refers to a consensually validated concept of the actual situation arrived at by discussion and negotiation between the two participants, patient and analyst. Gill, therefore, clarifies to some extent the working alliance concept, retaining its distinction from the transference, focusing on its present as opposed to its past determinants, and adding to it an emphasis on the "real," updated as realistic and negotiable.

To further elucidate the current version of the real relationship which Greenson has seen as the nucleus of the working alliance, we can refer to Kernberg's (1988) discussion of this concept, which he refers to as an aspect of the psychoanalytic "frame." For Kernberg, the "real" relationship:

[I]ncludes the analyst as an interested, objective, but concerned and sympathetic listener who respects the patient's autonomy, and the patient as one who expects to be helped to increase his own understanding of his unconscious conflicts. This realistic relationship . . . facilitates the development of the psychoanalytic process [p. 483].

Thus, there appears to be a division in present-day views of the working alliance. There are those who see it as a necessary construct to distinguish and offset transference phenomena from realistic phenomena, and there are those who dismiss the construct because of the inevitable nature of transference infusions into all mental life. Contributing to this dichotomy is the very way in which the process of its formation is described by Greenson. The alliance, he tells us, is formed and evolves almost imperceptibly, relatively silently and seemingly independent of any special activity on the part of the analyst. Kohut and Modell, among other developmentalists, have noted particular kinds of transference different from the transference of classical analysis, adding to the variety discernible in the analytic relationship. The point is, the selfobject transferences described by Kohut and the dependent/containing transferences described by Modell have similarities to Greenson's alliance: They, too, are silent, form imperceptibly, and require no special activity on the analyst's part. Moreover, they are seen to provide a background of support and safety.

To illustrate the potential for confusion between the alliance concept and these more recently identified, subtle transference manifestations, an idealizing selfobject transference, forming silently and without any special activity on the analyst's part, may contribute to the analysand's cooperation with the analyst in the analytic process; however, this manifestation would not be best understood as an aspect of the realistic relationship within the working alliance. Similarly, the narcissistic pleasures involved in being listened to, responded to, and resonated with by the analyst, long ago described by A. Reich (1950) and more recently formulated by Kohut as the archaic mirroring and/or alter ego selfobject transferences, are also not best understood as aspects of the realistic relationship. Finally, the dependent–containing and holding aspects of the analytic relationship are best understood not as realistic, but as symbolic gratifications and actualizations of the dependent–containing transference. Thus, they do not fall into the realm of the realistic relationship that forms the core of Greenson's working alliance. Yet these are all described in terms similar to the alliance.

It seems that there is a genuine problem, then, with the alliance concept; those who find it valuable and, in fact, irreplaceable, and those who find it problematic and, in fact, dismissable, are alike in the difficulty they identify of distilling it from the transference. Moreover, the addition of the new transference categories referred to above narrows the realm of patient–analyst experience that can be ascribed to the realistically based working alliance. There is, however, one aspect of the patient–analyst experience that is more clearly discernible as in that realm: a new object experience (Loewald, 1960; A. Freud, 1965; Ritvo, 1974; Shane and Shane, 1989). A new object experience derived from the psychoanalytic frame is a unique relationship never encountered before in the patient's lifetime and one which carries with it the developmental potential of the analytic situation. We believe Greenson might have categorized it as an aspect of the working alliance or the non-transference relationship (Greenson and Wexler, 1969). For example, the patient in analysis is told, however directly or indirectly, that he or she may express in words all loving, hating, angry, envious, jealous, tender, admiring feelings about the analyst, without the prospect of exploitation or retaliation in any form. This is, indeed, a unique experience never before encountered and destined to produce an increased psychological freedom that augments development in the direction of greater maturity. This new object experience can be seen, then, as in the realm of reality and as a constituent of the working alliance.

We will end this section with one further comment. The alliance concept has been criticized from another perspective—the quality of clinical examples provided to illustrate it. Zetzel has been criticized by Brenner (1977) and by Spence (1982) who view her interventions as psychotherapeutic rather than psychoanalytic. Greenson's clinical examples are also vulnerable, but for other reasons. Peterfreund (1983) has taken Greenson to task for seemingly allowing his theory to dictate too strongly his interventions. With all due respect for the difficulty inherent in communicating one's clinical work, for the fact that a given clinical example can neither prove nor disprove a theory but can only demonstrate it, and for the fact that Greenson stands among the few who have generously and courageously put forth detailed descriptions of their clinical practice, the illustrations of this particular concept are especially prone to the view that Greenson conducts himself as if he has privileged access to what is cooperative and what is uncooperative, what is genuine and what is false, and what is realistic and what is transference-imbued. Specifically, he describes in his text one patient with whom he refused to work on new material she brought in unless he was convinced that she was "in good alliance" with him, facing her, he states, with "her misuse of the basic rule and her blurring of the real purposes of free association" (p. 197). She eventually came around to Greenson's point of view. One might sum up the difficulty inherent in this particular example by noting that at times there may be a fine line between therapeutic *alliance* and therapeutic *compliance*.

Countertransference

Greenson defines countertransference in a clear and definitive way as all of the analyst's transference responses to his or her patient. These responses are based upon distorted and inappropriate reactions derived from unresolved unconscious conflicts from the analyst's own past. Thus, countertransference is a counterpart to an equivalent of the transference of the patient. Greenson separates himself from both the totalistic view of countertransference which includes all of one's responses to the patient, and, at the other extreme, from the limited view of countertransference which includes only those responses evoked by the patient's transferences.

In Greenson's vision, countertransference is a most important and ubiquitous phenomenon. During the course of psychoanalytic treatment, he tells us, "every psychoanalyst experiences many shades and degrees of love, hate, and indifference toward each of his patients" (Greenson, 1974a, p. 505), this range of feeling being necessary for the analytic work. Yet, he says presciently, countertransference has never achieved the place it deserves in our technique. He makes a distinction which is important to his concepts of the real relationship and the working alliance, the distinction between a transference to the patient, and a real reaction. By "real," Greenson means, in this context, "realistic," implying a capacity in the analyst to, by self scrutiny, separate his "realistic" from his "unrealistic" or "neurotic" responses.

Greenson makes a further distinction between what he terms the countertransference reaction and the countertransference neurosis, the latter referring to long-lasting transference involvements with the patient wherein the patient becomes persistently and inappropriately central to the analyst; for example, the analyst who falls in love with his or her patient, or who feels toward the patient intense hatred or persistent competitive feelings. When the counter-transference neurosis is more subtle, it is even more dangerous, because it becomes harder to detect, examples being the analyst who feels bored or who finds himself or herself forgetful of a given patient's material. Of particular interest is Greenson's insight that narcissistic needs in the analyst can create difficulties in the analysis: He or she may unconsciously seek to idealize patients in order to augment his or her own self-esteem, for example, or may feel unaccountably disappointed in patients who fail in this needed, self-aggrandizing function.

Citing Heimann (1950) and Little (1951), Greenson suggests that countertransference responses can make a positive contribution to the analysis, pointing to processes in the patient the analyst is unaware of consciously; but, Greenson warns, just as transference is an unreliable ally for the working alliance, so countertransference, its counterpart, is similarly unreliable. In Greenson's terms, counter-transference can interfere with the intuitively constructed "working model of the patient," depicted by him in a highly original and creative way as empathically conceived by the analyst and elucidated over the entire course of the analysis.

Vigilance is called for when the analyst perceives some difficulty with a given patient, requiring at the least self-analysis, and, should that prove unavailing, some monitoring of that self-analysis by a colleague. Greenson advises that when one's counter-transference has led to behavior hurtful to the patient, the analyst should apologize for causing pain even before the egregious interchange between patient and analyst is analyzed. He actively discourages, however, revelation to the patient of the content of any self-analytic efforts, here specifically disagreeing with Little (1951) and Searles (1965).

In terms of his understanding and articulation of counter-transference phenomena, Greenson was ahead of his time in presenting such responses as significant to achieving understanding of the analyst's role in the analytic venture, and we would add as a thought of our own, in the role it plays in stimulating self-analysis, a development-enhancing experience for the analyst as he or she participates in the analysis (M. Shane, 1979). He was remarkably frank and open in his description of his own errors and in indicating ways to make restitution to the patient so that the analytic process would not only

be reinstated, but actually furthered. Greenson's approach to countertransference anticipates Kohut's technical contributions in this
area. Kohut, too, points to the prevalence of empathic disruptions in
the analytic relationship, and to their significance in bringing about
transmuting internalization of analytic function and a strengthening
of self structure. Like Greenson, Kohut focuses on the necessity for
the analyst's recognizing his or her own part in the disruption and
exploring its meaning to the patient without revealing the content of
self-analytic efforts in this regard.

Kohut, like Greenson, focuses on the importance of the analyst's
countertransference responses in general, believing along with him
that the countertransference response in itself can reveal a good deal
about the patient with whom one is working. In this regard, Kohut
identifies two major countertransference responses to two of the
major selfobject transferences he specifies. A mirroring transference
is likely to stir up in the analyst irritation and boredom secondary to
feeling ignored as a person, perceiving himself or herself treated as
merely a psychological function of the patient's self. An idealizing
transference is likely to create feelings in the analyst of excitement
and anxiety at being so undeservedly and unreservedly admired and
esteemed. The counterreaction of the analyst, often stimulating
countertransference feelings, not only helps to diagnose the nature
of the patient's pathology, but also can lead the analyst into errors of
tact and timing. We believe that Kohut must be indebted to Greenson
in this regard for the latter's original contributions on boredom
(Greenson, 1953), empathy (Greenson, 1960), and tact and timing
(Greenson, 1967).

Other contributors indebted to Greenson regarding countertransference issues include Sandler (1976) and Modell (1984).
Greenson was at the forefront of a large trend toward openness about
one's errors that continues today, enhancing understanding of the
two-person interaction as well as enactments in the countertrans-
ference-transference.

Conclusion

Greenson's contributions to psychoanalysis are primarily and
quintessentially clinical. Much of what he has written has held up

remarkably well, requiring only addition and emendation rather than major revision to make his work consistent with current practice. Using his writings on transference, countertransference, and the real relationship as illustrative, Greenson emerges as a man *of* his time *ahead* of his time.

17

Countertransference and Counterdefense

Sanford M. Izner, M.D.

SINCE the time of the introduction of the term *countertransference* by Freud in 1910, psychoanalytic literature has been replete with many references to the phenomenon, along with numerous attempts to discuss, define, and otherwise elaborate conceptual formulations for the countertransference problem. These efforts have met with varying degrees of acceptance or rejection by most analysts and other therapists. It seems that as one follows the studies and literature on the subject, the varied forms of approach to the problem and the tendencies toward rather loosely structured conceptualizations have provided for some freedom of use of the term that is not especially conducive to the development of a functional, clearly representative picture of the countertransference phenomenon. It is my impression that the concept might be more clearly delineated, even at the expense of restructuring the scope of application of the term. In addition, any attempt at lending great specificity to the concept should fulfill the metapsychology requirements of the science, and descriptively conform with the requirements of the structural theory.

Freud first mentioned the countertransference problem in the following terms: "We have begun to consider the 'countertransference' which arises in the physician as a result of the patient's influence on his unconscious feelings--" (1910d, p. 289). There seem to be several elements of significance in relation to this fragmentary quotation from Freud. First, that it was expressed in his paper entitled "The Future Prospects of Psycho-Analysis" in the year 1910, at a time long before he had crystallized his formulations regarding the structural theory of the psychic appartus; and second, that he considered the countertransference phenomenon to be the result of the influence of the patient on the unconscious feelings of the therapist. This is the baseline position that I have selected in attempting to deal with the countertransference problem.

It is quite unnecessary to recapitulate the review of the literature on transference and countertransference by Orr (1954); rather it is more appropriate to relate some of these writings to the formulations to be expressed in this presentation.

Following Freud's two discussions of some of the counter-transference elements (1910d, 1915[1914] as he viewed them, many of the important contributors seemed to utilize Freud's definition as a working concept, and I would like to draw upon them for a similar purpose. Glover (1955) defined countertransference mainly in terms of the analyst's reaction to the transference reactions of the patient. He attempted to clarify a portion of the problem by the introduction of the term *counterresistance*, in an apparent effort to subdivide the more comprehensive term descriptively into phenomena of greater specificity. He defined counterresistance as the use of defense in the analyst, "in like kind and equal to the defensive resistances of the patient" (p. 92); for example, if the analyst were to meet projections with projections, repression with repression. In a further attempt to provide specificity, Glover considered the differentiation of positive and negative countertransference and counterresistances, which might be equatable with the use of predominantly libidinized or aggressivized defensive phenomena, rather than utilizing adequately neutralized processes in the analytic work. Tower (1956) limited the use of the term to those phenomena which are transferences of the analyst onto his patient, but she also discussed some of the analyst's defensive activities. Berman (1949) differentiated countertransference as the reaction of the analyst to the patient as though he were an important figure in the analyst's life; from the "attitudes" of the analyst, which he describes as "the emotional reactions of the analyst as a person during the treatment hour, including his reasonable and appropriate emotional responses and his *characteristic defenses*. It is assumed that the totality of the analyst's reactions, as in all interpersonal relationships, represents a blending, to a varying degree, of appropriate, defensive, and transference responses to the patient, but the appropriate ones largely predominate" (p. 163; emphasis added).[1] It is most important to differentiate appropriate and defensive responses from other reactions of the therapist. For there seem to be forms of defensive activity which may or may not be considered in the nature of a response or reaction, more characterologic, even possibly pathognomonic in type; and truly more definitely based on the conscious and unconscious fantasy life of the therapist, with little necessity for association to what might be transpiring within the patient. This form of emotional expression may be more closely linked to the therapeutic situation and position of the analyst, rather than be considered as the expression of an appropriate attitude in connection with the patient or analytic situation, and I will attempt to provide evidence for these comments later.

Some authors seem to include all of the feelings that the therapist experiences in relation to the patient as countertransference (Heiman, 1950). Sharp (1947) emphasized both the ubiquitous quality and the quantitative aspects of the feelings and reactions of the analyst. Other writers, such as Annie Reich (1951b) limited the use of the term *countertransference* to the unconscious feelings, attitudes, and expressions of the therapist. She emphasized that the patient must represent an object out of the past to the analyst in order that a true countertransference reaction might occur.[2] She differentiated countertransference phenomena in terms of "acute" and "chronic" countertransference activities, as additional criteria of significance, relating the latter to the acting out of characterologic behavior problems.[3] In a later publication (1960a), Annie Reich further emphasized that countertransference reactions must always

---

[1] The use of the term *characteristic defenses* borders closely on some of the important differentiating factors I have utilized in this thesis.

[2] The term *true* countertransference reaction is utilized, although it might just as appropriately be termed "analyzable" countertransference reaction.

[3] "Chronic" countertransference activities associated with characterologic behavior problems most closely approximate what I will attempt to describe as counterdefensive phenomena in this thesis.

be considered to be interferences with the analytic work, regardless of the fact that certain analytic insights may result. Gitelson (1952) utilized the differentiation of reactions to the patient as a whole, as contrasted to reactions to partial aspects of the patient. He referred to the former as transferences and to the latter as countertransferences. He describes "emergency defensive reactions," which he considers to be the nucleus of any manifestations of countertransference, rather than what is described as "whole responses" to the patient or case or patients in general, which he refers to as reactivations of "ancient transference potentials." Gitelson emphasized that these "transferences" are likely to become manifest early in the contact with the patient. These "transferences" also seem to closely resemble what I have chosen to term *counterdefense*. Gitelson states further that countertransferences occur later "and in the context of an established analytic situation they comprise the analyst's reactions to (1) the patient's transference, (2) the material that the patient brings in, (3) the reactions of the patient to the analyst as a person. . . ." Fliess (1953) also provided additional clarification of the phenomenon when he emphasized that countertransference "must be reserved for the equivalent in the analyst of what is termed 'transference' in the patient" (p. 28). He pointed up the regressive nature of the phenomenon and the elements of counteridentification involved.

It is the purpose of this presentation to attempt further delineation and clarification of the countertransference problem, based on the structural components involved. The approach utilized by Annie Reich in connection with her position concerning the unconscious and interfering qualities of countertransference phenomena seems to provide a most adequate definition for our purposes (Reich, 1951b, 1960a). As we are all aware, when we discuss countertransference, we discuss ourselves, and so I have elected to present the following material in the form of a somewhat personal communication, drawn from my own experiences and interpretation of the literature.

A situation taken from my own analytic work of many years ago, when I had been doing classical psychoanalysis for a relatively brief period of time, might serve the purpose of providing an illustration. The particular clinical experience was complicated by a number of elements, not the least of which was the fact that the patient was the first female analytic case I undertook as a part of my analytic training, with the further knowledge that the case was being supervised by a woman. In addition, I was commuting for this training from the city where I was now residing back to the city of my birth, with a considerable feeling of ambivalence over the need of travel. I will not go into all the facets of the problems involved, but a brief description of the case, along with some explanations in relation to the therapy, will suffice to illustrate the problem.

The patient in question was a financially successful unmarried woman, 41 years of age, who entered analysis because of the disruption of a love affair she had conducted with her married employer over a period of years, and because of the depression that accompanied this situation. In addition, the patient still resided with her aged mother, to whom she felt inextricably bound, and for whom she harbored considerable hostility in association with the conditions of dependence and infantilization under which she lived. She still felt a great deal of hostility toward her siblings, of which she was the youngest, and was especially hostile and depreciating of all of the men with whom she had been in contact throughout her life. She thought that her employer would not have attained his present status if she "had not made him," and that he really owed everything to her. Her masculine identification in this regard was quite clear. For all of her lifetime she felt unloved and unattended to by all of the important objects in her past experiences.

During the course of the first year of analysis, forward motion and progress in the analysis occurred, in spite of the patient's assumption of a somewhat stubbornly resistive anal position in the transference, and even though she suffered with considerable guilt in relation to her rich libidinal and aggressive fantasy life. After about one year of therapy, a period of marked slowing in productiveness to the point of stagnation seemed to develop, which was apparently related to the transference neurosis. This neurosis was structured around a reaction to the frustration of the patient's desire for love and attention spontaneously in the analysis, which was not forthcoming.

It was my practice to write notes following each visit of this patient, utilizing these notes for refreshing my memory in reporting the material to the supervising analyst. At this time, as I reviewed what I had written, I noticed a consistent and repetitive error in these notes. It was an error in the spelling of a most simple and common word, an error for which there appeared to be no logical explanation. With this observation on my part, coupled with the self-analysis that accompanied the explanation for the error, the entire course of the analysis was altered, because it enabled me as a therapist to develop certain insights into my own emotional position in relation to this patient, and to synthesize and integrate my own intellectual functioning and other ego activities in a different manner. This resulted in my being better able to assist the patient to deal with, and overcome, her rather stubbornly fixed resistive attitude in the treatment. An intellectual awareness of the problems in the transference and countertransference had existed for me before this time, but what seems of primary importance in connection with the countertransference experience is that it required further self-analysis and working through of these emotional components before this particular form of transference resistance could be dealt with in regard to this particular patient.

The word I had misspelled was the word *both*. How can one misspell this simple word? The form of the misspelling as well as the choice of word itself were of greatest significance in relation to the countertransference problem and the resulting self-analysis. I found that on several occasions I had spelled the word *bothe*. I had added the letter *e* to the word. With the advent of this observation, the self-analysis began.

In relation to this patient, intellectually I had been aware that my emotional position had been governed in part by certain rather specific elements in my own background. I was the younger of two children, the older being a girl very close in age to the patient, and obviously identified in my own mind with this patient (Fliess, 1953).[4] I will not go into the intimate details of the problem in relation to my own neurosis from childhood any further than to relate that my sister's name began with the letter *E*, and for all of my lifetime I have always referred to her by calling her *E*, and never by her given name. The significance of the particular form taken in the misspelling is now more clear, and we have some further clue as to the selection of *both* as the word to be misspelled. My sister and I were *both* mother's children, and *both* loved by mother and wanted and vied for mother's love. There certainly was a recapitulation of my own childhood desire for mother's love alone, and that it should not be given to *both*. In

---

[4] Elements of counteridentification as discussed by Fliess are clearly in evidence in this phenomenon.

addition, I was confronted with a patient who resided with, and was still bound to her mother, and for me this recapitulated what I must have experienced as a closeness of communication and attachment of mother and daughter in childhood that cannot easily exist for a mother and son, even though I may have been considered to be mother's favorite. So I had obviously resented the attention in the way of care and concern and interest this patient had described securing from her mother. Under these circumstances, without the analysis of this situation, it would be most difficult to comprehend the patient's reaction to these attentions in a way that could be meaningful and constructive. Although I was aware of these components in an intellectual way, the interference this problem set off in the course of the analysis could only be overcome by the self-analysis described. This was truly a countertransference reaction in every sense of the word, based on an emotional response related to unresolved elements of my own neurosis from childhood, and precipitated and recathected by the particular form of transference neurosis problem in the analysis of this patient.[5] Although it is evident that the countertransference feelings served an obstructive kind of function as far as the analytic work was concerned, the resultant self-analysis did provide for increased areas of synthetic and integrative functioning of my own ego in relation to this type of conflict, along with analytic progress on the part of the patient involving her own synthetic and integrative ego functions. We might speculate as to whether or not these changes might have occurred without the above-described reaction. Forward movement resulted in the analytic work from the time of the self-analysis, before any overt interpretive activity on my part, in relation to the transference resistance problem, was instituted. This does not mean to imply that expressions of a similar nature cannot occur again, in relation to the same or other patients, where transference neurosis problems of similar content might arise. But again, there would seem to be more potential for self-analysis and recognition of the problem with each successive attempt at working through on the part of both analyst and patient. After all, analysis is a continuing process for the analyst, and constant self-analysis is the rule.

[5] In order for a countertransference phenomenon to have occurred in the analyst, it would seem to have required the presence of an existing transference process, possibly even a "transference neurosis" as manifested by the patient.

Because an element of the childhood neurosis has been analyzed and has even undergone some working through, this does not preclude the return of this aspect of the conflict at some later date, or under other conditions or circumstances. The therapeutic (and sometimes supervisory) situation, with the demand for continuing regression in the service of the ego (Kris, 1952), seems to provide a most fertile area for this kind of recapitulation.

For additional discussion, dynamically, I might state that this reaction on my part occurred because of the presentation of this case material to a woman supervising analyst, whose interest in the case was experienced by me unconsciously as an expression of intense interest on the part of the supervisor (mother in this instance) in the patient (sister), in contrast to the desire, as a recapitulation of the childhood wish for all of mother's attention and interest in me, that she should give all of her attention to me and not to the patient. The unconscious feeling was extant that the supervisor should concern herself with my development as an analyst, and not with the treatment of the patient; after all, I could handle that! Need I emphasize further that the supervising analyst practiced in the city in which I had been born, where I had lived for most of my life, where my own mother still resided at that time, and the city I had always considered to be my home.[6]

As a second example of what I considered to be a true countertransference reaction, I would like to describe a situation presented to me several years ago by a young analyst. After over a year of his treatment of an attractive, apparently frigid hysterical woman, it became clear that her seductive maneuvers and remarks directed at him were increasing in intensity. The analyst managed to ward off these overtures with some difficulty. As a reaction to the frustration that she was experiencing, the patient resorted to further baiting the analyst with numerous comments concerning his masculinity. She expressed her feeling that his lack of response to her seductiveness must be based on his being either impotent or homosexual. The analyst gave no immediate response, but during a later visit, when vacation times came up for discussion, the analyst remarked that he

---

[6] For purposes of brevity, but not to negate the significance, I am omitting the influence of some of the factors associated with the supervisory situation in the resultant countertransference reaction.

would be taking additional time away from the office because his wife was pregnant and would be delivering their baby. The patient reacted with withdrawal and narcissistic hurt. The effect of the challenge by this particular patient, based on her developing transference neurosis, set in motion a regressive process in the analyst as an effort to contain the expression of his own libidinal interests in the patient. The resultant aggressive reaction mobilized as a defensive response by the ego was obviously designed to control unresolved aspects of the analyst's own neurosis from childhood. This neurosis, related to feelings of being unloved and rejected by his mother, and his response as indicated by his comments, affects, and actions, was once more reactivated by the transference activities of the patient. This example serves to further emphasize the effect of a patient's transference on a vulnerable therapist, vulnerable in the sense of a need to ward off inadequately analyzed (or inadequately neuralized) impulses too intense to be contained as internal manifestations of conflict, which vulnerability became evident via the defensive operations of the ego instituted to provide expression, regardless of the potentially counterproductive nature of these expressions.

Before going on to other things, I would like to emphasize two components of what I consider to be characteristic for the countertransference problem as presented in both of these situations; these components are characteristic of the phenomena as defined in my terms. First, it is probably most often dependent on the existence of a transference neurosis in a patient, which provides the impetus for the undoing of repression and resultant recathexis or reinstinctualization of unresolved components of the childhood neurosis of the therapist. And second, the end result is the expression, in action, as a piece of acting out, either in the form of emotional expression or physical action by the therapist of a derivative of the instinctual impulse in relation to some element of the transference situation. In my particular case, the action was confined to the misspelling of a word as representative of my resentment and hostility, along with my own regressive countertransference response to this patient's transference neurosis. This subtle misspelling reaction served to contain any other overt or direct response to the productions of this patient. Of course, emotional components came into play on other levels. In the second example, there was a similarly delayed response. In this instance, the response was more overt and directed at the patient in the form of a therapeutically unindicated intervention expressing the need to reveal very personal information to a patient. This counter-transference reaction occurred as a defensive recapitulation of aspects of the therapist's neurosis from childhood, surfacing in connection with the patient's developing transference neurosis and experienced both as an aggressive attack on the narcissistic defensive organization of the analyst, along with stimulating anxiety associated with his need to contain his libidinal interest in the patient; a patient who had come to represent for this analyst aspects of his early relationship to his mother.

We are now prepared to turn to another facet of our discussion regarding the actions of therapists in the therapeutic situation, closely allied to what are described as countertransference reactions, but not really of the same order of activity, and it is my belief that these *actions* (and I use this term rather than the term *reactions*) should be classed under the heading of what I choose to call counter-defensive phenomena, because they differ markedly from what we have described and defined earlier as countertransference. These activities are certainly a part of what is generally considered within the province of any discussion concerning countertransference, but rather important dynamic, economic, structural, and adaptive meta-psychological distinctions seem to exist in various counter-transference phenomena. In fact, it would seem that counterdefensive phenomena often precede in sequence the development of a true countertransference reaction. They would serve the defensive pur-pose of a prestage or precursor of a true countertransference, struc-tured to ward off anxiety associated with acting out by the therapist in the treatment situation, because these phenomena in reality repre-sent defensive activity by the therapist in an effort to ward off a development of transference phenomena on the part of the patient. I would consider it to be essential that some differentiations be made. The considerations in relation to our understanding of the psychic phenomena involved, along with the therapeutic implications of these distinctions, make the definition of these phenomena quite significant. Let us return to clinical situations to illustrate the point in question.

The following experiences involve conditions in which I was again in the role of the supervisor, and students being trained in therapy came to me for instruction. In one such situation, the student psychiatrist had been called on the phone by a patient with regard to making his first therapeutic appointment. The patient was afforded instructions regarding the appointment time and given directions for getting to the office of the psychiatrist. The patient failed to arrive for the appointment, phoning after the appointed time of the visit, to explain that he had become confused regarding the directions, had made a wrong turn, finding himself at the wrong location. In reviewing the information as the student presented it to me, I asked what had transpired in the student's phone conversation with the patient that might have led to this sort of confusion. What directions had been given to the patient? The student commented that he could not understand how this sort of confusion had resulted; he had carefully emphasized to the patient that the patient must "turn left"; in fact, he had repeated this at least three or four times on the phone. I asked further, "And what sort of impression or fantasy did you have concerning this patient's problems?" The student remarked that he had the thought, and felt almost certain, that this man's problems were predominantly of a homosexual nature. It is clear that the prospective patient had reacted to being told emphatically to "turn left" as a directive in relation to his homosexuality (for which left turns in dreams and the unconscious so often seem to have this connotation), and it was equally clear that this student's emphasis of the turning left to the patient was related to his own anxiety concerned with these unconscious and latent elements as a part of the constellation of his own internal conflicts.[7] We have difficulty in labeling this a countertransference reaction in the true sense of the word because it is predominantly determined or precipitated by the fantasy formation of the therapist, and is not set in motion by existing transference problems or a transference neurosis on the part of the patient. We have to seriously question whether or not some of these components had ever undergone repression in the first place, and although they are reactive, they are reactive on a much different level than true countertransference phenomena. Lastly, we are forced to recognize the defensive aspect of this behavior; a defense structured to prevent the

[7] I will not discuss the elements of anxiety in relation to the supervisory situation on the part of the student, and his defensive functioning concerned with this problem. It is apparent that anxiety, in connection with this kind of situation, could provide additional groundwork in connection with regression and reinstinctualization of impulses connected with earlier behavior patterns.

expression of the affect or impulse, in contrast to true countertransference reactions as dealt with here, wherein the affect and impulse are given expression, leading to a partial discharge.[8]

A second type of experience of this nature may further illustrate the point. Another student undergoing supervision reported his handling of the first interview with a very attractive young woman who had come to him for treatment. During his reporting to me, he remarked that "she could be even more attractive if she would make some attempt at doing something about it." In this first interview, as he discussed the initiation of treatment with the patient, he indicated that he had said, without knowing why, as he gave the fundamental rule to the patient, that "she should try to express everything verbally, and not get up and move around, but just talk." It is rather obvious from his comments that the student was having considerable difficulty in attempting to control his libidinal impulses, which seemed to have been organized around the assumption of a passive position, and thus told the patient in a sense, "don't do anything seductive or anything that might contribute to further arousal of these feelings in me, because your attractiveness already stimulates so many fantasies in me that I am afraid I won't be able to control my feelings in this area. In fact, I'm fearful I'll relinquish my passive position altogether." The student, in commenting that this woman could be more attractive if she would do something about it, indicated his feelings and position rather clearly. This again is a counterdefensive phenomenon based mainly on the fantasy formation of the therapist, and not at all necessarily in response to the conscious or unconscious fantasy formation in the patient, or especially as related to the character of a given transference neurosis or transference problem. This is one of the reasons for the selection of situations related to the first interview, where the details of differentiation could be more clearly made.[9] But more than this, we are able to note that in true countertransference reactions, some expression results leading to partial discharge of the

[8] Fenichel (1941, p. 73) points out how analysts strive for direct satisfaction in the analytic situation, and make use of the patient for a "piece of acting out" determined by the analyst's past, in relation to the countertransference phenomena, emphasizing the attempt to mobilize the activities in order to obtain partial discharge of affect or impulse.

[9] These last two examples coincide very clearly with what Gitelson (1952) has described as "transferences," and A. Reich (1951b) has described as "chronic countertransferences" based on characterologic behavior problems (both are referred to earlier in this thesis).

derivative of the disturbing instinctual impulses, in contrast to counterdefensive activity, which seems directed mainly at the warding off or defending against the expressions of derivatives of instinctual impulses which, if given even partial expression and discharge, could be extremely disturbing.

It would be incomplete to leave a discussion of this nature without going into some of the metapsychological aspects of the countertransference, counterdefense problem, because these theoretical formulations are fundamental to our understanding of and scientific approach to the problem. Dynamically, both true countertransference and those specific forms of countertransference I have chosen to refer to as counterdefensive activities are based on conflict, conflict related to the childhood neurosis of the therapist. But there is a marked difference in the two phenomena. True countertransference reactions are the result of regressive processes in the therapist, concomitant with the regressive process in the patient, and do involve the interposition of some elements of delay in gratification. As the patient undergoes regression in the analytic situation, so with the working analyst regression similarly occurs. Additionally, in the case of true countertransference reactions we are confronted with the recapitulation of a formerly repressed, unresolved childhood conflict in the therapist, most probably oedipal in nature, which return of the repressed conflict is based on the character and quality of the particular transference neurosis of the patient, and characterized by a quality of delay in response (probably associated with the process of undoing the repression). This repression, apparently being undone partly via the controlled regression (in the service of the ego)[10] that must occur in relation to any given patient in performing the analytic work and fostered toward deeper, relatively less well-controlled regression by intensification of the transference neurosis, projected onto the analyst by the patient. By contrast, in counterdefensive activity, we seem to be dealing with areas of conflict in the therapist, associated with his childhood neurosis but seeming not necessarily precipitated by the particular transference neurosis of the patient. This conflict seems also to include determinants which may have

[10] Kris (1952, p. 177) illustrates how regression in the service of the ego enables the ego to retain supremacy over the primary process mechanism, and relinquishes this supremacy in uncontrolled regression.

much more of a preoedipal coloring, and most importantly represent a way of dealing with conflict other than mainly by means of repression. The counterdefensive phenomenon seems more closely related to an armored sort of repetitive pattern of defense that has a more characterologic ego syntonic protective quality to it, and involves a more rigidly structured pattern of behavior. It seems to be more a form of activity called forth characterologically under any conditions of sufficient stress and anxiety, with little if any evidence of a capacity for delay. True countertransference involves the recurrence of some elements of an ego dystonic neurotic conflict, associated with the transference neurosis of the patient and often accompanied by increasing neurotic anxiety in the therapist. To contrast, counterdefense is characterologic in nature, associated with a process that has evolved to possess more ego syntonic qualities, and appears structured to ward off any form of anxiety which might be disruptive for the therapist. The end result would be directed at the avoidance of any feelings of closeness with a patient.

From the economic standpoint in countertransference reactions, the need for discharge of the highly cathected, hypersensitized formerly repressed emotional components of the instinctual impulse involved in the conflict is clear, and of course this discharge finds the most ready arena for displacement in connection with the situation, contributing most to the undoing of the repression, that of the therapeutic situation and the specific patient involved. To contrast, in counterdefensive phenomena, the mechanism is structured to ward off the discharge of the instinctual derivatives through the use of a characterologically ego syntonic, relatively fixed pattern of behavior that is brought to bear in any situation capable of providing sufficient stress and anxiety in the therapist. This may occur regardless of the transference implications of the therapeutic process, and may even at times be concerned mainly with a hypercathexis of the need to control the therapeutic situation.

From the adaptive standpoint, true countertransference reactions are geared to provide for a delayed form of partial discharge of affect in order to avoid anxiety attendant upon the exacerbation of emotions associated with unresolved conflict, residuals of the infantile neurosis of the therapist, by projection of the conflict into the therapeutic situation, all as a reaction to the transference neurosis of the patient. On the other hand, counterdefensive activities represent characterologic patterns of behavior organized adaptively to ward off the development of transference phenomena in the patient and subsequent regressive needs in the therapist. Thus, the development of anxiety associated with transference phenomena of the patient is virtually circumvented. Genetic factors differentiating countertransference and counterdefensive activities have already been discussed.

Topographically, it derives that a conflict in relation to fundamental instinctual need derivatives with all the attendant affect, which has been formerly relegated to the area of the unconscious mental life, has now been provided access in the countertransference to the area of preconscious and conscious mental life through the undoing of the defensive function of repression. To contrast, in counterdefensive action, the struggle revolves around the maintenance of what repression, isolation and displacement might exist in connection with the basic conflict through an already firmly established defensive pattern of behavior.

Finally, let us consider these theoretical formulations from the structural standpoint. We have already mentioned the elements of discharge associated with instinctual derivatives in relation to the struggle of the forces within the id. Superego functioning plays a significant role in the countertransference–counterdefensive problem. In true countertransference reactions, there seems to be a transitory suspension of some of the self-critical function under the impetus supplied by the heightened cathexis of the instinctual derivative, along with the decreasing capacity for defensive components on the part of the ego to adequately contain and limit expression. An accompanying transitory impairment of the capacity for self-observation results in a temporary relinquishing of identification with the ego ideal, and a transitory giving up of the identification with the ideal therapist superego model, the parental therapist imago (based possibly on trial counteridentification phenomena with the patient). The setting up of the patient as a transference object on the part of the ego during the regressive process occurring in the analyst results in these alterations of superego attitudes and positions in relation to the patient. The functional state of ego, superego, and id at this regressed level, related to the oedipal and preoedipal developmental periods, provides for a state where superego and certain aspects of the ego's development were in relatively primitive and formative stages, when at the same time certain aspects of ego development in relation to mobility of expression had progressed beyond this point. There is a decreased cathexis of superego aspects of mental functioning which would otherwise provide for some restrictive effects on the expression of affect and the psychic apparatus in general, and especially with regard to defensive functioning on the part of the ego, resulting in freer expression of instinctual derivatives. In counterdefensive activity the superego components appear to be involved mainly on the level of the regularly operative self-critical function, because there seems to be less regressive involvement of the ego. The ego's more rigidly structured defensive position does not provide for the infringement on the province of the more intolerant components of superego functioning. In addition, there seems to be a lesser development within the superego of the model of the therapist imago, with a more primitive position on the part of the superego in connection with the emotional position of the patient.[11]

We have arrived at a point in our discussion where we may consider the involvement of the therapist's ego functions in countertransference activities. The patient has now become a meaningful figure to the therapist in relation to his own neurotic conflicts. Inhibition of the ability to interpret in a meaningful and appropriate way, in connection with his patient, most often results. This follows a decreased ability to recognize, understand, and deal with the transference resistances arising out of the transference neurosis. In order to function with any degree of success analytically, special emphasis with regard to the development of certain ego functions on the part of both analyst and patient is required. The need for successfully controlled regression, in the service of the ego and important synthetic and integrative activities, along with a well-developed self-observing capacity related to the ego splitting (Sterba, 1934) phenomena in analysis are essential. We might readily trace the further results of temporary suspension of controlled defensive regressive functioning, with the accompanying transitory suspension of the reality testing capacity in connection with the patient, to the point where id–ego channels of expression become more readily cathected with primary

---

[11] Almost as if the defense were structured to ward off the development of empathic (nonregressive) feelings, and regressive trial identifications in the service of the ego by the therapist.

process activities, replacing what would regularly be translated into secondary process forms of expression. There results an impairment in the capacity to tolerate delay in gratification. With the inhibition of these ego functions, the important ability to form trial identifications with the patient seems lost, especially related to the impaired ego-splitting, self-observing functions. It is entirely possible that the "non-regressive identification involved in empathy" described by Fliess (1953) may provide the atmosphere for reestablishment of the propensity toward uncontrolled regression in the therapist. The use of judgment and interferences in the temporal sphere of ego activities are also involved, as with any form of transference or displacement phenomena, wherein primary process activities enable the individuals to suspend to a marked degree the awareness of the temporal-object–affect situation. This process only serves to further emphasize for us the degree of inhibition imposed on the reality-testing functions of the ego. It seems that counterdefensive activity is more primitively based on a relatively fixed pattern of behavior, established within the ego. This behavior results in greater immobilization of the functions mentioned before, so that some may not even come into play at all. Countertransference reactions involve a mobilization of the energetic forces in relation to id–ego activities, so that some suspension of the ordinarily active ego defensive functioning occurs, with resultant expression of instinctual derivatives. Counterdefensive activities are characterized by a lack of delay in response. There appears to be little interposition of defensive activity to modify the drive derivatives at all. They seem to be directed at immobilization of certain aspects of ego functioning through intensification of ego activities related to other defensive functions. This results in further immobilization and inhibition of other ego functions. The increased utilization of characterologic defensive functions seems structured to ward off any tendency to mobilize id–ego channels of expression other than the regularly utilized channels in relation to any situation of sufficient stress or anxiety. One final comment in connection with the therapeutic implications of this discussion: True or really analyzable countertransference phenomena appear to provide for much more potential for therapeutic success in the sense that they could be more readily accessible to analytic work and possible self-analysis and change. It seems clear that countertransference phenomena on all levels appear to be an integral part of the work of analysis, and that the development and recognition of true or analyzable countertransference reactions by the analyst seem to be as essential a phenomenon for the successful performance of the analytic work as are the elements of transference in our patients. This is in contrast to what I have described as counterdefensive activities, which seem to more closely approximate the situation of "true blind spots" for many therapists.

18

The Working Alliance Revisited: An Intersubjective Perspective*

Bernard Brandchaft, M.D.

Occupying a special place on my desk is a copy of Greenson's *The Technique and Practice of Psychoanalysis*. An inscription on the inside cover reads,
> "6/18/68—Father's Day (Also Grandfather's)
> To Bernie Brandchaft!
> Who Loves Psychoanalysis
> And Learning
> And Teaching
> And People
> From An Old Student
> (Bearded)
> Romey"

It is an inscription, I realize, more richly deserved by him. In response to this generous gesture I should like to return to the subjects that

*This paper is an extension of principles advanced in a previous paper, *Varieties of the Therapeutic Alliance* (B. Brandchaft and R. D. Stolorow), delivered before a joint meeting of the Los Angeles Psychoanalytic Society and the Southern California Psychoanalytic Society, March 16, 1989, and submitted for publication.

preoccupied Romey Greenson in his mature years. Foremost among these were problems of analyzability, the working alliance, and what he termed the "real relationship." To these Greenson brought his unfailing humanity and wealth of clinical experience which, together with a searching and challenging curiosity and intelligence, continue to animate his contributions even as one rereads them today. When one reexamines Greenson's most distinctive reflections one cannot but be impressed with how abundantly they provide support to his desire to be recognized and remembered as an innovator and "conquistador" (Greenson, 1978, pp. 313–357). At the same time a reconsideration of certain assumptions which shaped his observations and conclusions can continue to illuminate the problems with which he struggled. In a seminal paper on "The Origin and Fate of New Ideas in Psychoanalysis," Greenson described how Freud's creative genius evolved because of his constant recognition of the limitations of his knowledge and because he "was constantly at work revisiting, changing and amplifying his ideas" (p. 348). Greenson went on to observe:

Some analysts, other than Freud, also work in this way. What is characteristic of them is that they do not destroy old theories when they conceive of a new idea. They conserve the parts they consider useful, add their innovations and try to integrate them into a cohesive framework which is not closed off from further elaboration and emendation [p. 348].

It is in this spirit that the observations which follow are offered.

Throughout his career, Greenson's own love of analysis and people took the form of a preoccupation with and constant seeking to understand the factors that facilitated or impaired the analyzability of his patients. Increasingly his awareness of the analytic situation as one of an interaction between patient and analyst in which each participant played a constitutive role in the outcome came to influence his work and become ingrained in his thinking. More and more he sought to define precisely the role played by each. From the side of the patient, he first considered that "narcissistically oriented and psychotic patients are generally not suitable for psychoanalysis" (1967, p. 54). Subsequently he identified "a major defect in the capacity to form object relations and in the ego functions" as pathogenic factors militating against analyzability (p. 172). Still later, in reviewing experiences with patients who displayed "intractable transference reactions" he came to conclude that the single overriding factor in the patient's contribution was his ability, or lack thereof, to form a working alliance. In order for a successful analysis to occur, Greenson maintained, two developments of equal importance had to take place. "A patient must be able to develop a full blown transference neurosis and also establish and maintain a reliable working alliance. The working alliance deserves to be recognized as a full and equal partner in the patient–therapist relationship" (1978, p. 200).

In discussing intractable cases Greenson went on to refer to those "which have become so because of some subtle but important errors in technique. Most cases," he concluded, referring to insurmountable problems from the inadequate selection of patient and errors in the analyst's conduct of the cases, "will turn out to contain a mixture of both errors" (p. 337). It was only later that Greenson came to extend the principle that the impact of the analyst, especially the unintended impact on the analyzability of the patient, must occupy a central focus in the ongoing investigation and include more than errors in technique. He quoted Anna Freud (1969a) on the "lack of creativity among analysts today" and went on to note that he had been "impressed and depressed by the observation that applicants for training often seem to be more creative than the psychoanalysts who graduate from our training institute. . . . In all candor," he wrote, "we must face the possibility that our training programs and the atmosphere of our institutes may stultify the creative imagination of our students" (1978, p. 336). In the same paper, he referred to *the willingness to admit to oneself the possibility that one may have been pursuing the wrong path, the wrong material, or using a faulty theoretical and technical approach*. If one is sure that one has all the answers, there will be no doubt, no conflict, no discontent, but also no new ideas" (p. 342; emphasis added).

The concept of the working alliance derived from that of the "therapeutic alliance" described by Zetzel (1956) and Stone (1961), and Greenson endowed it with a new emphasis. Both concepts were part of a more general focus beginning in the 1950s and 1960s on the problems of resistance, which were threatening increasingly to narrow the criteria for analyzability and thus restrict its scope (Brandchaft and Stolorow, 1989). Greenson, following classical doctrine, defined psychoanalysis as:

[T]hat method of treatment of emotional disorders in which the relationship between the patient and therapist is so structured that it facilitates the maximal development of a transference neurosis. The analyst's interpretations are the decisive and ultimate instruments, used in an atmosphere of compassionate neutrality, which enables the patient, communicating via free association, to recapitulate his infantile neurosis. The analyst's goal is to provide insight to the patient so that he may himself resolve his neurotic conflicts—thus effecting permanent changes in his ego, id and superego, and thereby extending the power and sovereignty of the ego [Greenson, 1958b, p. 201].

It was the resistance to these insights—and to interpretations based upon them—that the working alliance was designed to overcome.

Transference, Greenson considered, as had Freud (1905a, 1909a, 1916-1917), to be "the experiencing of feelings, drives, fantasies and defenses towards a person in the present which are inappropriate to that person and are a repetition, a displacement of reactions originating in regard to significant persons of early childhood" (p. 201). He stressed that the designation, working alliance, emphasized the patient's capacity, in the throes of a transference neurosis, to work purposefully on his transference experience in the treatment situation. It is brought about when the analyst's interventions permit a split to occur between the patient's "reasonable" observing, analyzing ego and his experiencing ego. Its core is formed "by the patient's motivation to overcome his illness, his conscious and rational willingness to co-operate, and his ability to follow the instructions and insights of his analyst . . . the medium that makes this possible is the patient's partial identification with the analyst's approach as he attempts to understand the patient's behavior" (p. 202).

Central to the concept of resistance was this understanding of transference as a repetition of the past and inappropriate to the present. "Transference reactions are always inappropriate . . . the transference reaction is unsuitable in the current context but it was once an appropriate reaction to a past situation. . ." (1967, pp. 154-155).

It is this view of the patient's experience of the analyst with which the patient is required to identify that Greenson proposed was the determining factor in the patient's ability to form a working alliance. The goal of the analytic procedure to which such a working alliance is dedicated is to understand the distortions in terms of childhood displacement and trace them to their source in the unresolved pathogenic childhood neurosis and centrally the oedipal conflict. In the essential matters of transference as distortion and the goals of the working alliance, Greenson is in agreement with his classical colleagues, as he is with the Kleinian analysts with whom he registers sharp disagreement on other significant issues (1978, pp. 519–540).

Greenson's uneasiness with the concept of transference as distortion led him to attempt to sort out what in the patient's experience of the analyst might be "real" and therefore belonged to a "real" relationship (and thus by his definition "nontransference") and what was distorted and therefore belonged to "transference." In this endeavor he made extremely valuable contributions, as, for example, his dissent from "too literal acceptance of the concept of analyst as mirror and the rule of abstinence" (p. 202). He was acutely aware that purposeful imposition of abstinence could in itself create a milieu incompatible to a collaborative effort and contribute to an adversarial relationship too frequently mistaken for a "transference neurosis." With regard to such an analytic stance as well as other errors of technique that stemmed from empathic limitations in the analyst, Greenson understood and passionately advocated that the impact of the analyst had to be understood and evaluated not from the perspective of the conscious intent of the analyst, but from a perspective *within* the patient's subjective framework of experience. Together with his collaborator, Milton Wexler, Greenson recognized the damage done to the patient's confidence in perceptual abilities and to the essence of their selfhood, when experiences of damaging or unfeeling responses or abstinence evoked critical or angry expressions in the patient and when these were interpreted as transference material, evidence of distortion or displacement (Greenson and Wexler, 1970, pp. 143–150). For him, however, the analyst remained the final arbiter of what was "real" for the patient, and the purpose of the attempt to recognize and acknowledge the analyst's errors or misattunements remained to strengthen the working alliance so as to enlist the patient's cooperation in analyzing the transference neurosis. Those who failed to mobilize transference configurations recognizable as belonging to the triadic transference neurosis, or those who could not agree with the analyst's insights, rooted in classical doctrine, about their experiences and motivations, continued to be regarded by Greenson as unsuitable for analysis. For them he recommended a supportive psychotherapy (1978, p. 372).

In the paper previously cited, we proposed that in conceptualizing transference and the therapeutic bond in the way I have described, psychoanalysts, classical and Kleinian, illustrate "a basic and largely unchallenged assumption that has pervaded psychoanalytic thought since its inception, namely the existence of an 'objective reality' that is known by the analyst and distorted by the patient (Atwood and Stolorow, 1984; Stolorow, Brandchaft, and Atwood, 1987). This assumption lies at the heart of the traditional view of transference and its insistence on the dichotomy between the patient's experience of the analyst as distortion and the analyst's experience of himself as real" (Brandchaft and Stolorow, 1989). The same comment would apply to the criteria emphasized by Greenson as necessary to a definition of transference, an "inappropriate" reaction displaced onto the analyst from the past. It was not the philosophical assumption which concerned us, "but the serious and insufficiently acknowledged consequences of its clinical application."

We cited Evelyne Schwaber's (1983) view with which we are in complete accord and emphasized its significance. We then went on to suggest.

[T]hat the only reality relevant and accessible to psychoanalytic inquiry (that is, to empathy and introspection) is *subjective reality*—that of the patient, that of the analyst, and the psychological field created by the interplay between the two. The belief that one's personal reality is objective is an instance of the psychological process of "concretization"—the symbolic transformation of *configurations of subjective experience* into events and entities that are believed to be *objectively* perceived and known (Atwood and Stolorow, 1984). Attributions of objective reality, in other words are concretizations of subjective truth [p. 103].

While evoking critical reflection in many analysts from the beginning (e.g., Ferenczi, Balint, Fairbairn, Winnicott among others) the doctrine of an objective reality, known to the analyst, has found general acceptance among analysts of various persuasions and there has been wide agreement with the accompanying doctrine of distortion which sets the goal of analysis as that of bringing the patient's incongruent experience, against the resistance, into greater congruence with that of the analyst. Generations of analysts have proceeded on the basis of an unquestioned view of pathology as comprising processes and mechanisms located solely in the patient, and it is this fact, perhaps, that contributes to the lack of creativity in the graduates of psychoanalytic training institutes that Greenson deplored. The differences in competing schools of thought have generally been confined to concepts (pathological envy vs. oedipal rivalry, depressive and paranoid positions vs. castration anxiety and unresolved superego conflict, etc.) which emphasize one constellation of affects and defenses against another, together with considerations of technique based upon the specific concepts. The investigatory focus attempts to reveal what intrapsychic factors are at play to account for the patient's distortion of the analyst, and analyst and patient tend to be blinded to the ongoing impact of the observer on the observed as an intrinsic factor in the patient's experience and his expressions. Obscured are the ways in which the analyst and his reflection of the patient viewed from outside the patient's subjective framework, together especially with the theories which organize the analyst's view, are implicated in the phenomena he observes and seeks to treat (Brandchaft and Stolorow, 1984). Derivative configurations and affect states tend to be misidentified as primary, while the opportunity for illumination of the primary configurations and their transformation is by-passed.

No less an authority than Anna Freud expressed a compatible view in writing

So far as the patient has a healthy part of his personality, the real relationship to the analyst is never submerged. . . . I wonder whether our at times complete neglect of this side of the matter is not responsible for some of the hostile reactions we get from our patients and which we are apt to ascribe to "true transference" only. But, these are technically subversive thoughts and ought to be handled with care [A. Freud, 1969a, p. 27].

The invitation that the patient identify with the analyst's concepts as a condition for a working alliance with the work directed toward understanding the patient's resistance to the definition of himself reflected in those concepts is an invitation to cure by compliance, an outcome which Greenson specifically abhorred and warned against (1978, pp. 205–207, 433). Alternatively, it is a frequent trigger for the profound "resistance," to which Anna Freud alluded, which from the perspective of the patient may represent an important reaction to a perceived threat to an independent center of perception and affectivity. When the patient reacts adversely to the analyst's explanations, the idea that these disruptive reactions are to be explained by the same concepts that are producing the reactions sets the stage for the negativism that has been described as negative transference resistances or negative therapeutic reactions (Brandchaft, 1988; Atwood and Stolorow, 1984).

Perhaps most importantly from the perspective of the unfolding analytic process, invocation of the concept of objective reality and its corollary concept of distortion discourages the investigation of the subjective reality embedded in the patient's communications and thus the possibility of analytic transformation. Damage is thus inflicted not only upon the subjective reality of the patient but upon the potential of psychoanalysis itself to illuminate and transform.

Many patients enter analysis who have been exposed to severe developmental privation or trauma. With them, crucial aspects of self and object experience are inaccessible to a psychoanalytic process that requires that they "develop a full blown transference neurosis." Instead they are capable of forming attachments, sometimes of an intense kind, or alternatively they attempt to protect themselves against repetitions of traumatic childhood experiences or disappointment by various distancing measures. If these expressions are not subjected to preconceptions of resistance rooted in analytic doctrine, an analytic milieu can evolve which will be experienced by the patient as safe and nonjudgmental (Kohut, 1971, 1984). Stable transference configurations can then develop and these will be found to contain unfulfilled developmental strivings. The exact nature of these bonds and the specific developmental processes they are intended to reinstate lend themselves well to psychoanalytic inquiry.

"I want you to be my father" Tony said shyly during a recent session. I had been patiently exploring some reaction he was having as a consequence of a conflict that had arisen in his work. When he was a boy, any such problem, if it were addressed at all by a father too preoccupied with his own affairs, would invariably be explained in terms of what the boy had failed to do or done wrong. So Tony came to experience any setback as defining who he really was and he was therefore unable to sustain any positive sense of self that his abundant talents and achievements might otherwise have made possible. The analytic process which ensued made it possible for Tony to recognize that residues of the unconscious ties to his father and repetitively his father's reflection of him continued to shape his own sense of himself. The working alliance was directed toward helping articulate his experiences, especially in the transference, which tended either to reinstate or counteract the pathogenic influences, and thus to enable him to transform and redefine the principles upon which his sense of self had come to rest. A crucial step in the process of self-differentiation which had been derailed was revived and reinvigorated as a result of it coming to occupy a central focus of the working alliance.

The Intersubjective Approach

Considerations of this kind have led to the formulation of an alternative approach to psychoanalytic treatment.

In its most general form, our thesis ... is that psychoanalysis seeks to illuminate phenomena that emerge within a specific psychological field constituted by the intersection of two subjectivities—that of the patient and that of the analyst.... [P]sychoanalysis is pictured here as a science of the intersubjective, focused on the interplay between the differently organized subjective worlds of the observer and the observed. The observational stance is always one within, rather than outside, the intersubjective field ... being observed, a fact that guarantees the centrality of introspection and empathy as the methods of observation. ... Psychoanalysis is unique among the sciences in that the observer is also the observed ... [Stolorow, Brandchaft, and Atwood, 1987, p. 1].

The intersubjectivity principle was applied to the developmental system as well:

[B]oth psychological development and pathogenesis are best conceptualized in terms of the specific intersubjective contexts that shape the developmental process and that facilitate or obstruct the child's negotiation of critical developmental tasks and successful passage through developmental phases. The observational focus is the evolving psychological field constituted by the interplay between the differently organized subjectivities of child and caretakers... [p. 2].

The concept of intersubjectivity is in opposition to the tendency to view pathology in terms of mechanisms and processes located solely within the patient. It involves an extension in depth of the empirical data which led Greenson to postulate and attempt to distinguish between "real" and "transference" relationships. It brings psychoanalytic investigatory perspective into alignment with contemporary observational research into infant development (Sander, 1980, 1983; Stern, 1985).

The intersubjective approach requires a significant revision of the concept of working alliance. In place of a congruence between analyst and patient on the analyst's insights, the foundations of the working alliance are established instead by the analyst's commitment to seek to comprehend the meaning of the patient's expressions, his affect states, and most centrally the role and impact of the analyst, transference, not as displacement or inappropriate but from a perspective *within* rather than outside the patient's subjective frame of reference (Kohut, 1959). We have referred to this positioning as the stance of *sustained empathic inquiry* (Stolorow, Brandchaft, and Atwood, 1987). Such a commitment presents the analyst with great difficulties and perhaps adds weight to Greenson's description of analysis as "the impossible profession" (1978, p. 266). To see oneself and the world consistently through the eyes of another can pose serious threats to the analyst's personal reality and sense of self, exactly the same threat as that experienced by the patient when his expressions are treated as a distortion of reality. What is required of the analyst is the ability to hold conflicting perceptions of reality without either obliterating the other, in order for the investigation and understanding to proceed.

In a previous article (Stolorow, Brandchaft, and Atwood, 1987, pp. 47–65), I described a patient who in one phase of his analysis would appear consistently late for his sessions, sometimes not showing up at all. I described how one day he came in unusually late with an apparent indifference to my position or feelings in being kept waiting. I was especially vulnerable to irritation since he had spent much of the previous session deploring my lack of sensitivity to him and my lack of consideration in not complying with something he had wished of me. With that as background, and insufficiently aware of the impact of his criticisms on my own sense of self, I asked him if he was not aware of any lack of consideration in keeping me waiting so consistently when he so much hated to be in that position himself. Martin sat upright, looked squarely at me and said calmly:

Listen. If you are asking if I am upset about being late, the answer is yes. And if you are pissed off with me about it, tell me so and don't pretend what you are doing is part of the analysis. I have lived all my life with people being pissed off with me, and then saying they are not and always that it is for my own good! What I don't understand and don't like in you is not that you are upset but your subterfuge. You can insist that I have to come on time in order to keep you from getting out of joint and I will try to do it. If I can't, as I expect, then I will quit. But whether I came on time or whether I didn't, make no mistake about it, nothing fundamental about me would change!

Only after I could develop the ability to accept Martin's experience of me did it become possible to establish an analytic milieu in which the enduringly damaging effects of caretaker's critical and sometimes concealed attitudes upon Martin's development could be investigated and delineated. This proved to be a precondition of a working alliance that could then begin to investigate the reasons behind Martin's lifelong habits of procrastination and lateness. Only when Martin's lateness could be disentangled from constraints of pleasing or offending could his own frustration at not being able to come on time emerge; only then could he voluntarily engage in a process of analyzing the obstacles that subverted his own will, and only then gradually overcome them.

Disjunctions in analysis as a consequence of frustration and disappointment, in either party, or experiences of misattunement or misunderstanding on the part of the analyst are not to be considered as errors in any "objective" sense. They are testimony, if such were needed, of the "humanness" of both parties, providing indisputable evidence that the impact of the analyst and his understanding, or lack thereof, is central to the patient's subjective reality and thus they provide access to crucial areas of the patient's inner world. Such disjunctive experiences may not be expressed openly by the patient, and they may frequently even escape his conscious notation unless he has been specifically alerted to pay attention to them. Particularly is this likely to be so if the patient has sensed that the analyst prefers the working alliance to involve a commitment to see things from the analyst's perspective in order for harmony ultimately to prevail. It is necessary therefore for the analyst to remain alert to small shifts in the patient's affect state, to encourage processes of self reflection in the patient upon these shifts, and to open the investigation to include a focus on the intersubjective contexts in which such shifts are occurring.

Other analysts have recognized the importance of facilitating the expression of the patient's experience and his feelings in reaction to countertransference states that the analyst may not be aware of or able to control. Greenson has included the acknowledgment of such feelings or behavioral lapses as an important aspect of the "real" relationship (1978, p. 516) though he disagrees with Searles (1965) in the utility of disclosing its unconscious sources to the patient (p. 518). More important, perhaps, than the analyst's acknowledgment of his contribution to disruptions in the therapeutic bonds or his baring of his own private world to the patient, is his ability to reflect his unconditional acceptance of the patient's conscious experience as the basis of their shared understandings. Only then can attention be directed to the *meanings* that are activated by the disjunctive events and are encoded in the resultant dissonant affect states. In our previous paper (Brandchaft and Stolorow, 1989) we have described how viewing these experiences of disruption consistently from within the patient's subjective framework, with the observer as an immanent part of the experience, restores the therapeutic alliance. Such a procedure then provides access to the specific and idiosyncratic ways in which the patient is organizing his experience of the analyst and especially to the exquisitely personal meanings that this experience has come to encode. It is from a fresh look at these meanings and their invariance that "new beginnings" may take root.

The analyst's acceptance of the patient's perceptual reality in the ongoing delineation of intrapsychic experience, I stress, plays an indispensible role in helping to establish and maintain the working alliance as it permits the work of analysis to unfold. A threat to the validity of perceptual reality such as that imposed by the judgment of transference experience as distorted can constitute a deadly threat to the self and to the organization of experience itself. This more than any other factor is likely to usher in the conflictful transference–countertransference spirals so commonly described as resistances to analysis or negative transferences. These can be recognized as crises or impasses in which each partner in the would-be working alliance has become engaged in a defense of his own organization of experience against the threat to it posed by its counter-part. Patients generally anticipate that their discrepant experiences of the analyst and critical affect states will evoke invalidating adverse or defensive reactions. When they communicate such experiences and have them interpretively attributed to mechanisms of splitting, projection or displacement, by the analyst, they are likely to feel confused or betrayed. When such fearful anticipations are repetitively realized, the stage is set for symptoms of brittle psychological structure and violence of affect as traumatogenic experiences are revived and replicated.

Many of the patients who were once regarded as unsuitable for analysis can now be recognized as suffering from developmental interference in the area of self differentiation. Processes of self differentiation cover a very wide area, but among the more common and more fateful disturbances of this kind are those seen in patients who suffer from a primary sense of uncertainty about the reality of inner experience. For them the recognition and articulation of vaguely felt affect states of perceptions, and the analysis of the doubt and confusion surrounding these, constitutes an indispensible component of an analytic cure. In a previous paper I have described in some detail the case of Mr. N., a gifted composer.

Each time Mr. N.'s own efforts toward a creative solution to a compositional problem or in behalf of a better life for himself would initiate a sense of pride and enthusiasm it would invariably be followed by an uneasiness and then a feeling of unreality. Subsequently he would regularly repudiate the reality and significance of the effort that he had made and the sense of himself that he had experienced. During the course of a long analysis of the resultant intractable depression, this regular process emerged as the residue of a childhood relationship in which every hope for a distinctness of his own, every enthusiasm in a childhood achievement were relentlessly followed by a disparaging or humiliating response that conveyed the information, "That's not really you!" The archaic relationship was thus enshrined and perpetuated in the form of principle that invariantly, pre-reflectively and automatically continued to organize the patient's experience of himself as competent and talented as unreal [Brandchaft, 1988].

Many patients display a similar inability to sustain a belief in crucial aspects of their own subjective reality due to a derailment brought about because such emerging experiences and developments were threatening to caretakers. Threatening also were perceptions and reactions that were directly critical of caretakers because they contained information that the caretakers did not wish, or could not bear to hear. These perceptions and the triggered affect states thus became sources of continuing conflict and had to be repudiated.

The analyst's specific attunement to "the role of the analyst and of the surround, as perceived and experienced by the patient . . . as intrinsic to (his) reality . . . [parallels and] draws upon modalities which are significant components of the essentials of parental empathy . . . attunement to and recognition of the perceptions and experiential states of another" (Schwaber, 1984, p. 160). However, she also points out, and I wish to emphasize that, "it would be misleading to employ these terms (i.e., the analyst's and the parent's empathy) synonomously, or to suggest that the one 'corrects for' the failure of the other for they speak to two very different contexts" (p. 160). It is the failure to understand this point that leads to a variety of what I believe to be misguided enactments and provides the basis for criticisms of self psychology as being "supportive" or "psychotherapeutic," but not psychoanalytic.

A milieu in which the patient's perceptual reality is not threatened establishes the necessary security to encourage the patient to develop and expand his own capacity for self-reflection, with increasing confidence in his own center of perception and impression as a base. Access is thereby gained into unfolding patterns of experience reflecting structural weakness, psychological constriction, early developmental derailment, and archaic defensive activity—the specific patterns that await transformation.

Recognition of the intersubjective nature of the psychoanalytic field and the systematic tool of sustained empathic inquiry make possible a re-examination and re-formulation of the concept of transference. Transference in its essentials is an instance of the mental function of *organizing experience*, all aspects of which are equally "real." It refers to the "here and now" of experience, and also inevitably to:

[A]ll the ways in which the patient's experience of the analytic relationship is shaped by his own psychological structures—by the distinctive archaically rooted configurations of self and object that unconsciously organize his subjective universe. The transference is actually a microcosm of the patient's psychological life around which the patterns dominating his existence as a whole can be clarified, understood and transformed [Stolorow, Brandchaft, and Atwood, 1987, p. 36].

This concept of transference is responsive to the need of the patient for the analyst to be aware of his impact, a principle Greenson sought to establish with his concept of the "real relationship." At the same time it encourages ongoing inquiry into the psychological structures of the patient and especially to the unconscious invariant and prereflective principles that are embedded in these structures and communicated through them. Finally, it permits a more encompassing view of analysis than that provided by rigid orthodoxy of any school, fully satisfying Greenson's condition that "psychoanalysis is distinguished from all other therapies by the way it promotes the development of the transference reactions and how it attempts systematically to analyze transference phenomena" (Greenson, 1978, p. 151).

A specter that seems to haunt many psychoanalysts is that commitment to understand the patient's expressions and behavior consistently from within the patient's own subjective framework will result in an avoidance or diminution of the importance of the patient's contribution to his own circumstances. Thus the attempt to pursue a course of sustained empathic inquiry is ruled out as the path to "collusion." One supposes that some such concern underlay Greenson's persistent attempts to separate out the "real relationship" from the "transference relationship" by which he emphasized the attribute of distortion as the patient's contribution to his disorder, a legacy from Greenson's own roots in classical analysis. I believe this fear is unwarranted. In a previous article, this point was specifically addressed.

We emphasize that the patient's experience of the analytic dialogue is codetermined throughout by the organizing activities of both participants, with the analyst's organizing principles shaping not only his countertransference reactions but his interpretations and other therapeutic interventions as well. The patient's unconscious structuring activity is eventually discerned in the meanings that the analyst's activities—especially his interpretive activity—repeatedly and invariantly come to acquire for the patient. Thus, the patient's unconscious organizing principles become illuminated, first, by recognizing and comprehending the impact of the analyst's activities and, second, by discovering and interpreting the meanings into which these activities are recurrently assimilated by the patient. It is a paradox of the psychoanalytic process that the structural invariants of the patient's psychological organization are effectively illuminated and transformed only by careful analytic investigation of the ever-shifting flux of the intersubjective field encompassing the therapeutic dyad [Stolorow, Brandchaft, and Atwood, 1987, pp. 12–13].

Focus on the persistent inquiry into the subjective world of the patient leads to shared recognition that an indispensible part of the work of analysis involves the investigation of how conscious experience is organized according to hierarchies of unconscious principles. The illumination of these meanings, the discovery of the subjective truths and the ontogeny they encode in developmental traumata and derailments, provides the working alliance with its most generative purpose and transformational potential.

Consider, for example, a patient, Martin, referred to previously in this paper and described in greater detail elsewhere (Stolorow, Brandchaft, and Atwood, 1987, pp. 53–65). From early in his formative years, there had crystallized a persistent conviction that no one could really care for him and that any tie was ultimately based upon his having to organize his own course around fulfilling the needs of the other. Any experience of being cared about rendered him more vulnerable and raised the threat that he would ultimately have to abandon his own course and comply with an agenda I had in mind for him. In another, such experiences of being cared about might have acted to intensify and enrich his experience and especially the feeling of security. In Martin, however, they caused him to react automatically and regularly by either distancing himself or by attempting to counter the anxiety which was corroding his most cherished hope of being able to sustain a conviction of being cared for and therefore worth caring for. He was driven to place increasing demands on me or on an extra-analytic partner for expressions and enactments of selfless devotion. Each disappointment would confirm the unchallengeable "objective" validity of the underlying organizing principle while each new experience of being cared about would invariably lead to a raise in the ante.

An additional conviction that crystallized out of his early experience was that of a sense of himself as the principal cause of his mother's persistent and relentless unhappiness which frequently found its expression in irritability with him, nagging criticism of him for the trouble he caused her, and sometimes in physical abuse. Any success or achievement which temporarily enabled him to feel a sense of soundness, integrity, basic purity, and effectance continued to be followed inexorably by obsessive doubt of a tormenting quality. Any failure or limitation in him, on the other hand, was not experienced as delimited but as a confirmation of his essential "badness." To these he would react by attempting urgently to elicit responses, almost at any cost to himself, that would enable him to counteract the enveloping feelings of defectiveness; while to successes he would respond with a drivenness for ever more glorious and heroic accomplishments in the vain hope of sustaining a reliable and confident sense of himself. Only the encouragement to persistent self reflection provided by the working alliance gradually enabled Martin to recognize the contextual perspective in which these shifts were occurring. This in turn led to an increasing ability to trace the developmental history of the encodements to which he had fallen victim and gradually to free himself by the ability to consider reflectively new and more useful paradigms to explain the events which affected him. "*Developmental trauma derive their lasting significance from the establishment of invariant and relentless principles of organization that remain beyond the accommodative influence of reflective self-awareness or of subsequent experience*" (Brandchaft and Stolorow, 1989, p. 17).

The establishment of a working alliance based on the principles articulated above makes possible the consistent working through in the analysis of the developmentally determined, invariant organizing principles and the achievement of the structural change that was the terrain the conquistadors of our profession so passionately hoped to affect. It was a goal that Romey Greenson strove in his own inimitable way and with his own unceasing devotion to this patients and to his profession to advance. It is a goal which his efforts made more accessible to those who follow.

19

Problems of Termination

Ralph R. Greenson, M.D.

I BELIEVE that there are four vital areas which must be kept in mind when a patient is going through the terminal phase of analysis. The first point is to continually remind oneself that all the patient's material, no matter what else it may refer to, must have some reference to the fact that the analysis is terminating. This may not be the predominant problem but it will be omnipresent.

The second area requiring scrutiny is the fact that the patient is reacting to you in three different modalities simultaneously during termination. One must pay attention to the patient's transference reactions, to the state of the working alliance, and to the real relationship with you. New transference material will come up, both positive and negative in nature, regressive and progressive. Furthermore, there will be an increase in the working alliance as the patient, more and more, takes over the role of analyzing his or her own material. If this duality remains deficient, it should become a central focus of the analysis during this stage.

The last part of the patient's relationship to the analyst which has to be scrutinized during termination is the patient's real relationship with us. As patients approach termination, they have learned more and more about the analyst and also have gained the courage to express more and more about it. The analyst must also encourage them to express it during the final period of the analysis. It is important to acknowledge the patient's realistic reactions to the analyst from the beginning; for example, if, at the beginning of the analysis, a patient says that the analyst seems more reserved or more inhibited or more timid, I would be inclined to agree with them if these points seem valid. Or if a patient were to say the analyst seemed in the past to be more angry with them, I would tend to agree that there were such times in the past. Or, if toward the end of the analysis the analyst permits himself more emotional, natural responses to the patient, I would acknowledge to them that it is so because I feel at this point that the patient can cope with this. Or were I to decide, toward the end of the analysis, that I was going to be more silent and passive, I would tell the patient that at this stage of the analysis I thought it necessary to be helpful to be this way, and to see how it works. I stress these points in order to differentiate how a realistic relationship with the analyst can coexist along with the working alliance and the transference neurosis without it becoming friendship. I do not, by any means, wish to alter the professional nature of the relationship. The analytic relationship is by no means a social relationship and I do not think it is indicated to have extra-analytic contact with the patient. But the real relationship is a crucial component of the analytic relationship and must receive attention during termination.

The third area that has to be scrutinized at all times during termination is the particular form of the patient's depressive reaction to the notion of termination. Some patients react by becoming despairing, some become very clingy, others will become complaining, hostile, unclinging. However, there is a healthy depressive reaction that we expect our patients to be able to achieve; in other words, the patients should be able to recognize that they are going to miss the analyst and long for him and be able to remember him. This would be a relatively healthy aspect of a depressive reaction.

Finally, one must keep in mind that the patient will tend to do more acting out in the terminal phase. In part, this is a means of testing out the old neurotic patterns to see if they still give gratification, partly to say goodbye to the old neurotic pleasures, and partly to make a transition from reenactment to memory.

20

Termination:
A Case Report of the End
Phase of an "Interminable"
Analysis

Jack Novick, Ph.D.

ALPH Greenson, a most prolific and influential writer on psychoanalytic technique, never published anything on the subject of termination. This is not surprising since very little was
written on that topic until after his death. Despite Freud's (1913)
expressed interest in termination neither he nor his early followers
had much to say about termination as a phase of treatment. The view
that a standard psychoanalysis has three phases, a beginning, a middle, and a termination phase, was first proposed by Glover (1955) and
did not become widely accepted until the late 1970s. Writing in
1950, Annie Reich could find only two papers on termination and in
1966 Rangell commented on the scant literature. But in the past fifteen years a vast literature has appeared, providing psychoanalysts
with many useful suggestions on how to get into, through and beyond
a termination phase. Reviews by Blum (1989), Firestein (1978,

1982), Novick (1982, 1988, 1990a), and the Shanes (1984) cover most of the issues. The current emphasis on termination as a subject of study and clinical mastery is in sharp contrast with the prewar cavalier attitude toward the ending of an analysis.

The intensity of focus may have reached a peak and there are indications that a reaction to the plethora of articles may be occurring as some authors are suggesting that the importance of the phase may be overemphasized (Blum, 1989), that termination can occur without a formal setting of a date (Goldberg and Marcus, 1985), that termination is a misleading word and does not reflect what actually occurs (Pedder, 1988), and even that a termination phase itself need not be differentiated since termination is an issue from the very start (De Simone Gaburri, 1985).

Nevertheless, work continues on this phase of treatment with follow-up research raising interesting questions about goals of treatment and the role of self-analysis in the posttermination phase (Kantrowitz, Katz, and Paolitto, 1990). In recent work I have looked at the timing of termination and the factors related to premature or delayed termination (Novick, 1982, 1988). An extension of this work has led to a focus on the problem of "interminable analysis" (Novick, 1990b). In discussing this I described the case of Mr. M., a twenty-five year-old single man who was referred to me because he was seen as too disturbed to be a training case.[1] At his first session he pleaded, "I can't stand it. Please! Get it over with. Punish me, beat me." Mr. M. was the eldest of three children raised in a wealthy suburb of an East Coast city. His father was a successful professional and his mother was the beautiful, pampered eldest child of wealthy parents. When first seen Mr. M. was in a state of constant anxiety and tension. He supported himself with occasional house painting jobs and found temporary relief in a series of relationships with equally disturbed women who were initially allowed to play the role of a controlling mother and then were driven into a state of helpless rage by his passivity and covert sadism. Mr. M. initially experienced feelings of euphoria when I became the longed for good mother who would rescue him from his distress. By the first summer he felt so much better that he thought he could end his therapy. But, not surprisingly, he could not maintain his good feelings and soon we were locked in a sadomasochistic transference which reflected a "screaming relationship with a severely

[1] I want to thank Mr. M. for permission to use his clinical material. All identifying information has been omitted or disguised.

depressed, alcoholic mother and underscored the patient's masochistic pathology and life-long addiction to pain" (Novick, 1990b). I described the lengthy pretermination phase in which Mr. M. resisted for over a year picking a date and entering into a termination phase. Mr. M. had been in five times per week psychoanalysis for more than ten years and I suggested that an important factor in an interminable analysis is the patient's desperate need to cling to an omnipotent self-image. The need to maintain the "delusion of omnipotence" is central to masochistic pathology (Novick and Novick, 1987) and in a recent paper Kerry Kelly Novick and I used Mr. M.'s material and many other cases to trace the epigenesis of omnipotence (Novick and Novick, 1991). The work described allowed Mr. M. finally to pick a date. What follows is an account of the termination phase of his "interminable" analysis.

The Termination Phase

Mr. M. was in his eleventh year of analysis. After a year of work on his resistances to picking a date he finally decided upon, and I agreed with, a date in the middle of a working week three months or fourteen weeks away.

In the spirit of this "postmodern age" when no one theory or school is predominant in art, literature, or psychoanalysis and when a text can be read any which way with infinite meanings depending on the reader, I will present the material as follows. In the right-hand column are Mr. M.'s words quoted directly or summarized: My interventions are also in the right-hand column in italics, while the left-hand column contains my running comments on the text, kept to a minimum to allow the reader space to respond.

WEEK 1

He can experience, acknowledge, and contain the ambivalence, a major achievement.

Tension had always been a signal for rigid defense or rage. He had the fantasy that life

After making a firm commitment to a finishing date, Mr. M. reported that everything continued to go well in his outside world of work and family. But coming here now felt like a disturbance. "I had seriously con-

should be without tension. He now speaks of using tension to initiate work.

Idealization of analyst barely covering up disillusionment and anger.

sidered the idea," he said, "of selecting a date one month earlier, to get it over with. But I thought the *tension* is worth working with." "My first thought about finishing is that I'm not you. The fantasy, as you know, is that I would become you and be able to free associate and get in touch with my deeper feelings. I find that very hard. I need this kind of situation to be able to do it." As he became visibly tense and angry he said, "I can get to my anger but it's not smooth, effi- cient, effective." After some mumbling and more self blame he went on to say, "Back of my mind are some blaming feel- ings. I'm blocked. I can tell by the way I'm talking—stammer- ing, substituting words."

I said that he was angry at him- self and me for not making him into the perfect, magical person he imagines me to be.

The fantasy persists that I can give him the magical power.

"After all this time," he said, "shouldn't I leave as the bar mitzvah king, carried off on everybody's shoulders? If I don't, aren't you kicking me out?" The next day he reported a dream. "Some big guy was arguing against six other big guys. I was just watching. Sud- denly the guy grabbed me and said I was a hostage and he said, 'this guy is weaker than you guys.' My first thought is that I am weak, I'm a coward and I envy the big guys." He then related another dream of a bat coming at him. He is startled but doesn't panic. He related the dream to his recent experience of competently handling a bat in his house in contrast to a few years ago when he lost control and panicked when a bat flew in. He noted that he is not captive to his fears anymore but he can still work himself up into a panic.

I asked why he would do that here, with me.

"To explore the fear more fully but also to say 'I'm not in control. Watch me fall apart and then you'll rescue me.'"

I said that the bat dream reflected his competent handling of a realistic danger whereas the hostage dream reflected his fantasy that by becoming weak, helpless and fearful he will magically become powerful and protect himself from a deeper terror.

I interpret the masochism but also I'm looking for the underlying trauma.

He responded, "My mother and me. We can beat the other four or six big guys—the other members of my family. And here is where it gets out of control. This is my strategy. I'm just

Here is a major theme of the termination phase. Through his

masochism, i.e., his active pursuit of weakness, and victimization he omnipotently restores the object and thus ensures his own omnipotence.

standing there having a drink and then I become the decisive force. With me, this guy can fight off the other six. I'm the one who tips the balance. I make my mother or father strong. It's all magical and it gets out of control."

WEEK 2

He started the week by talking of his wish that during these last three months I would come up with one last trick which would fulfill his magical wishes. The wish was to be like me and he listed a set of idealized thoughts concerning my ability to do self-analysis easily, smoothly, without effort or obstacles.

Disillusionment is a necessary part of the termination process (Novick, 1982; Pedder, 1988).

I said that he was clinging to an idealized image because he was beginning to face his disillusionment with me and the analysis.

He said, "There's also the other idea. You work so hard, you don't have time for your kids." At first this seemed like a fleeting thought but he returned to this idea and then said, "Calling into question what you do, calls into question what I do. We both like to work, we both like to make decisions, we both enjoy going to the office. But the parallels are with my dad. He would come home late at

Still protecting me by sharing the sin.

night. It's hard even now to get beyond the boundaries you set up. You're this dynamic guy who teaches, writes, does service for the community, that's great! That's how I felt about my dad. He's president. That's great! I'm so proud of you. But that covers up my feeling of being left out and

The feeling of disillusionment is experienced,

deprived. But I don't feel that, I feel proud!" He paused, then in a sad voice he said, "I wanted more involvement, not a big, exciting dad. Even as I tell the

pushed away,

story I'm falling short of criticizing my dad. The aura of perfection is there for protection. What I hang onto with my father is the feeling of excitement when I'm around him. But my memory is of *not* being

and then returns.

around him. I suspect that it's not only that you're not perfect but that you're not perfect for me. My image of my father is a caricature. I don't really know my dad. With my mom or granny or [housekeeper] I had a gut to gut relationship, with my dad it was smile to smile— like with you." These thoughts were accompanied by a deep sadness and by anger. The anger emerged in the transference as he spoke of his feeling hurt and excluded by my vacations.

I said that he kept me perfect to

protect me from his anger.

"Yes. I'm afraid my anger will destroy the happy family."

WEEK 3

Defenses still operative but no longer unconscious. Present, analytic past and historical past are condensed in his words. He knows it and knows that I know.

"I'm not facing things, your deficiencies, dad's deficiencies. I'm overlooking things, idealizing things, compartmentalizing so the criticism flows to my mom. As a child I needed to do that. It was necessary to have happy good parents. Now it's a protection for me. Protect me from my anger."

A shared poetic language of allusion and shared myths, part of a terminal phase.

"My goal in life, my mission is to have a happy family. In that light my anger causes me nothing but trouble."

He then spoke, with deep feeling, of his memories of being yelled at by his mother. "I vowed never to do that to anyone," he said.

A further working through of trauma, an essential part of a termination phase. See the interesting work by Kinston and Cohen (1988) and Cohen and Kinston (in press) on the danger to the patient if the trauma is not worked through.

I said that the anger was overwhelming, devastating to the core.

He said, "My anger isn't shut off but I'm scared of it. I was yelled at daily and I would yell back. I know what it feels like to have someone berate and belittle you and I know what it feels like to have anger as the biggest feeling I have—to have it consume me, to be totally out of control." He went on to say that his father was never angry, in fact he was afraid of anger.

I said that he had held back his anger at father and me for fear it would overwhelm us.

He responded, "I hope you never heard such fights. Real hate, real destruction—we would rip up the relationship. I wouldn't want to do that to you or my dad. I definitely did have the capability of responding with an all out attack. Vicious! I don't want you to see me this way. I don't know if you'd collapse, but you'd be terribly disappointed." The next day he forgot the check and he realized that he was angry at me. "Yesterday I said I would risk my own survival to avoid anger at you. Today I'm saying you're as bad as my mom, just as controlling and inflexible. My anger feels palpable, as real as if you had really done some-thing I didn't like." He spoke with powerful feeling about getting what he had paid for but not what he had hoped for. He had given up so much to idealize me, to protect me from his anger so he should now get his magical wishes fulfilled "so now I'm not paying you, I'm getting back at you, pathetically."

Very angry but can step back, observe, and work with feelings. In termination phase the working alliance is at maximum efficiency.

WEEK 4

He started the week by trying to control his anger, his disappointment. He spoke in the conditional but soon the conditional became the present. What he *could* feel he *did* feel and he was shaking with rage as he expressed his need to control and boss. "The moral is I *can* provide for myself but the wish is you'll do it for me. I'll break down at the bottom of the street. You'll see me and you'll come and give me the best pep talk I've ever heard. The rescue will make all the angry feelings go away. You're not the depressed, incompetent mother. Look at what you can do and you're doing it for me."

Parental incompetence as a source of trauma which makes the disillusionment of the termination phase extremely difficult to face.

I said that his anger and his wish to build me up through his own failure follows his disillusionment.

"I was just thinking how I needed feedback." He continued to complain about the lack of feedback, that I could give him more and the analyst who first interviewed him did give him more feedback. Later he returned to what he perceived as my imperfections. "Seeing your imperfections derails me. You work too hard.

Though critical, this is actually a subtle form of fantasy that I really can give him what he needs and through his masochistic presentation he can force me to do so.

I'm deeply ashamed, I'm afraid to invite my friends home. I'm responsible for how you are. We're back into my feelings of shame and responsibility. Why can't I accept your imperfection? So you're not Mickey Mantle or Willie Mays— so what?"

I said he might be afraid that my imperfection would make him so angry he would ruin over ten years of work. How hard it is for him to fuse imperfections with the good things.

WEEK 5

He continued to focus on his struggle over facing my incompetence. He said, "I don't have to deny my mother's incompetence but I have to protect you and my dad." He spent some time talking about his agreeing to tape a program for his father. It made him furious that his father couldn't do it himself. He wanted to deny his disappointment and rage, or become totally incompetent himself.

I said that this was a struggle he was now having with his feelings about me.

During termination the

I was reminded of a fantasy he had reported a number of years

analyst's associations are more likely to be right on target and can be shared easily.

During termination old dreams or fantasies are reworked with new elements added, sometimes, as in this case, memories of reality events.

Week 6

Mother's failure was a theme throughout analysis, father's failure was not fully experienced until termination phase work focused on disillusionment with analyst.

before when on passing my office during a vacation he imagined he would see me on the roof with power tools.

I told him my association and suggested that separation seemed to intensify his need to protect me.

He recalled that fantasy and the work we had done especially in regard to the sexual associations and his feeling excluded from my "powerful sexuality activities." But now that fantasy had a concrete reference to his father's inadequacy. He said "that image reminds me that as a kid I noticed that my father couldn't hammer a nail or use any tool. He couldn't make toast or coffee. My mother's incompetence made my father look good. That's what I do. I build you and my dad up by being incompetent."

He continued to talk about his father's incompetence, he had never seen it so clearly. For years he had wondered why his father had stayed with his mother and he now understood that his father needed his mother in order to feel superior. He went on to speak of a seemingly unrelated event,

His masochism was understood throughout as including elements of identification with his "damaged and masochistic mother" and receptive feminine longings for his father. In the end phase transference it becomes emotionally clear to him that his "feminine masochism" is part of an omnipotent fantasy of denying and repairing the father's failure.

Reenactments of a central developmental trauma probably occur throughout treatment but the terminal phase allows the analyst the possibility of quickly recognizing and verbalizing transference/countertransference reenactments of what may be a developmental trauma.

The analyst cannot plan it, it just happens, but the analyst can learn to expect it and even welcome it as an important

when a friend had needed the name of a therapist and he had been too ashamed to give him mine.

I asked him to associate to why he felt shame.

His first thought was shame to reveal that he was seeing a therapist, then that his fantasy that we have the "perfect happy relationship" would be exposed and shown to be false and with this I would be exposed as an "incompetent fraud." He went on "so I must believe that if I expose you I would destroy you so I protect you by being incompetent, by fumbling and bumbling. I become weak, a failure, a woman, a homosexual who takes it up the butt so you can feel superior."

Then there occurred one of those split second reenactments of a central transference/countertransference drama. The next session I started to hand him my yearly vacation schedule. I hesitated when I realized he did not need it and I asked if he wanted it. He asked, "How far does it extend?" and I told him. The whole exchange took ten seconds yet he immediately saw that I had made an error. There was no need to give him a vaca-

means for working through during the terminal phase. See Sandler's (1976) concept of role responsiveness as related to the process I am describing.

tion schedule as he was stopping in seven weeks. As he said, either I had forgotten or I did not want him to finish. But in a split second he asked how far does the vacation schedule extend. After ten years he knew that the schedule extended for a full year and, furthermore, the question was irrelevant since he knew that he was finishing before any usual vacation date. He spent the next two sessions struggling with intense feelings of sadistic excitement and power, opposed by an equally intense wish to protect me by making himself the confused person who has to be rescued by me.

I noted that what he had presented as a possibility was something now deeply felt in the relationship. He had seen my incompetence and could feel the excitement and the wish to protect me.

He recalled the time he broke down in college and had to return home. He said "the excited wish to devastate can take secret paths. I broke down, came home and my parents had to rescue me but my breakdown devastated my parents."

I said that his wish to break down was also a wish to devastate me.

He said, "If I've sacrificed so much of my life for you and you're still not perfect then I have a right to rant and rave and devastate you."

WEEK 7

A week during which he could experience a forward surge in all areas, a week of integration and one in which he reported feeling "really good about my life, all of it: my work, my wife, my child."

In the sessions he continued to work on the theme of being able to destroy me by exposing my incompetence and the wish to protect me by becoming the damaged woman. He took it further through a piece of a dream in which a woman asks him to speak at a seminar.

I interpreted his joining the woman to attack me, his father.

The traumatic experience of seeing the analyst's incompetence can now be put into words and worked through. His word *catastrophe* during terminal phase work alerts us to the fact that termination can often result in failure or worse (Novick, 1982). Cohen and Kinston (in press) review the work on catastrophe and termination. They suggest that

He said that his mother could build up his father but she also took every opportunity to tear him down. "We're getting close," he said. "Seeing my mother nuts is bad. Having her attack me is horrible but to see her tear my father apart is catastrophe. So I make myself the target to preserve my family, preserve you." The price he paid for clinging to his

"catastrophe usually means that the trauma of the patient's life is being directly relived. . . . [This] may lead to growth or it may lead to a personal catastrophe such as illness, accident, death" (in press).

An example of what Greenson called "working through"—something we would expect in the termination phase.

Sometimes the power of positive parental feelings is the only force which can stand up to the self protective delusion of the omnipotent system.

WEEK 8

omnipotent fantasy was central to our pretermination work and had enabled him to enter into a terminal phase. This week he saw clearly how it did and could affect his relationship with his baby boy. At a play group his baby was involved in something other than what the teacher wanted and Mr. M. felt disappointed with his baby, began to get angry, and then withdrew. He suddenly connected this sequence with how he reacted to me when I disappointed him and he realized his anger was due to the fact that he felt he could not magically control the baby and make him do his every bidding.

Later in the week as he spoke again of ending analysis and what he thinks he will lose, he said, "I'll lose the magic, my fantasy that I can and should control your life. Like my breakdown in college and return home, there's a powerful pull back to the world of magic where I am king, I control everyone's life. It's quick, easy and exciting. But now I can see that the price includes my baby's life for he too has to become a willing subject."

His wife had decided to return to work and put the six-month-old baby in day care. His first response was to think that his boy would feel, as he still feels, rage at parents for finding something else more important than being with him. He kept calling his reactions "neurotic" and said that this was the price of clinging to magic. He was afraid that he wouldn't face reality and do what is right for everyone.

I said that calling his reactions neurotic left him helpless and in need of rescue. I then reminded him that he had said that they were introducing a new relationship in the baby's life.

"Did I say that? I didn't think of that but only of my baby's anger. The reality then is my jealousy, my being excluded. I can't stand people being separate. This is my neurosis."

I said that he is again dismissing his feelings as neurotic and so avoids looking at reality.

The next day he said, "I see that I have a choice. This 'neurotic' stuff is a defense against being a real person. Usually I feel I can't help it, but yesterday I saw I had a choice. You saying that when I act neurotic I can use that as a signal that I'm staying away from being real and seeing things realistically. I have a

It is becoming clear that the analytic method has become part of his masochistic perversion. At this point I know it but I am still pulled in by my own counterreaction, my need to rescue the baby.

choice! I can be neurotic and that's a choice or I can be competent and realistic. But I have a fear that I can't do it without you."

I said that last week he had said he would give up the magic; this week he is showing us he won't. Being neurotic is his way of being helpless and getting me to rescue him. But why? So that he doesn't have to look at me or his wife realistically. Why did I give him the schedule? Why does his wife want to change her relationship with the baby?

"As long as I keep things blurred about me, I don't have to look closely at you," he said. "You ask the price. The price is the same as the method. I play dumb and I become dumb. I give up the good feeling of clear insight."

Week 9

During the first part of the week he seemed overwhelmed by his feelings. At the same time he could observe and report his reactions. For example, he said, "I'm losing it. I'm mad without justification. I'm angry but I'm not using it as a signal. I'm depressed, angry, feeling overwhelmed. I don't want to deal with this, it's too much. I'm not being honest with myself."

I again focused on his denial of something he perceived.

He shouted, "Why does she want to go back to work?" The next day he could tell her that he was angry and disappointed but he quickly assumed the blame by talking of his neurosis, his high expectations of motherhood.

I reminded him that he had said her decision to return to work, "made no rational sense."

"I do blur things," he said. "The point is I don't think it makes sense but she does." He again fell into helpless despair but then could say, "I know there's something I'm avoiding." Finally he told me that the baby had not settled into a sleep pattern and his wife was up every two or three hours to feed him. It was clear that she felt helpless, unsupported by Mr. M., enraged at both of them and wanted to return to work to run away from her own feeling of failure. This was so close to his image of his incompetent mother that he was terrified of facing it. Having done so he could use what he had gained over the years to understand

Once again he had been
rescued by the analyst.

the situation and put his
understanding into action. He
spoke to his wife, together they
agreed on a plan for helping
the baby and within two nights
the baby was sleeping through
the night and the crisis
was over.

*I wondered what he was deny-
ing about me.*

"The fact is I've been trying to
convince you to change your
mind, to see that I'm not ready.
But the fact is, you're going to
let me go. My magic won't work."

*That's about you, I said, what
about me?*

"I'm not sure. The big issue
now for me is staying in contact
afterwards. I have little boy
insecure feelings, you won't
want to hear from me."

*I wondered what kind of person
I'd be to do that.*

He said, "A bad person, cold
and uncaring."

Week 10

The baby continued to sleep
through the night and Mr. M.
and his wife were feeling back
together again. He was proud of
his baby but also proud of the
work he had done. He said, "I
saw a side of my wife I don't

like to see so I gave up and forgot that I had ever seen it. In that way I can deny my mother was ever mean or my wife is ever mean."

I wondered if he had allowed the crisis to build up so that he could avoid feelings about leaving.

"I'll miss you," he said.

"Yes, but you're afraid I won't miss you," I answered.

The helpless feeling of being unloved covered up by the omnipotent fantasy defense.

He said, "That's a chilling thought. Most painful is the idea that all these years you didn't like me, you tolerated me. It feels like a new idea. What's new is the thought that my mother was looking forward to my going. I always emphasized how devastated she would be if I left her but it's not a big jump to see the reverse, that my mom not only didn't want kids, couldn't cope with kids, she was eager to get rid of me. I have the fantasy of over-hearing you saying to your wife that you're glad I'm going, glad to be rid of me. Why didn't I want to leave? The answer is clear now. Leaving is the moment of truth. If I have an inkling that you want me out of here, it will be seen when I leave. But I also want to keep in touch. You're an important per-

The link to resistance to separating/terminating.

He is now focusing on contact after termination. It sounds reasonable but, in addition, it is

a fallback position for the need to hang on to the omnipotent fantasy of control.

WEEK 11

He is not aware as yet that he is trying to enact a fantasy. Friday evening refers to a dream two years earlier in which he meets me when I'm visiting his hometown and he invites me home for a Friday meal. Behind the hospitality was hostile control of my life.

son to me. Do you reciprocate?"

He started the week by noting that all the pressing things were cleared out and he could now concentrate on his analysis. "Only four weeks left. I feel numb." He went on to talk of his sadness and pain and he went over the realization of last week that "leaving is the moment of truth."

I wondered if he was avoiding looking at the feeling that analysis had not fulfilled his expectations.

He said that he still expected that he should leave without conflicts. He returned, however, to the "pressing" question of keeping in touch after therapy. "I wonder about how often I should call you and would I be charged? I imagine I would be, especially if I did it on a regular basis. Let's say 6:00 o'clock on a Friday evening." He went on to say that he always had difficulty leaving and the struggle was to put together the old stuff and the new. How could he go to college and still maintain relations with his family? "I need rules" he said. "I need a model for separating. I never had a clean, good feeling kind of break." As he noticed that he was feeling angry and demanding he said, "I have to be careful I don't turn this into a fantasy that I can have all this free time and money and still have my analysis."

I asked what came to mind about "6:00 o'clock Friday evening."

He responded "You light the candles. It's the old analogue of keeping you trapped. Oh yes! The dream of [my home town] you thought you could get rid of me. Well you haven't. I'll show you. I'll invite you home for dinner. I'll break down and call you on Friday night and keep you under my control and take you away from your family and going out." He paused, sighed, and said, "Clearly there's more to separation than phone calls. It's one dot in the whole picture but I'm closing in on it so it occupies the whole space. What am I blotting out?" He spoke of the lifting of internal constraints, the new freedom and the new opportunities. As yet he doesn't feel the excitement, he wondered why. What he feels now is that it is a "humbling, humiliating

The use of vivid images and metaphors is often a feature of the termination phase and indicative of the increased creativity due to analytic work. At the start of his analysis his thoughts were almost concrete and unimaginative and his words were stilted and colorless.

In our paper on masochism and the delusion of omnipotence K. K. Novick and I (1991) note the many resistances to relinquishing the omnipotent system and living in the world of realistic, competent interactions. Mr. M. illustrates the humiliation and feared helplessness when making such a move.

feeling. The opportunities were always there. Most people enjoy the freedom. If I take this step I want to be the first! I feel as if I'm going into a different country and all my tricks aren't going to work in this new land. I need to be the first, to be the king, but in this new land I feel my identity blotted out. The same image of a dot of paint on a canvas. My feeling is that I'm a very special person but if I give up the magic then I'm afraid I'll become this vanilla guy disappearing among the million dots. This is clear when you compare me with my sister. Strip away my grandiosity and she can claim more attention than I can. What distinguishes me is that I'm the king, I'm the victim, and I am angry. I'm not engaging or attractive. I've established relationships by distortion, guilt inducement, tricks and manipulating. I'm giving up a system. Like a great basketball player switching to soccer. I want to play soccer but with basketball rules."

This interpretation is in the nature of a "mop up" operation, returning to deal with remaining pockets of resistance, a reworking of conflicts typical of

I noted that he has said that he doesn't feel excited about ending or the opportunities in store. I suggested that excitement, for him, belongs to the magic system, an indication that the magic system is at work.

end phase analytic work. If excitement remains exclusive to the magical system then there is little to induce a person to live in dull reality.

His wish for closeness is a derivative of his sadomasochistic wish to be the woman who submits to me and thus controls me and takes all my power. As a school child he had a day dream of sitting atop a flag pole with Indian princesses dancing around him. The fantasy was worked over from all angles and reference to it denoted the complex masochistic fantasy with all its determinants and functions.

WEEK 12

"Yes," he said. "Still, for me, excitement has to do with something dropping out of the sky—unexpected, dramatic."

I suggested that his wish to keep in touch might also be a wish to keep alive the hope of experiencing the excitement of having all his wishes granted.

"I never thought of that," he said. "For me it's a feeling of closeness, camaraderie. But there is something in what you say. There is a feeling that if I break contact I'll be out there *working* for what I want. What is lost is the aura of possibility. Without you I'll be left with what I am."

He started the week by talking of "trade-offs," what he imagines he gains and what in fact he loses by living in his magical system. He said, "I always felt it would take tremendous effort to live by reality but the other night I realized that it's much easier to live in reality, to see what I can and what I cannot control and not waste my life trying to control what I can't." He spoke again of the "trade-offs," of the cost.

During the termination phase it gradually became clear that his sadomasochistic stance had moved from the physical (pain, tension, heart attack, going blind) to the emotional (trapped in feelings of intense anger or envy or fear) to ego functions (figuring things out, remembering, differentiating, analyzing). The fantasy of rescue became realized when I responded to his confusion by acting as his memory, remind-ing him of what he had said or what we had understood at some earlier time. It is easy and tempting to be "brilliant" dur-ing the end phase and the clue to my collusion was the pleasure I had in these "brilliant rescues."

I said that now we can't avoid seeing that the major cost is what he does to his mind in order to retain the fantasy that he can get me to rescue him with my magical powers. I said that in the recent work on his baby's sleep problem, I had merely repeated what he had told me but he had experienced my words as brilliant insights and miraculous solutions.

He said, "This is the cost. I give up my ability to think and work things out. I let you screw me in the butt, mock me, and I kid myself into thinking it's excit-ing. You did it! You dropped from the sky and solved my problem. What I do pales in comparison."

This took place in the middle of the week and from this point there was a surge of hard work in the sessions and effective action outside. I had not planned to do so, but it felt right to remain silent for the rest of the week, in fact till the end of the analysis three weeks away.

Interpretation was effective for both patient and analyst.

WEEK 13

In the omnipotent magic system people are never lost and so mourning need never occur.

An attempt to abort the mourning process by moving back into the omnipotent system. Pain, deprivation, and justified anger open the doors to the world of fantasied hostile control over others.

One of the signs of being "on the path of progressive devel-

He had been thinking of the "flag pole" fantasy and that behind that conscious day dream was a secret fantasy of having sex without growing up. "What," he wondered, "is my secret fantasy about you? The goal of analysis was to become you. But now, there is a glimmer of a feeling that I can leave here and have learned from you but I'll become me. The hope is, I can leave here and recall you as human size and not a billboard size man, to leave here and not want to become you without feeling I'm rejecting you. I don't need to be you. I can incorporate things but I'm not you. I don't want to be you." He sighed and after a few moments of silence said sadly, "but then I'm faced with leaving, with the end. I can feel the mourning setting in. I can imagine the end. I thought of it last night and felt a real heartfelt missing of you and what I had here." This was followed by an attempt to convince us that he cannot do without me. "The thing I get here," he said, "is confirmation. I find that so important." He was on the verge of complaining about my lack of "feedback." He said, "You haven't said anything for over a week. It's *less hard*.

opment." The regressive pull of the omnipotent system has lessened, the progressive pull of the competent, reality system has increased, a sign we look for when considering termination (A. Freud, 1970a; Novick, 1990a; Novick and Novick, 1991).

That's not what I wanted to say. Why the slip? I wanted to say it's harder if you don't summarize, confirm. But I carry it too far and make your comments more important than doing it myself." He brightened, his voice was firm and he said, "There's excitement in finishing, in being challenged and rising to the occasion. I can feel it. There's excitement in the idea that I'll be worthy of dealing with life's problems. I now know when something feels right. It would be tremendous to have the validation in myself." He said that he realized that what I was doing was allowing him to find his own feelings about ending. "This is my leaving," he said. "It doesn't affect us the same. You remain the analyst, I become someone who does his own analysis. I'm going to take the last day off from work, make it a special day. No need for you to do that." Silence, then in a subdued tone he said, "But I want to wait for you. I want you to join me and if you don't I'll think that my leaving is not important. Reminds me of my first dream. I'm running the race, way out in front. I stop. I've gone too far. I have to wait for the others to catch up.

Reconstructed from his material and then confirmed. But this had happened at 2½ and he is referring to what Freud (1918b) called "deferred action" and Greenacre (1950) called the latency trauma.

We've talked about this dream many times but I have to recognize this desire. It's a contrived desire. I don't need you to validate the importance of the last day. I feel, honest to God, that there's something in me from way back that knows from inside what's right. I can recall a "show and tell" in kindergarten. The other kids brought toys and dolls to show and I just stood up and told everyone what I had planned to do after school. I had no hesitation in speaking out and saying what I wanted. Somehow this got overlaid by your feelings, my parents' feelings. My feelings had to be covered up. Another example, one we've talked about, a baby is born dead and everyone is sad and I'm happy. This is my leaving, it's special for me." Again he began to sputter, mumble, lose his train of thought, and then spoke of how he doesn't "beat himself up" as much as he used to. I felt the urge to speak, and confirm his hints that beating represented the masochistic fantasy that through pain he could keep the object. However, I remained silent and he rescued himself. He said, "There's a good feeling creeping back in," and he again

Termination is usually a time of review.

Week 14

Something I encourage people to do. The first date they choose is often one which allows them to deny the significance of the ending. The first date he had chosen was a Friday and his mother's birthday.

The thought of his parents dying used to be cause for a major panic.

At the end one not only relinquishes the object but more importantly, an image of the self as the omnipotent con-

recalled the "show and tell" incident in kindergarten. He then talked of this being the last weekend and he reviewed the importance of weekends and vacations through the course of analysis.

This was the last week, a short week since three months ago he had decided to end on a Wednesday so that the ending would stand on its own and not be another weekend.

He started the week by talking of a television interview with the eighty-year-old mother of a sixty-year-old sports celebrity. The mother said that she worries that her son will catch cold. He wondered about himself and his child, his parents and me. He said, "When my baby is forty, I'll be able to let him go, I'll know that he can take care of himself and I can take care of myself. I'll be sad when my parents die but I can take care of myself. As a dad I can let go and I've reached a point where I can let myself go. So I'm letting go of you and you can let go of me. It's a letting go of the relationship but also a letting go of the hope that on the eve of the last session something magical will happen. I

troller of objects (Novick, 1990b).

know that take away the pretense and there is excitement and freedom. But something keeps nagging at me. The idea of *Respect*. It's more respectful to feel that there is something more important than waking up every day and saying, 'it's my day'; something more important than my needs. There is US to consider, we will do it together, that is my mistake. Letting go of you is letting go of this fantasy that I'm not in charge of me but I'm in charge of the world as I conceive it, you, my sister, my wife, and baby. I'm on the verge of having a life that is mine. I don't know how many years I've said it but I know I can work toward that, though I'm not there yet. I'm excited but I want to say, 'forgive me for being glad for all I've accomplished, forgive me for being less attentive to you than I should be.' Again the idea from last week, it's my analysis and finishing is mine. Whatever feelings you have are different than mine. I can grieve or be excited or both. This kind of excitement and freedom keeps poking up but gets covered by clumsy, distorted, mumbled thoughts that there is a higher purpose, doing something for US. It's a crock, but these clumsy arguments carry a lot of force. I want them to carry force. All this reality stuff is not right. I want to take the easy route, the kingly route which, again, gets me into trouble." He then told me that he had thought about a gift for me, that he has a wish to thank me, that so much has changed in his life and that he wanted me to know that he was grateful for my patience, for my confidence in him when he didn't have any, and for my support and judgment. He then tried and quickly saw his repeated attempts to feel that in losing me he was losing something he could never do for himself, could never replace with others, in fact something magical. He was left then with the loss of me as a separate person who had been very important but he had now outgrown. "I'm just sad" he said.

As part of treatment, important human needs to communicate, share and be understood are released and experienced with the analyst. It is important that during termination the person can realize that these needs can and should be gratified with others (Bergmann, 1988; Novick, 1990a).

"I can take away the memories and feelings of accomplishment but I'm sad. You're a friend, you won't be there for me. I feel close and part of feeling close is wanting to be around. But, that doesn't mean I can't replace that in part." He left in tears.

On the last day he brought a gift, a beautiful sweater, with a card thanking me for helping him find his own way.

Fantasies of bringing a gift at the last session are common (Calef and Weinshel, 1983). Actually bringing a gift is seldom reported as occurring though it is not unusual in work with children. He is the only one of my adult patients to have done so.

He can now experience the excitement and contain the ambivalence.

On the last day of a ten-year plus analysis the patient is still on the couch, still bringing dreams, and using his self-analytic skills. He is continuing to do analysis to the very end.

Many analysts vary the technique at the end but the material of this case suggests that it is advisable to analyze to the very end.

I thanked him but said nothing regarding the meaning of the gift. He said, "I feel all choked up. I've tried in the last few weeks to tell you how appreciative I am, I didn't want my feelings to pile up." He began to cry and then spoke of his gratitude to his wife and to his parents for their support. "I'm sad and I'm excited," he said. "It's a beginning as well as an end." Again, he cried and said, "Sad seems to be the bigger feeling at the moment." He went on, "I'm lying here expecting my feelings to come gushing out but there's been a lot of work preparing for this day. I dreamt last night that one of the big guys in my field was impressed with an impromptu remark I made at a conference. It was a good feeling. My work felt good to me and was judged good by others. That's the way I feel here. I feel good about what I've accomplished and I think you feel good too. But I won't stop there. I still have a lot of work to do. I know my wish to hang on to my delusions and fantasies, but I also know the good feeling of knowing what I've really accomplished and that the choices are mine. The idea that somehow the great insight will occur has

Review of the shared analytic history is a frequent occurrence during the termination phase and is part of the mourning process.

The gift can and does have multiple meanings but just as the patient continues to work after the analysis is terminated so too can the analyst keep wondering and learning. The gift represents something which words alone could not encompass. It felt like an enactment of his deepest wish and fear, to be intimate yet separate. The sweater was my size, color and style and not his.

Again this points to the importance of deidealization and disillusion before the working alliance can be transformed into a self-analytic function.

passed. It's a silly idea and if a great insight should occur it would mean I was not ready to leave." He went on to recall our first meeting, and the many life events he had shared with me. He wondered again about keeping in touch, especially to tell me of further major events. He then spoke of the gift, the fact that it was uncalled for and was a "drop in the bucket" compared to all the money he had paid over the years. He realized that there were many motives, some of them magical but, "I had fun looking for the sweater. You know I hate shopping but I really wanted to do it, my heart was in it. I feel sad now, but it's a warm sad." He spoke again of his joyful anticipation of the next phase of his life and then said, "One of the things I've been thinking about is the way I used to come down on myself for not doing analysis by myself as well as I did it with you. But analysis is work! It's not easy. You're skilled and trained so you could give those turns and prompts which are important. It was a great relief to realize I wasn't a failure for needing your skills and now these are skills I can take with me." He then turned his thoughts to the analytic work he will carry on alone after termination.

"I feel the next few days and weeks I'll understand better what leaving means. I think it's going to be possible to be running my own life when I'm away from here. Being here I'm always trying to compromise. Leaving here *is* the moment of truth. It's going to college only this time I'm prepared and I'll take advantage of my being on my own. I'll seize the responsibility, something I can't do while I'm here. All the talking and working things through won't help if I'm here waiting for miracles."

Some things cannot be worked through until the termination phase but, there may be many things which cannot be worked through until the analysis is over.

He can now accept the reality and limits of psychoanalysis.

He spoke again of our having shared his deepest moments, how much he relied on my presence and then said, "I've not thought about a different support system for myself. My wife is the person I can now share things with but I've been so wrapped up here that I've let things slide. I would like someone I could lean on. I'm thinking of friends where the potential of a warm, meaningful relationship is possible. It'll take work but worthwhile work."

Again, the importance of finding someone else to meet those paraverbal aspects of the analytic situation, the safe holding, containing, sharing, supporting, reflecting, etc.

"There's one request," he said. "You don't have to respond. If you move, I'd like to know. I'd

Erna Furman (1982) quotes Anna Freud as saying that, "a mother's job is to be there to be left." In her beautiful paper Mrs. Furman looks at the mother's ability to be left throughout the course of development and Mr. M. alerts us to the possibility that the analyst's job is to be there to be left.

Termination experienced as death has been mentioned in the literature (Stern, 1968; Laforgue, 1934). Here it would seem closely related to accepting reality, including our helplessness in relation to death.

like to know how to get in touch with you. It's easier to hold on to what I've got from here knowing I could get in touch. Maybe I'll get to the point where I don't need that, but I feel I need it now." It was near the end of the hour, he sighed and said, "It's like saying goodbye to a grandparent who is dying. This is like a death. This relationship will be no more. I'm left with memories."

I said, "It's time to end."

He got off the couch, shook my hand and at the door turned to look at me. He smiled, tears running down his face and said "Thanks."

I too was very moved.

Conclusion

There has been relatively little written on the topic of interminable analysis despite the fact that Freud's case of the Wolf Man (1918) would fall into that category. Difficulty with the Wolf Man was probably one of the motivations for Freud's rather pessimistic paper, "Analysis Terminable and Interminable" (1937). The fiftieth anniversary of the publication of that paper was commemorated at the 1987 International Psychoanalytic Congress in Montreal and a number of articles appeared (Anzieu, 1987; Berenstein, 1987; Blum, 1987; Burgner, 1988) which addressed some of the issues and raised more questions than can be answered in a single paper. First, it is important to recognize that many analysts are reluctant to admit that they have cases which have been in analysis for over ten years. They may be afraid of being accused of fostering a pathological dependence, for, at a time when there is a great deal of professional and third party pressure to shorten therapy, to admit openly that a course of four to five times per week psychoanalysis can last for over ten years might be considered professional suicide by some. It would confirm the worst fears of most people looking for a therapist, it would add substance to the wishes of insurance companies who want to deny payment for psychoanalysis, and it would be a windfall for antianalytic mental health professionals who offer a smorgasbord of fast, painless cures. In 1987, *New York* magazine published an article entitled "Prisoners of Psychotherapy" and the cover had a photograph of a woman tied by thick ropes to the couch.

It is my impression that there are many long-term (over ten years) psychoanalytic cases and perhaps this report may encourage others to share their material. There might be many more such cases, but some analysts set a time limit at the outset of treatment to avoid what may seem like the trap of an interminable analysis. Patients like Mr. M. often bring about a premature termination as part of the sado-masochistic transference and the accompanying negative therapeutic reaction (Asch, 1976) or negative therapeutic motivation (Novick, 1980). We need reports of long-term cases to differentiate among the many factors involved. There are those who seem to respond well to treatment but relapse soon after termination. The Wolf Man was one such case (Freud, 1937) and the case Greenson (1965b) used to illustrate difficulties in working through is another. Perhaps closer attention to termination issues and criteria might be helpful. Some of these are suggested in Greenson's paper and in the work of Kinston and Cohen (in press) whose formulations are especially relevant to cases which break down or relapse after treatment. In a recent paper (Novick, 1990a) I looked at a case of reanalysis to illustrate some criteria not usually discussed. This, however, would lead to longer treatment and again the "embarrassing" problem of interminable analysis. There are evidently patients who can never terminate, where therapy of some sort will be needed throughout life. Perhaps, if we could accurately isolate those who fall into this category, we could apply the method of "intermittent analysis" recommended by Mahler and others for use with children (Kramer and Byerly, 1978). These cases then could be of briefer duration with the expectation that analysis will resume in the future and intermittently for many years. There are also a large number of patients who after making substantial progress reach a stalemate. The stalemate may be due to intense resistance in the patient and/or countertransference issues and technical limitations in the therapist. Mr. M. might be viewed as such a case for by his eighth year he was, by most criteria, ready to stop. He was happily married, planning a family and successful in his career. There are many analysts who would have suggested termination at this point and picked a date (Brenner, 1976). Had I done so, the analysis could have ended two years earlier. There are many who might claim that my leaving the decision to the patient is a technical error unnecessarily prolonging the length of treatment. In an earlier paper I described Mr. M.'s attempt to have me choose the date and his subsequent reactions when his attempt failed (Novick, 1990b). Having him take responsibility for setting the date allowed for the clear emergence of his omnipotent fantasy. Based on his struggle over entering into a termination phase I suggested that "the interminable analysis of adults such as Mr. M. involves the necessity to do what was not done in adolescence—take leave of the omnipotent self, give up the impossible task of magically controlling people and find pleasure in the exercise of real skills in a real world" (p. 22). Near the end of his analysis Mr. M. said, "I don't regret how long it took to get to where I am. I know I could have finished two years ago but then I wasn't where I am now." I would suggest that Mr. M. falls into the category of patients who take a long time to change and to work through conflicts and trauma, especially around issues of independence, change, separation, and termination. Such patients need time and the analyst needs patience and trust. When Freud first turned his attention to the problem of working through he said, "This working through of the resistance in practice may turn out to be an arduous task for the subject of the analysis, and a trial of patience of the analyst" (1914, p. 155). His recommendations to the analyst apply to the pace of material of people like Mr. M. "The doctor has nothing else to do than to wait and let things take their course, a course which cannot be avoided nor always hastened" (p. 155).

After over ten years of analysis what is there left to do during the terminal phase? Having accomplished so much and having finally accepted that the analysis must end, would it be preferable to not prolong the agony and end it quickly, as they used to do, perhaps at the long summer break, with a handshake and a glint in the eye that would indicate that it is all over (Gardiner, 1983)? Mr. M.'s material illustrates the importance of the terminal phase regardless of the time spent before it. If the timing is right (Novick, 1988), if the phase is started not when the goals of analysis have been achieved but when progressive forces are in the ascendant (Novick, 1990a), then the terminal phase can be a most stimulating and fruitful period of work for both analyst and patient. As illustrated by Mr. M.'s material, the reality of an ending date intensifies and revives conflicts and anxieties. At the same time the working alliance is at peak efficiency and both analyst and patient have much more available to resolve conflicts and work through potentially traumatic events. The termination phase is a time when the analytic achievements can be seen and can be tested. A large range of affects can be experienced, owned, and used as a guide and spur to further action. Affects such as disappointment, disillusionment, and sadness are particularly intense during this phase and detailed work on defenses against and working through of these affects allows the patient to endure and grow from the experience. In particular a mourning process sets in, during which the working alliance can be internalized as a self-analytic function, the crowning achievement of the analysis and the main outcome of the work done during the terminal phase of analysis.

21

About Clinical Issues in the Treatment of Primitive States: From Gigolo to Self Realization—The Turning Point

Rudolf Ekstein, Ph.D.

Introduction

Deuten heisst, einen verborgenen Sinn finden.
Sigmund Freud (1900)

FREUD'S (1900) definition of interpretation is: Interpreting means to find a hidden meaning. It is more than twenty years ago that I published *The Nature of the Interpretive Process* (1966) and I was occupied then, as I am now, with clarifying for myself and my readers the concept of interpretation, a poor translation when I thought of the German word *Deutung*. At that time I referred to St. Augustine, who stated in his *Confessions* that he knew what *time* was only as long as nobody asked him (Pusey, 1907). Of course, we must assume that he was then familiar with the usage of the concept of time, although he could not offer a satisfactory definition. I propose then and propose again all these years later, that we might do well to take the same attitude concerning the concept of interpretation. A review of the literature draws our attention to the German word *Deutung* being translated as interpretation, sometimes used in terms of explaining or translating, to expand, to elucidate, and occasionally it is used as a verb, *to construe*. Freud never used the word *interpretation* and we can see from these few examples of the use of the word *interpretation* that we deal here with a diffuse logical climate and therefore we find it difficult to decide whether the word belongs in a scientific or prescientific context.

Freud (1900) seemed closer to prescientific dream interpreters, noting that its origin is prescientific, religious, or superstitious, and subjective in nature. Analytic interpreters show us that which is hidden, that which is unconscious, gives meaning to that which seems to have no meaning otherwise. But we also know that Freud (1900) referred to interpretation as an art and stressed that interpretation is more than mere logical inference. He (Freud, 1900) spoke about the lack of strict rules and brought to our attention the necessity for tact and skill, to "catch the drift of the patient's unconscious with his own unconscious." Artistic intuition, empathy, evenly suspended attention of the analyst, all are used in order to get to the hidden meaning of the patient's communications.

Freud (1900) spoke about psychoanalytic work as comparable to the work of the archaeologist. Others, such as Robert Waelder (1939), spoke about interpretation as detective work. Siegfried Bernfeld (1932) characterizes the interpretive work in terms of putting together the total structure, all the manifestations of the patient, *Gestalt*. They refer to other aspects of the patient's system of defense, attempting to wipe out the clues or the tracks and this work is countered only by the clues, not always being wiped out.

As one follows these metaphors, one will find that they usually lead to certain basic theoretical assumptions, characteristic for the different schools of psychoanalysis or psychotherapy which populate today's marketplace of mental health. In other words, one might well say that the interpretation used not only uncovers something new about the patient, but helps us to throw light on the patient's communications. It helps him, so to speak, see the light, and also throws light on the analyst's way of thinking, his theories, or, in other words, his way of communicating with the patient. It is not only the language of free association and the language of interpretation, but sublanguages as well.

I have suggested in other communications (Ekstein, 1979, 1987), as I will in this communication as well, that one must listen to a patient and say to oneself that his diagnosis is also his way of talking. Furthermore, one can also say that the analyst's, the psychotherapist's way of interpreting, of communicating, of confronting, is seen as the language that he has chosen in order to make contact with the patient. If he has no choice of language, is tied to but one simplified way of speaking, one way of interpreting, must belong to one way of dogmatic thinking, to one special school, he will not be able to fully communicate.

Our field does not present a simple culture, a land, so to speak, with but one language spoken. We speak and hear many languages, many dialects, problems of communication. Can we learn to be multilingual? Can we be free enough to listen to children, adolescents, adults, older persons, to the many different languages related to the various emotional and mental illnesses? Or, are we to be stymied by the lack of spontaneity, the lack of the capacity to adapt ourselves to our patient's needs, his languages?

My communication (1966) begins with a quote of Ludwig Wittgenstein: "I should not like my writing to spare other people the trouble of thinking; but, if possible, to stimulate someone to thoughts of his own."

I refer to my own philosophical education in the *Wiener Kreis*, which never saw philosophy as a closed system, as the only way of thinking, but as an attempt at eternal clarification. Remember then that the treatment which I will describe and discuss is not a final view. Rather it is to illustrate my struggle with this special problem. Every patient offers a special problem which does not permit us to have a technique applicable to all patients.

I suggest to my reader that he read the communication to follow in perhaps the same way that he listens to a play, an unfinished stage production. He might try to live himself into the hero of the story, the patient. Or, he may wish to identify with the analyst, the psycho-therapist. He may follow the process, the back and forth of the dialogue, the spontaneous script that the two of them develop. I hope he will read it with the wish to understand, to read between the lines, and not expect a final solution, but to allow himself to develop, as Wittgenstein suggests, thoughts and methods of his own.

Perhaps, had he been the therapeutic partner of the patient, he would have developed an entirely different scenario, and the two of them would have written a different script. In order to allow such thoughts, critical or supportive, insight giving, or struggling with the resistance of the reader, I have tried to use a number of verbatim hours. It is, of course, difficult to watch a play, a therapeutic dialogue, and not wish quite often to enter the scene. I will use this paper then as a kind of private seminar where the dialogues and the monologues lead to one's own working through of the multitudes of interpretive interventions, the mistakes and the successful moves. Let us move then to the Village Green of the theater and expect the curtain to rise.

Prologue

A European comes to Japan and sends for a Japanese tree expert to have a garden planted. On the first day, the gardener sat on a bench all day long and did not do anything. On the second day, it was the same. And the same on the third, fourth, fifth day—all week long. Then the European asked: "When are you going to get started on the garden?" "When I have taken in the scenery." It is the same with analysis. One first has to take in the scenery of every new psyche [Freud, 1985].

In a communication (Ekstein, 1985), I dealt with the concept of borderline, speaking of it as a borderline concept. I suggested that the borderline patient forces us to new methods of treatment. The patient who fluctuates back and forth between psychoticlike adjustments, borderline adjustments, or neurotic adjustments, demands that we who travel with him help him to acquire an inner passport which will permit him to move from one psychological territory to the other, without being caught in the land of psychoticlike regression. He is then enabled to build a bridge between primary and secondary process thinking. The task then is to follow such a patient, using verbatim hours and the back and forth of the psychoanalytic dialogue, the work of the free associative process, transference development, resistances, and the interpretive attempts of the analyst who tries to throw light on the process. Thus, we help the patient become a master of his inner world, a man with a psychological passport, a border crosser. My own attempt is to allow the reader to put the emphasis on the process, the back and forth, not only to understand the patient, but also the problems of the therapist. He may be guided by insight, and is often misguided by countertransference problems which are not always in the service of empathy. He lives himself into the soul of the patient, but may be led to the kinds of regression which are not in the service of the therapeutic ego but are in the service of the kind of countertransference which serves but therapeutic resistance rather than adaptation to the patient's characteristic ways of dealing with himself, his world and with the analysis. The reader may identify himself with the patient's dilemma or with the therapist's attempt to help. He may put himself in the place of the patient, or the therapist, or perhaps even the therapist's supervisor. As I delve into the material, I will also try to identify with these three functions and thus follow an old advice of Anna Freud (1936). She suggested that the analyst will do best if he keeps himself equidistant from id, superego, and ego. Let us see how he tries to live up to this recommendation, or whether he deals with a patient who is not represented by an equilateral triangle, but perhaps characterized best through the kind of triangle in which the point of gravity changes constantly. He, the analyst, is hardly ever safe and only very rarely has an opportunity to maintain the kind of psychoanalytic situation which allows for equidistance.

Prelude to the Theater

In a previous publication (Ekstein, 1966) dealing with the problem of termination and working through, I compared the analytical process with a stage play. Allow me to share the fantasy with you, and I want you to participate in it, which brings us all to the Village Green of the Globe Theater, the stage of Shakespeare's plays. Before we enter the theater and take our seats, we find ourselves in front of it, waiting for our friends, taking refreshments, and noticing suddenly that all the actors in the play are out there greeting the arriving audience. They are in costume and we recognize some of the actors, the cast of characters. We try to delve into the plot that we are to experience but which is still unknown to us. We hope that we have learned from Freud (1985) that we must first take in the scenery of every new psyche, of all the players, the internal object representations that dominate the patient's inner stage, the play of his life that will soon unfold.

Soon, the players go to the stage door, just as the patient moves out of the waiting room and into the consulting room, his stage, the psychoanalytic couch. We follow and take our seats, being now the audience who expects the play to unfold.

The curtain is still closed and we notice, left and right on the stage, the masks which represent Tragedia and Comedia. We see the pained mask and the smiling mask, the split, the conflict in the patient's life, a view of which we don't know whether the one mask presents the external disguise, the diagnostic picture, or whether perhaps refers to the core self, or vice versa.

I might suggest that I first saw my patient on the Village Green before the real show began.

Actually, Dr. Ben Miller had been known to me some time before his treatment started. I am not quite sure whether the meeting on the Village Green in front of the Globe Theater, although not yet official treatment, was not actually a foreplay of the treatment situation.

My knowledge of Dr. Miller goes back to about 1979 when I helped him and the family assess the needs of his son who was an adolescent suffering from schizophrenia. I saw the boy for several months and attempted a therapeutic program but it turned out that the situation in Dr. Miller's home made it impossible to continue office treatment. The boy had to be hospitalized in one of the residential treatment centers in the East. He has occasional contact with the father but very little contact with the mother who is divorced from Dr. Miller. There is very little contact between the boy and my patient's second wife. I had a second opportunity to help Dr. Miller, namely with his adolescent daughter. She could not live with either the mother or father and stepmother, and finally made an adjustment in the East which was precarious at first but later seemed to succeed quite well.

Thus, about January 1984 a situation developed out of these contacts, both young people being taken care of by their respective therapeutic programs, that necessitated Dr. Miller's pleas to have treatment with me. He felt he was in a desperate situation at that time and I personally experienced all the difficulties one has, having been on the Village Green and having gotten to know a number of other members of the family. I played with the idea of being their therapist, having known some of Dr. Miller's circle of people quite well, the cast of characters who were to dominate the scene, not only on the Village Green but also on the psychoanalytic stage as well. In other words, I said "yes," I would accept him and the treatment began. From the beginning there was a fluctuating quality of contact that did not permit me to decide whether psychoanalysis, intensive psychotherapy, or, at times, of a compassionate support system would succeed. Even his behavior in the hour expressed these therapeutic fluctuations of the role he wanted to play, and did not quite allow me to establish a therapeutic situation in such a way that he could be truly thought of as a psychoanalytic patient.

But first, a few words about him. He is a cardiac surgeon, extremely skilled and knowledgeable, working as a private practitioner in one of the larger hospitals in our city. When he came for treatment, he suffered from acute anxiety states, an extremely troubled marriage, his third marriage. His anxiety states, fear of the operating room, worries about his colleague, and his marriage, coupled with suicidal fantasies, also expressed themselves in the way he used the couch. Sometimes he would lie down but often he would sit up. Occasionally, his beeper would signal and he would jump up and run to the telephone. Then an unbelievable change of personality would take place. He spoke on the telephone and one suddenly had the impression that the patient, tortured by suicidal thoughts, with shame and disgust for himself (associations one could hardly follow because they often seemed nearer the primary process than the kind of material that one gets in conventional psychoanalysis), changed now and became the perfect physician. Every response on the telephone was adequate, whether he spoke to a nurse about a dangerous treatment situation, a colleague, his patient, or the relative of his patient. I can best describe it by saying that if I were to need his services, measuring his competence from these telephone contacts, I would have no doubts and use him. I found two personalities, not only the sick patient, but also the professional specialist who had been able to develop his professional self and become an expert. But that was not the feeling he had about himself. He often despaired about his work, felt he had no friends and lived in a terrible marital situation.

Which mask was I to believe? The mask of the perfect specialist and surgeon or the mask of the gigolo that he was in his private life? He fluctuated back and forth and one never knew what was the core and what was the mask. What is the defense and what is the true self? I almost felt that he dictated to one the kind of treatment he would need at any given moment, fluctuating between these extreme positions.

A few things must be said, of course, about his past. He grew up in the East with fairly well-to-do parents. His father was a physician, his mother a strong woman who did not mind if he had the one or the other professional or scientific goal, but also constantly preached that it was more important for him to go into the kind of profession which would allow him to marry a rich woman. He was to become a doctor or a lawyer. He would go to this or that university. The only thing that counted was his finding an opportunity to meet a rich woman. She herself was dissatisfied with her husband because he did not allow her the standard of living that she aspired to. Now it was the son, Dr. Miller, who was to make up for it. He was tortured and allowed the mother to win. The kinds of aspirations that he had as a young man were to drive expensive cars, sail, participate in the activities of rich people. But at the same time, he felt pained at the fact that he was literally not allowed to follow his heart's inclination, to choose a girl that he could love because whoever she was she had to be stone rich, had to have rich parents. His struggle then was between the position of the gigolo and his wish to accomplish something of himself in life, achieve independence, contribute to science and to medicine.

At that time the gigolo, the playboy, succeeded. He married a woman whose parents belonged to the richest families, a woman who, like his mother, had power over him, not only in terms of money but in the kind of experience that made her literally into his teacher when it came to sexual activity. She truly dominated him, a tragic person herself, and neither of them could manage the marriage even though they had four children (two of whom I described, and two others, young men who are presently in college).

The marriage ended in divorce and was followed by endless legal struggles that he could not really win. The divorce created a wall of hostility between him, his wife, and their parents. It brought him face to face with the constant demand of his own family that he apologize and keep the marriage intact. The children went where the gold was. Only the daughter mentioned earlier escaped and wanted to live with him. She could not stand the hostility of the mother who herself was involved with another woman in a lesbian relationship. The second marriage was similar, again a rich woman. Finally, a third marriage of the same type, which is of concern to us now. His colleagues all thought of him as the man who always looked for rich women, who lived off these rich women or off the money of their relatives. He tried to free himself from it, felt the pressure of his mother, his sister, all of them hoping that would pump the financial wealth of the in-laws in order to allow the family to benefit from the gold of the rich. But instead of becoming King Midas who turned whatever he touched into gold, a kind of modern fetish of "the more dollars the better," he was pursued by anxiety, by outbreaks of sweating when he was working, and by suicidal thoughts. That was the situation in which he found himself, a man without friends, with deep anxiety, depressive states, yearning for the advantages of wealth, but with an even deeper longing to master life.

We are ready to move now from the Village Green, the meeting of the characters who populate his social and his inner world, into the consulting room, the stage of the analysis, paraphrasing Shakespeare by saying that "all of psychoanalysis is but a play and we are only players." Now we move with him into the play, as an analyst must, at a time when he will be in the patient's mind, one of the actors during the development of the transference, one of the different people of the patient's inner life. Let us study one of these hours which can best be characterized as the opportunity for a turning point, a time where there must be a clash between the gigolo and the task of self-realization. Is the gigolo the true character, the man who hunts rich women and then becomes their passive victim? Or, is it the talented physician who may be able to move beyond the infantile position and struggle, ceaselessly struggle, toward the independent, mature self? Or, will the child remain forever the father of the man? Or will the man be capable of achieving an adult role?

First Part of the Tragedy

In the beginning of the analysis a desperate man, hounded by thoughts of suicide, depression, deep anxiety states, outbreaks of sweating in the operating room, tried to save himself and run away from the position of the gigolo. For hours he could be found in the library studying, going to lectures, spending endless time in the hospital morgue dissecting cadavers, studying the heart, trying to perfect himself as he worked with arteries, veins, by-passes, trying to regain strength, new information, self-esteem, and knowledge. But it also alienated him from his marriage, the rich life, and the endless encounters with temptation. Slowly, as he identified with the analytical work and supported by the analyst, he withstood these temptations. For example, his father-in-law invited the whole group of families and friends on a cruise to the Mediterranean, the Near East or to the Orient. At first he promised that he would go along. He wanted to meet the high and mighty and to enjoy that pleasant experience. But at the last moment, moved by the wish to work, to overcome his difficulties and by the increasing power of the developing transference, he canceled the trip or said that he would only go for part of the trip. He wanted to continue the analysis and begin his work as a physician, a surgeon, in earnest. Endless struggles developed between him and his wife. But it was more than that. Both of them had children from their first marriages. His wife, Gloria Rich, had brought up her children without their father. Her first husband died, suiciding after a deep depression. She did her best and wanted to give her two daughters as much time as possible. He, too, wanted to be a good father and take care of his children, wanted them to feel at home in the new house in the Canyon, and the conflict began. Gloria did not want the sick boy, by whom she felt threatened, to come. She wanted to spend most of the time with her own children. She found that his children, when they visited, misused the privilege of being in her home, that she, so she felt, allowed her husband to use. From time to time, her rich father would invite the family on these various cruises chartering a boat for the family. Dr. Miller was always tempted to go but at the same time struggled with the wish of building up his practice, to please his partner and colleague, Martin, and to be faithful to his patients as well as to continue with his analysis. Gloria wanted interruptions, saw the analysis as an obstacle to their being together, and felt that either drugs and/or group psychotherapy rather than psychoanalysis would be preferable for him. She felt that he was in bad hands, that he should stop the analysis, and she interfered whenever she could. They also had some marital counseling, fortunately with a colleague who was an analyst and understood the situation. He did not undermine the work that was to be done here. But nevertheless, at the time the work was carried on, accompanied by so much acting out by every family member, I occasionally felt like my analytical colleagues in London in the days of the Second World War during the Blitz. I was in an almost impossible position, trying to stay with the inner conflict when it was outer conflict that threatened life and any form of safety, any capacity and opportunity for reflection. At times, the struggles were so bad that she told him to leave the house, once or twice she herself left the home and stayed elsewhere overnight. Occasionally, he would take a hotel room or go to the beach, and later rented a small apartment near the ocean and it seemed that the marriage had come to an end. But there was also the yearning for the good days, a belief in his love for her, but the struggle did not seem to cease. She accused him of lack of sexual interest, and in rages scratched his face bloody, leaving marks to be seen by all, spit at his body, his genitals, as if to say that she despised him. The struggle went on within him between the image of the despised gigolo and the one of the proud man who aspired to be a good physician. Thus, it was as if the whole treatment situation moved from the consulting room, from the couch into the external world. Could one think of an exciting drama, a stage, where suddenly the intermission allowed all to go out to the Village Green and to wait there for the next act? But then, could the moment come when the actors also emerge and turn the bloody contest of the drama and play into real action?

I will move away from the plays of Shakespeare to the plays of Bert Brecht, who wanted the audience to participate, and carry the protest of the play into the street.

But it was also during that time that the violent action turned into insight concerning the meaning of that action.

The verbatim parts of the hours of that time bring to life the analytical events.

Dr. Miller, in that hour, is desperate and depressed and whatever he says is self-accusation, the voice of the punitive superego, the voice of despair, and the voice of self-condemnation. The analyst does not suppress the voice of condemnation but tries to help the patient to see that his self-accusations are disguised insight. The self-accusation is in the service of insight on the one side, but on the other side a kind of self-accusation which tries to keep the insight repressed, and to replace it with helplessness, the desire to give up, the hopelessness and, of course, also the struggle against the analyst. It is as if to say that he, the analyst, cannot help him, that he would need to do all he could in order to return to the source of support, the mother, the wife, the money of the in-laws, the life of the gigolo. Sections of the hour go as follows:

Dr. Miller: You know, Rudi, what I was thinking of since I left here, is that one of the interesting things in my life and the one thing which I feel that is the most related to the relative failure of my practice, is the sense that I had to go outside of the normal referral pattern to establish a base in my practice, is that at no time in my lifetime did I make meaningful, lasting relationships. There were people that I used, but I never, I'm talking about in grammar school, in high school, I don't have a single friend from college. I had roommates I was friendly with for a brief while and then we went our separate ways. Umm, medical school, no friendships. Residency, no friendships.

Dr. E.:   Was this your wish or do you think you yearned for friendships but could not develop them?

Dr. Miller: I think that I was so aggressive in terms of wanting something other than what I was doing, wanting to be in a world beyond my world, and that I was really only partially in my world and looking beyond it. Then sometimes, say when I talk, looking around the room or something, and I think that one of the reasons that I really decided to go back with Gloria is that Gloria was quite distraught over my leaving her, in spite of, and let's assume that everything I say it was all her fault, partially her fault, she was a little neurotic, whatever, but one of the things that interested me is that if there's been a recurring pattern in my life, it's been one of not being able to establish a relationship with anybody within my family, outside of my family, in my first marriage, during my residency, in my high school and I can give you all types of excuses that could even have some partial validity to them.

Dr. E.: But you mean the fact remains that you did not make friends?

Dr. Miller: Right.

Dr. E.: My thought was for a moment, that there are some people who need to be by themselves.

Dr. Miller: No, I don't think that was it, Rudi.

Dr. E.: What was your deeper goal?

Dr. Miller: I think my deeper goal was social climbing and then . . .

Dr. E.: You mean to just use friends to climb . . . ?

Dr. Miller: To get somewhere. Do you know what I'm saying?

Dr. E.: Yes, I certainly know.

Dr. Miller: Right. And I think that I was always using someone as a rung up the ladder. That is, use them, get rid of them, and go to the next person. And I don't think I ever really did anything for someone where I didn't expect to get something back in return. And with big dividends.

Dr. E.: In other words, you would try to get to know someone, not so much because you needed a friend, but he was a piece of the ladder?

Dr. Miller: Absolutely. And . . .

Dr. E.: But where does that end? You know, I mean, how high can a ladder go?

Dr. Miller: Well, I think that at age forty-eight, you find yourself having almost nothing but very, very superficial relationships and I would be different if I was a loner or someone who liked to be alone. But that really isn't me. I rather enjoy people, but I think I have been so aggressively . . .

Dr. E.: But obviously the purpose in mind is to use them.

Dr. Miller: Absolutely.

Dr. E.: That's sort of what you might have called in the past sort of the complex to use them, such as when you speak about reaching the rich woman or the rich situation, where then something, however, very strange happens, because how can a user become a gigolo? I mean I can

	think of a powerful president of the United States who is known to have used people around him for political ambitions, but nevertheless he is not a gigolo. And that second part I don't understand, how that fits.
Dr. Miller:	Well, I think I wanted to gain friendships to find a soft spot for myself, so that I could use other people's achievements and rest easy. I think that was really the basis, to a certain extent, for my relationship with my office partner, Martin, part of it was my admiration of his work, but you know, one of the reasons when I look back and think that I should have been happy. I wasn't that happy, but what I was aware of is that the real, basic gist, the frustration that Gloria feels toward me, has such a repetitive tone to it, notwithstanding everything that Gloria might be doing is wrong, let's say all that's a give up, I'm concerned about something different from that. I'm really concerned about my total lack of relationships from age five to forty-eight.
Dr. E.:	Except the one to use others.
Dr. Miller:	Right. Whoever, at the moment, is someone I'm using.
Dr. E.:	Useful to you.
Dr. Miller:	I have absolutely no relationships with anybody. And I would say that Martin and I are going to split up as partners in January and I think that it's been . . .
Dr. E.:	Years of using him . . .
Dr. Miller:	Many years of using him and one might even say that at a time when he rarely needed to use me, and even though I felt he was through with me, *I* really broke off the relationship. Umm, but more important than that, I mean I can remember when I was in high school, I'd be afraid to be with girls or guys who weren't rich because I wanted to climb, I never, ever had in mind what I was doing. It was always on who was out there that could advance me.
Dr. E.:	Toward what?
Dr. Miller:	Toward being really a playboy. I really, when I look at it, my real goal was to marry a very rich person and take over the family business.
Dr. E.:	So you could play.

Dr. Miller:	Pretty much.
Dr. E.:	So you became ...
Dr. Miller:	No, I think I wanted to be a very rich businessman, really, and I thought that if I could take over somebody's business, that then I could get the feeling that I could verbally impress people, make a first impression, and by the time they were aware of what I would have done, I would have taken care of them too. And taken what they had. I think I wanted to be a crook. I wanted to steal. I was afraid to steal but I think that's what I really wanted to do.
Dr. E.:	Sort of legal ways of doing business and getting more money.
Dr. Miller:	Right. A white collar crook. And it's interesting because I am very, very critical of anybody who does anything that isn't very ethical or moral, but really my basic desire was to cheat and steal.
Dr. E.:	And what drove you then, in spite of all, into the profession of a doctor? A heart surgeon.
Dr. Miller:	So that I could marry a rich girl and take over her family's business. That's really true. So that's ...
Dr. E.:	So that was just a sideshow to impress her?
Dr. Miller:	That's right.
Dr. E.:	And in that way get to the money.
Dr. Miller:	Sure. As a matter of fact, when I was married to Susie and we were at med school, I really wanted to drop out of that school and go to law school but I was afraid that then the Richmonds wouldn't let me stay, that they wanted a doctor, and then when Susie's brother committed suicide I thought now they're going to ask me to take over the family business. What a stroke of luck and I felt so awful because I'd been very envious of her brother and now he'd gotten himself out of the way by killing himself. And I really, really thought now I'm going to be the head of the Richmond Foundation. I used to read the paper and I'd see that there was the one in the family and the other and the son-in-law was the one to be the head man. And I thought I would be the president of the organization. And it was as though it

was a dream come true. That was what my life's work had been. And I think I was terribly disappointed when that didn't work out. And I think I was very, very angry at Susie and the Richmonds that it didn't work out. But I really didn't have at that time in my life a thought of being a doctor, but more than that, Rudi, when I was in high school I really hadn't thought of being a high school student.

Dr. E.:   So what you're really saying to be a student or to become a doctor was almost like camouflage.

Dr. Miller: It was a camouflage. I mean it was absolutely, it was more than a subconscious thing, Rudi. It was openly talked about between my mother and myself.

Dr. E.:   Your mother spoke openly about it?

Dr. Miller: Oh, absolutely.

Dr. E.:   But then you started to stand up against mother and in spite of your wish to be a gigolo who uses people, you became a competent physician, who suddenly started out on a new track, namely . . .

Dr. Miller: Rudi, I don't agree with what you're saying. I can tell you truthfully now, I mean, you know again, and I remember Ralph Greenson's book when he said when someone says "really" he doesn't mean "really," but to my way of thinking, I have never considered myself a doctor and I will tell you why. Umm, I always was afraid that I would hurt a patient. I always felt there were people who were better than I was and I really always felt that I was in the wrong profession. But I happen to like being a doctor.

Dr. E.:   Then you spoke about that very often.

Dr. Miller: Right.

Dr. E.:   I say in addition to feeling you are in the wrong profession and you do that only as camouflage, you also, at least since you were working with me, went down to the morgue to study the corpses, to study the heart, read the books. How does that suddenly come? Because it is so much of a contradiction to the rest of what you feel and think.

Dr. Miller: Well, I went there because I felt that I was incompetent

	really. And when I got there, a great deal of the area that I felt incompetent has been diminished. I really know a great deal more about the heart itself. I still sweat thinking about operating on it, but I must tell you, Rudi, that my fear of being incompetent was justified. You see, I'm not . . . I know you're going to say flip-flop, I'm not. There is a consistency in what . . .
Dr. E.:	No, please, I don't speak about flip-flop. I speak about the struggle between two positions. I am an incompetent gigolo, I am a doctor only for camouflage but . . .
Dr. Miller:	Oh, no, no, no, no. Wait a minute, time out. You misunderstand. When I started out in my twenties, I was a doctor in camouflage. I promise you that.
Dr. E.:	Right.
Dr. Miller:	That is . . .
Dr. E.:	Clear.
Dr. Miller:	Clear. Clear, to me, at least. My basic goal was to become the head of Richmond Foundation. That was my goal. And when Susie's brother committed suicide, I thought that my goal had been realized. I continued, I was very interested in psychiatry, I continued in surgery because the Richmonds didn't like psychiatrists, but I really thought at some point I would be out of surgery. And I liked studying the acute abdomen and it wasn't that hard. You don't have to be that smart as a surgeon. It was only really much, much later that I began to realize that I was really gonna have to be a doctor. And as a matter of fact, it was midway through my surgery residency when I nearly quit and went into business. When I came in to see you I, the only thing I really had was surgery and then I really wasn't a surgeon, I didn't have a practice of any sort, I was really living off Martin, and that it was going to have to be organized pretty soon or my camouflage was gonna be over. And that's when I did all this work and I feel now that my fears of incompetence are no longer justified. I really feel now that I'm intellectually up to doing the work.
Dr. E.:	But the point that I want to make is it slowly became a conflict between two wishes. One: I use the camouflage

to be with the rich woman because mother wants me to and the other was out of the camouflage of the doctor who uses that as a kind of trick suddenly became a desire more and more to be competent, and now the man who wants to be competent as a professional person and the other one who wants to take over the Richmond Foundation, etc., are in conflict with each other.

Dr. Miller: Yeah. I think that that may be true but I don't see it that way. I see that the conflict I feel that I've resolved. And I feel comfortable with the idea that I like to be a doctor. O.K.? And also I feel comfortable with the idea that I'm now at a point where my training has really been reasonably full and I'm competent to start a practice.

Dr. E.: What's then left over of the old?

Dr. Miller: O.K. What's left over of the old and what I feel is really the last phase of my analysis that I feel is tremendously important is that what is separating me now from a reasonably good practice, and I think I'll have a reasonably good practice, is not people's opinion of me as being competent or not. The camouflage I did was reasonably good so that even when I really didn't know what the hell the heart looked like, people thought I was smarter than what I was. But, people never liked me. They felt that I had airs, I was above them, they felt that I was rich enough that they didn't have to send me patients, whatever. But there are certainly many, many doctors, Rudi, who married heiresses and who've been very, very successful as doctors, so that's a very lame excuse. Something that I do, that I've done all my life, that's made it so I haven't made friendships. Basically, most people, it would be wrong to say they don't like me, they're just not comfortable with me. And most people would feel that I was aggressive, that I tend to take over, that I don't listen, I talk a lot.

Dr. E.: Tell me, is it possible to make friends when they perhaps sense the old unconscious desire to just use them?

Dr. Miller: Well, I don't think it is, that's part of the problem and I think that that requires demonstrations over a period of time that you're really not trying to use them and I think that one of the reasons that I went back with Gloria, quite frankly, was that it seemed to me that a significant part of my problem with Gloria was really related to the sense of frustration that I personally have with my career and with my frustration with what I have or have not accomplished. I've really sat and thought to myself on Friday, if I were successful in heart surgery and had a practice that I would like to have, would some of the things which Gloria does upset me, and I was aware that I don't think they would. I wouldn't be so dependent on her praise or lack of praise. And I'm very much aware, Rudi, that if you do the rounds, that the people who don't refer to me, it isn't because they don't think I'm capable, they don't like me, they're not comfortable with me is better. They don't feel at one with me, and it's interesting because a lot of doctors, Rudi, are snobs, do you know what I'm saying? It's not like doctors have good practices are such wonderful nice guys.

Dr. E.:	Why do you think they don't like you?
Dr. Miller:	I think they feel I'm using them.
Dr. E.:	Excuse me?
Dr. Miller:	I think they recognize that I use people and have used people.
Dr. E.:	Then that's the problem then that one must overcome?
Dr. Miller:	Well, I think one that I need to understand. I'm not certain that what I'm saying is correct, you know what I'm saying? But I know that something in terms of my, I think it's unusual for a person to be my age and to not have a single friend. I think that's unusual.
Dr. E.:	Only shallow acquaintances.
Dr. Miller:	That's right.
Dr. E.:	That might turn into friendships but are not now.
Dr. Miller:	That's right. I mean, I know what I mean by the difference and I, you understand what I'm saying. It isn't that there aren't a lot of people who I know to say hello to, etc., but there's nobody . . . I can understand that someone like Gloria may have a multiple group of people who consider themselves friends and that may not really be true friendship also, but Gloria does have one

	or two people who are very special in her life. I don't have any. The closest thing I have to a friendship is Martin. I think that's very unusual.
Dr. E.:	Sort of like a second father to you.
Dr. Miller:	Right. I think it's unusual that outside of that there is nobody that I have a close enough relationship with to talk to, to feel comfortable with, to exchange ideas with, nobody, I mean, I remember when, you know, I went through Harvard. I mean my daughter has a couple of friends from Harvard, I have none Rudi. Zero.
Dr. E.:	And you are always striving for the external success, that is, you try to fulfill the demands of your mother, not of your father.
Dr. Miller:	Well, the whole time at Harvard, rather than engaging in what was going on at Harvard, everything I did was in terms of how I could get a rich woman, this business, this business I could take over, and I think that everything that I've always done has been separate from my work. I mean, just like right now I was saying to Gloria, we have to go away in December to this Worker's Compensation meeting in Hawaii and I want to go because I want to see if I could meet the people and become friendly with them and I'm certain, in a sense that I use them because I would like them to refer to me, but there's another thing. I'd like to mix with the people that I'm working with and not feel above them and get involved with them. And sort of enjoy the Worker's Compensation area, maybe that's all intellectually that I'm capable of doing. I just want to be involved in something, I want to really taste life a little bit.
Dr. E.:	What keeps you from that? Because, you know for some people that may sound like an easy obligation, an easy task.
Dr. Miller:	Well, I think that what is keeping me from it, Rudi, is that all of my life I really wanted to be super rich, I want to be part of the jet set. I was never satisfied with what I had. I wanted what other people had and I think now, just like you were asking me, was I going on this trip to patch up my marriage? No. No. I'm going on this trip

because I'm a little tired and I've always loved driving and seeing things. I've never seen this part of the southwest and I want to take a drive, it's the last trip I'll be able to take where my partner will be doing the work and I'll be earning while I'm gone. Beginning January 1, we'll be separate and I want to enjoy this trip for the trip's sake. I'm ready to stop for a little while. I think I see what I have ahead of me. I'll be having a lot of trips, business trips. I'll be going December 26 for a week on a Worker's Compensation thing, I'm gonna go away the first week of March for a medical fraternity and I want to mix with the people who are my colleagues. Not just to get them to refer to me but I'd like to be part of the group now. I want to mix with them, I want to be with them. And then when I get back I'll be home a week and I want to go to a meeting in Hawaii on the heart where there are people coming in, they don't want me to present a paper, but I want to talk to them. I want to meet them. And so I'm sort of taking this trip to take a break now. It's been a long and an exhausting year.

Dr. E.:   And what then do you hope to accomplish after the break?

Dr. Miller: After the break, Rudi, I hope to really get down to work and get some surgery going, working again on the heart, my mind, you know it's a little bit tired, not emotionally, I just want to see some trees and some fresh air for a while. What I hope to do is more of the same and I'm really focusing in on the heart now, really, really focusing in and there's two things I want to do. I want to focus on my work, I want to go in there and sweat in that operating room. You know, you've heard the doctors say how he was operating on the guy and told him how he sweated during the operation. And I want to sweat in there. And the other thing I want to do is that I'd like not just to make friendships, but I want to meet some doctor friends and I want to know them, I want to know them, I want to be part of the community. I never have been. I don't want to be afraid to live in the world I'm in. I don't want to feel that I have to be rich. I want to live in my world. And I want to spend a little bit of time trying to understand, more important to me than building up my practice at this point, is that I've done that work now. Well, the practice should begin to develop. I was afraid I didn't have the knowledge to develop that practice. The real problem that I have now is in relating to people. That's been the problem all my life.

Dr. E.:   Of course, that also includes then the marital situation itself.

Dr. Miller: Yes it does. But I really consider the marital situation as a symptom of the general problem. Do you know what I'm saying, Rudi?

Dr. E.:   Yes, it's quite clear to me. That I just use my wife instead of being a friend of hers.

Dr. Miller: Exactly. In other words, because of the closeness of the relationship in a marriage, her feelings are an intensity of what the general public friendships feel. They just magnify.

Dr. E.:   She would feel neglected and used.

Dr. Miller: Exactly what people would say who come near. Do you understand what I'm saying, Rudi?

Dr. E.:   Yes. Neglected and used.

Dr. Miller: Exactly. So, I mean, even though I can come in here and I can point out to you what you're doing may be wrong and how neurotic, and all those things, all that has validity. But, there's another side to it and that is that what she's saying is the same thing that everybody else says about me, except with greater feeling. That greater feeling may be a sense of frustration on her part and so I've sort of had a feeling that what I want to do is to try and understand what it is that makes me literally use people. But I'm also a very giving person so it's a very ambivalent situation. Do you know what I'm saying, Rudi? It's not like I use and use. I'm working very hard. Well, as long as you're working very hard, why do you have to use people so much? And I really think . . .

Dr. E.:   It's only the gigolo who has to use people. The competent doctor who realized his professional ambition doesn't have to.

Dr. Miller:	Right. And I feel that part of my using people has been my frustration at my incompetence or my lack of success. But it's a vicious circle because the one may be causing the other. It goes round and round. Do you know what I'm saying, Rudi? It seems to me, I can remember in high school, that when I first got out of high school I was made an officer of the class and then when the class was all assembled and we came from different grammer schools, I never won any election where people knew me. Never. I would be acquainted with them by teachers but never won an election. And when I got to Harvard, I had interviews and I knew that I would be selected into the freshman governing body, the freshman council, and I was. But I couldn't get myself elected to office. Ever. There's something . . .
Dr. E.:	Sort of like an appointed by the rich but not elected by the nonrich.
Dr. Miller:	Not so much that. It was always that my first impression, people's first impression of me was always that he's knowledgeable, he's attractive, he's bright, he knows what he's doing, he speaks well, he's great. But when they got to know me they didn't like me. And I always felt that I was sort of a lot of hot air.
Dr. E.:	For your own purposes but not for friendship.
Dr. Miller:	Right. A user.
Dr. E.:	But struggle then became later when you struggled between being a user and being a contributor to society.
Dr. Miller:	Right. But I sort of have a feeling that's really the reason that it's characteristic of this thing with Gloria is that I have a feeling that part of the problem that I have with Gloria is that same problem that I have in relating to everybody. And that's got to be analyzed.
Dr. E.:	That is the task of the analysis.
Dr. Miller:	Yes.
Dr. E.:	What are you doing with Gloria so that she feels used and misused while you want to have a relationship that would be true love and true friendship.
Dr. Miller:	And Rudi, you know, where I didn't develop friend-

ships in my former life, I really was trying to use people. Now, I suppose, in a sense, I think when I first met Gloria, I may well have been wanting to use her. But as I came to you, I really tried hard to reverse that. To make it so that she would feel that I was supportive of her. But I did use Gloria to help me with my daughter, to help me with my son. A lot of things. But I'm, I must tell you, Rudi I am not as concerned about my marriage as I am that if you gave a thousand people who have known me, a hundred people, fifty people, ten, three, five, any number, multiple choices, ask if I was dumb, brilliant, superbright, they'd mark down I was bright. If you ask them if I speak well, they'd say I could speak well. If you ask them attractive, they'd say attractive. If you ask them if I was a good friend, they'd say "no." If you ask them if I was a user, they'd say "yes." And that would include Gloria, that would include everybody who has known me. Now, I think that for a long time, I was a user. I really think I've tried not to be. And I think that I've slowly overcome that. But I think a great deal of my problem is that I don't know how to relate to people, to have relationships. Like Gloria said to me, you know you want people to like you so much that when you come on you come on so strong then you get tired and then you just drop them. Why don't you just be you? People would like you. You're so afraid they won't like you. I can feel what she's saying because I have done that.

Dr. E.: Well, it would be, if one is too self loving, one cannot love other people. If one is only for one's own goal, like money or cars, one cannot love other people. It's sort of a struggle between narcissism and the capacity to love. A self without objects, without people. (long pause)

Dr. Miller: To me that's the biggest flaw in my life. Right now.

Dr. E.: It's a flaw that you sound as if you really work on it and change it.

Dr. Miller: To me I think it's most important.

Dr. E.: And you wonder whether you can.

Dr. Miller: No. I think I can if I really put my mind to it.

Dr. E.: And your heart and soul. The mind alone doesn't do it.

Because that becomes calculated. (Very long pause here) . . . Here you have a true agenda.

Dr. Miller: It's funny, you know Rudi, because sometimes in the last year or so, I'll lie in bed and I'll think to myself, you know, there are a lot of people, men and women, that I avoided my feelings with because I wanted to concentrate on getting ahead. And when I look back on it, I'm very much aware that I could have accomplished the same thing in terms of my position in life, no matter whom I'd married because I'm heavily in debt and I must work to earn a living. But it really doesn't make any difference who I'm married to in terms of the work I'm doing. I really felt I had to marry someone so I could have the family business, but I could have gone right on with medical school, married whoever my childhood sweetheart was, and really could not have come out materially, financially worse off. I might have been better off, I might have had a more pleasant life, and I think that I feel a tremendous amount of anger about that. But I think there is something else that I feel at this point. And that is once you come to that awareness, there's nothing to say that at this point, as long as I'm aware of that, that I can't live now. You know what I'm saying, Rudi? It's not like . . .

Dr. E.: Well, it's sort of a bit as if you were guided in the past to express it in a rough way, by greed. And you want to be guided by love and competence.

Dr. Miller: Right. I just sort of feel like okay, now let's get on the road. And I don't think that leaving Gloria would have been anything more, quite frankly, than having found that Gloria doesn't serve a particular useful function to me.

Dr. E.: In other words, she doesn't serve the greed and the love, for a while that was not that important.

Dr. Miller: Right. Therefore, I could get along without.

Dr. E.: But then you would be without love and without support.

Dr. Miller: Right. But what I also saw, was I saw how hopelessly unhappy Gloria also was. And it seemed to me that

	what I was missing was I had organized her now, with seeing a therapist, but I *had* married her, she had made a choice to marry me. We do have the potential of a good life and I had to think a little bit, Rudi, that part of my anger that I've expressed here, was that gosh when I had to sell my Mercedes, they did nothing to help me.
Dr. E.:	Right. But that was the old self.
Dr. Miller:	Right. But it caused me a lot of anger.
Dr. E.:	And not the new self, that could mobilize her love and interest.
Dr. Miller:	Right. And so it seems to me that if I'm really sincere in wanting to stop using people . . .
Dr. E.:	The time has come.
Dr. Miller:	The time has come and I'm a little bit concerned that part of my anger at Gloria was due to my anger that she wasn't permitting me, she wasn't giving me what I wanted, I had to work. You understand what I'm saying?
Dr. E.:	Right. The old self, for a moment, was in danger of winning and the new self might have lost.
Dr. Miller:	And that's when all of a sudden, I said: wait a minute, wait a minute, there's something, I hear a familiar song. I can get along without her, she isn't, look I'm driving a Honda, I can't drive much less. I found a place at the beach, I can stay there without her, I can do this work, I don't need Gloria to do the work. Well, wait, maybe she's nice to some of my friends, maybe she makes things nice, you know. All of a sudden, I really thought to myself, I've never had any friends. My relationships have always ended up like what's going on here with Gloria. How, would it be possible for me to become Gloria's friend and if I could become her friend, would it translate into other areas? You know what I'm saying, Rudi?
Dr. E.:	That would be the burial of the gigolo.
Dr. Miller:	Exactly. That's really what suddenly came into my head. If I can become Gloria's friend, and Gloria now feels about me the way everybody else does, if I can turn her around I can turn them around. And the difference in

now and before is that now I have been resigned to "failure," I don't necessarily mean by failure, I don't feel I'm a failure, but I mean that I'm done worrying if I'm going to be a rich man. Okay? To be rich in what I'm capable of doing.

Dr. E.:   You can now change into inner richness rather than an external richness.

Dr. Miller: And what I'd like to do now is that while it could happen that if Gloria became my friend, and the other doctors became my friends, that I might prosper inside as well as out, I really am doing, and again Ralph Greenson says we say "really," that it's a lie, you don't really mean what you say.

Dr. E.:   I'm glad you remember that quote of his.

Dr. Miller: I remember it so much because it always bothers me when I say "really," but it strikes me that at least what I'm interested in right now, my goal is, is that I've been so successful being such a user, I wonder at least if I wouldn't be happier making some relationships. And if it happens that I become successful financially, wonderful, but I'm already at a point now where I've given up the *myth* of being successful financially. I'd like to be successful, happy.

Dr. E.:   Well, what can one say but, "join you."

Dr. Miller: Well, it's interesting, you know, I really feel like Gloria is a good experiment in that area. She right, hurt, exaggerated. But it may be exaggerated because Gloria, because of all types of things that come up.

Dr. E.:   Maybe she provoked you the right way.

Dr. Miller: It could be. But it could also, I really, I see the challenge that I see in my analysis directly related, that Gloria, the problem I'm having with Gloria, the core problem is so similar together, that I'm interested in. . . .

Dr. E.:   It's just a replay of the past, but we want now a different ending. See you tomorrow.

Dr. Miller: At 9:00.

We see in this session the move from self accusation to insight, from desperate and self-destructive inactivity to action. Can we now speak of adaptation? Or, should we speak about repetition, the compulsion to repeat?

There is again the idea of proving that he can take care of things, as things go better in his life, to invite them all, the entire family to go to Hawaii at his expense. Is he trying to say to them that he doesn't want to be taken care of, he can take care of them? And does he try to use the trip to make serious contacts with colleagues, a convention taking place which will allow him to build up his practice? Does he still hope, as he hints somewhere, that the father-in-law will pay for the trip, that perhaps some birthday he will get an expensive car for the one that he had to give up in order to pay for his son's college expenses? Or, does he really mean it? Does he still play with the fantasies of the gigolo, or, can we speak about a turning point? The danger of the analyst's work consists of the possibility that he may be tempted to take sides in the battle between the gigolo and the competent physician. But can he really avoid that? And is it not true that the patient identifies with his analyst, and now relies on the kind of working alliance where both work on a goal that they have recognized together as one that the patient really wants? But does the patient want that goal? Or, does regression not force him to go back to the days where mother's breast, the gold of the rich women are to allow him the kind of life that mother wants him to become accustomed to? Will he identify with the weak father who could not satisfy the mother? Will he see the rich fathers-in-law as those who will feed him, his dreams and his expectations? Or, can he identify with the task of analysis? That is, to bury the gigolo, to bury the childhood and to move on?

The Second Part of the Tragedy

A few weeks later, Dr. Miller finds himself in a new predicament. His external tragedies never end and his internal response to these tragedies brings the analytical work to a new phase. He had seen the ability to restore somewhat his situation with the mother as a goal of his analytical work. At the beginning of the analysis, he tried to separate from her, tried to be independent, live on his own, and not allow her to make him into a gigolo. He should supply the funding, the money that would make his life rich and beautiful, a life of play, a life of the very rich. He had severed the bond with his mother fairly well, having made clear what he wanted, and that he needed some distance. But he also wanted her love, not as a gigolo, but as a doctor who has succeeded, who does not need the rich woman, who can be helpful. He promised to pay for an improved apartment for mother, now in her early eighties. She responded to this happily and moved into this Fifth Avenue apartment overlooking Central Park. But there are new problems. She has serious heart symptoms, and he begins to fear for her as he did very often in the past. Was it a wish to get rid of her, to see her dead? Or, was it the realistic fear of her condition? She might die, she might need him, and he would want to have her love, her recognition of him, her acceptance of his change. But he also wants that from all the other people in his life, including the father-in-law, his wife Gloria, his children, his friends and colleagues. He no longer wants to be the fortune hunter and he wonders whether he can convince the world that he is different. But can he convince himself that he is different? Or, does he only play up to my expectations, the analyst? Are they truly his expectations? Is he identified with me? Or, is he still the pretender whom he despises?

Hour after hour is filled with preoccupation, the money, the gold, the income, the question of whether he can ever make it, namely the gold. We discover, among other things, that even now he has an income of $20,000 per month, some $200,000 per year, but that he cannot live within a budget trying to be a doctor who lives a life of the newly rich, the life of the playboy. Again, a later hour will be conveyed:

Dr. Miller: Oh, Rudi, it looks like I will be going away tomorrow so don't, I think I'll have that Monday, but if you don't fill it, just bill me. I'm leaving tomorrow, I'm leaving tomorrow.

Dr. E.:   Uh-huh. I will try to fill it.

Dr. Miller: You may not be able to. You know, Rudi, I think I solved, I am so freaking angry, mostly at myself. I, now, you know all year I've been saying to you, how can I be working so hard and be so absolutely broke. I haven't been taking salaries, I sold, you know, Rudi, I bought that new car because I had done a very good case and I thought it would bring in easily another $50,000 or $60,000 a year in income from the insurance company. I had operated on the wife of one of their head claims people whose heart had really been screwed up and she did very well. And I waited about a month, and she did very well, and that's when I bought this new car 'cause I love pretty cars and I've enjoyed cars. When I sold that car, Rudi, I lost $14,000, and I absolutely needed the cash to live on. I really lived on that $34,000, or less. And I spoke to my partner and I remember coming in here and talking to you and I asked him could he help me with part of the office cost or something, I was just buried financially. And Gloria withdrew her financial support. And here I was working my ass off and was absolutely broke. It's fascinating what happened to me in the last twenty-four hours. First, I went home and Gloria and I were talking and I said, look I really just want to go away, you know. I think your daughter's going to be all right, blah, blah, blah, let's go away. And I said to her, I said, you know it's interesting because Rudi asked me, am I going away to try to patch up our marriage or what have you. I told him, really, I'm just tired.

Dr. E.:   You told her . . .

Dr. Miller: I told her, I'm just, and told you, that I'm really just tired, I just want to go see some trees and smell some air and I'm just, it's enough really, whether our marriage works, doesn't work, I want to go away and I enjoy going away more with you than without you. So Gloria said to me, she said you know I have lots of money in the bank, let me put some of mine in your account for the trip. And I said, Gloria. . . . She said, you know I'll put $5,000 or $6,000 in. And I said, whatever you want, I don't really care. She said, I'll put $5,000, no $6,000, lots of money in my account. And I thought about it and we're preparing dinner and I said, you know Gloria, if you don't mind I'd rather you don't do that. She said, why, what's the money for? I said, well you know, I've been working awfully hard and I feel like going away a little bit and I can't believe that somebody can work like I have worked and not be able to do that. I'm going away now and I have to go away to Hawaii in December, I'm going to Vail in March, the beginning of March and I've got to go back to Hawaii the end of March for some meetings and I actually want to go. And so one of the things you've pointed out . . .

Dr. E.:   You want expensive things?

Dr. Miller: Right. I said one of the things you'd pointed out to me is that I never, I haven't given, I don't do anything, I'm not fighting with you, I'm just telling you.

Dr. E.:   You speak to her?

Dr. Miller: To her. I really prefer that you let me take you with me on this trip. And it just doesn't make sense that I can't afford to do that. That's what you said. She said, well but I want you to buy this and that. I said, Gloria, you do whatever you want to do but I prefer you don't put money in my account. If at some point we want to reorganize our entire living arrangement here, we can sit down and talk, but right now, you know, just leave everything alone. And I said, but I don't want to fight with you about it, you know, if it's something you want to do, but I prefer that you don't. Okay. Then she asked what if I want to buy this or that, I said take some checks with you and you want to buy some things, you know, I just thought I'd take us a drive and see the countryside. You want to buy some things for the house, or something, you'd better bring some money. You know, bring a separate check. And I go to the office today, and it was very interesting, as I go to the office a woman said to me, Dr. Miller, you don't know me, but I'm Mrs. MacCarey, you saved my mother's life, whatever, and it was very nice. Now, I'm in the office and my secretary, I had asked her about three or four weeks ago, I think I mentioned it to you, to analyze my billing for the last year because it looked like Martin and I were going to be splitting up and I want to have some idea what I was really earning. And I don't want to keep just exactly what I earn, I don't mean my split money with Martin over cases, just put down whatever surgeries I did and whatever patients I saw. Just put down that billing. She gave it to me this morning. Most of my work, Rudi, was consultations and things. There was not that many surgeries. There could have been more but I chose not to because I wanted to build up a volume and be very selective in the cases I operate on. My billing, Rudi, was $21,000 a month. Okay? That's a lot, that's an incredible amount of money to be billing.

Dr. E.:   How much?

Dr. Miller: $21,000 a month.

Dr. E.:   Multiply that by 10 and you have about $200,000.

Dr. Miller: More than that.

Dr. E.:   Remember, I said yesterday, just by 10.

Dr. Miller: Now, and she looked at me and she said my God, there's hardly any surgeries, incredible amount. And I said, well it'll, that's a nice base for the office. I said okay. And I gave her a little money, for you know, separate from her regular work, and I left. And I really was so fucking mad, Rudi, because I could be mistaken, but I feel that a year ago in July, Martin and I split up and I was working with you at the time, and I did a lot of surgery, and I must have put $40,000 or $50,000 on the books in that one month, you know how it happens, sometimes in surgery you can work harder on one day. And Martin came back and he was very angry, he felt that I had cheated him. I remember discussing that with you. And I said, look Martin, I love being your partner, of course, I didn't cheat you. That's ridiculous. Everything I've been doing has been over a long time, I happened to do a few extra surgeries. If you want a partnership again, I'll put it back again, and you can take the monies I earned while you were gone, we'll just put it in the common pool. He said, Oh, that would be very nice. But then over the last eight or nine months, Martin was really gone more than he was home. This past month he's been home, he's done a lot of surgeries lately, I've helped him on a lot of surgeries. During the time that I had the car for sale, Rudi, I told Martin, I said, look I don't understand it, I'm busy and I have no money. Can you even help me with my office expenses? No, I don't want any part of your office expenses. Apparently, he was, you know Martin was in surgery, not in surgery but he was gone a good deal of the time. When I sold that car, Rudi, I took a $14,000 loss, I didn't have money to live on and it was a mystery to me what the hell was going on. And I sort of feel like, and I could be mistaken, that Martin decided that he was going to, that Martin had sort of supported me for a long time whether it was intentional on my part or not, I wasn't hurting that much. And I think whether consciously or subconsciously he decided that he was entitled to just take it easy, he was worried about his health, what have you . . . .

Dr. E.:   To turn it around.

Dr. Miller: To turn it around. But I think that it went beyond the point of being appropriate. For a person to be putting over $20,000 a month billing into an office and have to lose $14,000 selling a car to have money to pay basic bills, while the partner is going off building a house and doing whatever, vacationing in Palm Springs, I think it stinks. And I guess . . .

Dr. E.:   It's that he became a gigolo to live on you.

Dr. Miller: Now you know he's such a wonderful surgeon, that it's hard for me to say that. I'm certain I'm wrong. I must say that's sort of the way I feel and I think what's really bugged me about it, see when I spoke to him about it, he told me that if I handled my marriage better, I wouldn't have any financial problems. I said, what do you mean? He said, well your wife is very wealthy, what difference does money make? And I think that's what he really felt, Martin reminds me a lot of my mother when it comes to money, he wanted all of his children to marry wealthy people. They all didn't but he has one son who is a very fine violinist who is in love with a ballerina and when he came home with her his father went crazy. And a week later the boy was engaged to marry a very wealthy girl. Okay? That he'd known for a long time. And I think that Martin in his mind honestly felt that if I was appropriate with my in-laws, he said to me, you handled the first marriage all wrong, that if I handled the in-laws properly. . . .

Dr. E.:   They would pay. . .

Dr. Miller: They would pay and that would be that.

Dr. E.:   That you could milk them instead of having debts.

Dr. Miller: And I've got to tell you something. It's funny, I went home today and saw Gloria for a few minutes . . .

Dr. E.:   Excuse me . . .

Dr. Miller: I saw Gloria for a few minutes. And I said well, now I think I understand things. And I told her what I just told you, because Gloria is, I mean Gloria's liberal. She said, well don't you think that it's been very hard on me, she said, you know, I know how busy you've been because I've watched you working and she said, but you know it's very hard on me, I wish you'd let me put some money in the account. I said, Gloria, I really don't want your money in my account. I said, if we happen to have some game plan, that here is how we want to live, I'm earning, I'm billing over $20,000 a month and I think next year I'll do $30,000 a month. I mean, I'm hardly doing any surgeries. This is almost entirely an office practice. I said if you and I decide that we want to do something, I want to sit down and I want to do it, I don't want it pulled out from under and I don't want you to hand me some money so I can take you on a trip. But now, at least, I understand what the hell is going on. This is absolutely crazy. I have such anger, I feel the same anger toward Martin that I used to feel toward my mother. I honestly feel . . .

Dr. E.:   You felt with your mother she was exploiting you by sending you after money and Martin is exploiting you going and building a house while you work your ass off.

Dr. Miller: Right. And saying to me if you handle your marriage right, you don't have to worry about money.

Dr. E.:   Yeah, you don't need it from him, take it from your in-laws.

Dr. Miller: Right. But I know he's a brilliant surgeon. But you know, Rudi, I have to tell you something. I also think, and I know this is wrong of me, but I also sort of feel that it was totally stupid and inappropriate of Gloria, I seem to be complaining and raving at everybody, and raging at everybody, but here I was working my ass off, clearly had a problem, we had a financial arrangement and all of a sudden the thing gets pulled out from under me and all Gloria kept saying to me this week is I feel awful, I think it's because of me that you did this office. And I said, Gloria, I needed the office, that's a matter between my partner and myself. And the office is no problem, it's just you know, now I see I could have been able to support your office, but you know, Rudi, what I did do, and what Gloria really was responsible for is, not only did I hire her girl friend who was a decorator and give her $10,000 to decorate the office, but I gave Gloria part of the office to use on a sublease and there are a lot of things that I did based on a financial arrangement which we had. Or I really felt that while I was working my ass off because I wanted to build up the practice because I didn't think Martin would live forever, never mind his goofing off, and I just wanted to practice. And everybody pulled the rug out from under me at one time. But what I have to find out, Rudi, is . . . (long pause)

Dr. E.:   Am I correct, that what you tell me is that it was always a one-sided partnership?

Dr. Miller: Always.

Dr. E.:   You know, either you felt that you used or you felt you were used.

Dr. Miller: Well, you know, it's hard to say that because . . . admiration . . .

Dr. E.:   I understand that isn't it, but we speak about . . .

Dr. Miller: Because I felt that I either I was using him . . .

Dr. E.:   At first you felt that you were using your wife and your in-laws. Then, under her pressure of your own unconscious, you yielded to a new arrangement and felt now that you were asked to finance $400 dinners and with him about the same. At first you used him, and then you felt, feel now, the man goofs off and he turns it around.

Dr. Miller: Well, you know, I think what I feel, Rudi, is that I'm most interested in is that I told you yesterday that I feel like I'm a total failure. And . . .

Dr. E.:   In spite of your hard work and the many positive comments that you make about saving their lives . . .

Dr. Miller: Right. Whatever. But a total failure. And now I'm seeing, all of a sudden, I come and I have the passbook in front of me and what I'm seeing is that somehow or another, Gloria says I internalize my anger, you may have mentioned it to me, it seems to me that I had a lot of anger and at a lot people. What I've done and I've permitted myself to feel total, totally worthless. And I damn near died.

Dr. E.:   Like you said yesterday . . .

Dr. Miller: I felt like dying . . .

Dr. E.:   Is it worthwhile living?

Dr. Miller: Well, because I just had no more energy to fight. And when all of a sudden they show me this thing I must tell you that I'm certain it's paranoid on my part, but I wonder if when Martin came back from his trip last July, I don't mean three months ago, I mean fifteen months ago, if he decided to, because he's the one who broke up the partnership, then he came back and wanted together, I wonder if he didn't decide, wait a minute, now Miller is doing well and I want part of this. And I feel very, very angry for having had to lose $14,000 and having had to live on borrowed money. But more than that, what's interesting to me is why, instead of seeing that the problem wasn't totally of my own doing, I . . .

Dr. E.:   It's sort of an interesting battle, isn't it, it goes back and forth between you and all these people and it goes of course back to the question that you voiced yesterday, how come I have no friends because either I feel exploited and they might feel they're exploited. A real battle. And of course also inside of yourself a battle. Yesterday it was depression and today it's $20,000 a month billing. That makes for more than $200,000 a year. Like I told you yesterday.

Dr. Miller: And yet, Rudi, I've had to live on about $1500 or $2000 a month. It's crazy. Yeah.

Dr. E.:   In other words, one earns $200,000 and lives on $24,000 for twelve months.

Dr. Miller: That's crazy, absolutely crazy. But what's interesting to me, Rudi, is that I felt like being dead. I felt worthless.

Dr. E.:   And how it fluctuates back and forth between that belief and the occasional lightening that comes to you but isn't true. I work hard, I have learned, I know something, people say very positive things about it and then I fall down again and say I'm utterly worthless. It's like I put it yesterday, that the endless struggle between the gigolo who thinks of himself as worthless and the competent physician who doesn't know how come he has no money. And you must fall back again of course on a position somebody ought to give it to me.

Dr. Miller: But Rudi, I'm so tired from all this work. But I must go away. But really I've just reached the end of the line, and I just thought well, okay, I better see what my earnings really are because maybe . . .

Dr. E.:   Maybe what?

Dr. Miller: Maybe I really am finished. I mean, if after all, when I'm still partners with this man who has such a wonderful reputation and he is a very, very fine surgeon . . .

Dr. E.:   Well, I think sometimes, is he finished or does he now really start a way to success. And occasionally you talk that way too. And it's sort of interesting that one side always wins and you fluctuate back and forth between hope and inner acceptance and despair.

Dr. Miller: Well, my despair, Rudi, seems to me, interestingly enough, to always be centered around money.

Dr. E.:   I know. But remember you said that you had a new account and it looks like the money will come and you have tremendous hope, and I'll buy myself a Mercedes, isn't it? But two days later, you say, oh, God, I cannot do it, you've got to sell the car and you lose $14,000 and there's something, you know there is a method to this madness. And we've got to discover the method that gets you back and forth between being a successful physician and a man who has, thinks he has to live on handouts from a rich woman . . . (pause). Truly puzzling . . . (pause). What does all that make you think about?

This is a dramatic account of Dr. Miller's slowly turning to a consideration of reality, his true yearnings, and his problem of living within the budget, and of course, I don't mean merely the financial aspect of a budget, but the emotional budget as well.

It's an interesting move that he makes, and we see in it both sides. He must convince the family that he can now give, that he is able to supply the vacation in Hawaii, but internally he hopes that the father-in-law might help him. He is deeply disappointed and even more disappointed about the discovery of his not yet having gotten rid of the gigolo who wants to be given while at the same time he earnestly attempts to be the one who gives, who takes care of others.

Here the therapist has, of course, the main problem of trying to interpret in terms of the inner struggle without taking sides. But, can he do it with this type of patient? As I reread my own material, I can see that in a way the patient does everything he can to create me in the image he needs in his analyst. I must be the counter-conscience. I must not be like the mother who expects him to marry the rich woman, the woman made of gold, but I must be the one who reminds him that he cannot be King Midas if he wants living people in his environment, not people of gold, but people with a heart. It is as if I were to slowly help him identify with the anti-Midas complex. And I say parenthetically that this is not alway easy for psychoanalysts in our culture which puts so much value on income and being rich. It is an interesting problem to discuss in terms of these aspects of countertransference which allow for empathy, for better understanding, and those aspects of countertransference that secretly identify with the pathology of the patient, and then struggle with the dilemma.

This is now a period of time where he literally deals with the problem of perhaps losing his mother soon, the one who taught him, he believes, what he must fight against. This is the time where he may regain a true partner in Gloria, even if her last name is not "Rich." He must bury that part of mother that he hated, that demanded of him that he become a gigolo. And he would like to remember the part of mother, and to have definite proof of it, that recognizes him as a physician, as a person who is competent, and who can take care of himself and others.

If I had to write the last part of this tragedy, I would love to be able to write about it, not as a *Tragedia*, but as a *Comedia*, in the sense of a play that has a happy outcome. Can there, will there be a happy outcome, a successful termination?

Epilogue

Freud (1937), in a late work of his, wrote in "Analysis Terminable and Interminable," and spoke in pessimistic terms, so it seems, about the results of psychoanalysis:

But we also learn from this that it is not important in what form the resistance appears, whether as a transference or not. The decisive thing remains that the resistance prevents any change from taking place—that every thing stays as it was. We often have the impression that with the wish for a penis and the masculine protest we have reached bedrock, and that thus our activities are at an end. This is probably true, since, for the psychical field, the biological field does in fact play the part of the underlying bedrock. The repudiation of femininity can be nothing else than a biological fact, a part of the great riddle of sex.[1] It would be hard to say whether and when we have succeeded in mastering this factor in an analytic treatment. We can only console ourselves with the certainty that we have given the person analysed every possible encouragement to re-examine and alter his attitude to it [pp. 252-253].

One may well wonder whether the resistance to change, the move from the gigolo to the adult, can really and completely take place. Or, will we reach bedrock, and thus will have to bring our activities to an end? My patient, for example, speaks now about the possibility of ending his treatment within a few months. Can I force him to remain passive, to stay with me forever, having had five years of analysis with someone else before? Or, would I yield to him, in the same way that one would hope that mother and wife would finally let him be what he wishes to be?

A footnote to "Analysis Terminable and Interminable" (Freud, 1937) concerning the great riddle of sex, suggests that:

[1] We must not be misled by the term "masculine protest" into supposing that what the man is repudiating is his passive attitude (as such)—what might be called a social aspect of femininity. Such a view is contradicted by an observation that is easily verifiable—namely that such men often display a masochistic attitude—a state that amounts to bondage—towards women. What they reject is not passivity in general, but passivity towards a male. In other words, the "masculine protest" is in fact nothing else than castration anxiety. (The state of sexual "bondage" in men had been alluded to by Freud in his paper on "The Taboo of Virginity" [1918a], *Standard Edition*, 11, 194.)

Do we deal with an essentially masochistic attitude, and, in a surgeon at that, who cannot escape bondage, whether it is to women or to gold that emanates from the eternal promise of the breast?

And do we perhaps have to say to ourselves, and once more I quote Freud (1930): "We can only concern ourselves with the certainty that we have given the person analysed every possible encouragement to re-examine and alter his attitude to it."

Are we to be pessimistic or optimistic? And while I continue my work with this patient, I do not want to be on the optimistic or the pessimistic side. Rather, I want to be committed to my kind of analytic attitude which I hope characterizes my work. Many analysts are always sure that they know what they are doing, and they may say with the philosopher Descartes: "*Cogito ergo sum.*" May I paraphrase the philosopher and say about my own sense of existence: "*Dubito ergo sum.*" I allow myself doubt and therefore I am. And thus I have come to the end, quoting Freud (1930) once more. In "Civilization and Its Discontents," Freud said:

The fateful question for the human species seems to me to be whether and to what extent their cultural development will succeed in mastering the disturbance of their communal life by the human instinct of aggression and self-destruction. It may be that in this respect precisely the present time deserves a special interest. Men have gained control over the forces of nature to such an extent that with their help they would have no difficulty in exterminating one another to the last man. They know this, and hence comes a large part of their current unrest, their unhappiness and their mood of anxiety. And now it is to be expected that the other of the two "Heavenly Powers" (p. 133), eternal Eros, will make an effort to assert himself in the struggle with his equally immortal adversary. But who can foresee with what success and with what result [p. 151]?

Afterthoughts

Another few months have passed since I finished the first draft of this paper. Dr. Miller is still in treatment with me, perhaps nearing the ending phase, filled with uncertainties but also filled with new and realistic hope. Should I have done things differently? As I look through this manuscript I ponder, how much have I learned? I am speaking not only about the countertransference problem of the therapist but also of the scientific curiosity which requires one to better understand the process between patient and therapist, and to gain professional knowledge that will be useful with other patients for the purpose of teaching, of communicating with one's colleagues, and thus gain help with one's own work and deepen one's own critical insights.

At the time that Dr. Miller came to me for treatment and for a long time thereafter, he was playing with suicide, endless destructive outcomes of his career and his private, more personal life. His present clinical problems, his anxieties, depressive attacks, are mere shadowy reminders of the days past, each one of them, each hour filled with impending catastrophe. As I reread the epilogue of the original paper, I now find myself much less pessimistic. I no longer think of the never ending struggle between thanatos and eros. Rather, I see the emergence of new stability and, a competent expert in his medical speciality, a man who no longer wants to be a gigolo, dependent on rich women and fathers-in-law. I see a man who is convinced that he can develop a true partnership of love, of mutual respect if he does not need to feel dependent on a Mrs. Rich with a rich family behind her. He could rely on his own secure income, his expertise, and no longer need to be seduced with fully paid vacation trips around the world while he escapes from his medical and surgical work. He can recognize that the anxiety, the enormous fear, the sweat and the somatic symptoms which threatened his expertise, was caused by escaping from work, leading a life of island hopping and the pleasures of the idle rich, feeding his dependency on them, and the fear of autonomy.

What the future will bring, what his wife might be able to do in order to adapt to the new man, the competent man, is, of course, still uncertain. We deal not only with his inner life but also with the reality that he faces.

Some of this is played out in this ending phase. He feels that I saved his life, that I am the replica of those protectors that his mother wished for him. At times he stands up and criticizes and is angry with me, and he has become a man who moves from dependency to autonomy. At the same time he doubts about his love life, his lovability and his ability to maintain the marriage, or other relationships of friendship and professional comradeship.

Recently, he returned to the East and visited his old home, the house that the primary family possessed then. The thin memory dominated that it was a shabby home, one that he would not want to show his friends. He remembered his mother being critical of his late father, criticizing that he did not provide her with a decent home, hoping that her son would find good providers and do better. He rediscovered the home, brought photographs back, actually picturing a beautiful home, by no means comparable to the memories he had, distortions of the past. The past suddenly seemed to be a different one, and a picture of his father emerged, a new, much improved edition. Digging through the reconstructed process one will sometimes discover not only the repressed and open traumata of the past, but also positive aspects that one had repressed, denied in order to live up to the mother's expectations. I think for a moment of Joseph of the Old Testament, at first chosen by the father, but rejected by the brothers, slowly going through the process of growing up, of overcoming traumata, and finally becoming Joseph, the Provider. This man has to provide now for the children of his first marriage. They are all students who become more successful, even though one of them is a schizophrenic young adult whom he still sees in terms of the danger of becoming like that product of the first marriage. At times he is enraged with the in-laws who so easily could have helped him with his finances. At times he turns the rage into work, hinting that he no longer wants to be helped, that he will pay his debts off by himself, take care of his own expenses for the analysis, evidences in his favor, a new turn toward genuine autonomy.

This then is an unfinished play, an unfinished piece of work. I think of some actors who played one of Shakespeare's dramas, interrupting the rehearsal of the play, trying to think of another dialogue, another outcome. I would like the reader to step into my play, interrupt it here and there and think of another dialogue, another interpretive language, another way to participate in the process of recovery and renewal. Would he do the same?

To interpret means to throw light on the material of the patient. But the light should never blind us, it should not be so strong that we cannot see aspects of the material, cannot understand the more subtle aspects of the play, the dialogue. Interpretation, *die Deutung*, is directed not only to the patient, but is also directed to oneself. Interpretation offers not only more light to the patient, but to us as well, since we must listen not only to the patient but we must also listen to ourselves. Perhaps then it takes not only the third ear with which we listen to the patient, but also a fourth ear that hears our own interpretations, not only the interpretation that is expressed out loud, but also the one that is known only to us, as we listen and follow the process, the therapeutic dialogue. What a task! If I listen too much to the patient, I cannot hear myself. As I listen too much to myself, I cannot hear the patient. This precarious balance is what we must look for, a balance that can be in danger of being lost. Our successful balance act, however, will lead us to new truths, to new insight, to new ways of being helpful in the search for better methods of treatment, if we are willing to learn from our mistakes.

22

Screens, Splits, Frames, and Keys: The Analysis of an Omnipotent Man

Vann Spruiell, M.D.

Introduction

A N exceptionally talented and successful young professor came to see me years ago. He was distraught because he believed he would never reach the pinnacle of honor in his science. I shall use one vignette from an extract of the long and ultimately successful psychoanalytic work to illustrate the clinical and theoretical value of the metaphors of psychic screens and screening. To some extent, these evocative metaphors overlap several other metaphors (and proposed conceptions) commonly used in the description of the more disturbed of analyzable patients: alterations of the ego, splits and splitting, pathological isolations or separations of some mental functions for others, "primitive," "defense mechanisms," alterations of boundaries within the mind, lack of development of distinctions between representations of self and objects—or refusion of these representations.

There are advantages to metaphors, if there weren't they would be dropped. Each of those mentioned refers to internal activities or functions of the mind. Most of these functions can't be experienced, or if they are, only in disguised or substitute forms. But people *do* imagine things like screens: blank walls, veils, nothingness, curtains, emptiness, or screens themselves. It is sometimes possible to "see" figures or shadows that seem to be on the other side of a screen, or shadows projected upon it. Or else it seems opaque and solid as a stone wall. These are representations, or part representations, of unconscious ego–superego functions that filter, disguise, distort, or otherwise completely blot out conscious registrations of dangerous impulses, wishes, fantasies, and feelings. Without the functional separation, the screen, the conflicts among these elements might spell danger, or they might be seen to conflict with other motivations; for example, the perceptions of necessities or moral demands. Conflicts must be compromised in some way, even desperate evasions that stop short of complete disorganizations and breakdown are products of multiple causes. Quantities of anxiety or depression (or erotic excitement that cannot be released) that reach unbearable levels signal imminent dangers of destabilization (Freud, 1923a, 1925; Waelder, 1936; Brenner, 1982).

Surely everybody knows that metaphors speak inexactly. Each of those mentioned carries misleading connotations about the nature of the mind. But some are less misleading than others. The argument to be presented is that these overlapping metaphors have one important thing in common: It is one that defines pathology. Each, if chronically held, represents permanent or temporary *separations* of communications (seen in the widest sense of regulated material or energic exchanges of "information") among psychic functions and systems. Such separations produce perturbations of buffering and other influences among the systems. In an organismic approach to psychoanalysis, which, in fact, Freud's last structural theory is (Freud, 1923a; Arlow and Brenner, 1964; Loewald, 1971a; Spruiell, 1990): Everything is connected with everything; every system in a sense buffers or otherwise influences every other.

As seen here, psychopathology is analogous to (but cannot be exactly equated with, certainly not reduced to) physiological pathology. Communications within and among systems become functionally disrupted (or actually interrupted in the case of neural pathology), and new pathways of function must be found. In the case of psychopathology these interferences may be only temporary. That is, they are functional disruptions which serve the multiple purposes of internal adaptation, but create these at a high cost to some external adaptations. They may remain as chronic organizations or integrations of compromises—parts of compromise formations that have become "frozen."

Preliminary Remarks About the Patient

The man to be discussed had an overriding secret ambition to be awarded a Nobel Prize. It was not enough that he was undoubtedly successful by ordinary standards. However, he began to doubt that his secret ambition was possible to achieve. When he sought treatment he believed, probably correctly, that his entire future was threatened. From the narcissistic aspect of his internal and external relations with others, he acted as if he were omnipotent, and for those who idealized him *seemed* so. Omnipotence coupled with intense ambitions to achieve tangible results usually results in tragedy. From the aspect of intimate object relations he felt detached, although he could usually disguise this isolation from those about him. He thought that something like a wall or a screen made out of glass or plastic stood between himself and other people he would have liked to love—or hate.

The account of this long analysis was prepared more than twenty years ago, in part during the work, in part soon afterward.[1] It was presented at the Hampstead Clinic in 1973, and since then in other places. The purposes of the presentations varied, but the story has not been altered. Originally, I used it to focus upon soaring visions of omnipotence which in response to seemingly minor frustrations could be replaced with terrible fantasies of helplessly falling. In imaginations that felt prophetic, "something worse than death" would happen. Annie Reich (1960b) once said of the fragile self-esteem of some narcissistic individuals that it could be blown up like a big balloon; and one pin-prick could collapse it. The same analogy could apply to my patient's omnipotence.

---

[1] Some psychoanalytic clinical reports can satisfy reasonable standards of evidential validity, and I admire them. But this presentation could not be such an effort. Too much had to be left out. The purpose of this essay is merely to seek to illustrate a specific point of view, with the hope that other analysts' experiences will resonate with it.

I used the same vignette later to demonstrate some difficulties in the transference and countertransference reactions encountered with similar patients. And on still another occasion I used the material to illustrate certain aspects of the potential growth and the potential downfall of creativity.

This material could not be published in the past, but the constraints no longer apply. A few facts, none important to the understanding of the man, have been altered. Although the vignette still illustrates some of the ideas mentioned above, I now want to relate it particularly to ideas presented in three papers by colleagues that have been neglected in the past, and in more partial ways to the works of other writers who have written about "the broadening scope" of analysis (especially, see Weinshel's recent papers [1988, 1990] on this subject).

Primarily, my scientist–patient demonstrated many of the features described by Ralph Greenson in "On Screen Defenses, Screen Hunger, and Screen Identity" (1958a). But in certain other ways he could also have been a prototype of the patients described by Helen Tartakoff (1966) in "The Normal Personality in Our Culture and the Nobel Prize Complex." Finally, the account illustrates some of the dilemmas brought to our attention in Paul Pruyser's classical paper (but one that has been neglected even more than the others), "What Splits in 'Splitting'?" (1975).

After the clinical and developmental material has been presented, I shall return to the ideas put forward by Greenson, Tartakoff, and Pruyser, along with comparable ideas put forward by Winnicott, Annie Reich, Helene Deutsch, some Kleinian authors, object relations theorists, and self psychologists. I shall also present some of my own ideas.

A Clinical Vignette

For seven long years I worked with this brilliant and erratic scientist who may have had an actual *chance* to win a Nobel Prize (although I never knew with any objectivity how large that chance was). He had, side by side with the omnipotent fantasies, a fine ability to conceptualize the abstractions of his discipline.

When, at thirty-two, he became privately convinced that he would never become preeminent in his field, he struggled with this miserable conclusion by himself. But finally he decided that analysis was his only hope. It was not that he believed that he had exaggerated his abilities but that there were mysterious causes that blocked his way. Fortunately, he did not believe that these blocks existed in the external world. Rather, he thought they existed within himself. Thus, psychoanalysis might somehow remove the imperfections inside. Only his work bothered him, he thought, and only his work was important. He knew, of course, that he was highly regarded professionally, but this was little solace for the secret certainty of failure. The rest of his life, including married life and relations with two then young children, was "entirely satisfactory."

I had initial doubts about whether he could endure an analysis. However, it was easy to believe that the unmanageable disillusionment within himself might grow and grow. He did not have a depression of a transitory sort. Rather, he was confronted with a general and inescapable failure of those aspects of his personality we would regard as narcissistic. His entire future, not merely his scientific work as he thought, seemed literally in jeopardy. Even if by chance he *did* receive a Nobel Prize, the outcome would have been no different. Yet, along with numerous other strengths, he was a courageous and determined man.

The professor was big, tall and slightly fleshy. His clothes were usually rumpled, the shirts frayed, the tie loosened. He looked older than thirty-two; probably he had been a handsome boy and younger man. Before we met, I had heard of his local renown as a teacher, and that he was thought to be eccentric. He amalgamated a commanding presence with slight awkwardness, messiness, and unnaturally fluent speech. His accent was "academic," pleasant, with faintly British embellishments. Not a trace remained of its poor, rural origins in the southern seaboard. He was both witty and humorous. But the humor was fundamentally cruel, never ironic, never poignant, never warm. Nor was it ever at his own expense; it was always targeted other people.

He read widely, and had an appreciation of art and serious music. His mind was wonderfully inventive, and when he was in a "good mood," his ideas were probably original and certainly charming. When he was in a "bad mood" he seemed "flat" and even boring.

In telling more of his story, I will take the license of an essayist, that is, I will not try to provide a story organized tightly into categories and sequences. One dramatic fantasy that occurred during the *middle* of the analysis will be used to organize what happened earlier and later. These happenings illustrate the brief dreamlike condensation of parts of the analysand's motivations, character, conflicts, fantasies, and transferences—parts that also emerged at different times throughout the work. These chronic transference-countertransference phenomena persisted. Yet, in small increments, they slowly changed over the years. But during a concluding portion of the analysis they changed dramatically. I will save the developmental reconstructions for the last, although they were of course slowly assembled, gradually corrected, and constituted a major part of the whole work.

For almost four years the work was grindingly slow, often confusing, and occasionally seemingly hopeless. I shall describe this frustrating work in more detail later. Yet, for some reasons, that even now I can only partly understand, neither one of us seriously considered stopping. As if in reward the analysis gradually began to make sense. Sometime before the end of the fourth year, the patient understood something with great surprise. His surprise surprised me. The insight had seemed so obvious I presumed he knew it also: that he had only pretended to say everything that occurred to him during sessions. He claimed, believably, that he had "known but not known" that he was withholding very important fantasies and impulses.

Similarly, he regularly switched from one strip of associations to another—"knowing but not knowing" that he was changing the subject. Usually, neither he nor I could identify the missing links. Freud stressed that maneuver as characteristic of obsessional thought (1909c). As Freud put it, what was repressed—and here he was speaking of repression in the old, broad sense, synonymous with all defenses—was not the content but connections.

Of course I understood that certain universal and "obligatory" fantasies were not emerging, but I ascribed their absence purely to repression (in the later sense, as only one of several "defense mechanisms"). And I interpreted them as such, not understanding that the patient was, in effect, saying to himself, "Yes—but I already do know that. I simply haven't told you."

Despite these inexact interpretations the professor eventually, after almost four years of work, reached a decision: He consciously determined to "give in," accept his fantasies, whatever they were, and explore them verbally without censorship. But when he began to try to do that, he also began to experience inner pain that became intense. The content of the fantasies did not necessarily bother him— it was that dangerous feelings were then closer to consciousness and therefore acknowledgment. But the feelings were "free-floating," he said; they weren't connected to anything. The terrible feelings consisted of anxiety, a sense of doom, and feeling of crushing evil.

His protestations to one side, the feelings and the fantasies gradually become joined. Most of the fantasies, which sometimes accompanied masturbation, were manifestly "tame," at least from the point of view of an outsider. They were poorly defined, without vividness. And they constantly shifted. On the surface they represented homosexual holding and mutual masturbation. At that time it was unclear to me, and I believe to the analysand, who did what to whom. Even the nature of his partner was uncertain. Intellectually, he "supposed" the partner stood for me.

A Waking Dream

One morning, after a brief separation from the analysis to make a scientific presentation in another city, he slumped half-asleep during a long ride in a taxicab. His mind drifted, but became slightly more alert when a vivid imagination that he was sucking my penis seemed to swim into consciousness. He felt warm inside, but only mildly erotically excited. And he had an unaccustomed awareness of shameless closeness. He could feel the erect, perceptually defined penis filling his mouth; his lips felt exquisitely sensitive. But suddenly the peaceful feeling were interrupted—he lost control of the fantasy. In a rush the penis grew to an enormous size. This monstrous phallus, as big as a man's arm, rammed straight down his gullet all the way to his stomach. It was as if he had no separate mouth, throat, or esophagus. One tube led to the stomach. The great phallus was blank, without features. It spread warmth within. At that instant he felt *at one* with the phallus. Distinctions were gone. Time changed. Everything was immediate.

The exquisitely terrifying experience lasted, he thought, only a few seconds. It was hard to describe later. It was, he said, something akin to an orgasm, though he did not actually have an orgasm. But unlike such a climax, it was more, in his words, an "implosion" rather than an "explosion." It was without localizable pleasure. Yet it seemed extraordinarily "real." "I think it was the most real experience I can remember," he said. At the same time he was awed, filled with terror. "I have no words that seem right," he said. "There is no way I can tell either you or me much about it in words."

In the taxicab, he physically shook himself, startling the driver. He got out, walked for a long, long time, attempting to come to terms with the experience. He wondered if he should call me on the telephone. He never had called in distress before, and as he calmed down decided not to. By the time of the early evening appointment he was outwardly composed but inwardly still profoundly shaken. "I think I went crazy, but at the same time it was the most real thing I can remember." By "real thing" he meant "sane thing." As he described the feelings he felt them again in an attenuated form on the couch. I did not feel any need to interpret anything or even say anything. He said it was enough that he could be with me and that I understood. I am not sure how much I understood. But I felt no alarm at all.

What did the experience mean? Gradually, as the work went on, it came to mean almost everything. It was a screen fantasy, a communicative interchange of associations from many levels, like the crossroads Freud called "nodal points" of associations (Freud, 1900). But it was also *itself* a screen. It was like an especially memorable dream, or like an insistent screen memory pierced, then remade into another screen. As we learned over many months, the various meanings screened other meanings, and they, in turn, screened still others, revealing and concealing, veils upon veils.

The patient analyzed and reanalyzed the fantasy and derivative fantasies. We began with a joint preconscious bank of memories, assembled together over hundreds of hours of analytic work. The half-dream, half-fantasy, and the awakening from it, stimulated poignant associations to old memories and new associations, previously disregarded as unimportant. Our joint memory bank became much richer.

The Context

To reiterate, the professor's fantasy lurched into consciousness during a return from a brief separation from the analysis. The fantasy began with intense wishes to lovingly, physically, reunite with the analyst, first known distinctly as a man, by sucking his penis. Familiar and documented clinical theory suggests the outlines of what happened: As one of the reverberations of the earlier work that identified, partially analyzed, and allowed the relaxation of resistances, he had become less afraid of homosexual fantasies. But in the middle of the serpentine irruption in the taxicab, he wittingly or unwittingly lost control. The anxiety that ensued led to a regression to a more infantile version of fantasied literal incorporation and merging, first with a sort of blank phallus, then with something more distinctly maternal, a breast, but a giant, intrusive breast that entered and fused with his gullet. Phallus-breast and gullet *became* each other. But other realities intruded, external ones like freezing rain on an ocean beach: in the form of the immediacies of the taxicab and its driver, in the form of memories of the analyst, in the form of fear of craziness. He "awoke" to "reality."

Before summarizing the clinical course, I shall mention some general characteristics of the man.

Verve, poise, bearing, and wit in strong mix make analysts cautious. They wonder if they might be dealing with a scoundrel, and are not reassured to note a flamboyance that seems contrived. But these same traits made my patient notable in other than analytic arenas. They added to his reputation; in a way they might be thought of as advertising. And in a small city it is not possible to avoid hearing about academic "characters."

As a graduate student, he had made the first of several minor, though substantial, scientific contributions. Once he became a professor, younger graduate students tended to attach themselves to him. However, most of them sooner or later deserted. Their mentor found these desertions perplexing and hurtful. He was not popular either, at least for long, with most of his professional peers; they saw him as aloof, domineering, and controlling—or obnoxious.

Those who came closest to knowing him were impressed with his almost religious devotion to science in general. At the same time they sensed a seemingly fundamental indifference to people. A few of his less friendly colleagues told him as much, to his consternation and puzzlement. It was another thing he "knew but did not know." But there were also a few colleagues who remained surprisingly loyal. He made himself subject to idealization and there were people there to idealize him, no matter how he treated them. To a few disciples he confided that ordinary happiness was trivial; more important things called. Nor (so he told them, and later, me) did bouts of feeling totally "empty" or "dead" worry him. Intellectually, he had always thought suicide a "likely and rational option in life."

This physically brawny man usually impressed others as brave physically, as he was courageous intellectually. Actually he was extremely afraid of physical confrontations and of pain of any sort. He was not counterphobic. Rather, he consciously disguised his fearfulness with bombast. Fear was shameful and effeminate. In these ways, among still others to be mentioned below, he was *not* like the patients described by Greenson.

The reasons he sought and continued analysis were cast in almost mythic terms, as if he were a Greek hero battling fate. Sometimes he did feel like a hero. But vague feelings of purposelessness and lack of integrity were much more awful to experience than he admitted to others. The private belief that he either had already, or might in the future, fail—that he wasn't really a great man, that, in fact, he was something of a fraud, was almost unbearable.

The forlorn hope that psychoanalysis might not only save his chances for the Nobel Prize, and thus, for him, a sense of integrity, was gradually eroded. But he could not reconcile himself to ultimate failure. He had no intentions, he said, "to adjust to reality." By that he meant, as he said and as I believed he meant, that suicide was preferable to ordinariness.

Of less importance to him, so he thought for a long time, was a recognition that he was unable to love another person, excepting the two young children. I believe the exception was crucially important; at least it indicated a sort of foothold that might become expanded. He yearned for contact with his own and others' feelings but felt an automatic and irresistible need to control them. But the coldness did not necessarily apply to nonintimate contacts. At a distance, from a position of safety, he could on occasion be exquisitely sensitive and show warmth and tact that seemed quite genuine.

With others, even by himself, he felt a stranger. For example, he rarely felt released orgastically. He hated the "numbness" and wished for explosive outbursts. And he was concerned about the fact that the masturbation fantasies occasionally included, along with the adolescentlike homosexual wishes, rudimentary and inhibited sado-masochistic fantasies. He had never enacted these, and because they seemed so bizarre and incomprehensible he never seemed consciously afraid that he would. But he did look upon them as secret marks, awful imperfections.

A prideful man, he felt a keen humiliation in allowing another person to look behind his masks. But he was courageous in his eventual willingness to do so verbally within the analysis. As a result I eventually learned that he not only sought perfections for himself, but that the wishes to master the laws of nature signified barely disguised fantasies of controlling the *whole universe*. He felt part of a scientific movement, one of the disciples of what was actually for him a religion of science. It was a religion that not only would some day provide material mastery, but make all contemporary moral systems obsolete. Never was he more expansive, after securing some measure of trust in another person, than when he talked about these things. He glowed. Except for acknowledging the importance of what I elliptically termed his values, I never otherwise commented about them or interpreted their functions. Later, he interpreted them himself.

On the other hand, beneath the flamboyance and seemingly imaginative freedom was (necessarily) a rigid psychic organization. Although his character seemed predominantly organized along obsessional lines, I would characterize it as "brittle" and "global," not "wishy-washy" and "meticulous," not perpetually racked by doing and undoing. Just as he rarely could feel released by orgasm, except for righteous anger he could not allow other strong feelings to burst forth. He could not seem to avoid a sense of self-consciousness and blankness at times most people would laugh or cry.

Late in the analysis, having regained awareness of the private parts (really, secret parts) of his body (he had almost ignored them previously) he experimented with some of his most shameful wishes. He gave himself a few experimental enemas, consciously trying to reexperience their repeated administration by his mother well into his school years. At other times, in moments of private mortification, he made himself vomit. After retching, he could sob convulsively. At no other time since he was small had he been able to weep. But toward the end of his analysis he could experience grief in my presence.

Thus, in public act and private thought, he manifested a "specialness," a belief in a right to transcend the ordinary rules and morals that govern ordinary men, while at the same time experiencing, paradoxically, a dim, chilling fear that he was in fact in bondage to inexorable inner rules that he did not understand. He was a failed Faust.

Careful never to be caught in delinquencies, which included occasional dubious research practices, he was constrained by a sense of external danger to career and reputation, not by inner prohibitions or concern for others. The corrupt practices were petty: He cut corners; to some extent he exploited associates.

Summary of the Analytic Course

The analysis was maintained four, then five times a week for over seven years. The technique was "classical"—more "classical" than would seem reasonable to me now (although he apparently forgave me anyhow). During the first months he produced a flurry of dreams, fantasies, and transitory transference reactions. They seemed patently oedipal in nature. He interpreted them for himself on the basis of his reading. Obviously, these productions and "interpretations" were defensive maneuvers on a conscious level. Whatever affective verity they might have had was beyond consciousness. The surface needs to please me had a hollow quality; he wanted to bribe me to hold off, stay away, disappear.

Most of the time he was almost insufferably "nice" and cooperative, patronizing, even unctuous. But some other element would usually make an appearance—punctuations of wit, some humorous remark that was malicious, derogatory, or intellectually arrogant. Occasionally, the superficial screen of niceness would break down entirely. Then he would try to cover bursts of derision and open hostility with what he called, with a combination of sarcasm and irony, and a lot of affected pomposity (I may not be quoting him exactly but I am not caricaturing his words), "the remorse that comes with the burden of maturity." Nor would he pay any attention to remarks I might make in return. What he then called remorse, was, if anything, fear. Control was the most important of life's modes of being.

Over the first three years, my analytic interventions were almost entirely confined to "tending the analytic frame" (Spruiell, 1983, 1984) and making occasional interpretations of resistances as they appeared (and as I thought I understood them). "Tending the frame," means, without losing an analytic stance, coping with the patient's unconsciously shrewd attempts to prevent an analytic situation from being set up or clearly defined, or, failing that, to disrupt what had been established. He wanted special arrangements of all sorts: the setting of the fee, payments, time, the withholding of some information regarded as "too confidential," the belief that some scientific obligations were too important to be overridden by the analytic requirements placed on "one poor, unimportant individual." He fought the everyday, necessary arrangements as though they were entirely matters of my bureaucratic nature. While he never pushed demands so far they could not be dealt with as resistances, it was clear that in each case he finally only complied without conscious understanding. At least this was true for a long time. Otherwise, by interpreting resistance I mean finding ways to show the patient how he resists whole parts of his own inner life. One of the major resistances was a common one: He wanted to think of resisting *me* and the *analysis* externally. These pressures to externalize resistances finally subsided, and, contrary to first expectations, he did not act any more impulsively than he always had. The seemingly sociopathic qualities also became less a source of concern, especially after he resolved (and kept to the resolve more consistently than most patients) to renounce conscious censorship. After this, I became, in part, an externalized conscience.

He remained, however, sensitive and easily mortified. Once, before I had read Kohut's first works on narcissism (1966a, 1968), I interpreted a proffered gift as, in effect, a bribe. The interpretation was correct but premature, and the fact of the prematurity was related to a transitory countertransference reaction. My patient nursed that hurt for years, and it took me years to understand why.

During what seemed to be the darkest part of the work, between three and four years, the "gaps" between strips of associations came much more frequently He would put together short strips of relatively free associations, report dreams that he analyzed, report fantasies. A strip of associations made "psychological sense," except that he was aware of little feeling outside of the little bursts of hostility and ill-defined experiences of anxiety and depression. The fragmentations of the lines of association were bewildering. A strip of analytic interaction would suddenly seem to be switched off and replaced either by a period he called "deadness," or replaced by another strip of analytic work, which neither he nor I could connect to the previous strip. Often the "switching off" or "switching over" occurred within a single session. More often, one session would seem to have little to do with the next session.

Some might regard this as evidence of a thought disorder, a defect in the machine. I did not and do not now see such fragmentations as anything but dynamically relevant and at least potentially understandable, potentially alterable, *functional* separations. But too often I was unable to make sense of them. Material, clearly transferential in nature, appeared, disappeared, and became replaced by other transferences. Occasionally, I attempted to interpret some seemingly oedipal or preoedipal transference, usually approaching it by way of alluding to some resistance. Those forays might be met by a putatively cordial interest, or perhaps by an irritated outburst of ridicule. Neither reaction could be put to the purposes of the work.

The analysand seemed to "slide" easily among the levels of organization, from oedipal, through all the preoedipal levels, and it was usually not possible for me to guess the causes of these shifts. Beyond pointing them out, no intervention seemed to make sense of them. The results of the "switching" and the "sliding" amounted to confusion—endured patiently by the analysand if he recognized it at all. But the confusion particularly troubled me. My "trouble" amounted to a reaction that, even then, had already become familiar with some other relatively disturbed patients. On the one hand, I would find myself doubting that I knew how to conduct this analysis, or doubting that I knew how to conduct any analysis, or, more seriously, that I knew anything at all. At those latter times I even felt momentarily as if I were being fraudulent to attempt to analyze such a person. Nowadays, but not then, I would identify this reaction of mine as analogous to the effects of what is meant by others, particularly Kleinian and Bionian authors, as projective identification.

Despite the doubts, if there were anything consistent it was in terms of the growth of a stable bond between us. I became the first man with whom, as an adult, he could sustain close contact. I had understood from the beginning that this tortured man had more complex problems than those of a clear-cut psychoneurotic, or those of a patient with obsessional–depressive characterological problems. I also understood, after trying, that most interpretations of content, as opposed to resistance, were useless. But a number of inferences about unconscious operations were possible: The patient not only used defensive patterns that included intrapsychic acts of repression, intellectualization, isolation, displacement, and undoing, he also used special forms of denial and disavowal.

Along with the obsessional capacity to "repress" the connections between particular associations, this man also apparently had an internal world representing external reality that was not entirely comparable to the internal worlds of others. He could change from one frame defining a particular kind of social situation (in the broad sense of the meaning of social) to another without recognizing that he was doing so. An interaction that a partner might understand to be one between peers might be seen by the analysand as one between an authority and a subordinate at work—or more secretly as one between himself and a dangerous rival. *Within* a frame he might be reenacting verbally, he shifted bewilderingly among the various abstract levels, or *keys* (Spruiell, 1983), from the highest levels of rational thought to the crudest language of the small child's body. For example, the partner who framed the situation as one between peers might be dealing with a man who saw himself to be coping with a dangerous, imaginary, rival sibling. I must emphasize that these interactions did *not* demonstrate psychotic thought. They represented small and usually unacknowledged "misunderstandings." My patient knew what was expected of him and rarely acted inappropriately.

Usually, he could see no connections between the various keys, or hierarchical levels of abstraction. If made aware of the shifts and their possible relationships, or if made aware of the possible incompatibility of the two different frames, he denied the reality of the similarity or difference, or disavowed the meanings of either. Even when he *did* recognize these dissonant, seemingly incompatible frames or keys, he was unable to exploit them for new insights, as more creative individuals often do.

More than leading to "misunderstandings," his assumptions about reality (his "folk philosophy") within the various frames (not merely two) often contradicted each other in fundamental ways. He could not, at any rate for years did not, allow the acknowledgment of these contradictory views of reality. When he finally began to, for a time he thought he was "crazy." I do not remember if we ever used the word *split*. I think we talked about "switches in ways of thinking," which, when he recognized them he at first assumed "just happened," and later that he came to "own" as ways he used to protect himself.

The shifting object-related transferences included equally shifting narcissistic transferences. Aside from the periods of "deadness," in which I was "wiped out" as an object (and *felt* "wiped out"), the patient could and did eventually idealize me in seemingly authentic rather than purely defensive ways. He could and did use me as a sort of alter ego to reflect and respond to his marvelous qualities. These interactions could easily have justified the patient being diagnosed as one or the other sort of narcissistic personality described in Kohut's earlier formulations (1971). And it seemed that the nature of the patient's aggressiveness, his rage, and aspects of his omnipotence were not merely a reaction to narcissistic injuries.

I did not interpret these narcissistic phenomena (Spruiell, 1975) then, although I steadily interpreted defenses against them—the hauteur, mockery, distancing. They covered his fear of his own impulses. Later, he could understand that they covered his fearful wishes for affection toward me and from me.

It would be pleasant to report that the last three years amounted only to a "mopping-up operation." In fact, the analysis became more alive and more understandable. But at the same time it became turbulent and extraordinarily painful as preoedipal and the central oedipal "resolution" were analyzed; that is, the massive denials that went with it together with the almost intense, unconscious fantasy that he had "defeated" the oedipal dilemmas completely. Having made a "core" relationship with me, he could no longer evade the fact that he also hated me murderously. In particular, sadomasochistic fantasies dissolved into raw, destructive impulses, manifested in new, vivid ways. But the fantasies were not carried into action. Matters of control, domination, submission, and fantastic power struggles filled the sessions, but came to be confined to them.

These struggles built to a final crisis, the second nodal point of the analysis. It had to do with both of us finally coming to grips with his almost psychotic need to do me harm, to literally destroy me by destroying the analysis itself. After repeatedly "going to the wall," so to speak, we managed to preserve the work, neither of us omnipotent, each surviving the coexistence of needs to love and destroy one object (Winnicott, 1965). I believe that the work that came after the first nodal point made the second possible. This period represented still another temptation to institute "parameters," to close off, to avoid the "realness" of the condensed oedipal and preoedipal efforts to obliterate the intruder. Sometimes these are indeed necessary, but not always.

Developmental Considerations

As analyses deepen it becomes possible to identify more accurate outlines of the intimate biography, including what is not known and probably never can be known. At least more reliable and plausible reconstructions become possible, and while they can never more than approach personal historical "truth," they can, especially when compared and coordinated with other reconstructions and verifications made in *other* analyses by other analysts, amount to more than "narrative truths" merely agreed to by one analyst and one analysand.

Nothing is known of my patient's earliest infantile development. He was told that he was a happy, rather placid baby, and photographs seemed to confirm this. Even without knowing the early "facts," I would have speculated, on the basis of assorted dreams and fantasies, and what is known developmentally about similar patients, that some catastrophic event had happened early in life. There was strong inferential evidence of close and prolonged exposure to primal scenes, that intense anal fixations had come into being, and that the negative oedipal dispositions were strong.

He had been an only child, born on a family farm. Like the neighboring farms, it had gradually become greatly reduced in worth. When he was about a year and a half, his mother contracted a serious illness. Neither its nature nor his reactions to it were ever revealed to him, but he knew that she was away for weeks or even months. A screen, more like a thick curtain, was never lifted from these family secrets. Whatever the secrets, my patient speculated that his mother had had a psychotic break, *the separation from his mother was his first great loss.*

Yet, the family biographical lore was rich in other ways. It included many tales of infantile precocity, supported by abundant early memories. For example, he remembered teaching himself to read at about the time of his fourth birthday. As he matured he understood that his brilliance served as a point of orientation and consolidation for an emotionally deprived family.

The parents had little use for each other. The mother, apparently indifferent to everyone but her son, claimed that she lived only for him. He believed it, but as a boy was unable to recognize her cold hatefulness. The bitterness was countered by the heat of ambition. Yet it seemed to be ambitiousness without qualities. Her son was destined for unspecified glories. The father also went to great lengths to advance the golden child. As a young man he had had intellectual aspirations of his own, but a combination of character pathology and external circumstances had reduced him to a mean inheritance, the marginally self-sufficient but worn-out family farm.

The picture provided of the father, at least for a long time, ranged from the sad to the sordid. Distant, submissive when sober, rageful and even violent when he went on alcoholic binges several times a year, he was a mostly silent, failed man. The frantic, periodic drinking, with its occasional violence, was simply taken by his son as the norm, and not consciously understood until prepubescence. When he was thirteen years old his father died after a short illness. No grief was expressed at the funeral or afterwards.

The subsequent reissues of the templatelike unconscious fantasies, of which the conscious fantasy in the taxicab was one variation, suggested that they had developed and become fixed during the phases in between the early preoedipal and late oedipal periods. Even without new memories, some that had been conscious all along were mentioned in the analysis for the first time, having become imbued with new meanings and importances. The patient's biography, as is typical if analyses are successful, became changed in the process. For example, as a new patient he thought of his father, literally, as a "nothing," merely a horrible burden. Much later we learned that the father had taken over many maternal functions, before and after the mother's illness. But with her return, she apparently battled to regain the boy. She finally won and the father retreated. With the retreat, the son sustained a new loss, a *second loss*; and so did the father lose. Both buried their losses.

And in the course of remembering and partly reconstructing the account of those struggles and those losses, we also learned that the boy had been indulged to an extent most people would find bizarre. It had been his privilege to invade the parental bed on any whim (usually, he thought, displacing the father), eat what he liked, when he liked, where he liked, even on the floor if he wanted to. He could break anything, do anything, in his home or anywhere else. This tyranny was enforced by temper tantrums and they always worked. The parents were his absolute servants and his Imperial Guards. He was like the "enfantes terribles" Maher (1949) wrote about.

And he was like them when he had to go to school. The first time there he became completely unmanageable, completely intransigent, completely disruptive. He could not be calmed, and his mother stayed on the premises for several days. The semipublic life of school had displaced part of the life of family, and he had sustained *a third loss*. But then he abruptly changed, or seemed to, for what reasons we never learned. Loud became quiet; absolute rebellion became sweet conformity; a total refusal to learn turned into an endless demand to take in whatever the teachers had to offer. Some of them made him a pet. In later life, however, he doubted that the rural and small town teachers had felt warmly toward him. He did not experience the sort of personal care he had seen them show other children. The undeniable gifts coupled with conformity made him invincible, but he could not be sure that anyone really liked him.

As for men who might have served as alternates to his father, he never seemed to become intimate with any. I was curious about this apparent lack; no male teachers, coaches, uncles, ministers, scout masters became his heroes. It is possible that some memories having to do with idealized older men may have continued to lurk behind screens, never to be uncovered. What we could make out, however, were vivid fantasies during late latency and early adolescence; stimulated by voracious reading; he made up his own imaginary masculine ideals.

Years later his children were invested with some of his ideals. Yet, in some way that is mysterious to me, these children were not seen predominantly in transference terms, either as independent (and therefore dangerous) objects or as narcissistic manifestations of his own person. To my knowledge the children were the first creatures with whom he could feel intimacy without self-consciousness. If that had not happened, I do not believe he could have been analyzed.

Well into the work, as a result of the analysis of transference fantasies, he recovered connections between other, earlier memories. These were among the most important secrets of all. He had dismissed them earlier, leaving the fragments unassembled. His mother had taken an overt and direct interest in him sexually. Well into latency she gave him frequent enemas, smiling and "fussing" in a teasing way while he whined and begged her to stop. The life between the two revolved about the bathroom, with all its sights, smells, and activities. It was important also that he frequently saw her sitting on the toilet, knew about her pubic hair, copied her way of sitting, like her, hid his own genitals when he sat there. He played at hiding as she watched him hide, just as she called attention to the hiding of her own genitals.

Several times, with great excitement and many warnings to keep their secret, she shared nude sunbaths with him in a sheltered part of the backyard. There were also long, wonderful tub baths, followed by the mother toweling him. As she did, she rubbed harder and harder, until he began to squeal and yell and beg. His skin turned red as she "fussed" at him for not washing well. She held him tightly with one arm: He was dirty; she showed him the dirt rubbed off and he "saw" the dirt—but couldn't see the dirt. It was like a perverse version of Freud's mother demonstrating human mortality by rubbing her hands together and showing the apparent dirt that was actually dead skin. Only, Freud could see *something*; my patient had to imagine it.

In one analytic session, a visual image of a screen at first appeared as completely blank, but took on texture. It became a towel, and he experienced an almost unbearable traumatic experience of anxiety for a few moments on the couch. Later, he realized that it was unbearable because he *wanted* the masochistic experience of being rubbed so hard. He wanted me to do it. And he had to recognize that what he thought (but "unthought") had been a clear memory of dirt on the towel had been hallucinatory. In that humble but scrupulously clean house, there couldn't have been dirt on the towel. Nor was it possible that he *never* saw his nude mother frontally. But he remembered her pubic hair and her buttocks; her back too was a screen. Everything was all right as long as certain secrets were kept. Selective uncertainties of memory are common enough; extreme versions are described by Shengold (1989), in victims of soul murder.

During the same times just before and just after latency, as the father drifted away the mother openly used the boy as her "protector" against his hateful interests. She maintained domination of her son both by the hardly disguised seductions and by fearsome threats: stories of his father squeezing and grabbing and hurting her in bed; the fact that she would "go crazy" and surely die before the next Christmas.

The intensity of the patient's castration anxiety became unmistakably documented in the transferences, as did inferences for radical compromise formations, including regressions to oral and anal fixations, parallel narcissistic functions, and accompanying fantasies. The most tightly kept secret fantasies were about "successful" incest. The overt incestuous interactions with the mother hid an even deeper set of fantasies—searing urges, unbearable for more than seconds but as "real" as the specimen fantasy in the taxicab—of incest with the little boy and the man: wishes to be ultimately castrated and presented in the transference to a rapacious father.

Capacities to isolate affective states and utilize a gifted mind probably saved him from much more severe disturbances, as they often do with very obsessional patients. Productivity was more than amply rewarded. It is no wonder that he could maintain the myth that he had "won" the oedipal struggle. The "victory," of course, partly turned Pyrrhic by adolescence, but even then, all might be salvaged by the award of the magical Prize. Desperately afraid of the evil that felt to him as if it dwelt like a living thing in his chest, the future scientist finally protected himself by "seeing through" his mother's martyrdom and into her seductions and threats. He came to the conclusion that his mother was a monster who did not love him at all. Yet, he still believed that she had saved him from his father and really did live her life for him. In a way this was true, but she had also saved him from the father's love.

Abdicating during the latter part of his life, the father gradually became less overtly rageful and more depressed and indifferent. Ironically, only his outbursts of rage were remembered as "real"—

until the analytic work exposed the necessary distancing that had replaced a much earlier closeness. After that, during termination, grief welled up through the medium of transference. The total blankness he experienced following the man's funeral covered a fourth loss, a loss dealt with in familiar ways.

The losses were condensed into one another, stacked pieces of paper wadded up like a clumsy ball.[2] Together they reinforced a near-psychotic determination to personally reconstruct the universe. My patient had truly consecrated his soul to science.

As an early adolescent, now in a nearby town, now a big boy, he briefly became a "regular fellow," temporarily even a leader in athletics. In his memory, it was only an act. He retreated into books and chemical equations and experiments, which almost alone seemed "real." One other thing seemed so—he built a "wall of hatred" for his mother. He treated her politely, but as far as he knew silent hatred was all he felt.

Before entering graduate school, he defied her openly by marrying a woman who seemed "perfect on paper," and was not in any way like his mother (and, oddly, as nearly I could tell, he was right). He wanted to love his wife, but could not. He hoped "it would come some day." Occasionally, she complained that he was erotically mechanical and these accusations drove him to frantically elaborated and seemingly interminable efforts to please her. But for the most part she was stable and supportive, if wan and retiring, proud to be married to a man accepted as a genius. She recognized, without much openly expressed resentment, that the only emotionally alive features in his life were work and the two children, who were adored and adoring— and surprisingly well adjusted then and subsequently.

The professor was an attractive man to women, and he had many opportunities for extramarital affairs, but he never followed through with them. During the termination of the analysis he discovered a tenderness for his wife and began to express it. Whether that tenderness had been there all along, hidden behind screens on screens, or whether this was a totally new experience, he never knew.

---

[2] A metaphor used by Milton Horowitz, M.D., at a meeting of the Center for Advanced Psychoanalytic Studies in Aspen, October 1986—in place of the familiar but misleading metaphor for the analysis of developmental levels: the unpeeling of layer after layer of an onion.

Formulations

Eventually, I reached a fair clinical understanding of this patient's life, at least as it developed after babyhood. But it took a long time to mesh the clinical understandings, and understand that they wee indivisibly related to an integrated set of theoretical assumptions and concepts. Speculations about the earlier months seem fruitless. Despite the coldness and detachment imputed to the mother, nothing was really known about the quality of her maternal care. It may have been adequate, or it may have been provided largely by the father.

What is almost certain is that *after* the first year—probably beginning about the middle of the second year—the patient experienced the four major separations mentioned above.

These losses were condensed in the adult's associations, and were highlighted by memories of some of the phenomenal indulgences of infantile wishes during early childhood. The creation of an *enfante terrible* by the focus of both parents' libidinal (and aggressive) interests (Mahler, 1949), also favored fixations on early patterns of self-love, early regulations of self-esteem, and, above all, the failure of modifications of the "flowering of omnipotence" from about eighteen months (Mahler, Pine, and Bergman, 1975; Spruiell, 1975) on. These dreaded and wished-for possibilities of the disappearance of either mother or father accentuated the intensity of the conflicts of preoedipal, oedipal, and postoedipal triangular relationships, and led to the near-balancing of positive and negative oedipal organizations of fantasies.

The separations undoubtedly stimulated intense and persistent greed. Omnipotence coupled with golden possibilities coupled with infantile hungers make together a mighty force. That provided the emotional context of feverish oral, anal, and phallic excitements brought to a climax by the grossly seductive incestuous genital and sadomasochistic exchanges.

At least as important as the overt seductions by the mother was the steady retreat by a depressed and alcoholic father, culminating in his death during the future patient's riotous new world of early adolescence. It was only during later adolescence, after the death of the father, that he also withdrew from the mother—into the hubris of self-sufficient fantasies to worship (and be worshipped by) a higher "collective alternate" in the form of a scientific universe. In that realm he would at the very least share all power (keeping in mind that "sharing" was an empty word for him).

The intensity of the chronic castration anxiety, in terms of both negative and positive oedipal organizations, was illustrated by the outwardly "normal" but inwardly bizarre extremes of the "solutions" (according to the principle of multiple function or compromise formations [Waelder, 1936; Brenner, 1982]). The prices paid in terms of anxiety, guilt, and deprivation of genuine gratifications were indeed excessive, thus pathological. They were pathological *quantitatively* in the sense of "too much" sacrifice of transferences and "too much" suffering. They were also pathological qualitatively in that they represented chronic interferences with communications among the suborganizations of the mind. A psychologically ill person is not fundamentally different from a supposedly healthy person. But when quantitative intensities reach extreme levels they amount to qualitative impairments of external adaptations (Freud, 1900, 1937).

I assume that these processes imply an organismic theory of the mind, another word for Freud's last structural theory (Freud, 1923a; Loewald, 1971a). That theory encompasses both functions in interactions (*processes*), and concepts of structures and substructures (but, as in physiology, not necessarily localized in space).

Analysts at work do not often think in terms of such abstractions. Rather, they usually remain in a receptive mode and allow their thoughts as much freedom to drift as feasible. They do not "try too hard" to understand the therapeutic exchanges in terms of strictly logical or rational thought. Rather, they allow as much free play of the many variables as possible; they watch the interactions; they attend to fantasies; they remain conscious of multiple determinations and functions; they pick up the intrapsychic resistances, especially to transferences; above all they look for what is missing. They look for "obligatory fantasies" which simply seem absent; they look for failures to make ordinary connections between outside life, the transference, and the past. Then, from time to time, Gestalten seem to "well up" from within, without effort, rather from forced reasoning.

Sometimes this form of thought is called "nonlinear." This is a somewhat strained mathematical metaphor, but one that allows for pattern recognitions and associations unlike the reductionistic and highly organized thinking of "higher rationality." One can and should think theoretically about these mental operations, which might seem loose and "dreamy" to some, but resemble free associations to analysts, a surrender to another kind of order in terms of the complexity of the multidetermined variables, the hierarchies of organizations, representations, conflicts, internalizations and externalizations, displacements, transferences—particularly the leading edge of resistances. But theories about the "nonlinear" mode make closer use of clinical observations than more abstract operations of structure and function.

Nevertheless, these abstract operations are *also* intimately related to the psychoanalytic situation. It is important to move from time to time from the more "subjective" state of mind within the field of operations, and to take a more "objective" point of view outside it— to shift to a form of thought often called "linear." Serial abstract "snapshots" can allow the distinction of structures with boundaries delineated by conflicts, estimated intensities, representations, and identifications. The more abstract views help integrate the picture of mind; they provide an abstract overview that allows comparisons with other patients (Friedman, 1988).

Both parts of the organismic theory, processes in interaction and the delineation of structures, are necessary. Together they make up psychoanalytic theory as an entity itself, from which most of the principles of practice are derived—in the same way that theory is in large part derived from clinical experience. The two are mostly (but not exactly) identical; each largely entails the other; changes in one require, or should require, changes in the other (Spruiell, 1990).

It would not be difficult to formally summarize my patient's case in these terms, but it is more important to note that such a summary, about this patient at least, would seem rather bleak; in analytic work most attention is by necessity paid to impairments rather than relatively autonomous assets. My patient's severe psychopathology was buffered in several ways. Not only infantile wishes, fears, and conflicts were screened—on the "other sides" of the screens, to speak loosely, were much more "normal" and "realistic" abilities to relate to others. He could turn to an inner discipline that had been finely honed by an excellent education and tangible professional rewards. He was unusually intelligent. He had capacities for intense aesthetic pleasures (and psychoanalysis knows next to nothing about the nature of these capacities). Providing there was no threat of intimacy, he could divine the wishes and problems and desires of other human beings. Of crucial importance was his ability to love his children, and tolerate a tolerant wife. Together they signified at least a foothold in an advanced level of development. Finally, he had a strong will (also a subject about which psychoanalysis knows little) that enabled him to seek out psychoanalysis— and he endured it, though not without hazards. If his analysis were to be deeply effective therapeutically, it had to reactivate the screen fantasies, within the therapeutic relationship, that he was totally self-sufficient, and that his will and talents were strong and that he was capable of irresistible genius. Behind that screen fantasy was the unconscious fantasy that he could maintain closeness with one other person (eventually represented by his "collective alternate," science) and that he had successfully erased any third person. This was his most fundamental unconscious "reality." Anything outside this implied murder and death.

But he was living on borrowed time; the analysis failed to produce the Prize, and the analysis and the analyst became themselves intrusions, and threats.

Is there a single quality that these seemingly disparate intrapsychic examples of psychopathology have in common? I have been alluding to intrapsychic separations—*gaps*—in which both object and self representations were continually disrupted. Internally, these were represented by the experiential phenomena and the structural distortions which reflected the costly compromises. From an external view, they were represented by disorders in his object relations.

All that meant he could not play with other people, nor could he work cooperatively with peers. He required years to develop a reliable analytic relationship, one that could allow enough of a feeling of safety to "play" within the analytic frame, to reenact verbally other frames of his life. It was only then that we could identify and interpret the resistances (which he also experienced as screens) against the apparently missing (repressed, denied, disavowed) transferences. This changed most dramatically in the dreamlike experience in the taxicab, and its successful analysis later.

No analysis can be more than relatively successful. And any analysis that must finesse confrontations with evidences of destructive aggression, and many analyses must, is sharply limited.

With my patient the real progress in the first and most lengthy segment of the analysis made it possible to experience more dangerous possibilities than he had ever consciously contemplated: a vivid experience of almost unbearable (for him and for me) murderous impulsions from early childhood that had been rendered even more dangerous by omnipotence. During this stormy time, it seemed to me that I was no longer a person to him. I was to him a *part* of a psychotic transference life that was dominated by almost overwhelming wishes to do me literal harm (Bird, 1972). It was only after both of us endured that he accomplished a truly successful analytic result, whatever its other shortcomings.

A "totally successful analysis" is a dangerous myth that implies that humans can become transfigured. Although the professor came to savor his actual story rather than the heroic myth, became able to enjoy his excellent reputation and his family life, he retained a certain self-conscious distance, a certain inability to play, a certain humorlessness about himself.

Screens, Frames, Boundaries, Splits, and Membranes

Ralph Greenson's 1958 paper, "On Screen Defenses, Screen Hunger, and Screen Identity," is rarely cited in the contemporary literature. It deserves to be. Originally called "Characters in Search of a Screen," the older title might have been more memorable, but it would not have been as descriptive as the one finally chosen. The focus of the paper actually took the screen metaphor far beyond mere searches or appetites.

The patients Greenson described, and in most ways the patient described here, had qualitatively similar characteristics at all structural, economic, and historical levels. The analyses were long and difficult, but one did not get the impression from the descriptions that they were particularly stormy. My patient's analysis, during its last year or two, was exceedingly stormy. Greenson specifically avoided an attempt to delineate a new diagnostic entity, rather, he delineated a syndrome. My patient had this constellation of features, but other problems as well in the realm of his sense of mission, preoccupations with power, and impaired object relationships.

The paper offered, and still offers, a fresh perspective on the subject of narcissism. Written from a viewpoint within the mainstream structural and drive theories, it is particularly important because it approaches narcissism without fundamental alterations of psychoanalytic theory. Its beautifully condensed, multileveled descriptions should not be further condensed by me. Better to encourage people to read his paper.

But in a capsule summary, he described patients who nosologically could be labeled combinations of hysteria and depression (although the depression turned out to be a special mix of neurotic depression and impulse disorder). These analysands organize their lives about the shielding and gratifying disguises, the filtering purposes, of "psychic screens."

Screens were first used, of course, in references to memories, but they have also been applied to affects, the provision of derivative discharges, their applications to hide or disguise moods, the use of "screen identifications," their function in character structure, their economic and dynamic functions. Screens not only hide but falsify. "In ordinary language the word screen may mean to conceal, to filter or to camouflage" (Greenson, 1958, p. 248). They are thus *symptoms*, the products of multiple functions (Waelder, 1936); instances of compromise formations (Brenner, 1982). They maximize defenses, minimize pain, and often enough they provide hidden gratifications.

All people make use of screen formations, but the patients described make very extensive uses of them in an effort to maintain psychic equilibrium. More than utilize screens to disguise major parts of the mind from themselves and from others, these individuals have only temporary appeasable hungers for almost endlessly new experiences and sensations. They turn soon from them to other, new screens. A common characteristic is a tendency toward counterphobic reactions. These people are apt to be intelligent, successful in outside life, talented, likable, sensitive, well motivated—and more optimistic than they "should" be. There is much apparent or disguised depression.

They grasp the nature of psychoanalytic work rather easily, and persist in it despite the frustrations of what seem to be mazes of screens. Searches for new screens provide a large part of their motivations to analyze. Yet these patients also have countervailing forces within—to penetrate and rip down the screens. Complicating their analyses is the great hunger they have for objects. "They need objects as witnesses to testify to the fact that the patient's aggression has not damaged the object; they use witnesses to give permission for instinctual activity. Furthermore, the object offers them an opportunity to belatedly master their anxiety in regard to objects. The screen-hungry patients libidinize their anxiety; and for this purpose, too they need objects" (pp. 254–255).

My patient manifested most of the characteristics mentioned by Greenson, except that he was a more disturbed person. In particular, his ambitiousness went far beyond that of Greenson's patients. In fact, my analysand could have served as a prototype for Helen Tartakoff's classical 1966 paper, "The Normal Personality in our Culture and the Nobel Prize Complex." She described the contemporary cultural influences which stimulate some parents with specific narcissistic disturbances, especially those with beautiful and talented children, to gratify omnipotent fantasies through their magical child to extreme degrees. Too often, such children not only feel impelled to satisfy the parental ambitions but believe themselves capable of it. The most pretigious recognition of extraordinary scientific accomplishments is the Nobel Prize. Tartakoff's descriptions of the dynamic and economic developments which result in such disordered, grandiose, omnipotent fantasies are masterful.

Other Terms and Metaphors

The relatively less disturbed patients described by Greenson, the "omnipotent" patients described by Tartakoff, and the patient described here make up part of the "widening scope" of therapeutic analysis. Yet, the larger congeries of more disturbed, but analyzable patients do not make up a coherent group (Abend, Porder, and Willick, 1983). The diagnostic distinctions are not clear and the range is wide, from neuroticlike characters through patients with severe superego, narcissistic and pathological relations with other people.

To "locate" Greenson's analysands, they seem almost identical with the narcissistic patients described by Annie Reich (1953, 1960b). They are not as disturbed as Helene Deutsch's "as-if" personalities (1942), or as many of the patients described by self psychologists or object relations theorists as "borderline personalities."

They bear some resemblances to Greenacre's (1958) imposters, but compared to them my patient was much more reliably organized and analyzable.

I suspect the patients described by Greenson, Tartakoff, Reich, and myself have certain important features in common with Arlow's patients with character perversion (1972). Chasseguet-Schmirgel (1983) believes that specific, pathological alterations of reality are always encountered in genuine perverse organizations: the lack of erotic distinctions between the generations and the sexes, along with the important symbolic equation of the phallus with the stool. Greenacre (1957) described the presence in many highly creative individuals of blurring of boundaries between the erotic developmental phases (and one might add, if it were possible to define them, the aggressive phases). Finally, the patients under discussion have something in common with the analyzable schizoid individuals described by Winnicott (1965).

Splitting

I have not made use of another pair of common metaphors that are better known than "screens" and "screening." They are "splits" and "splitting." Freud (1923a, 1927, 1940[1938]) believed that the ego is capable of altering itself—including "splitting itself" organizationally. Kohut (1971) spoke of a "vertical split" of the personality. Kleinian analysts refer to splits—originally the poles of the dual instinct theory. Some authors use the word in place of ambivalence. Kernberg (1967) and others use it to refer to a postulated "primitive defense" associated with future "borderline pathology."

It is not that I doubt the existence of most of the clinical observations that give rise to these metaphors. Rather, it is the belief that they are heuristically too misleading. In a classical paper, Paul Pruyser (1975) studied the uses of the terms *split* and *splitting*, from Charcot, Janet, Breuer, and Freud, in reference to developmental psychology, schizophrenia, schizoid phenomena, fetishism, and ordinary neuroses. He took up Fairbairn's and other object relations theories' use of the terms to describe selves, part-selves and objects, "primitive defenses," and the various uses made by Kleinian and

Bionian theorists of spatial metaphors (as entities that could be split, digested or undigested, contained or be contained, inserted into others, or carry on as quasi-autonomous, space-occupying homunculilike entities within the mind, fighting little civil wars or making love, or conducting business). Above all, Pruyser wonders, *what does the splitting*? Must we infer that the ego as a whole, or some agency within it, conducts this action? Pruyser believed that the spatial metaphor of splits—with its organizational and material vagueness— shuts down understanding, calls a halt to further inquiry, or leads in false directions.

Must we return, as some developmental researchers seem to wish, to old ideas, such as Janet's, that the mind comes preformed—a whole entity, at least in outline? If we presume that, we are taking at face-value clinical observations that psychic functions, formerly parts of whole entities, are *actually* (rather than relatively and functionally) separated and out of communication with each other. Deeper explanations do not seem necessary. Freud's thought offers a different possibility, that the whole mind is *assembled* out of parts which, like neutral networks, come to be related and increasingly differentiated. Hence he emphasized regression to earlier fixation points, which are markers of the movements from one developmental phase to another. This point of views allows us to see that, aside from toxic or material neural damage, analyzable patients can come to understand that most of psychopathology is of their own construction and subject to their own alterations.

My patient's mind was functionally divided in *multiple* ways, and frequently the parts came into conflict with one another—in fact, multiple conflicts. Usually the latter necessitated further separations in the form of denials or disavowals. In a system, everything depends upon the nature of the compromises of inevitable conflicts and their relationships. The metaphor of screens carries connotations of inner construction, movability, filtration, distortion, total disguise—and the capacity to be undone. The other metaphors carry for me, as they often do for other analysts, too many implications of permanence and mechanical indestructibility.

But in "good-enough" analyses, a wholeness, an inner freedom, an inner increase of options, develops in the shelter of the analytic situation.

A Digression on Creativity

Greenson's patients (1958a) had developmental experiences in childhood which are more often found in much more disturbed patients. He speculated about why they had been able to do so well in life—relatively speaking, even before analysis. His tentative answer was that, despite the severity of the distressing experiences, the patients also had many opportunities for gratifications.

The same question may be put to my clinical account—and the same possible answer given. If anything, my patient had a much worse time in development than Greenson's or Reich's patients, and he had much more dangerous psychopathology. He also had more gratifications, but some of them were overwhelming and traumatic; rather than mitigating pathological trends they added to them.

Greenacre maintained (1957, 1958, 1969) that at least five conditions are necessary for an individual to be creative: (1) the possession of a marked sensitivity to relevant areas of perception; (2) an unusual ability to link ideas or images, possibly implying "a greater sense of the gestalt"; (3) an unusual capacity for empathy, implying a responsiveness to one's own body states; (4) a childlike propensity to anthropomorphize inanimate objects and animals; and (5) "adequate sensorimotor equipment."

Greenacre presumed, and I presumed in the case of my patient, there were innate constitutional gifts, including unusual abilities to construct Gestalten. And my patient, also, was able to develop a "love affair with the world"—for him, science. Like Greenacre's creative patients, he had a perverselike "blurring" or diffuseness in the boundaries of stages of development. Just as their biographies include an inordinate number of experiences of extreme separation, my analysand had them too. Greenacre's subjects also had special gratifications, but again, as far as I know, these came later, in the form of mentors who recognized genius and did everything to further it in later childhood and adolescence. My patient's incestuous gratifications had nothing to do with the recognition of talent or genius.

My scientist–patient was creative in familiar, everyday ways, but he could not be the genius he so desperately believed he had to be. He couldn't peer into a chasm and come back with a vision. He couldn't imaginatively project original Gestalten into the seeming emptiness of his screens. He needed their very blankness too much. Potential visions were for him, I suspect, too risky.

Therefore, the differences between our speculations about the developmental histories of creators who are truly revolutionary in their offerings, and my patient, are great. His gratifications reached traumatic proportions in the erotic ministrations of his mother. He did not "need" to put together associations in new, linking forms; he had to separate them. Some individuals can find support in imaginative fantasy; he found danger. There is a related difference of possible importance: Just as most "screen patients" have counterphobic tendencies, the professor did not. He would grapple directly with problems mostly with words; he tended to avoid major actions that were chancy. Finally, one set of character traits never changed. The lack of change suggested a continuing internal organization that would not allow total immersion in his vocation. He never could lose a certain kind of anxious self-consciousness. He never could become the subject of his own humor. He could appreciate the tragic but not the comic qualities of his life.

Actually, the professor accomplished more than most people dare to hope they might, and he eventually came to accept his right to be proud.

Summary

The primary purpose of this essay is to discuss the extensive uses put to certain alterations of conscious perception in which one or more sets of psychic realities seem to be missing, but actually are unconsciously screened off from others (Greenson, 1958a). These phenomena are illustrated by fragments from a long but successful analysis, conducted by ordinary, "standard" means, with a gifted, but narcissistic person, an "omnipotent character" very similar to those described by Tartakoff (1966). Thus, the second purpose of the essay is to illustrate the phenomena of omnipotence as it emerges when a standard psychoanalytic approach is used. This brings up a third purpose, the demonstration that Freud's last structural theory is literally an organismic theory which encompasses process explanations and structural explanations. From this point of view, psychoanalytic theory and practice are intimately related: Everything is connected with, and influences, everything. The fourth purpose is to advance the proposition that the metaphors of various kinds of "defense mechanisms" and "splits" are much less heuristically useful and carry too many false metaphorical leads than the metaphor of the screen. The latter is closely related to clinical observations, and the underlying nonexperiential, organismic events; it is flexible, carries the possibilities of construction and removal, the possibilities of partial filtering, distortion, and total opacities, which can indeed be discerned at least inferentially during analyses. The heuristic uses are much more promising for the future study of how, when, and for what purposes, that is, for what aims of particular compromise formations, the psyche *seemingly* divides itself into *seemingly* separate, independent realms. Last, I included a discussion of the necessary antecedents of a certain kind of creativity (Greenacre, 1969; Spruiell, 1977).

References

Aarons, Z. A. (1962), Indications for analysis and problems of analyzability. *Psychoanal. Quart.*, 31:514–531.

——— (1965), On analytic goals and criteria for termination. *Bull. Phila. Assn. Psychoanal.*, 15:97–109.

Abend, S., Porder, M., & Willick, M. (1983), Borderline Patients: Psychoanalytic Perspectives. *The Kris Study Group of the New York Psychoanalytic Institute,* Monogr. 7. New York: International Universities Press.

Abraham, K. (1919), A particular form of neurotic resistance against the psychoanalytic method. In: *Selected Papers on Psychoanalysis.* London: Hogarth Press, 1927, pp. 303–311.

Abrams, S. (1974), The meaning of "nothing." *Psychoanal. Quart.*, 43:115.

——— (1987), The psychoanalytic process: A schematic model. *Internat. J. Psycho-Anal.*, 58:441–452.

Aiza, V., Cesarman, F., & Gonzalez, A. (1966), Discussion of Rangell's An overview of the ending of an analysis. In: *Psychoanalysis in the Americas,* ed. R. E. Litman. New York: International Universities Press, pp. 166–167.

Alexander, F., & French, T. M. (1946), *Psychoanalytic Therapy.* New York: Ronald Press.

Alvarez de Toledo, L. C., Grinberg, L., & Langer, M. (1966), Termination of training analysis. In: *Psychoanalysis in the Americas,* ed. R. E. Litman. New York: International Universities Press, pp. 174–192.

Angel, K. (1971), On analyzability and narcissistic transference disturbances. *Psychoanal. Quart.*, 40:264–276.

461

Anzieu, D. (1987), Some alteration of the ego which makes analysis interminable. *Internat. J. Psycho-Anal.*, 68:9–19.

Appelbaum, A. (1972), A critical reexamination of the concept "motivation for change" in psychoanalytic treatment. *Internat. J. Psycho-Anal.*, 53:51–59.

Appelbaum, S. A. (1973), Psychological mindedness: Word, concept, and essence. *Internat. J. Psycho-Anal.*, 54:35–46.

Arlow, J. A. (1953), Masturbation and symptom formation. *J. Amer. Psychoanal. Assn.*, 1:45–58.

——— (1972), Character perversion. In: *Currents in Psychoanalysis*, ed. I. Marcus. New York: International Universities Press.

——— (1979), The genesis of interpretations. *J. Amer. Psychoanal. Assn.*, 27(Suppl.):263–288.

——— (1987), The dynamics of interpretation. *Psychoanal. Quart.*, 66:68–87.

——— Brenner, C. (1964), *Psychoanalytic Concepts and the Structural Theory*. New York: International Universities Press.

Asch, S. S. (1976), Varieties of negative therapeutic reaction and problems of technique. *J. Amer. Psychoanal. Assn.*, 24:383–407.

Atwood, G., & Stolorow, R. (1984), *Structures of Subjectivity: Explorations in Psychoanalytic Phenomenology*. Hillsdale, NJ: Analytic Press.

Bacal, H. (1985), Optimal responsiveness and the therapeutic process. In: *Progress in Self Psychology*, ed. A. Goldberg. New York: Guilford Press, pp. 202–227.

Bachrach, H., & Leaff, L. (1978), "Analyzability": A systematic review of the clinical and quantitative literature. *J. Amer. Psychoanal. Assn.*, 26:881–920.

Balint, M. (1936), The final goal of psycho-analytic treatment. *Internat. J. Psycho-Anal.*, 17:206–216.

——— (1950), Changing therapeutical aims and techniques in psycho-analysis. *Internat. J. Psycho-Anal.*, 31:117–124.

——— (1968), *The Basic Fault: Therapeutic Aspects of Regression*. London: Tavistock.

Benedek, T. (1955), A contribution to the problem of termination of training analysis. *J. Amer. Psychoanal. Assn.*, 3:615–629.

Berenstein, I. (1987), Analysis terminable and interminable: Fifty years on. *Internat. J. Psycho-Anal.*, 68:21–35.

Bergmann, M. S. (1988), On the fate of the intrapsychic image of the psychoanalyst after termination of the analysis. *The Psychoanalytic Study of the Child*, 43:137–153. New Haven, CT: Yale University Press.

Berman, L. (1949), Countertransference and attitudes of the analyst in the therapeutic process. *Psychiatry*, 12:159–166.

Bernfeld, S. (1932), Der Begriff der "Deutung" in der psychoanalyse. *Zeitschrift f. Angewandte Psychologie*, 42:448.

Bion, W. R. (1970), *Attention and Interpretation: A Scientific Approach to Insight in Psycho-Analysis and Groups*. New York: Basic Books.

Bird, B. (1957), A specific peculiarity of acting out. *J. Amer. Psychoanal. Assn.*, 5:630–647.

——— (1972), Notes on transference: Universal phenomenon and hardest part of analysis. *J. Amer. Psychoanal. Assn.*, 20:267–301.

Blum, H. P. (1976), Acting out, the psychoanalytic process, and interpretation. *Annual of Psychoanalysis*, 4:163–184. New York: International Universities Press.

————— (1977), The prototype of preoedipal reconstruction. *J. Amer. Psychoanal. Assn.*, 25:757–786.

————— (1987), Analysis terminable and interminable: A half century retrospective. *Internat. J. Psycho-Anal.*, 68:37–48.

————— (1989), The concept of termination and the evolution of psychoanalytic thought. *J. Amer. Psychoanal. Assn.*, 37:275–295.

Boesky, D. (1982), Acting out: A reconsideration of the concept. *Internat. J. Psycho-Anal.*, 63:39–55.

————— (1989), The questions and curiosity of the analyst. *J. Amer. Psychoanal. Assn.*, 37:579–604.

Bonaparte, M., Freud, A., & Kris, E., eds. (1954), Letter #61, Draft L. In: *The Origins of Psycho-Analysis: Letters to Fliess by Sigmund Freud.* New York: Basic Books.

Bornstein, M. (1983), Values and neutrality in psychoanalysis. *Psychoanal. Inq.*, 3:547–550.

Brandchaft, B. (1988), A case of intractable depression. In: *Learning from Kohut: Progress in Self Psychology*, Vol. 4, ed. A. Goldberg. Hillsdale, NJ: Analytic Press.

————— Stolorow, R. (1984), The borderline concept: Pathological character or iatrogenic myth? In: *Empathy*, Vol. 2, ed. J. Lichtenberg, M. Bernstein, & D. Silver. Hillsdale, NJ: Analytic Press, pp. 333–357.

————— ————— (1989), Varieties of therapeutic alliance. Paper presented before Los Angeles and Southern California Psychoanalytic Societies, March 17, 1989.

Brenner, C. (1973), *An Elementary Textbook of Psychoanalysis.* New York: International Universities Press.

————— (1976), *Psychoanalytic Technique and Psychic Conflict.* New York: International Universities Press.

————— (1977), Working alliance, therapeutic alliance, and transference. *J. Amer. Psychoanal. Assn.*, 37(Suppl.):137–157.

————— (1982), *The Mind in Conflict.* New York: International Universities Press.

————— (1987), Working through: 1914–1984. *Psychoanal. Quart.*, 56:88–108.

Breuer, J., & Freud, S. (1893–1895), Studies on Hysteria. *Standard Edition*, 2:vii–309. London: Hogarth Press, 1955.

Brodsky, B. (1967), Working through: Its widening scope and some aspects of its metapsychology. *Psychoanal. Quart.*, 36:485–496.

Buhler, C. (1962), Goals of life and therapy. *Amer. J. Psychoanal.*, 22:153–175.

Burgner, M. (1988), Analytic work with adolescents: Terminable and interminable. *Internat. J. Psycho-Anal.*, 69:179–188.

Calef, V., & Weinshel, E. M. (1983), A note on consummation and termination. *J. Amer. Psychoanal. Assn.*, 24:425–436.

Chasseguet-Smirgel, J. (1983), Perversion and the universal law. *Internat. Rev. Psychoanal.*, 10:293–301.

Cohen, J., & Kinston, W. (in press), Understanding failures and catastrophes in psycho-analysis. *Internat. J. Psycho-Anal.*

Coltrera, J. T. (1980), Truth from genetic illusion. The transference and the fate of the infantile neurosis. In: *Psychoanalytic Explorations of Technique*, ed. H. Blum. New York: International Universities Press, pp. 289–314.

Cooper, A. M. (1986), Some limitations on therapeutic effectiveness: The "burnout syndrome" in psychoanalysis. *Psychoanal. Quart.*, 55:576–598.

De Simone Gaburri, G. (1985), On termination of the analysis. *Internat. J. Psycho-Anal.,* 12:461–468.

Deutsch, H. (1942), Some forms of emotional disturbance and their relation to schizophrenia. *Psychoanal. Quart.,* 11:301–321.

Dewald, P. A. (1972), The clinical assessment of structural change. *J. Amer. Psychoanal. Assn.,* 20:302–324.

———— (1972), *The Psychoanalytic Process.* New York: Basic Books.

———— (1976), Transference regression and real experience in the psychoanalytic process. *Psychoanal. Quart.,* 45:213–230.

———— (1982), The clinical importance of the termination phase. *Psychoanal. Inq.,* 2:441–461.

Eidelberg, L. (1945), A contribution to the study of the masturbation fantasy. *Internat. J. Psycho-Anal.,* 26:127–137.

Eissler, K. R. (1953), The effect of the structure of the ego on psychoanalytic technique. *J. Amer. Psychoanal. Assn.,* 1:104–141.

Ekstein, R. (1965), Working through and termination of analysis. *J. Amer. Psychoanal. Assn.,* 13:57–78.

———— (1966), Termination of analysis and working through. In: *Psychoanalysis in the Americas,* ed. R. E. Litman. New York: International Universities Press, pp. 217–237.

———— (1979), Further thoughts concerning the nature of the interpretive process. *S. Freud Hse. Bull.,* 3:12–19.

———— (1980), Robert Waelder's criteria of interpretation (1939) revisited. *J. Phil. Assn. Psychoanal.,* 7:113–128.

———— (1985), Fundamental concepts: Prolegomena to the study of the languages of psychoanalysis and psychotherapy. In: *New Ideas in Psychoanalysis,* ed. C. Settlage & R. Brockbank. Hillsdale, NJ: Analytic Press, pp. 56–67.

———— (1987), Reflections on the meanings of "borderline": Between metaphor and concept. In: *The Borderline Patient,* ed. Grotstein, Solomon, & Lang. Hillsdale, NJ: Analytic Press, pp. 95–104.

———— Wallerstein, J. (1954), Observations on the psychology of borderline and psychotic children. *The Psychoanalytic Study of the Child,* 9:344–369. New York: International Universities Press.

Erard, R. (1983), New wine in old skins: A reappraisal of the concept "acting out." *Internat. Rev. Psychoanal.,* 10:63–73.

Erikson, E. H. (1950), *Childhood and Society.* New York: W. W. Norton.

Fenichel, O. (1941), *Problems of Psychoanalytic Technique.* Albany: Psychoanalytic Quarterly.

———— (1945a), Neurotic acting out. *Collected Papers of Otto Fenichel,* 2:296–304. New York: W. W. Norton, 1954.

———— (1945b), *The Psychoanalytic Theory of Neurosis.* New York: W. W. Norton.

Ferenczi, S. (1926), *The Theory and Technique of Psychoanalysis.* London: Hogarth Press.

———— Rank, O. (1925), *The Development of Psychoanalysis.* New York: Nervous and Mental Disease Publishing.

Firestein, S. K. (1974), Termination of psychoanalysis of adults: A review of the literature. *J. Amer. Psychoanal. Assn.,* 22:873–894.

———— (1978), *Termination in Psychoanalysis.* New York: International Universities Press.

———— (1982), Termination of psychoanalysis: Theoretical, clinical, and pedagogic considerations. *Psychoanal. Inq.,* 2:473–497.

Fleming, J. (1972), Early object deprivation and transference phenomena. *Psychoanal. Quart.,* 41:23–49.

Fliess, R. (1942), The metapsychology of the analyst. *Psychoanal. Quart.,* 11:211–227.

———— (1953), Countertransference and counteridentification. *J. Amer. Psychoanal. Assn.,* 1:268–284.

Freud, A. (1936), *The Ego and the Mechanisms of Defense.* New York: International Universities Press, 1966.

———— (1949), Certain types and stages of social maladjustment. In: *Searchlights on Delinquency,* ed. K. R. Eissler. New York: International Universities Press, pp. 193–204.

———— (1954a), Problems of technique in adult analysis. *Bull. Phila. Assn. Psychoanal.,* 4:44–69.

———— (1954b), The widening scope of indications for psychoanalysis. Discussion. *J. Amer. Psychoanal. Assn.,* 2:607–620.

———— (1965), Diagnostic skills and their growth in psychoanalysis. *Internat. J. Psycho-Anal.,* 46:30–38.

———— (1966), *Normality and Pathology in Childhood: Assessments of Development.* New York: International Universities Press.

———— (1969a), Research at the Hampstead Child Therapy Clinic and other papers. *Writings,* 5. New York: International Universities Press.

———— (1969b), Difficulties in the path of psychoanalysis: A confrontation of past with present viewpoints. *Writings,* 7:124–156. New York: International Universities Press, 1971.

———— (1970a), Problems of termination in child analysis. *Writings,* 7:3–21. New York: International Universities Press, 1971.

———— (1970b), The symptomatology of childhood: A preliminary attempt at classification. *Writings,* 7:157–188. New York: International Universities Press, 1971.

Freud, S. (1900),The Interpretation of Dreams. *Standard Edition,* 4 & 5. London: Hogarth Press, 1953.

———— (1905a), Fragment of an analysis of a case of hysteria. *Standard Edition,* 7:116–117. London: Hogarth Press, 1953.

———— (1905b), Three essays on the theory of sexuality. *Standard Edition,* 7:125–245. London: Hogarth Press, 1953.

———— (1905c), On psychotherapy. *Standard Edition,* 7:257–268. London: Hogarth Press, 1953.

———— (1908), Hysterical phantasies and their relation to bisexuality. *Standard Edition,* 9:155–166. London: Hogarth Press, 1959.

———— (1909a), Family romances. *Standard Edition,* 9:235–241. London: Hogarth Press, 1959.

———— (1909b), Analysis of a phobia in a five year-old boy. *Standard Edition,* 10:3–149. London: Hogarth Press, 1955.

———— (1909c), Notes upon a case of obsessional neurosis. *Standard Edition,* 10:155–318. London: Hogarth Press, 1955.

———— (1910a), The future prospects of psycho-analytic therapy. *Standard Edition,* 11:139–151. London: Hogarth Press, 1957.

——— (1910b), A special type of choice of object made by men. *Standard Edition*, 11:163–176. London: Hogarth Press, 1957.

——— (1910c), *Three Contributions to the Theory of Sex*. New York: Nervous and Mental Disease Publishing Co.

——— (1910d), The future prospects of psychoanalytic therapy. In: *Collected Papers of Sigmund Freud*, Vol. 2. New York: Basic Books, 1959.

——— (1911), The handling of dream interpretation in psycho-analysis. *Standard Edition*, 12:91–96. London: Hogarth Press, 1958.

——— (1912a), The dynamics of transference. *Standard Edition*, 12:98–108. London: Hogarth Press, 1958.

——— (1912b), Contributions to a discussion on masturbation. *Standard Edition*, 12:239–255. London: Hogarth Press, 1958.

——— (1913), On beginning the treatment. *Standard Edition*, 12:121–144. London: Hogarth Press, 1958.

——— (1914), Remembering, repeating, and working through. *Standard Edition*, 12:145–157. London: Hogarth Press, 1958.

——— (1915[1914]), Observations on transference love. *Standard Edition*, 12:157–171. London: Hogarth Press, 1958.

——— (1916), Some character types met with in psychoanalytic work. *Standard Edition*, 14:309–333. London: Hogarth Press, 1957.

——— (1916–1917), Introductory Lectures on Psycho-Analysis. *Standard Edition*, 15 & 16. London: Hogarth Press, 1963.

——— (1917a), Mourning and melancholia. *Standard Edition*, 14:237–258. London: Hogarth Press, 1957.

——— (1917b), A metapsychological supplement to the theory of dreams. *Standard Edition*, 17:222–235. London: Hogarth Press, 1957.

——— (1918a), The taboo of virginity. *Standard Edition*, 11:191–208. London: Hogarth Press, 1957.

——— (1918b), From the history of an infantile neurosis. *Standard Edition*, 17:1–122. London: Hogarth Press, 1955.

——— (1919), Lines of advance in psychoanalytic therapy. *Standard Edition*, 17:159–168. London: Hogarth Press, 1955.

——— (1920), Beyond the pleasure principle. *Standard Edition*, 18:7–64. London: Hogarth Press, 1955.

——— (1923[1922]), Two encyclopedia articles. (A) Psychoanalysis. *Standard Edition*, 18:233–254. London: Hogarth Press, 1955.

——— (1923a), The ego and the id. *Standard Edition*, 19:12–66. London: Hogarth Press, 1961.

——— (1923b), Remarks on the theory and practice of dream-interpretation. *Standard Edition*, 19:109–121. London: Hogarth Press, 1961.

——— (1924), The dissolution of the Oedipus complex. *Standard Edition*, 19:173–179. London: Hogarth Press, 1961.

——— (1925), Some additional notes on dream interpretation as a whole. *Standard Edition*, 19:127–138. London: Hogarth Press, 1961.

——— (1926a), Inhibitions, symptoms, and anxiety. *Standard Edition*, 20:87–174. London: Hogarth Press, 1959.

——— (1926b), The question of lay analysis. *Standard Edition*, 20:177–258. London: Hogarth Press, 1959.

———— (1927), Fetishism. *Standard Edition,* 21:152–157. London: Hogarth Press, 1961.

———— (1930), Civilization and its discontents. *Standard Edition,* 21:57–145. London: Hogarth Press, 1961.

———— (1933[1932]), New Introductory Lectures on Psycho-Analysis. *Standard Edition,* 22:1–182. London: Hogarth Press, 1964.

———— (1937), Analysis terminable and interminable. *Standard Edition,* 23:209–253. London: Hogarth Press, 1964.

———— (1938), Moses and Monotheism. *Standard Edition,* 23:1–137. London: Hogarth Press, 1964.

———— (1940[1938]), Splitting of the ego in the process of defense. *Standard Edition,* 23:275–278. London: Hogarth Press, 1964.

———— (1985), Quoted by Princess Maria Bonaparte in her unpublished journals—as mentioned by Daniel Goleman: Freud's Mind: New Details revealed in Documents, *New York Times,* Sept. 12, 1985.

Friedman, L. (1985), Towards a comprehensive theory of treatment. *Psychoanal. Inq.,* 5:589–600.

———— (1988), *The Anatomy of Psychotherapy.* Hillsdale, NJ: Analytic Press.

Furman, E. (1982), Mothers have to be there to be left. *The Psychoanalytic Study of the Child,* 37:15–28. New Haven, CT: Yale University Press.

Gardiner, M. (1983), *Code Name "Mary."* New Haven, CT: Yale University Press.

Gaskill, H. S. (1980), The closing phase of the psychoanalytic treatment of adults and the goals of psychoanalysis: "The myth of perfectibility." *Internat. J. Psycho-Anal.,* 61:11–23.

Gedo, J. (1979), *Beyond Interpretation.* New York: International Universities Press.

———— Goldberg, A. (1973), *Models of the Mind.* Chicago: University of Chicago Press.

Gill, M. M. (1954), Psychoanalysis and exploratory psychotherapy. *J. Amer. Psychoanal. Assn.,* 2:771–797.

———— (1982), The Analysis of Transference: Theory and Technique, Vol. I. *Psychological Issues,* Monogr. 53. New York: International Universities Press.

———— Hoffman, I. Z. (1982), The Analysis of Transference, Vol. II: Studies of Nine Audio-recorded Psychoanalytic Sessions. *Psychological Issues,* Monogr. 54. New York: International Universities Press.

———— Newman, R., & Redlich, F. (1954), *The Initial Interview in Psychiatric Practice.* New York: International Universities Press.

Gitelson, M. (1952), The emotional position of the analyst in the psycho-analytic situation. *Internat. J. Psycho-Anal.,* 33:1–10.

———— (1962), The curative factors in psychoanalysis. The first phase of psychoanalysis. *Internat. J. Psycho-Anal.,* 43:194–205.

———— (1963), On the present scientific and social position of psychoanalysis. In: *Psychoanalysis: Science and Profession,* ed. M. Gitelson. New York: International Universities Press, 1973, pp. 342–359.

Glenn, J. (1978), General principles of child analysis. In: *Child Analysis and Therapy,* ed. J. Glenn. New York: Jason Aronson, pp. 29–66.

Glover, E. (1954), The indications for psychoanalysis. *J. Ment. Sci.,* 100:393–401.

———— (1955), *The Technique of Psychoanalysis.* New York: International Universities Press.

Goldberg, A. (1988), *A Fresh Look at Psychoanalysis*. Hillsdale, NJ: Analytic Press.

——— Marcus, D. (1985), "Natural termination": Some comments on ending analysis without setting a date. *Psychoanal. Quart.*, 54:46–65.

Gray, P. (1973), Psychoanalytic technique and the ego's capacity for viewing intrapsychic conflict. *J. Amer. Psychoanal. Assn.*, 21:474–494.

——— (1982), "Developmental lag" in the evolution of technique for psychoanalysis of neurotic conflict. *J. Amer. Psychoanal. Assn.*, 30:621–655.

——— (1986), On helping analysands observe intrapsychic activity. In: *Psychoanalysis: The Science of Mental Conflict: Essays in Honor of Charles Brenner*, ed. A. Richards & M. Willick. Hillsdale, NJ: Analytic Press, pp. 245–262.

——— (1987), On the technique of analysis of the superego: An introduction. *Psychoanal. Quart.*, 56:130–154.

Greenacre, P. (1950), General problems of acting out. In: *Trauma, Growth and Personality*. New York: W. W. Norton, 1952, pp. 224–226.

——— (1952), The prepuberty trauma in girls. In: *Trauma, Growth and Personality*. New York: W. W. Norton, pp. 204–223.

——— (1954), The role of transference: Practical considerations in relation to psychoanalytic therapy. *J. Amer. Psychoanal. Assn.*, 2:671–684.

——— (1956), Re-evaluation of the process of working through. *Internat. J. Psycho-Anal.*, 37:439–444.

——— (1957), The childhood of the artist: Libidinal phase development and giftedness. *The Psychoanalytic Study of the Child*, 12:47–72. New York: International Universities Press.

——— (1958), The family romance of the artist. *The Psychoanalytic Study of the Child*, 13:9–36. New York: International Universities Press.

——— (1966), Problems of over-idealization of the analyst and of analysis: Their manifestations in the transference and countertransference relationship. *The Psychoanalytic Study of the Child*, 21:193–212. New York: International Universities Press.

——— (1969), The fetish and the transitional object. *The Psychoanalytic Study of the Child*, 24:144–164. New York: International Universities Press.

Greenson, R. R. (1953), On boredom. In: *Explorations in Psychoanalysis*. New York: International Universities Press, 1978, pp. 45–60.

——— (1955), Forepleasure: Its use for defensive purposes. *J. Amer. Psychoanal. Assn.*, 3:244–254.

——— (1958a), On screen defenses, screen hunger, and screen identity. *J. Amer. Psychoanal. Assn.*, 6:242–262.

——— (1958b), Variations in classical psychoanalytic technique. *Internat. J. Psycho-Anal.*, 39:200–201.

——— (1959), Phobia, anxiety, and depression. *J. Amer. Psychoanal. Assn.*, 7:663–674.

——— (1960), Empathy and its vicissitudes. In: *Explorations in Psychoanalysis*. New York: International Universities Press, 1978, pp. 147–162.

——— (1961), On the silence and sounds of the analytic hour. In: *Explorations in Psychoanalysis*. New York: International Universities Press, 1978, pp. 163–169.

——— (1965a), The working alliance and the transference neurosis. *Psychoanal. Quart.*, 34:155–389.

——— (1965b), The problem of working through. In: *Drives, Affects, Behavior*, Vol.

2, ed. M. Schur. New York: International Universities Press, pp. 277–314.

—— (1966), Discussion of Parres' and Ramirez' Termination of analysis. In: *Psychoanalysis in the Americas*, ed. R. E. Litman. New York: International Universities Press, pp. 263–266.

—— (1967), *The Technique and Practice of Psychoanalysis*, Vol. 1. New York: International Universities Press.

—— (1968a), Disidentifying from mother: Its special importance for the boy. In: *Explorations in Psychoanalysis*. New York: International Universities Press, 1978, pp. 305–312.

—— (1968b), The use of dream sequences for detecting errors of technique: A clinical study. In: *Explorations in Psychoanalysis*. New York: International Universities Press, 1978, pp. 313–331.

—— (1969), The origin and fate of new ideas in psychoanalysis. *Internat. J. Psycho-Anal.*, 50:503–515.

—— (1970), The exceptional position of the dream in psychoanalytic practice. In: *Explorations in Psychoanalysis*. New York: International Universities Press, 1978, pp. 387–414.

—— (1972), Beyond transference and interpretation. *Internat. J. Psycho-Anal.*, 53:213–217.

—— (1974a), Loving, hating, and indifference toward the patient. In: *Explorations in Psychoanalysis*. New York: International Universities Press, 1978, pp. 508–518.

—— (1974b), On transitional objects and transference. In: *Between Reality and Fantasy: Transitional Objects and Phenomena*, ed. S. Grolnick & L. Barkin. New York: Jason Aronson, 1978, pp. 203–210.

—— (1974c), Transference: Freud or Klein. In: *Explorations in Psychoanalysis*. New York: International Universities Press, 1978, pp. 519–540.

—— (1978), *Explorations in Psychoanalysis*. New York: International Universities Press.

—— Wexler, M. (1969), The non-transference relationship in the psychoanalytic situation. *Internat. J. Psycho-Anal.*, 50:27–39.

—— —— (1970), Discussion of 'The non-transference relationship in the psychoanalytic situation.' *Internat. J. Psycho-Anal.*, 51:143–150.

Greenspan, S., & Cullander, C. (1973), A systematic methodological assessment of the personality—its application to the problem of analyzability. *J. Amer. Psychoanal. Assn.*, 21:303–328.

Grinberg, L. (1980), The closing phase of the psychoanalytic treatment of adults and the goals of psychoanalysis: "The search for truth about one's self." *Internat. J. Psycho-Anal.*, 61:25–37.

Grinstein, A. (1983), *Freud's Rules of Dream Interpretation*. New York: International Universities Press.

Grossman, W. (1989), Hierarchies, boundaries, and representation in a Freudian model of mental organization. The Maurice Friend Lecture, Psychoanalytic Association of New York, October 12, 1989.

Guttman, I. K., & Guttman, S., eds. (1987), Robert Waelder on psychoanalytic technique: Five lectures. *Psychoanal. Quart.*, 56:1–67.

Hanly, C., & Masson, J. (1976), A critical examination of the new narcissism. *Internat. J. Psycho-Anal.*, 57:49–70.

Hartmann, H. (1955), Notes on the theory of sublimation. In: *Essays on Ego Psychology*. New York: International Universities Press, 1964, pp. 113–141.

———— Kris, E. (1945), The genetic approach in psychoanalysis. *The Psychoanalytic Study of the Child*, 1:11–30. New York: International Universities Press.

———— ———— Lowenstein, R. M. (1946), Comments on the formation of psychic structure. *The Psychoanalytic Study of the Child*, 2:11–38. New York: International Universities Press.

Heimann, P. (1950), On counter-transference. *Internat. J. Psycho-Anal.*, 35:163–168.

Hoffer, A. (1985), Toward a definition of psychoanalytic neutrality. *J. Amer. Psychoanal. Assn.*, 33:771–795.

Holzman, P., & Schlesinger, H. (1972), On becoming a hospitalized psychiatric patient. *Bull. Menn. Clinic*, 36:383–406.

Huxster, H., Lower, R., & Escoll, P. (1975), Some pitfalls in the assessment of analyzability in a psychoanalytic clinic. *J. Amer. Psychoanal. Assn.*, 23:90–106.

Izner, S. (1959), On the appearance of primal scene content in dreams. *J. Amer. Psychoanal. Assn.*, 7:317–328.

Jacobson, E. (1954), Transference problems in the psychoanalytic treatment of severely depressive patients. *J. Amer. Psychoanal. Assn.*, 2:595–606.

James, M. (1960), Premature ego development. *Internat. J. Psycho-Anal.*, 41:288–294.

Jones, E. (1955), *The Life and Work of Sigmund Freud*, Vol. 2. New York: Basic Books.

Kantrowitz, J. L., Katz, A. L., & Paolitto, F. (1990), Follow-up of psychoanalysis five to ten years after termination: Stability of change. *J. Amer. Psychoanal. Assn.*, 38:471–496.

———— Singer, J. G., & Knapp, P. H. (1975), Methodology of prospective study of suitability for psychoanalysis: The role of psychological tests. *Psychoanal. Quart.*, 44:371–391.

Karush, A. (1967), Working through. *Psychoanal. Quart.*, 36:497–531.

Keiser, S. (1969), Superior intelligence: Its contribution to neurosogenesis. *J. Amer. Psychoanal. Assn.*, 17:452–473.

Kennedy, H. (1971), Problems in reconstruction in child analysis. *The Psychoanalytic Study of the Child*, 26:386–402. Chicago: Quadrangle.

Kernberg, O. (1967), Borderline personality organization. *J. Amer. Psychoanal. Assn.*, 15:641–685.

———— (1972), Early ego integration and object relations. *Ann. N.Y. Acad. Sci.*, 192:233–247.

———— (1974), Further contributions to the treatment of narcissistic personalities. *Internat. J. Psycho-Anal.*, 55:215–240.

———— (1975), *Borderline Conditions and Pathological Narcissism*. New York: Jason Aronson.

———— (1976), Technical considerations in the treatment of borderline personality organization. *J. Amer. Psychoanal. Assn.*, 30:795–829.

———— (1983), Object relations theory and character analysis. *J. Amer. Psychoanal. Assn.*, 31(Suppl.):247–272.

———— (1988), Object relations theory in clinical practice. *Psychoanal. Quart.*, 57:481–504.

———— Burstein, E., Coyne, L., Appelbaum, A., Horwitz, L., & Voth, H. (1972), Psychotherapy and psychoanalysis. *Bull. Menn. Clinic*, 36:3–277.

Kinston, W., & Cohen, J. (1988), Primal repression and other states of mind. *Scand. Psychoanal. Rev.,* 11:81–105.

Klauber, J. (1972), On the relationship of transference and interpretation in psychoanalytic therapy. *Internat. J. Psycho-Anal.,* 53:385–392.

Klein, M. (1957), *Envy and Gratitude.* London: Tavistock.

———— (1975), *Love, Guilt and Reparation.* New York: Basic Books.

Knapp, P., Levin, S., McCarter, R., Wermer, H., & Zetzel, E. (1960), Suitability for psychoanalysis. A review of 100 supervised analytic cases. *Psychoanal. Quart.,* 29:459–477.

Knight, R. P. (1941–1942), Evaluation of the results of psychoanalytic therapy. *Amer. J. Psychiatry,* 98:434–446.

———— (1952), An evaluation of psychotherapeutic techniques. In: *Psychoanalytic Psychiatry and Psychology,* ed. R. P. Knight & C. R. Friedman. New York: International Universities Press, 1954, pp. 65–76.

———— (1953), Borderline states. In: *Psychoanalytic Psychiatry and Psychology,* ed. R. P. Knight & C. R. Friedman. New York: International Universities Press, 1954, pp. 97–109.

Kohut, H. (1959), Introspection, empathy and psychoanalysis. *J. Amer. Psychoanal. Assn.,* 7:459–483.

———— (1966a), Discussion of Alvarez de Toledo, Grinberg, and Langer's Termination of training analysis. In: *Psychoanalysis in the Americas,* ed. R. E. Litman. New York: International Universities Press, pp. 193–204.

———— (1966b), Forms and transformations of narcissism. *J. Amer. Psychoanal. Assn.,* 14:243–272.

———— (1968), The psychoanalytic treatment of narcissistic personality disorders. *The Psychoanalytic Study of the Child,* 23:86–113. New York: International Universities Press.

———— (1971), *The Analysis of the Self.* New York: International Universities Press.

———— (1977), *The Restoration of the Self.* New York: International Universities Press.

———— (1980), Summarizing reflections. In: *Advances in Self Psychology,* ed. A. Goldberg. New York: International Universities Press, pp. 473–554.

———— (1984), *How Does Analysis Cure?* Chicago: University of Chicago Press.

Kramer, M. K. (1959), On the continuation of the analytic process after psychoanalysis (a self observation). *Internat. J. Psycho-Anal.,* 40:17–25.

Kramer, S., & Byerly, L. J. (1978), Technique of psychoanalysis of the latency child. In: *Child Analysis and Therapy,* ed. J. Glenn. New York: Jason Aronson, pp. 205–236.

Kris, E. (1951), Some comments and observations on early auto-erotic activities. *The Psychoanalytic Study of the Child,* 6:95–117. New York: International Universities Press.

———— (1952), *Psychoanalytic Explorations in Art.* New York: International Universities Press.

———— (1956a), On some vicissitudes of insight in psycho-analysis. *Internat. J. Psycho-Anal.,* 37:445–455.

———— (1956b), The recovery of childhood memories in psychoanalysis. In: *The Selected Papers of Ernst Kris.* New Haven, CT: Yale University Press, 1975, pp. 301–340.

Kubie, L. (1948), Instincts and homeostasis. *Psychosom. Med.,* 10:15–30.

Laforgue, R. (1934), Resistance at the conclusion of analytic treatment. *Internat. J. Psycho-Anal.*, 15:419–434.

Lampl-de Groot, J. (1950), On masturbation and its influence on general development. *The Psychoanalytic Study of the Child*, 5. New York: International Universities Press.

———— (1967), *Man and Mind*. New York: International Universities Press.

Langs, R. (1973), *The Technique of Psychoanalytic Psychotherapy*, Vols. 1 & 2. New York: Jason Aronson.

———— (1976), Acting out. In: *The Therapeutic Interaction*, Vol. 2. New York: Jason Aronson, pp. 73–90.

Leider, R. (1983), Analytic neutrality: A historical review. *Psychoanal. Inq.*, 3:665–674.

Levy, S. (1987), Therapeutic strategy and psychoanalytic technique. *J. Amer. Psychoanal. Assn.*, 35:447–466.

———— Inderbitzin, L. (1990), The analytic surface and the theory of technique. *J. Amer. Psychoanal. Assn.*, 38:371–391.

Lewin, B. D. (1948), The nature of reality, the meaning of nothing, with an addendum on concentration. *Psychoanal. Quart.*, 17:524–526.

———— (1950), *The Psychoanalysis of Elation*. New York: W. W. Norton.

Lichtenberg, J. D. (1983a), The influence of values and value judgments on the psychoanalytic encounter. *Psychoanal. Inq.*, 3:647–664.

———— (1983b), *Psychoanalysis and Infant Research*. Hillsdale, NJ: Analytic Press.

———— (1989), *Psychoanalysis and Motivation*. Hillsdale, NJ: Analytic Press.

Limentani, A. (1972), The assessment of analyzability. A major hazard in selection for psychoanalysis. *Internat. J. Psycho-Anal.*, 53:351–361.

Lipton, S. D. (1961), The last hour. *J. Amer. Psychoanal. Assn.*, 9:325–330.

———— (1977), The advantages of Freud's technique as shown in his analysis of the Rat Man. *Internat. J. Psycho-Anal.*, 58:255–273.

Little, M. (1951), Counter-transference and the patient's response to it. *Internat. J. Psycho-Anal.*, 32:32–40.

Loewald, H. (1960), On the therapeutic action of psychoanalysis. *Internat. J. Psycho-Anal.*, 41:16–33.

———— (1971a), On motivation and instinct theory. *The Psychoanalytic Study of the Child*, 26:91–128. New York: International Universities Press.

———— (1971b), The transference neurosis: Comments on the concept and the phenomenon. In: *Papers on Psychoanalysis*. New Haven, CT: Yale University Press, 1980, pp. 302–314.

———— (1973), Comments on some instinctual manifestations of superego formation. *Annual of Psychoanalysis*, 1:104–116. New York: International Universities Press.

———— (1980), *Papers on Psychoanalysis*. New Haven, CT: Yale University Press.

Lower, R., Escoll, P., & Huxster, H. (1973), Bases for judgment of analyzability. *J. Amer. Psychoanal. Assn.*, 20:610–621.

Luborsky, L., Crits-Christoph, P., Mintz, J., & Auerbach, A. (1988), *Who Will Benefit from Psychotherapy?* New York: Basic Books.

MacDougall, J., & Lebovice, S. (1969), *Dialogue with Sammy*. London: Hogarth Press.

Mahler, M. (1949), Les "enfantes terribles." In: *Searchlights on Delinquency*, ed. K. R. Eissler. New York: International Universities Press.

—— Furer, M. (1968), *On Human Symbiosis and the Vicissitudes of Individuation*. New York: International Universities Press.

—— Pine, F., & Bergman, A. (1975), *The Psychological Birth of the Human Infant*. New York: Basic Books.

Masterson, J. F. (1981), *The Narcissistic and Borderline Disorders*. New York: Brunner/Mazel.

McLaughlin, J. T. (1981), Transference, psychic reality, and countertransference. *Psychoanal. Quart.*, 50:639–664.

—— (1987), The play of transference: Some reflections on enactment in the psychoanalytic situation. *J. Amer. Psychoanal. Assn.*, 35:557–582.

—— (1988), The analyst's insights. *Psychoanal. Quart.*, 57:370–389.

Modell, A. H. (1976), "The holding environment" and the therapeutic action of psychoanalysis. *J. Amer. Psychoanal. Assn.*, 24:285–308.

—— (1984), *Psychoanalysis in a New Context*. New York: International Universities Press.

—— (1988), The centrality of the psychoanalytic setting and the changing aims of treatment: A perspective from a theory of object relations. *Psychoanal. Quart.*, 57:577–596.

Nemiroff, R. A., Sugarman, A., & Robbins, A. (in press), *On Loving, Hating and Living Well: The Public Psychoanalytic Lectures of Ralph R. Greenson, M.D.* Madison, CT: International Universities Press.

Norman, H. F., Blacker, K. H., Oremland, J. D., & Barrett, W. G. (1976), The fate of the transference neurosis after termination of a satisfactory analysis. *J. Amer. Psychoanal. Assn.*, 24:471–498.

Novey, S. (1962), The principle of "working through" in psychoanalysis. *J. Amer. Psychoanal. Assn.*, 10:658–676.

Novick, J. (1980), Negative therapeutic motivation and negative therapeutic alliance. *The Psychoanalytic Study of the Child*, 35:299–320. New Haven, CT: Yale University Press.

—— (1982), Termination: Themes and issues. *Psychoanal. Inq.*, 2:329–365.

—— (1988), The timing of termination. *Internat. Rev. Psychoanal.*, 14:307–318.

—— (1990a), Some comments on termination in child, adolescent and adult psychoanalysis. *The Psychoanalytic Study of the Child*, 45:419–436. New Haven, CT: Yale University Press.

—— (1990b), The significance of adolescent analysis for work with adults. In: *The Significance of Child and Adolescent Analysis for Work with Adults*, ed. S. Dowling. Madison, CT: International Universities Press, pp. 81–94.

—— Novick, K. K. (1991), Some comments on masochism and the delusion of omnipotence. *J. Amer. Psychoanal. Assn.*, 39:307–331.

Novick, K. K., & Novick, J. (1987), The essence of masochism. *The Psychoanalytic Study of the Child*, 42:353–384. New Haven, CT: Yale University Press.

Oremland, J. D. (1972), The fate of the transference after the psychoanalysis. Paper presented at fall meetings of the American Psychoanalytic Association, New York.

—— Blacker, K. H., & Norman, H. F. (1975), Incompleteness in "successful psychoanalyses": A follow-up study. *J. Amer. Psychoanal. Assn.*, 23:819–844.

Orr, D. W. (1954), Transference and countertransference: A historical survey. *J. Amer. Psychoanal. Assn.*, 2:621–670.

O'Shaughnessy, E. (1983), Words and working through. *Internat. J. Psycho-Anal.*, 64:281–290.

Panel (1960), Indications and contraindications for psychoanalytic treatment, reported by S. Guttman. *J. Amer. Psychoanal. Assn.*, 23:90–105.

———— (1968), The assessment of change resulting from psychoanalytic treatment, reported by J. S. Beigler. *Bull. Phila. Assn. Psychoanal.*, 18:95–100.

———— (1969), Problems of termination in the analysis of adults, reported by S. K. Firestein. *J. Amer. Psychoanal. Assn.*, 17:222–237.

———— (1973), On the fate of transference after the termination of analysis, reported by H. T. Hurn. *J. Amer. Psychoanal. Assn.*, 21:182–192.

———— (1974), The fate of the transference neurosis after analysis, reported by A. Balkoura. *J. Amer. Psychoanal. Assn.*, 22:895–903.

Paniagua, C. (1985), A methodological approach to surface material. *Internat. Rev. Psychoanal.*, 12:311–325.

Parens, H. (1979), *The Development of Aggression in Early Childhood.* New York: Jason Aronson.

Pedder, J. R. (1988), Termination reconsidered. *Internat. J. Psycho-Anal.*, 69:495–505.

Peterfreund, E. (1983), *The Process of Psychoanalytic Therapy.* Hillsdale, NJ: Analytic Press.

Pfeffer, A. Z. (1959), A procedure for evaluating the results of psychoanalysis: A preliminary report. *J. Amer. Psychoanal. Assn.*, 7:418–444.

———— (1961), Follow-up study of a satisfactory analysis. *J. Amer. Psychoanal. Assn.*, 9:698–718.

———— (1963), The meaning of the analyst after analysis: A contribution to the theory of therapeutic results. *J. Amer. Psychoanal. Assn.*, 11:229–244.

Poland, W. S. (1984), On the analyst's neutrality. *J. Amer. Psychoanal. Assn.*, 32:283–299.

———— (1986), Insight and the analytic dyad. *Psychoanal. Quart.*, 57:341–369.

Pruyser, P. (1975), What splits in "splitting"?: A scrutiny of the concept of splitting in psychoanalysis and psychiatry. *Bull. Menn. Clinic,* 39:1–46.

Pusey, D. D., trans. (1907), *The Confessions of St. Augustine.* London: Dent.

Rado, S. (1925), The economic principles in psychoanalytic technique. *Internat. J. Psycho-Anal.*, 6:35–44.

Rangell, L. (1959), The nature of conversion in hysteria. *J. Amer. Psychoanal. Assn.*, 7:632–662.

———— (1966), An overview of the ending of an analysis. In: *Psychoanalysis in the Americas,* ed. R. E. Litman. New York: International Universities Press, pp. 141–165.

———— (1968), A point of view on acting out. *Internat. J. Psycho-Anal.*, 49:195–201.

———— (1980), Contemporary issues in the theory of therapy. In: *Psychoanalytic Explorations of Technique,* ed. H. Blum. New York: International Universities Press, pp. 81–112.

———— (1987), A core process in psychoanalytic treatment. *Psychoanal. Quart.*, 56:222–246.

Rapaport, D. (1967), *The Collected Papers of David Rapaport,* ed. M. M. Gill. New York: Basic Books.

———— Gill, M. M., & Schafer, R. (1968), *Diagnostic Psychological Testing*, ed. R. Holt. New York: International Universities Press.

Reich, A. (1950), On the termination of analysis. In: *Psychoanalytic Contributions*. New York: International Universities Press, 1978, pp. 121–135.

———— (1951a), The discussion of 1912 on masturbation and our present day views. *The Psychoanalytic Study of the Child*, 6:80–94. New York: International Universities Press.

———— (1951b), On countertransference. *Internat. J. Psycho-Anal.*, 32:25–31.

———— (1953), Narcissistic object choice in women. *J. Amer. Psychoanal. Assn.*, 1:22–44.

———— (1960a), Further remarks on countertransference. *Internat. J. Psycho-Anal.*, 41:389–395.

———— (1960b), Pathologic forms of self-esteem regulation. *The Psychoanalytic Study of the Child*, 15:215–232. New York: International Universities Press.

Reich, W. (1949), *Character Analysis*. New York: Noonday Press.

Ritvo, S. (1974), Current status of the concept of the infantile neurosis. *The Psychoanalytic Study of the Child*, 29:159–181. New York: International Universities Press.

Rosenfeld, H. (1965), *Psychotic States: A Psychoanalytic Approach*. London: Hogarth Press.

———— (1966), The need of some patients to act out during analysis. *Psychoanal. Forum*, 1:19–29.

Sander, L. W. (1980), New knowledge about the infant from current research: Implications for psychoanalysis. *J. Amer. Psychoanal. Assn.*, 28:181–198.

———— (1983), To begin with: Reflections on ontogeny. In: *Reflections on Self Psychology*, ed. J. Lichtenberg & S. Kaplan. Hillsdale, NJ: Analytic Press, pp. 85–104.

Sandler, J. (1960a), The background of safety. *Internat. J. Psycho-Anal.*, 41:352–365.

———— (1960b), On the concept of superego. *The Psychoanalytic Study of the Child*, 15:128–162. New York: International Universities Press.

———— (1976), Countertransference and role-responsiveness. *Internat. Rev. Psychoanal.*, 3:43–48.

Saul, L. J. (1972), *Psychodynamically Based Psychotherapy*. New York: Science House.

Schafer, R. (1983), *The Analytic Attitude*. New York: Basic Books.

Schlesinger, H. J. (1973), Interaction of dynamic and reality factors in the diagnostic testing interview. *Bull. Menn. Clinic*, 37:495–517.

———— (1985), Some ingredients of effective interpretation. Plenary Address, Fall Meeting, American Psychoanalytic Association, December 20, 1985.

———— (1988), Historical overview of the mode of therapeutic action of psychoanalytic psychotherapy. In: *The Therapeutic Action of Psychoanalytic Psychotherapy*, ed. A. Rothstein. Madison, CT: International Universities Press.

Schlessinger, N., & Robbins, F. P. (1974), Assessment and follow-up in psychoanalysis. *J. Amer. Psychoanal. Assn.*, 22:542–567.

———— ———— (1975), The psychoanalytic process: Recurrent patterns of conflict and changes in ego function. *J. Amer. Psychoanal. Assn.*, 23:761–782.

———— ———— (1983), *A Developmental View of the Psychoanalytic Process:*

Follow-up Studies and Their Consequences. New York: International Universities Press.

Schur, M. (1960), Phylogenesis and ontogenesis of affect and structure formation and the phenomenon of repetition compulsion. *Internat. J. Psycho-Anal.,* 41:275–287.

———— (1966), *The Id and the Regulatory Principles of Mental Functioning.* New York: International Universities Press.

Schwaber, E. (1983), Psychoanalytic listening and psychic reality. *Internat. J. Psycho-Anal.,* 10:379–392.

Searles, H. F. (1965), *Collected Papers on Schizophrenia and Related Subjects.* New York: International Universities Press.

———— (1986), *My Work with Borderline Patients.* Northvale, NJ: Jason Aronson.

Sedler, M. J. (1983), Freud's concept of working through. *Psychoanal. Quart.,* 52:73–98.

Segal, H. (1973), *Introduction to the Work of Melanie Klein.* London: Hogarth Press.

———— (1981), *The Work of Hanna Segal.* New York: Jason Aronson.

———— (1985), The Klein-Bion model. In: *Models of the Mind,* ed. A. Rothstein. New York: International Universities Press.

Shane, M. (1979), The developmental approach to working through in the analytic process. *Internat. J. Psycho-Anal.,* 60:375–382.

———— (1980), Countertransference and the developmental orientation and approach. *Psychoanal. & Contemp. Thought,* 3:195–212.

———— Shane, E. (1982), Psychoanalytic theories of aggression. *Psychoanal. Inq.,* 2:263–281.

———— ———— (1983), The strands of aggression: A confluence of data. *Psychoanal. Inq.,* 4:263–281.

———— ———— (1984), The end phase of analysis: Indicators, functions and tasks of termination. *J. Amer. Psychoanal. Assn.,* 32:739–772.

———— ———— (1989), The opening phase: A developmental perspective. In: *On Beginning An Analysis,* ed. T. J. Jacobs & A. Rothstein. Madison, CT: International Universities Press.

Shapiro, T. (1984), On neutrality. *J. Amer. Psychoanal. Assn.,* 32:269–282.

Sharpe, E. F. (1930), The technique of psychoanalysis. In: *Collected Papers on Psychoanalysis.* London: Hogarth Press, 1950, pp. 9–106.

———— (1947), The psychoanalyst. In: *Collected Papers on Psychoanalysis.* London: Hogarth Press, 1950, pp. 109–122.

———— (1950), *Collected Papers on Psycho-Analysis.* New York: Brunner/Mazel.

Shengold, L. (1974), More about the meaning of "nothing." *Psychoanal. Quart.,* 43:116–119.

———— (1989), *Soul Murder.* New Haven, CT: Yale University Press.

Shevrin, H., & Shectman, F. (1973), The diagnostic process in psychiatric evaluations. *Bull. Menn. Clinic,* 37:451–494.

Spence, D. (1982), *Narrative Truth and Historical Truth.* New York: W. W. Norton.

Spruiell, V. (1974), Theories of the treatment of narcissistic personalities. *J. Amer. Psychoanal. Assn.,* 22:268–278.

———— (1975), Three strands of narcissism. *Psychoanal. Quart.,* 44:577–595.

———— (1977), Creativity: Psychoanalytic studies. In: *Encyclopedia of Psychiatry, Psychology, and Neurology,* Vol. 3, ed. B. Wolman. New York: Aesculapius, pp. 437–440.

———— (1983), Rules and frames of the psychoanalytic situation. *Psychoanal. Quart.,* 52:1–33.

———— (1984), The analyst at work. *Internat. J. Psycho-Anal.,* 65:13–30.

———— (1990), The analytic situation: Sheltered freedom. Presented at the Freud Lecture of the Psychoanalytic Association of New York, May 21, 1990.

Stein, J. (1981), The unobjectionable part of the transference. *J. Amer. Psychoanal. Assn.,* 29:869–892.

Sterba, R. F. (1934), The fate of the ego in analytic therapy. *Internat. J. Psycho-Anal.,* 15:117–126.

———— (1940), Aggression in the rescue fantasy. *Psychoanal. Quart.,* 9:505–508.

Stern, D. N. (1985), *The Interpersonal World of the Infant.* New York: Basic Books.

Stern, M. (1968), Fear of death and neurosis. *J. Amer. Psychoanal. Assn.,* 16:3–31.

Stewart, W. A. (1963), An inquiry into the concept of working through. *J. Amer. Psychoanal. Assn.,* 11:474–499.

Stoller, R. J. (1979), *Sexual Excitement.* New York: Pantheon.

Stolorow, R., Brandchaft, B., & Atwood, G. (1987), *Psychoanalytic Treatment: An Intersubjective Approach.* Hillsdale, NJ: Analytic Press.

Stone, L. (1954), The widening scope of indications for psychoanalysis. *J. Amer. Psychoanal. Assn.,* 2:567–594.

———— (1961), *The Psychoanalytic Situation.* New York: International Universities Press.

———— (1973), On resistance to the psychoanalytic process. Some thoughts on its nature and motivations. *Psychoanal. & Contemp. Sci.,* 2:42–76.

Strachey, J. (1934), The nature of the therapeutic action of psychoanalysis. *Internat. J. Psycho-Anal.,* 15:127–159.

Szasz, T. S. (1956), The experience of the analyst. *J. Amer. Psychoanal. Assn.,* 4:197–229.

Tartakoff, H. (1966), The normal personality in our culture and the Nobel Prize complex. In: *Psychoanalysis—A General Psychology: Essays in Honor of Heinz Hartmann,* ed. R. Loewenstein, L. Newman, M. Schur, & A. Solnit. New York: International Universities Press.

Tausk, V. (1912), On masturbation. In: *The Psychoanalytic Study of the Child,* 6:61–79. New York: International Universities Press, 1951.

Ticho, E. A. (1966), Discussion of Rangell's An overview of the ending of an analysis. In: *Psychoanalysis in the Americas,* ed. R. E. Litman. New York: International Universities Press, pp. 171–173.

———— (1972), Termination of psychoanalysis: Treatment goals, life goals. *Psychoanal. Quart.,* 41:315–332.

Ticho, G. R. (1967), On self-analysis. *Internat. J. Psycho-Anal.,* 48:308–318.

Tower, L. E. (1956), Countertransference. *J. Amer. Psychoanal. Assn.,* 4:224–256.

Tyson, P., & Tyson, R. L. (1990), *Psychoanalytic Theories of Development: An Integration.* New Haven, CT: Yale University Press.

Tyson, R. L., & Sandler, J. (1971), Problems in the selection of patients for psychoanalysis: Comments on the application of the concepts "indications," "suitability," and "analyzability." *Brit. J. Med. Psychol.,* 44:211–228.

Valenstein, A. F. (1983), Working through and resistance to change: Insight and the action system. *J. Amer. Psychoanal. Assn.,* 31(Suppl.):353–373.

Volkan, V. (1987), *Six Steps in the Treatment of Borderline Personality Organization.* New York: Jason Aronson.

Waelder, R. (1936), The principle of multiple function. In: *Psychoanalysis: Observation, Theory, Application,* ed. S. Guttman. New York: International Universities Press, 1976.

——— (1939), Criteria of interpretation. In: *Psychoanalysis: Observation, Theory, Application,* ed. S. Guttman. New York: International Universities Press, 1976.

Waldhorn, H. F. (1960), Assessment of analyzability: Technical and theoretical observations. *Psychoanal. Quart.,* 29:478–506.

——— (1967), *Indications for Psychoanalysis and the Place of the Dream in Clinical Psychoanalysis.* New York: International Universities Press.

Wallerstein, R. S. (1964), The role of prediction in theory building in psychoanalysis. *J. Amer. Psychoanal. Assn.,* 12:675–691.

——— (1965), The goals of psychoanalysis: A survey of analytic viewpoints. *J. Amer. Psychoanal. Assn.,* 13:748–770.

——— (1986), *Forty-Two Lives in Treatment: A Study of Psychoanalysis and Psychotherapy.* New York: Guilford Press.

——— (1988), Psychoanalysis and psychotherapy: Relative roles reconsidered. *Annual of Psychoanalysis,* 16:129–151. Madison, CT: International Universities Press.

——— (1989), Psychoanalysis and psychotherapy. An historical perspective. *Internat. J. Psycho-Anal.,* 70:563–591.

Weigert, E. (1955), Special problems in connection with termination of training analysis. *J. Amer. Psychoanal. Assn.,* 3:630–640.

Weinshel, E. (1988), The many borders of borderline: On the virtues of modesty in psychoanalytic diagnosis. *Psychoanal. Inq.,* 8:333–352.

——— (1990), How wide is the widening scope of psychoanalysis and how solid is its structural model? Some concerns and observations. *J. Amer. Psychoanal. Assn.,* 38:275–296.

Weiss, J., & Sampson, H. (1986), *The Psychoanalytic Process: Theory, Clinical Observations and Empirical Research.* New York: Guilford Press.

Windholz, E. (1955), Problems of termination of the training analysis. *J. Amer. Psychoanal. Assn.,* 3:641–650.

Winnicott, D. W. (1949), Hate and the countertransference. *Internat. J. Psycho-Anal.,* 30:69–74.

——— (1953), Transitional objects and transitional phenomena. *Internat. J. Psycho-Anal.,* 34:89–97.

——— (1955), Metapsychological and clinical aspects of regression within the psycho-analytical set-up. In: *Collected Papers: Through Paediatrics to Psycho-Analysis.* New York: Basic Books, 1958, pp. 278–294.

——— (1958), *Collected Papers: Through Paediatrics to Psycho-Analysis.* New York: Basic Books.

——— (1963), The development of the capacity for concern. *Bull. Menn. Clinic,* 27:167–176.

——— (1965), *The Maturational Processes and the Facilitating Environment: Studies in the Theory of Emotional Development.* New York: International Universities Press.

Wolf, E. (1983), Aspects of neutrality. *Psychoanal. Inq.,* 3:675–689.

Wolff, P. H. (1966), The Causes, Controls and Organization of Behavior in the Neonate. *Psychological Issues,* Vol. 5, No. 1, Monogr. 7. New York: International Universities Press.

Zeligs, M. (1957), Acting in. *J. Amer. Psychoanal. Assn.*, 5:685–706.

Zetzel, E. R. (1956), Current concepts of transference. *Internat. J. Psycho-Anal.*, 37:369–376.

——— (1966), The analytic situation. In: *Psychoanalysis in the Americas*, ed. R. E. Litman. New York: International Universities Press, pp. 86–106.

——— (1968), The so-called good hysteric. *Internat. J. Psycho-Anal.*, 49:256–260.

Name Index

481

Subject Index